GarageBand® '09 Power!: The Comprehensive Recording and Podcasting Guide

Todd M. Howard

Course Technology PTR
A part of Cengage Learning

COURSE TECHNOLOGY
CENGAGE Learning

Australia • Brazil • Japan • Korea • Mexico • Singapore • Spain • United Kingdom • United States

COURSE TECHNOLOGY
CENGAGE Learning™

GarageBand® '09 Power!: The Comprehensive Recording and Podcasting Guide
Todd M. Howard

Publisher and General Manager, Course Technology PTR: Stacy L. Hiquet

Associate Director of Marketing: Sarah Panella

Manager of Editorial Services: Heather Talbot

Marketing Manager: Mark Hughes

Acquisitions Editor: Orren Merton

Project Editor/Copy Editor: Cathleen D. Small

Technical Reviewer: Marc Schonbrun

Editorial Services Coordinator: Jen Blaney

Interior Layout Tech: Macmillan Publishing Solutions

Cover Designer: Mike Tanamachi

Indexer: Larry Sweazy

Proofreader: Brad Crawford

For product information and technology assistance, contact us at
Cengage Learning Customer & Sales Support, 1-800-354-9706

For permission to use material from this text or product, submit all requests online at **www.cengage.com/permissions**
Further permissions questions can be emailed to
permissionrequest@cengage.com

GarageBand is a registered trademark of Apple Inc. All other trademarks are the property of their respective owners.

Library of Congress Control Number: 2009924520

ISBN-13: 978-1-4354-5420-0

ISBN-10: 1-4354-5420-0

Course Technology, a part of Cengage Learning
20 Channel Center Street
Boston, MA 02210
USA

Cengage Learning is a leading provider of customized learning solutions with office locations around the globe, including Singapore, the United Kingdom, Australia, Mexico, Brazil, and Japan. Locate your local office at: **international.cengage.com/region**

Cengage Learning products are represented in Canada by Nelson Education, Ltd.

For your lifelong learning solutions, visit **courseptr.com**

Visit our corporate website at **cengage.com**

Printed in the United States of America
1 2 3 4 5 6 7 11 10 09

This book is dedicated to Erika Norton Stone, my lovely wife, partner, and best friend. You help to make all things possible! I am eternally grateful for your constant support, love, laughter, and encouragement. What's next? ww.

This book is also dedicated in loving memory to two dear members of my family who have gone before me unto the next great adventure: my "Uncle Bob," Robert Joyce, and my brother-in-law, Justin Noel Stone.

Acknowledgments

Writing a book is a fascinating and exciting endeavor and also a painful, arduous, detail-oriented process. Without my masters, muses, and maestros at my side, on my shoulder, and perpetually in my memory and imagination, I would most certainly be a flailing crazy person, bouncing willy-nilly from one creative enterprise to the next without any solid sense of my ability to draw each project to conclusion. The physical anchors and spiritual breezes that my family, friends, gurus, mentors, and colleagues provide for me—in specific ways many of them might not even be aware of—are in fact both the cornerstones and the tethers-released of my day-to-day thoughts and feelings. I want to thank them all deeply. It is this power of my community that propels me toward anything I set my heart on and my mind to. Without that fuel, I'd be pushing an awfully heavy load up the hill in a rickety old wagon with square wheels. I'd get there, but it would most certainly take several more lifetimes.

I would like to express my deepest gratitude to my family for their loving support of my many creative endeavors over the years, and for helping to cultivate a place for me to learn, grow, and express myself: Erika Stone; Paul Howard; Sandi, Jack, Jon, and Lane Rossi; Jesse, Kate, Bailey, and Chloe Howard; Peter, Heidi, Nick, and Peter Howard; Leanne Joyce, Jim, and Debbie Stone; my "Grampa Norm," Norman Johnson; and of course … Betty Graybelle and Hugo Long.

Special thanks to my incredibly supportive and inspirational family of friends—I am truly blessed to have a list this long: Eric Tully and Liz Pachuilo; Don and Kirsten Gunn; Karmen Buttler; Paul Westfall; Jim Vasquenza; Glen and Sue Nelson; Tina Peterson; Jeff and Keith Palmer; Christopher Eddy; Michele Goodson; Jesse Moore and Patty Foley; Aaron and Laura Murray; Samantha Libby Sodickson; Stuart Baker; Hugh Sutton; Angela Cardinali; Sarah McNair; Caroline Streeter; Michael Card; Kathy O'Mara; Clark Semon; Libbie Pike; Lisa Hill; Jed Gramlin; Deidre, Najla, and Nevin Nassar; Jim Parr; Tim Van Ness and Eve Capkanis; Edward Cating; Lindsay Brandon Hunter and Chris Guilmet; Raouldook, Niena, Wexxa, and Pressto for a year of great Thursday nights; and the members of The Brethren on Khadgar.

A big tip of the hat and a huge B♭sus2 chord on a 13-foot grand piano with the damper pedal down hard to all of my musical cohorts for keeping me honest and for years of sweet spots welcoming of my busy melodic bass lines and vocal harmonies: Jesse, Dad, Mom, Don, Karmen, Tom, Phil, Glen-e-bones, Sue, Christopher, Jimmy V, Guy Leon, Jammer, Dennis, and Peter & Heidi.

I'd like to thank Eric Tully specifically for his indispensable help with wrangling the exhaustive lists of Apple Loops in the appendix and for his great friendship and support of my creative and professional development for more than two decades now. Eric, thanks for always taking the time to explain things, even when it's the third time, and for telling me your thoughts about my work—even when it might be critical! Your critical thinking has helped me out of innumerable jams, and I really appreciate our friendship.

A round of pant-flapping applause to my musical-soul-brother Don Gunn, not only for years and years of work on songwriting and recording together, but also for being my mentor and guru in my audio engineering and recording endeavors. Don is truly the master; he is the one I look up to and trust in matters of sonic capture, manipulation, presentation, and appreciation. He was also kind enough to help me with the descriptions of the new stompbox guitar effects. Don, thanks for turning me on to recording, for teaching me to use everything from the old Ross 4×4 cassette four-track to Logic 8 Pro, and for mentioning my name to Orren as a potential author for this book. Also, for being a major muse for me in my composition all the way back to high school. Writing music to your lyrics has been a huge part of my creative life and an incredible inspiration.

The most special thanks I can give to my mom, Sandi Rossi, for teaching me about harmony—in music and in life—is by living it. It's far too difficult to immortalize a thank you to a mother as inspirational, caring, loving, and supportive as you are like this, in a book's acknowledgments, but let me say that I think about all that you've done for me every day of my life, and I feel so much gratitude for the relationship we have. You are the truest of blessings and the purest of hearts.

A huge hug and banner-wave to my dad, Paul Howard, for helping with the definitions of the major and minor scales in this book and for a lifetime of musical inspiration and encouragement. From the ukulele, to the acme bass, to the Ibanez, to the Taylor six-string, and most recently to the Bodhrán, he has always endeavored not only to keep me in good instruments, but also to keep me listening to music in the joyous, fan-like way that he adopted as a teenager while watching The Beatles on *Ed Sullivan*. I have to say there's nothing quite like leaning in to sing a tenor vocal part on a full-tilt rendition of a song you love and looking slightly to your right and seeing your pop's bearded mug there singing the lead part and wailing on that six-string rhythm.

I'd like to lovingly thank my brother, Jesse Howard, my sister-in-law, Kate, and their two beautiful kids, my nephew Bailey and niece Chloe, for their never-ending patience with me and their understanding about the kind of time it has taken to get my media business off the ground and make my way through the writing of this book. I finally have some time to come down and play! Just as Jesse was writing the screenplay for our first feature film, *The Trouble with Boys and Girls*, while I simultaneously wrote my first book, *Who's Afraid of HTML?*, I wrote *GarageBand '08 Power!* while he was writing multiple drafts of his second feature-length screenplay, currently titled *Halfway Down the Stairs*. We went into pre-production on *Trouble* the same month I turned in my completed HTML book in the winter of 1997. So Jesse, now that the second edition of my GarageBand book is done, does that mean we get to start working on the new film project?

Last but not-on-your-life least, I would like to sincerely thank Orren Merton, my acquisitions editor, for giving me the opportunity to write this book and for his support and understanding along the stream of delays we rode toward getting this book out the door. Heaps of gratitude (and milkshakes!) go to Cathleen Small, my talented and tireless editor, who was there for me every step of the way, even mere days after bringing her baby boy, Theo, into the world! Appreciation and thanks also go to Marc Schonbrun, my technical editor, for his astute comments and peanut-butter-and-butter wit, and to Brad Crawford for proofreading the manuscript. I can't thank the four of them enough for their immense help in bringing this book to fruition. I could not have done it without their knowledge, understanding, and professionalism.

About the Author

Todd M. Howard is an accomplished songwriter, musician, and performer and is the bassist/vocalist in the acoustic American roots quartet Last Fair Deal. Todd co-produced the band's most recent album, *True Tales*, which he also mixed using Logic Pro. In addition, Todd is the bass player in the family-friendly rock band Spaghetti Cake, and he wrote and recorded original music with Seattle-based drummer, producer, engineer, and lyricist Don Gunn for more than 20 years. He has written and performed in acoustic-fourpiece-turned-acoustic-duo Mobile Home with his brother, Jesse P. Howard, since the early '90s. He was also a member of the bands Gaillion, Caribou, Understanding Thomas, and High Adventure.

Todd is founder and principal of Howard Digital Media, a Massachusetts-based creative media development company. The company works in the fields of film and video production, DVD authoring, website design and development, music composition and production, and Mac software training. He has conducted training seminars and one-on-one instruction on Mac OS X, Final Cut Pro and DVD Studio Pro, GarageBand, iLife, Logic, and Photoshop, as well as HTML/CSS and principles of website design. Also an independent filmmaker, Todd was the producer and co-editor of the feature film *The Trouble with Boys and Girls*, which was written, directed, and co-edited by his brother, Jesse. After the film's premiere screening, Scott Foundas of *LA Weekly* called the film "the most engaging, endearing film" in competition at the 2003 Dances with Films festival.

In addition to creating a graphic design and animation training podcast series for Adobe in 2007, Todd was the author and instructor on four DVD-based training titles in the Digital Media Training Series produced by Magnet Media (creators of Zoom In Online) and released between 2006 and 2008: *Inside Mac OS X: 10.4 Tiger, Inside iLife '06, Adobe Dreamweaver CS3 Jumpstart*, and *Mac OS X: 10.5 Leopard Jumpstart*. The *Inside Mac OS X: 10.4 Tiger* training title garnered Todd a 2006 Videographer Award of Distinction. He also served as tech/film/music blogger for Zoom In Online during most of 2007/2008. He first became a published author in 1999, with *Who's Afraid of HTML?*, published by Morgan Kaufmann. *GarageBand '09 Power!* is the second edition of his second book.

Todd currently lives in the Berkshires of northwestern Massachusetts with his wife, Erika, and two cats, Betty and Hugo. He enjoys film, cooking, astronomy, history, video games, words, late-night conversation, good serial TV, and spending time with his family.

Contents

Introduction xv

Chapter 1
Software Installation and Getting Connected   1

System Requirements.. 1
    Software 1
    Hardware 3
GarageBand Installation 4
Connection Protocols 5
    USB (Universal Serial Bus) 6
    FireWire (IEEE 1394) 6
    MIDI (Musical Instrument Digital Interface)...................................... 7
    Audio Line In 8
    Bringing It All Together 9
System Preferences: Sound 12
    Sound Effects 12
    Output 14
    Input 15
Let's Get Started! 16

Chapter 2
Choosing Your Project Type   17

The New Project Interface.. 17
    New Project 19
    Creating Your Own New Project Templates 26
    Learn to Play.. 27
    Lesson Store: Basic Lessons 29
    Lesson Store: Artist Lessons 31
    Magic GarageBand 32
    iPhone Ringtone 33
    Open an Existing File 35
    Quit 36
An In-Depth Look at Project Types in GarageBand 36

Music Project 37
Podcast 41
Magic GarageBand 43
What's Next? 45

Chapter 3
GarageBand Preferences and the User Interface   47

GarageBand's Preferences Window 47
Preferences: General 47
Preferences: Audio/MIDI 54
Preferences: Loops 57
Preferences: Advanced 59
Preferences: My Info 60
The GarageBand '09 Menus 61
The GarageBand Menu 62
The File Menu 63
The Edit Menu 65
The Track Menu 66
The Control Menu 67
The Share Menu 69
The Window Menu 70
The Help Menu 71
The GarageBand '09 Application Interface 71
The Arrange Window 71
The Transport Controls 73
The Track Editor 73
The Loop Browser 73
Track Info Panel 74
The Media Browser: Audio 74
The Media Browser: Photos 74
The Media Browser: Movies 76
The LCD Display 77
Let's Make Tracks 83

Chapter 4
Working with Tracks   85

What Is a Track? 85
Real Instrument Tracks and Software Instrument Tracks 87
Creating and Naming New Tracks 88
Creating a New Track 88
Editing a Track's Name 89

Duplicating and Deleting Tracks 90
    Duplicating a Track 91
    Deleting a Track 91
Reordering Your Tracks 92
Working in the Timeline 92
    Playback Control 93
    The Playhead and the Timeline Grid 93
    Scrolling and Zooming 96
    Trimming and Looping Audio 97
Tracks and Track Mixer Controls 102
    Track Volume and the LED Level/Clipping Indicators 103
    Panning 104
    Enable Recording 104
    Mute 105
    Solo 105
    Lock 105
    View/Hide Track Automation 105
Track Automation 105
    The Master Track 107
    The Ducking Function 107
Track Info 108
It's Time to Do Some Recording 110

Chapter 5
Real Instruments and Electric Guitar Tracks   111

Check Those Sound Prefs! 111
    System Preferences Check 111
    GarageBand Preferences Audio/MIDI Check 112
Setting Up the Input Source, Monitor, and Recording Level 112
    Input Source 113
    Monitor 114
    Recording Level 114
Effects 115
Electric Guitar Amps 120
Electric Guitar Stompbox Effects 123
    Phase Tripper 123
    Vintage Drive 124
    Grinder 124
    Fuzz Machine 125
    Retro Chorus 125
    Robo Flanger 125
    The Vibe 126

Auto-Funk 126

Blue Echo 127

Squash Compressor 128

Recording 128

Undo and Re-Record 129

Experiment with Post-Processing 130

Punching In 131

Additional Tips for Punching In 133

The Power of the Editor 134

Splitting a Recorded Region 135

Recording Multiple Takes 138

The Step-by-Step Process of Recording Multiple Takes 140

Give Yourself Some Breathing Room 141

Select Your Take 142

Combine Different Parts of Different Takes 143

Tuning and Timing Enhancers 144

Enhancing Tuning 145

Enhancing Timing 146

Next Up: Software Instruments 147

Chapter 6
Software Instruments　　149

Check Those MIDI Prefs! 149

Create a Software Instrument Track 151

Tracking with Your MIDI Controller or Keyboard 152

Let's Record Some MIDI Data 153

Using Cycle Recording and Multiple Takes to Build a Drum Beat 156

Renaming a Region in the Editor 159

Using the Editor for Editing MIDI Information 159

Piano Roll and Score 160

Piano Roll View 161

Score View 164

Now on to Apple Loops 165

Chapter 7
Working with Apple Loops　　167

What Is a Region? 168

What Is a Loop? 169

What Is an Apple Loop? 170

The Loop Browser 173

The Process of Browsing Loops 174

Scales 179

Importing Loops 181

Setting Loop Preferences 183
Adding Loops to the Timeline 183
Moving, Looping, Splitting, and Copying Loops 185
Swapping Apple Loops 186
Editing Software Instrument Apple Loops 188
Saving and Browsing Favorites 189
Becoming a Conductor: Magic GarageBand 190

Chapter 8
Magic GarageBand Jam Walkthrough

193

Apple and Inspiration 193
Choosing a Song Genre 194
The Genres and Style Options in Magic GarageBand 197
    Blues 198
    Rock 201
    Jazz 205
    Country 208
    Reggae 212
    Funk 215
    Latin 219
    Roots Rock 222
    Slow Blues 226
Auditioning a Band and Creating Your Project 229
    Basic Blues Song Structure in Magic GarageBand 230
    Basic Rock Song Structure in Magic GarageBand 231
    Basic Jazz Song Structure in Magic GarageBand 231
    Basic Country Song Structure in Magic GarageBand 232
    Basic Reggae Song Structure in Magic GarageBand 232
    Basic Funk Song Structure in Magic GarageBand 232
    Basic Latin Song Structure in Magic GarageBand 234
    Basic Roots Rock Song Structure in Magic GarageBand 235
    Basic Slow Blues Song Structure in Magic GarageBand 235
Jamming Along and Overdubbing More Parts 235
Open in GarageBand 238
Changing Keys and Tempos 239
Constructing Your Own Arrangements 241

Chapter 9
Arrangements

243

Song Form and Song Arrangement 243
Creating Arrangements with the Arrange Track 248
    Creating an Arrange Region 249
    Naming an Arrange Region 249

Resizing an Arrange Region 250
Deleting an Arrange Region 250
Moving an Arrange Region 250
Copying an Arrange Region 252
Opening GarageBand Projects with Arrangements in Logic Pro 253
Ready to Create Your First Podcast? 254

Chapter 10
Podcasting   255

Creating a Podcast 256
Creating an Episode 256
Creating a Video Podcast 257
The Media Browser's Role 259
The Podcast Track 260
Episode Artwork 261
Markers: Chapters and URLs 262
Ducking Audio in Podcasts 263
Working with Episode Information 264
Exporting Your Project as a Podcast Episode 266
Submit Your Podcast to the iTunes Podcast Directory 267
The Nitty Gritty: Mixing and Automation 267

Chapter 11
Mixing and Automation   269

A Perspective on Learning to Mix 269
Some Food for Thought about Mixing Audio 270
Mixing with GarageBand 273
Getting Started with Your Mix 274
No Undo with Mixing—What Gives?! 275
Zeroing/Flattening Out Your Levels 275
Your First Pass 276
Subsequent Passes and the Cycle Region 277
Muting and Soloing 278
Final Decisions about Software Instruments 278
Using Effects and Post-Processing 281
Presets versus Effects 281
GarageBand Effects 282
Adjusting Guitar Stompbox Effects and Guitar Amps 293
Audio Unit (AU) Effects 293
Creating Nodes and Basic Automation 294
Track Volume 295
Gradual Automation Changes over Time 297
Deleting Nodes 298
Track Pan 299

The Add Automation Menu 299
   Automating Effect and Instrument Parameters 300
Visual EQ 302
Master Effects 305
Automation in the Master Track... 305
Automating Changes in Tempo and Pitch... 306
Mixing Your Own Mash-Ups 307
What's Next: Sharing and Archiving... 308

Chapter 12
Sharing and Archiving Your GarageBand Projects   309

Sharing GarageBand Projects 310
   The Share Menu 310
Saving and Archiving GarageBand Projects.. 320
Compacting GarageBand Projects 322
Sharing GarageBand Projects with Logic Pro 323
Allow Yourself to Write Bad Ones 324
Links for the Author 325
What's Next: GarageBand Learn to Play Music Lessons................................. 326

Chapter 13
GarageBand Learn to Play Music Lessons   327

Getting Started with Learn to Play 327
   Piano Lesson 1: Intro to Piano 328
   Guitar Lesson 1: Intro to Guitar 329
Lesson Store: Basic Lessons 329
   Piano Lessons 331
   Guitar Lessons 331
   Learn... 332
   Play 332
Lesson Store: Artist Lessons 337
   Learn Song 338
   Play Song 340
   Story 341
The Appendixes 342

Appendix A
GarageBand Jam Packs   343

Installing Jam Packs 344
Using Jam Packs.. 345
Troubleshooting Missing Loops 346
   GarageBand Preferences File 347

Default Location of Apple Loops 348
A Walkthrough of Apple's GarageBand Jam Packs 348
GarageBand's Default Library 348
Jam Pack 1 351
Rhythm Section 353
Symphony Orchestra 357
Remix Tools 373
World Music 386
Voices 393

Appendix B
GarageBand '09 Keyboard Shortcuts   397

Keyboard Shortcut Comprehensive Reference Guide 397
Playback and Navigation 397
Tracks 398
Track Info Panel 398
Learning to Play 399
Arranging and Editing 399
Recording 400
Score View 400
Adjusting Master Volume 400
Showing Windows and Editors 401
LCD Mode Commands 401
File Menu Commands 401
Application Menu Commands 402
Help Menu Commands 402

Index 403

Introduction

Welcome to *GarageBand '09 Power!* If you're reading this sentence, chances are you've realized that your Mac computer came with an incredibly powerful application called GarageBand for recording, composing, and sharing digital music. Chances are also pretty good that you thought it would be fun and interesting to learn how to use this application, and wouldn't it be cool to find a book that would walk you through the process in an understandable and enjoyable way? I have endeavored to write a book that will both educate and entertain, and I am confident that you will get a lot out of it. If you make your way through this whole book—or even the sections that are of most interest to you—you will be up and running with GarageBand in a matter of hours, and you will be writing and recording your own music on your computer.

In this era of swapping MP3s, watching and listening to media on portable devices and mobile phones, and posting videos on websites such as YouTube, Google, and your own personal and professional blogs, audio production and editing have become skills that are no longer only the domain of the high-priced professional studio. It's something that many more of us than ever before have a need for…even a desire for. While these creative pros are, in fact, trained and practiced artists with highly honed senses of sound, timing, creative expression in the audioscape, and deep understanding of the often arcane knowledge of bringing an audio project from raw idea to market, there is no reason why the rest of us can't work on musical projects at home with our own gear and produce pieces that sound fantastic and represent our creative impulses, without having to invest thousands of dollars in studio time or pro-level hardware and software. GarageBand is here for the embracing, and embrace it we will in this book! I want to thank you for picking up *GarageBand '09 Power!*, and I encourage you to put your most creative and energetic hat on, boot up your Mac, launch GarageBand, and come along on a journey that will have you composing and recording your own music in no time at all.

Who Is This Book For?

This book is written for Mac users who want to explore their creativity in the areas of music composition and recording, podcasting, audio blogging, remixing/mashing, learning to play the piano or guitar, and even sound design in the context of video editing and DVD creation. The new features of GarageBand '08 and GarageBand '09 (a.k.a. GarageBand versions 4 and 5, respectively) have raised the bar for "pro-sumer" applications to such a degree that many users will ultimately find no need to take a step up to other, more expensive, commercially available digital recording applications. Although these applications have merit (that's an understatement, actually—I'm a Logic Pro user as well as a GarageBand user, and I love working with Logic, too), GarageBand '09 is so powerful and achieves such a high level of quality that a majority of people who want to compose and record music on their computer will find all they will ever need right inside GarageBand '09. This book is the first revision of *GarageBand '08 Power!* While it does cover all of the new features in GarageBand '09 and all of the functions that may have changed since GarageBand '08, it remains incredibly relevant for users of GarageBand '08. There are a vast number of functions and techniques that remain identical in the '09 version, and others may have only changed in their appearance or location within the application interface. Throughout the book, I will mention things that are new in GarageBand '09, so if you are using GarageBand '08, you will be alerted to things that might've been handled a little differently back in the '08 version of the application. Many sections of the book are of value to users who are still using version 3 as well, but there are other books by other authors that focus on GarageBand versions 1, 2, and 3. Whenever space and time permit, I will briefly describe the way a particular function may have operated in GarageBand '08.

In the past, GarageBand has tended to be somewhat underrated or looked down upon by critics as "that free consumer app that comes with every Mac" and therefore seen as somehow unsuitable for real work. What people who hold such opinions fail to realize is the empowering nature of the program, which, paired with its ability to record and create audio at bit rates and sample rates much higher than CD quality, makes it a revolutionary product. It's so easy to sit down and start using it that its actual value is often dismissed. I took on this book project initially because I believe that a vast majority of people have some creative inclinations, and these days we are so surrounded by music, movies, and TV shows that a lot of our creative impulses seem to direct us toward these endeavors. GarageBand is the bridge between having a nascent desire to be creative with one's computer in the area of music and being able to do so out of the box, with very little help.

Let me also say thank you for buying this book. I put a lot of time, energy, and heart into the original edition, as well as this revision, and it's great to know that someone is out there reading it. I hope you enjoy it, and I hope it is of some help to you in your desire to create music on your Macintosh. If you have any questions for me or comments on the book, please contact me through my website, www.toddhoward.com, email me at garageband@toddhoward.com, or become a fan of *GarageBand '09 Power!* on Facebook. To become a fan, just search on GarageBand '09 Power! in the Facebook search bar. I'd be happy to hear from you.

Why Is This Book Necessary?

I see two reasons why this book is necessary—or three, actually. The first is that some people—you may be one of them—just love to have a book that is not provided by the purveyor of the product in question, so they know they are getting a clear, unbiased perspective that will be written in a way they can easily understand. Although Apple's help documentation hits a fairly high mark in terms of quality and clarity, it's still written like a manual, and some GarageBand users will find more aid in mastering the program by looking at it through the lens of a third party—someone presumably more like them than the folks at Apple who actually write the software documentation.

The second reason is a desire for mastery. Although GarageBand is very easy to learn to use, even if you just start poking around at it a bit, some readers will appreciate the goal of this book, which is to cover every feature of the application and provide some real-world mental criteria for why and when to use each of these advanced features and suggestions for how to go about considering a secondary approach when the first one isn't providing a desired result. The help docs for Garage-Band, including the tutorial videos on Apple's website, are preliminary, direct, and basic. The idea of those efforts is to get you started. The idea of this book is to get you started in a few easy-to-read chapters and then really dig into the meat of the app, allowing you to master GarageBand's many techniques so you can easily begin crafting anything that comes into your creative mind.

The third reason that comes to mind when pondering the value and efficacy of this book is that it's an opportunity for me, your guide, to share with you my passion for music, for creativity, and for working with, creating, capturing, sculpting, editing, and publishing sound. Yes, sound—that old thing we take for granted. The miraculous encoding and decoding process of the movement of air molecules in vibrational waves and the ways in which those waves meet our eardrums and are then translated by our brains, hearts, minds, and bodies into meaningful expressions of human consciousness. I love working with sound, and as a musician and songwriter, I deeply love the process of editing audio—of using the fragments of sound waves that I have captured or created like colors on a painter's palette, put into my own personal masterpiece. And I use the word "masterpiece" easily not because I think anything I have ever created would be seen by the world at large as a work of genius, but because when I am working on a project in GarageBand or in Logic Pro, or when I am just sitting there with my bass guitar in my hand, it's that precious to me. It's that important. The acceptance of my own work, by me, as a personal masterpiece can be equated to the degree to which I experience hope and joy around the process of creativity. If I can help bring just one more ounce of your own creativity out of you, dear reader, then the many months of working diligently to bring this book to fruition will have been completely worth it. If the book helps you in that way, I'd love to hear about it. There is no greater thrill for me than hearing from a reader whom I have helped take a step forward.

With the recent explosive success of podcasting, millions of podcast listeners who are also Mac users have been hearing scores of program hosts say, "We use GarageBand to record and edit our shows." This has dramatically increased the number of Mac users who start poking around their Applications directory, wanting to see what this GarageBand thing is all about. The simple answer to the question "Who is this book for?" is beginner/intermediate Mac users who want to dig in and explore their own creativity with this all-but-free, full-featured digital recording studio that they already own.

Apple includes GarageBand bundled in the iLife suite that ships free on every Mac, and if you use a Mac, it's probably sitting in your Applications directory right now, ready to be explored. It is aimed at complete musical novices, yet it also has features desirable to professional musicians who are looking for a simple, high-quality sketchpad for their musical ideas. It has a straightforward interface and a wealth of features, including an enormous library of effects plug-ins, modeled amplifiers, synthesized and sampled sounds, and a whole spectrum of professional-quality digital effects that make it easy to create a song, podcast, or radio show or score a digital movie. GarageBand makes it just as easy to plug a keyboard or guitar into your computer and just jam. GarageBand '09 takes the whole thing even further by introducing the Learn to Play music lessons feature, which can teach a beginner how to play the piano or the guitar and even lets you purchase and download lessons created by some of the top recording artists of the day, who will teach you how to play one of their popular songs.

What Is GarageBand?

GarageBand is a digital multitrack recording application designed by Apple, Inc., in Cupertino, California, for the purpose of recording music, MIDI sequencing, looping, podcasting, downloading interactive video-based music lessons, and scoring your digital movies. It has been bundled on every new Macintosh computer shipped since January 2004 as part of Apple's iLife suite of "digital lifestyle" applications, which includes GarageBand, iPhoto, iTunes, iMovie, iDVD, and iWeb. See Figure I.1. It has also been available in stores and online for purchase by those who have an older Mac and might desire to upgrade to the most recent major release of the suite at the $79 price point. As of the writing of this book, GarageBand is at version 5.0.1, and each iteration of the application has introduced enhancements that have surprised and delighted its devoted user base, even those of us—myself included—who are accustomed to using a more professional-level (read: costly and deeply feature-rich) application for media production and creation.

GarageBand allows users to create a song using prerecorded musical clips, called Apple Loops, as well as to record their own instruments and vocals. Users can browse, select, and use whichever Apple Loops they wish; superimpose—or "overdub"—their own audio recordings and MIDI performances (if any); arrange them however they choose; add effects, such as reverb, EQ, or

Figure I.1   iLife '09 software packaging, courtesy of Apple.

distortion; and then export the completed song to their iTunes library for later listening, sharing with friends, creating ringtones, loading onto their iPod, posting to their Facebook page, blog, or RSS feed, and so on.

One of GarageBand's claims to fame is that the user does not necessarily need to know anything about music to construct a complete song out of these Apple Loops. The prerecorded, repeatable audio clips (often only seconds long) of talented drummers, guitarists, keyboardists, and so on will automatically fit themselves into the tempo and key of the user's own song, without the user even needing to know what a tempo and a key actually are! Rest assured, if you don't know what these are, we will be covering them thoroughly in the coming chapters. Additionally, more advanced users can record themselves playing several parts of an arrangement on various instruments of their choosing and then preview and select Apple Loops to flesh out "the band" on their song. For example, a user who can play guitar and keyboard but not bass or drums could record real guitar and MIDI synthesizer parts, then use Apple Loops of drums and bass to create a complete song from their musical sketch. GarageBand users of all levels of skill will be able to do this after reading this book.

Helping to fuel the recent explosion of podcasting, Apple added a full-featured podcasting studio to GarageBand in version 3, which was released in January 2006. This allows a user to record voiceover narration, add jingles or stingers from a library of high-quality radio-style sound effects and music bumpers, add chapter markers, and display artwork and still images within iTunes or on a listener's mobile device, iPod, or iPhone screen. To round out the podcasting studio, GarageBand has made it a one-step process to upload and announce the podcast directly to the iTunes Store's Podcast Directory—the one-stop shop for browsing, sampling, and subscribing to podcasts—so podcast fans from all over the world can find the user's original audio—or video—program, subscribe to it, and hopefully become a devoted listener and fan!

This book is an easy-to-understand, detailed guide on how to get the most out of GarageBand. It fully explores the application in what I hope is a lighthearted, non-intimidating style. Through the use of screenshots, tutorials, creative jumping-off points, and real-world examples, I hope to teach you how to use GarageBand to create music, record and publish podcasts, and even use the application for live performance. If you're new to the piano or the guitar, I will show you how to use Learn to Play and get your feet wet as a guitarist or pianist. If you've been playing for a while and want to learn some new songs directly from some of today's top artists, the Learn to Play Music Lessons feature will be covered in detail in Chapter 13.

I bring an intense passion for creativity to the writing of this book. I feel that all people are creative and that while being creative, we are building our lives quite literally out of the matter of our creative thoughts. Any time I discover that there is a new way for people to bridge the gap between their own innate creative desires and actually holding something in their hand that they created—or, better yet, giving it to someone else to enjoy—I am right there on board with helping to bring that thing deeper into people's minds and hearts. Enter GarageBand...

GarageBand is an important application because it is one of the most powerful tools for capturing and manipulating sound that has ever been made available to the public. Furthermore, it's built in such a way that almost anyone with even the most basic understanding of how to use his computer can launch it, select a project type, and begin creating and expressing himself artistically. I often think of how incredible it would have been for me when I was a teenager and just starting to get into playing, recording, and writing original songs to have had a tool like GarageBand at my disposal. GarageBand makes it simple and fun to work with music and audio. Music is such a deep part of our lives, and making music is something that I feel is at the heart of every person. Garage-Band is a hip, innovative, modern, powerful way for anyone to begin to explore his own musical creativity—and *GarageBand '09 Power!* will help build a bridge past fear for anyone interested in pursuing his creativity in this way.

For the intermediate or more advanced user, GarageBand is a topic that has an incredible amount of depth to it. If you really dig in and get to the meat of this tool, there is an amazing level of power and sophistication that can be explored. If a user feels comfortable using GarageBand in some basic ways, there is so much more that he can do with the software than he may even realize. This book will help those people take their knowledge and understanding of GarageBand much further.

This newly revised second edition of *GarageBand Power!* will serve the rapidly growing segment of creative computer users who are taking advantage of the ability to record music, audio, and podcasts and create their own mixes and mash-ups using Apple Loops, MIDI sequencing, and analog and digital source material. The application is preinstalled on every Mac, and most average users who I have spoken to in my consulting and training business consistently say things to me such as, "Oh yeah, I can't wait to figure out how to run that program." It's an application that almost any Mac user can find a use for. If the user is not a musician, maybe he wants to record his old vinyl records into his computer so he can listen to them on his iPod. If he's not a podcaster, maybe he wants to create an edit of excerpts from several of his favorite podcasts and create his own sampler mix of clips from shows by other people. If he doesn't know how to play the guitar but always wanted to learn, he can download interactive guitar lessons right inside of GarageBand to start on that journey. Or maybe he isn't musically inclined, but he heard from a friend that you can make a song of your own by browsing and sampling thousands of drum, bass, guitar, and horn parts and putting them all together like some kind of creative puzzle.

Apple has been very vocal about the idea that users don't have to be musicians to create a song in GarageBand, and from what I can tell, many of these people—perhaps you're one of these—are aching to figure out how to do it but feel somewhat daunted by how difficult it may have been in the past to learn other, more complicated music software applications. Maybe you haven't dug too far into it on your own because you are unsure about how you will fare. This book will show you that you can't break GarageBand, and all you need to do is get in there and start playing with it to create your own personal masterpieces. This book will teach you everything you need to know to use the entire application, but it will also be useful if you only want to explore a few of the facets of GarageBand.

I would also like to mention that the basic cost for any Mac user who does not yet have an updated version of GarageBand is a mere $79, and if you can manage it, I'd recommend paying the price. The fact that this tool (and its five counterparts in the iLife suite) can be upgraded so affordably is a striking reminder that many of the people who have an older version of GarageBand can easily move up to the new one. Anyone with even a slight inclination toward using this tool for creating music would most likely at least consider upgrading at that price point.

Personal Note: Why *GarageBand '09 Power!*? Why Now?

A friend of mine from Seattle, Kathleen McGinnis, once moderated a panel I was part of—an independent film production Q&A that took place after a screening of the 2003 independent feature film that I produced and co-edited, *The Trouble with Boys and Girls*. During the discussion, she looked at me and my brother, Jesse (the director, writer, and co-editor), and asked us, "Why *Trouble*? Why now?" We answered the question as best we could, and we talked about the reasons for the timing of that project and so on, but afterward, when I complimented Kathleen on that question, she didn't take credit. She said she had been asked the same question in an interview sometime in the past, and the person who had asked her the question said that she, too, had been asked it at some past event. I was intrigued by both the ask-it-forward nature of this good question and also the content of the question itself and the consideration it poses. Kathleen urged me to always ask myself this question before beginning any new project, and that is why this section of the introduction exists at all. Why am I writing *GarageBand '09 Power!*, and why now?

It's a time like no other for anyone and everyone who feels called upon to make his or her voice heard in the world. With technology such as this so close at hand, there is no longer any viable reason why one cannot decide to reach out with a media content element of some kind. Whether it be something artistic, something political, something educational, or something devoted to a particular niche, there are other people out there using tools such as GarageBand to make their voices heard, so why not you, too? There is a deluge of content available on the Internet today, and we all agree that much of it is of questionable value. Let's all (at least those with a desire) work together to produce some exceptional and interesting content. It's our legacy. Let's flesh out our niches. Let's contribute to the conversation! If any of what I'm saying here resonates with you, allow me to encourage you to listen to that nudge and produce something that you would like to share with others and get it out there. Add it to the stew. It's your turn. Still need some more encouragement? Keep reading *GarageBand '09 Power!*

1 Software Installation and Getting Connected

Now that you have a brief background on GarageBand and you have a sense of where your creative desires and GarageBand's capabilities converge, let's take a quick look at the installation process so you can start creating! This chapter will cover installing iLife '09 (the software suite that includes GarageBand '09), and getting your devices, speakers, and instruments connected to your computer for use in recording. If your Mac came with iLife '09 and GarageBand '09 preinstalled, or if you already have GarageBand up and running and you have your audio interface or mic, guitar, or MIDI keyboard connected, you can skip ahead to Chapter 2, "Choosing Your Project Type." If you are not yet up and running, or if you would like a refresher on the system requirements and software installation process of iLife '09 and GarageBand '09, then this chapter will help you get the software installed and your audio devices connected and communicating with each other.

System Requirements

Before you jump into installing iLife '09 on your computer, you need to consider its specifications. While iLife will run fine on many of the Macs sold in the past several years, there are some software and hardware requirements you'll want to consider. This is especially true if your computer is a little on the older side or somewhat lacking in RAM or processor speed, and you are updating to iLife '09 from a previous version.

Software

On the software side, your main concern should be your operating system version. iLife '09 will not run on Mac OS 9 or in Classic, nor will it run on Mac OS X 10.0 (Cheetah), 10.1 (Puma), 10.2 (Jaguar), 10.3 (Panther), or 10.4 (Tiger). You will have to be running Mac OS X 10.5.6 (Leopard) or later. Leopard users will need to make sure they are updated to version 10.5.6 or later. Any earlier versions (10.5.5 or before) will not be compatible with iLife '09. If you do not have Mac OS X 10.5 Leopard, you will need to purchase a copy from your local Apple retail store, the Apple Store on the Apple website (www.apple.com/store), or another Apple software retailer to be able to run iLife '09 and GarageBand '09. Mac OS X typically costs $129 for a single user license, and Apple offers family license packs for $199 that authorize you to install Max OS X Leopard on all of the computers in one household. A similar family pack license is available for iLife '09 as well.

To make the whole process of upgrading even simpler, Apple has introduced the Mac Box Set. This software suite includes Mac OS X 10.5.6 Leopard, iLife '09 (iPhoto '09, iMovie '09, GarageBand '09, iWeb '09, and iDVD), and iWork '09, Apple's productivity suite (Pages '09, Numbers '09, and Keynote '09). The Mac Box Set retails for $169, and a family pack license for installation on all the computers within one household is $229. Purchasing the Mac Box Set offers a savings of more than $100.

If you have Leopard but are running any version previous to 10.5.6, you need only open up System Preferences, found in the Dock, in your Applications folder, or in the Apple menu at the top-left corner of your screen, as shown in Figure 1.1.

Figure 1.1 Choosing System Preferences from the Apple menu.

In System Preferences, choose Software Update (see Figure 1.2).

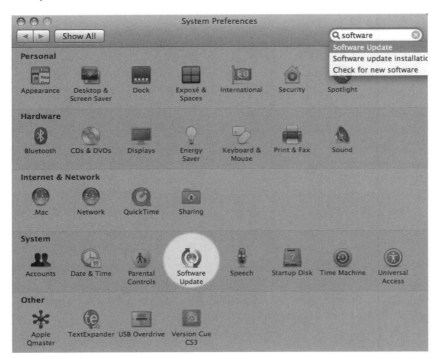

Figure 1.2 Update your Mac OS X Leopard system software by choosing Software Update from the System Preferences window.

In this Preferences window, you can set the frequency with which your computer automatically checks for updates to your system software (and any other Apple software you have installed), and you can also initiate a manual check. Click the Check Now button in the Software Update pane to see whether there are indeed any updates to your OS or Apple software applications available (see Figure 1.3).

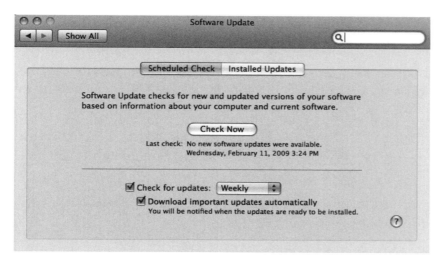

Figure 1.3   Click Check Now to update your version of Mac OS X Leopard.

Hardware

On the hardware side, you have to think about the CPU, processor speed, RAM, a DVD drive for the installation DVD, as well as hard drive capacity. Apple's published system requirements for installing iLife '09 are available at www.apple.com/ilife/systemrequirements.html and are as follows:

- Mac computer with an Intel, PowerPC G5, or PowerPC G4 (867 MHz or faster) processor.

- iMovie requires an Intel-based Mac, Power Mac G5 (dual 2.0 GHz or faster), or iMac G5 (1.9 GHz or faster).

- GarageBand Learn to Play requires an Intel-based Mac with a Core Duo processor or better.

- 512 MB of RAM; 1 GB recommended. High-definition video requires at least 1 GB of RAM.

- Mac OS X v10.5.6 or later.

- Approximately 4 GB of available disk space.

- DVD drive required for installation.

- QuickTime 7.5.5 or later (included).

- AVCHD video requires a Mac with an Intel Core Duo processor or better. Visit iMovie '09 Camcorder Support for details on digital video device and format support.

- 24-bit recording in GarageBand requires a Mac OS X–compatible audio interface with support for 24-bit audio. Please consult the owner's manual or manufacturer directly for audio device specifications and compatibility.

- Burning DVDs requires an Apple SuperDrive or a compatible third-party DVD burner.

- iPhoto print products are available in the U.S., Canada, Japan, and select countries in Europe and Asia Pacific.

- Some features require Internet access and/or MobileMe; additional fees and terms apply. MobileMe is available to persons age 13 and older. Annual subscription fee and Internet access required. Terms of service apply.

- GarageBand Artist Lessons are sold separately and are available directly through the GarageBand Lesson Store in select countries.

- Flickr service is available only in select countries.

GarageBand Installation

Chances are that iLife '09 came preinstalled on your Mac or you already installed it before reading this book. If you are upgrading from a previous version of GarageBand, you need only to run the installer on the iLife '09 DVD and follow the steps in the dialog boxes that display during the process. Installing GarageBand '09 is part of the larger installation of the suite of applications known as iLife '09. iLife '09 includes the latest versions of GarageBand, iPhoto, iMovie, iDVD, and iWeb.

Although it is possible to install GarageBand by itself without installing the other applications in iLife '09, I recommend proceeding with the full installation if you don't have some specific need to save on hard drive space or you know from experience that you have no need for the other iLife applications. The main reason I am recommending you do this is that Apple has gone to great lengths to make these five applications (or six, if you include iTunes) work very well together. For example, if you are using GarageBand to create a podcast episode, this integration of the applications within the complete iLife suite allows you to easily browse your iPhoto library right from within GarageBand. Selecting and embedding artwork for each of your chapter markers—a crucial step when producing an AAC-enhanced podcast—becomes a one-click process, instead of a fairly involved one requiring you to switch between multiple applications and possibly even go hunting for images on your hard drive and using graphics editing software to crop or resize your images manually.

A good example of a follow-up step, taking advantage of the seamless integration of the apps in the iLife suite, is that with a single click, you can post your new podcast episode directly to your website from GarageBand using iWeb. Or, you can use a song you created in GarageBand as the background music for a video that you are editing in iMovie and, with only one more click, move the whole project to iDVD for burning. The integration and intermingling of the applications in the iLife suite truly enhance creativity by removing long series of steps (which I believe can often become full-blown obstacles!) from the process of utilizing assets from one application or media library while working on a project in another.

For the purpose of checking to be sure GarageBand is installed and running properly, you can launch GarageBand. (Look in your Dock, which is the row of application icons along the bottom of your screen, or in your Applications folder, which resides inside your Home folder for the GarageBand application icon. Alternatively, when you are in the Finder, you can press Command+Shift+A to go directly to the Applications directory.)

You can skip the Welcome to GarageBand screen that you see just by clicking the Close button in the lower right, and then choose Piano from the New Project dialog box. If you don't see a choice called Piano, be sure that you have selected New Project in the left column. Once your GarageBand project opens, choose File > Save As and save a test project into a folder for your GarageBand projects on your hard drive. If that worked, you can most likely assume the installation went as planned, and GarageBand is ready for use. You can quit GarageBand and read on to find out how to get all of your connections and protocols in order.

Connection Protocols

Now we're going to jump right in and look at the first thing you need to do before you can start working with audio on your Mac—connect all of your audio and music devices to your computer. The first thing you need to know is what interfaces—what specific connection protocols—your computer supports. Any Mac (not including the MacBook Air) that ships with GarageBand '08 or GarageBand '09 installed supports four main types of interfaces (you may require adapters or an additional hardware interface to utilize all of these connection protocols):

- USB (*Universal Serial Bus*)

- FireWire (IEEE 1394)

- MIDI (*Musical Instrument Digital Interface*)

- Audio Line In

I will discuss these interfaces briefly so you will be able to determine which types of devices and connectors you may want to use in conjunction with GarageBand in the exciting and creative pursuit of producing music on your Mac. I will not be going into a lot of technical detail about these protocols—much has already been written about them, and you can investigate them fully by searching online. For the purpose of helping you start working with GarageBand as quickly and easily as possible, I will not dwell on the technical ins and outs; I will try to favor the practical principles involved and explain some of the choices you have.

USB (Universal Serial Bus)

USB, a connection protocol used for audio interfaces, external hard drives, CD-ROM and DVD-ROM burners, and even your keyboard and mouse, comes in two flavors: USB1 and USB2. USB 1.0 was released in 1995, and you will encounter this version on some machines still in use today. USB 2.0 was released in 2000 and is a faster, more reliable version of the protocol. All Intel-based Macintosh computers sold today have one or more USB 2.0 ports on them. USB can be extended by attaching a USB hub, which comes with four or more additional USB ports (see Figure 1.4).

Figure 1.4   USB 2.0 port and USB jack (6-pin).

FireWire (IEEE 1394)

FireWire is Apple's brand name for their implementation of the IEEE 1394 protocol. Sony introduced it to the camcorder marker in 1995 and dubbed it i.Link. On Macintosh computers, FireWire currently comes in two flavors. Known as FireWire 400 (IEEE 1394a) and FireWire 800 (IEEE 1394b), these protocols are used primarily for connecting external hard drives, CD/DVD burners, audio interfaces, and digital video cameras to your computer. FireWire is a faster, more robust connection protocol than USB. This is a generalization, but many Mac users doing audio work tend to prefer hard drives and other devices that use FireWire to those that use USB. The truth is that on most machines, either protocol (FireWire or USB) in its current incarnation is perfectly suitable for connecting drives, audio interfaces, and burners. Check the documentation of any devices that you are planning to incorporate into your recording setup for any specific information pertaining to its use for your desired purpose, and see whether the FireWire or USB protocol is recommended for that purpose. Most devices that have both protocols built in will work well using either, and in that case it will come down to the physical existence of the ports on your computer itself or the requirements of the application being used. In this case, we're talking about GarageBand, which works well with either FireWire or USB for your device connections. See Figure 1.5.

FireWire 400 Jack

FireWire 800 Jack

FireWire 400 Port

FireWire 800 Port

Figure 1.5   FireWire 400/FireWire 800 ports and FireWire 400/FireWire 800 jacks.

Be aware that all Macs made after 2009 only come with FireWire 800 and no longer include FireWire 400, but you can acquire a special adapter cable to interface with FireWire 400 from a post-2009 Mac.

MIDI (Musical Instrument Digital Interface)

MIDI has been around since the early days of electronic music. It debuted in 1983, when it was a proposal brought to the Audio Engineering Society by Dave Smith of Sequential Circuits, Inc., who is regarded as the father of MIDI. MIDI allows electronic instruments to communicate with one another. The MIDI implementation most likely to be part of your GarageBand setup will be a controller device (typically a piano-style keyboard or some other MIDI-enabled device, such as a MIDI guitar or a wind controller) communicating with your Mac.

If you are using one of the software instruments in GarageBand—for example, the grand piano—MIDI allows you to press keys on your MIDI controller keyboard, and those key presses trigger notes to be played by the grand piano software instrument. This process allows you to perform and record music. (Keep in mind that when I mention pressing keys on your keyboard to trigger notes in this context, I don't mean your computer's QWERTY keyboard—I'm referring to a piano-style keyboard controller connected to your Mac with a MIDI or USB cable.) Your piano keyboard—your MIDI controller—becomes your interface to the library of software samples and sounds that ships with GarageBand. I don't wish to further complicate the issue by mentioning this, but there is a feature in GarageBand called *musical typing* that does, in fact, allow you to use your QWERTY keyboard to play or record MIDI notes, using any chosen software instrument (such as the grand piano software instrument in the earlier example). This can be used in the absence of a MIDI controller. To access this feature, choose Musical Typing from the Window menu. Musical typing is further explained in Chapter 3, "GarageBand Preferences and the User Interface," in the section called "The Window Menu."

If you import additional software instruments into your library—a number of Jam Packs are available for purchase that significantly add to your collection of sounds—you will be able to choose from among those sounds as well as the default group that comes with GarageBand. You will use your MIDI controller to trigger any of these software instruments, and you can record these triggers—sometimes referred to as *MIDI data*—into GarageBand in real time. This process allows you to play back your MIDI recording and select different software instruments to be triggered at any time. This flexibility is part of what makes MIDI such a desirable tool for composing and performing. You might have recorded a little melody with the grand piano sound, but that data is saved, and you can just as easily change the sound to a lead guitar, a flute, or even a marimba or drum set. Then you can audition these sounds to your heart's content, until you find the exact sound you want to use in your final recording.

MIDI data takes up far less hard drive space than recording actual real-world sounds into your computer with a microphone, through your audio interface, or directly into your Mac using the Audio Line In port, which we'll discuss in the next section. See Figure 1.6 to see a MIDI port on a keyboard and an audio/MIDI interface.

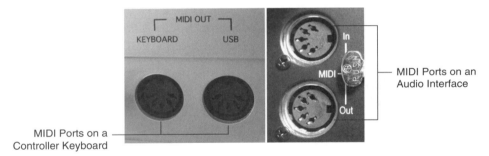

Figure 1.6 MIDI port on a keyboard and an audio/MIDI interface.

Audio Line In

The last type of interface protocol common to all Macs is the Audio Line In. It's a ⅛-inch stereo input and combines optical digital input and standard audio line level in into one jack. The Audio Line In is something you might use for any source that does not have preamplification, and it uses the soundcard built into your Mac. For example, you might use it for connecting a cassette deck or another component or device that has a line out—which often uses RCA-style connectors. You will need an adapter to turn those RCA jacks into a ⅛-inch stereo jack for the end that connects to your Mac. Adapters like these are available at any electronics store or directly from Apple. It's worth mentioning here that a guitar or bass cannot be plugged directly into the Audio Line In; it needs to pass through an audio mixer, audio interface, or direct box (often called a *DI box*) to change the high-impedance unbalanced output signal produced by the guitar (a rather low level) into a signal that is appropriate to the input level required by the Audio Line In jack on your computer. See Figure 1.7 for a visual of Audio Line In.

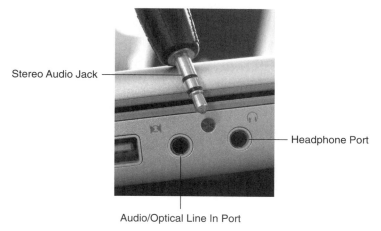

Stereo Audio Jack

Headphone Port

Audio/Optical Line In Port

Figure 1.7   An optical digital input/Audio Line In port and a stereo audio jack.

Bringing It All Together

These methods of connecting external devices to your Mac are all available to you out of the box. Keep in mind that the list of possible devices you might connect to your computer to use while recording and mixing audio is extensive—much more extensive than what would be practical to print here (and constantly expanding). You will have to do some investigation of the products available today to determine which is right for you and your system.

It wouldn't be prudent to suggest what hardware you should use, given the wide range of possible needs, budgets, brand loyalties, and quality requirements that could describe each musician or producer wishing to use GarageBand to record audio on his Mac. There are many resources on the Internet that will not only provide a far more exhaustive list of possible choices, but will also be updated with the most current version of each product; a book like this can't provide that level of immediacy. Use Google or another search engine to try some searches for terms such as "USB condenser mic," "analog to digital converter," "digital I/O," "audio interface," and "microphones for home recording," and you are bound to find a wealth of products to investigate. If you shop at the Apple Store or you purchased your computer there, you might also want to investigate the products they carry and speak with a salesperson about your specific needs and budget.

To tackle the process of choosing your audio hardware on your own, you can start by thinking about all of the things you might want to record. If you want to record voice, you'll need a microphone. There are mics that have USB jacks built right in, which will allow you to plug in the mic, create a track in GarageBand, and begin recording immediately. Other mics might require a preamp or phantom power and may need to run through a mixer before they hit your Mac. If you want to have a keyboard to play and you intend to trigger software instruments and use sounds available inside of GarageBand—such as the many available Jam Packs (covered in depth in Appendix A, "GarageBand Jam Packs")—then you'll need a MIDI controller keyboard. There are scores of different MIDI controllers available, starting at less than $100 for simple three- or four-octave plain-Jane controllers and ranging to many thousands of dollars for fully programmable MIDI sequencers and synthesizers.

At a bare minimum, you'll probably want to pick up a four- or five-octave MIDI keyboard controller, some type of analog-to-digital audio interface, a decent condenser microphone, and a guitar/bass patch cable. If you're running your guitar or bass though an amp, you always have the option of positioning (focusing) a microphone in front of the amp to record it, avoiding the line-in situation entirely for recording your "real-world" instrument. This technique will also give you the live room sound of your amp. But keep in mind that if you record your guitar through your amp with a chorus effect or a distortion pedal effect on it, for example, then there will be no way for you to remove those effects and experiment with other tones once you have everything recorded. Recording a clean, unprocessed (un-effected) signal offers you more flexibility after the fact for experimentation with GarageBand's vast library of amplifiers, digital processing, and stomp box effects. This is your creative decision, of course. If you know the exact sound that you want to record and you have the effects pedals or sound processing that achieve "your sound" built into your amp, then by all means get a mic in front of your speaker cabinet and track it!

There are many professional studio-quality effects and stomp boxes available to you in GarageBand, including amplifier modeling, distortion, chorus, reverb, delay, and so many more. Unless you have a specific reason for recording your real-world instruments with effects processing already on them, I suggest you try to get a good, clean, unprocessed signal recorded, and then begin to tweak your sound in GarageBand during the mixing phase of your project. I will cover how to accomplish this in detail in Chapter 11, "Mixing and Automation."

If you have any trouble getting iLife '09 installed or running properly, once you've connected all your devices and instruments, you have some really great resources at your fingertips. My recommendations follow:

- **Apple Discussions.** Visit discussions.apple.com. On the main page, there is a section called iLife; under that heading, you will find GarageBand. There are separate discussions for GarageBand versions 1, 2, 3, '08, and '09. Be sure you're in the GarageBand '09 discussion group before doing a search or posting a question.

- **Apple Support.** You can try calling 1-800-MY-APPLE or 1-800-APL-CARE and telling the representative that you recently purchased iLife '09 and would like some help getting it installed and running. Although they will likely sidestep direct questions about getting any specific third-party hardware running, you can potentially eke out some info from Apple's helpful support reps by explaining where you're coming from and what you're trying to do. Be creative in your question-asking, and you just might get what you're looking for. There is also an Apple GarageBand support website at www.apple.com/support/garageband.

- **Audio/MIDI/Music Forums.** There are a number of web forums that might be useful to you in tracking down a specific solution. These may require you to first search the forum to see whether anyone else has had your issue (which is likely). If you come up empty-handed, you might be required to register on the forum, and then you can leave a posted question and see whether anyone answers it for you. Most well-traveled forums seem to generate answers within a few hours, and it is often not more than a day. In fact, if the forum you are on has many hundreds of members and you ask a question and no one posts a response within a day or so, it usually means that your question was poorly articulated, your question has been answered on the forum a dozen times already and everyone's ignoring you because you should have searched the forum for the answer first, or you haven't listed your system specs as part of your posting. On behalf of forum posters everywhere, I ask you to please, when posting a question on a web forum, always list what type of machine you are using (specifically and exactly—everything but your serial number), the version of the OS you are running, the version of the software in question, how much RAM you have installed (and whether it's third-party or shipped with the computer), which hard drive and how big, which processor and how fast, and each and every device you have plugged into the machine, along with pertinent model numbers or version numbers. If you've done all of this and you get no answer within a day or so, then you're probably on the wrong forum—try another one. Some good ones are www.bigbluelounge.com, createdigitalnoise.com, macjams.com, and macusersforum.com, among many others.

- **Google.com.** When all else fails, try Googling your issue. If you've received an error box with a message in it, try Googling the exact phrase that was in your error dialog box. If you have no error, type in phrases such as "trouble installing GarageBand '09," "iLife '09 installation issue," "no MIDI in GarageBand '09," and the like. Try a few different searches before you give up. Chances are very good that if you're having an issue with getting things working properly, someone else has had the same issue and has written about it online somewhere. Give it a shot. Google searches will often turn up Apple Discussion forum posts as well as other various resources.

System Preferences: Sound

After you have GarageBand installed and any hardware devices connected, including any updated software drivers that are required for use, you'll want to instruct your Mac to use the input and output devices you've connected. To accomplish this, return to the System Preferences application in the Apple menu. From the Hardware category, choose Sound (see Figure 1.8).

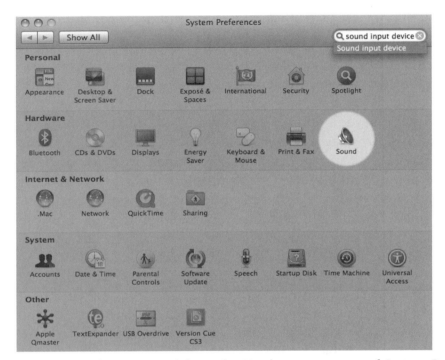

Figure 1.8 Choose Sound from the Hardware category of System Preferences.

The Sound panel has three tabs or subcategories—Sound Effects, Output, and Input. We'll look at the Sound Effects tab first, which governs the sounds your operating system makes, and then move on to Output and Input, which pertain directly to the process of getting sound into and out of your computer (see Figure 1.9).

Sound Effects

The Sound Effects tab of the Sound panel in System Preferences is for choosing which alert sound you want the computer to use when something is wrong. It's that "system beep" type of sound we're all used to hearing when the computer is saying, "Um, I don't think so." You can click on each effect, such as Basso, Blow, Bottle, Frog, and so on, and the computer will play a test tone for each one as you click on it. The last one you click on will be the one used for your system's alert sounds.

You can choose which output device to play these alerts through in the Play Alerts and Sound Effects Through drop-down menu just below the list of alerts. The choices

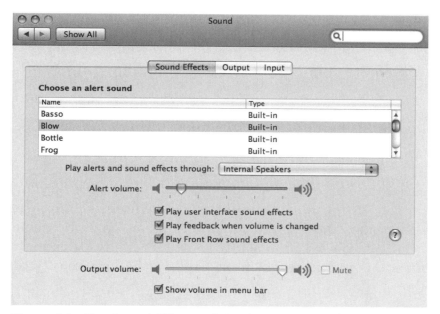

Figure 1.9 The Sound Effects tab in the System Preferences Sound panel.

begin with Use Selected Sound Output Device, which refers to the category called Output. Using this setting will play the alert tone of your choosing through whichever output device you choose in the Output tab. We'll get there in a moment. Choose this if you want your system alerts to update whenever you change an output setting in the Output tab.

The next choice is Internal Speakers, which refers to the speakers that are built into your laptop or desktop machine. Below that in the drop-down menu are listed any devices for which you have installed audio drivers. One thing to keep in mind is that many people play their system alerts through the built-in speakers, and they play their "important" audio (such as iTunes music, GarageBand playback, DVDs, YouTube videos, and so on) through their sound-output devices. For example, my input/output device of choice these days is a Lexicon Omega USB audio interface. I use this for my sound input and sound output. I plug guitars and microphones into it for recording into GarageBand or Logic Pro, and I have my Wharfedale Diamond Studio 8 Pro monitors (speakers) connected to its output. Whenever I play sound out of GarageBand, iTunes, my web browser, or my software DVD player, the audio comes out of my high-end speakers instead of out of the built-in speakers on my iMac.

Still other users look to the next series of check boxes and further customize how their alert audio is played back. You can set your alert volume in this Sound Effects tab. This allows you to have your alerts play very softly, for example, and other audio play at a different level. You can turn on or off the Play User Interface Sound Effects option by checking the box for on and unchecking it for off. These sound effects are things such as the "finished" sound that happens when you copy a file from one place to another or the crumpling sound of paper when you empty the trash.

The Play Feedback When Volume Is Changed option is for hearing the sound that plays when you adjust your system volume using the keyboard volume up and volume down function buttons. If you have a Mac with Front Row on it, there is a series of sound effects that application uses that you can activate or deactivate by checking or unchecking the box.

Finally, you can set your overall system volume with the slider at the bottom of the Sound Effects pane. Some hardware sound input/output devices (my Lexicon is one of them) disable the slider here by making it gray. This is because an optimized line-level signal is sent to the I/O device, and typically, you can control the volume of your whole system by adjusting a hardware volume knob on the device itself. This system volume setting is the same slider that appears in the main menu bar, up on the right side, next to the date and time, if you have the Show Volume in Menu Bar option checked. You can also mute your system sound from here by checking the Mute check box.

Output

The Output device settings pane is located in the second tab, which contains the Choose a Device for Sound Output list. If you have installed a hardware audio I/O on your system, the device will appear in this list. Choose it by clicking once on it. By the way, if you plan to use your system's stock soundcard, it is perfectly fine—don't get the idea that you must have higher-end gear to use GarageBand. A better interface may produce overall better sound recording, but it is entirely user preference. If your hardware output device has any unique proprietary controls or settings, they may appear here as well. See Figure 1.10.

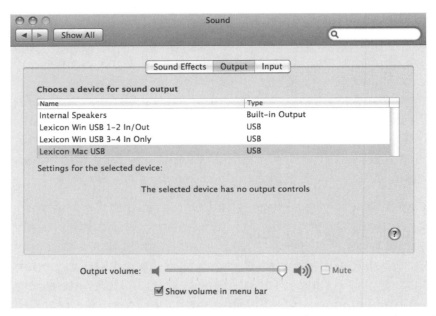

Figure 1.10 The Output tab in the System Preferences Sound panel.

Input

The Input tab lets you once again select your hardware I/O, if you have one connected, or the built-in soundcard on any Mac. Click on the input device once from the list to choose it. Your input setting will need to be set to your microphone or hardware I/O and can also be set to built-in if you're using the line-in port on your Mac. Remember, these settings are for your system at large, and not specifically for GarageBand. You can set things here one way, and in GarageBand's preferences (covered in depth in Chapter 3), you can override these settings for use in GarageBand exclusively. After you choose your microphone or sound device input from the list, if your device grants you the ability to set a global input level, you can set that here by clicking and dragging the Input volume slider. If your I/O handles that part of things itself, the Input volume slider will be grayed out.

If you can adjust global Input volume here, as you speak into your microphone, headset, or built-in mic, you will see the Input volume meter bouncing up and down in response to the loudness and proximity of your voice. I usually keep mine set to about 75%, but you will have to judge for yourself, given the sensitivity of your mic. See Figure 1.11.

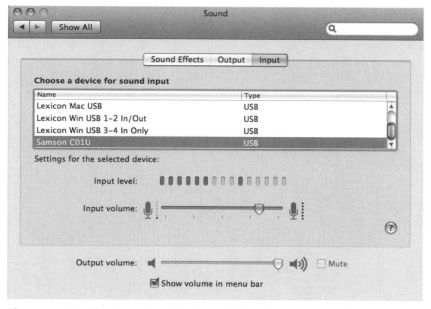

Figure 1.11 The Input tab in the System Preferences Sound panel.

You have access to the Output Volume, Mute, and Show Volume in Menu Bar settings from all three tabs of the Sound panel. You can see these options at the bottom of Figures 1.9, 1.10, and 1.11. If you ever have issues with your input or output sound devices, start your troubleshooting by going back to Apple menu > System Preferences > Sound and investigating the Output and Input tabs to be sure your devices are still selected. Mac OS X notoriously drops settings in this box from time to time when you restart, install new software, or your system crashes and you have to reboot. It's always good to start here when trouble arises and see whether everything is working properly on your system before you tackle the question of whether it's working properly in GarageBand.

Let's Get Started!

Now that you have GarageBand installed and running, all of your system preferences assigned, a mic line level set for your system, and sound coming out of your built-in or external speakers, it's time to talk about actually using the application! The next few chapters will teach you how to explore and modify GarageBand's settings and preferences to your liking, as well as how to choose a project type and design your project. They will also take you on a brief tour of GarageBand's user interface and how to work with tracks, mixing controls, and the timeline. Let's dig in!

2 Choosing Your Project Type

GarageBand was originally designed as a music- or song-recording application. As Apple evolved the application, some additional work modes were added. For example, Movie Score was introduced in GarageBand 3 in iLife '06. That mode was designed to generally behave like the standard music-recording mode, but it displayed a Video Track that allowed for importing a video clip, alongside which you could easily compose music and record it to picture, meaning visually in sync with the image. This work mode behaved much like good old GarageBand, but it had some specific new features and functions activated and unique tracks, such as the Video Track, set to show. As time has gone on, even more work modes have been introduced. Also in GarageBand 3, Apple introduced the Podcast Episode mode, and new to GarageBand '08 was Magic GarageBand. In GarageBand '09, Apple redesigned the Choose Project Type interface to operate a little more like iTunes or iPhoto does, in that you can choose a category of GarageBand use on the left and then make a choice from the right pane to create your new project. Through all of the versions of GarageBand, this initial window allows you to specify the type of project on which you would like to begin working.

The New Project Interface

The first time you launch GarageBand '09, you will see the Welcome to GarageBand window. By clicking Video Tutorials in the upper-right corner, you will be connected to Apple's online Video Tutorials library, where you can get in-depth instruction right on your Mac with dozens of tutorials for GarageBand, iPhoto, iMovie, iWeb, and iDVD. In the lower-right, you can click Hands-On Help to learn about One to One personal training, the Genius Bar, and free workshops at the Apple Retail Store. In the center, you can click on the button labeled Click to Play to watch a Getting Started video to see how easy it is to make, record, and learn to play music. To prevent this screen from coming up every time you launch GarageBand, you can uncheck the check box labeled Show This Window When GarageBand Opens. Click the Close button to close the window (see Figure 2.1).

When you close the Welcome to GarageBand window, you will be presented with a window that requires you to select which type of GarageBand project you'd like to begin working on. The interface has changed considerably since the last version of GarageBand. In GarageBand '08, there were only four buttons to choose from.

Figure 2.1   The Welcome to GarageBand window in GarageBand '09.

They were Create New Music Project, Open an Existing Project, Create New Podcast Episode, and Magic GarageBand. I believe the reason Apple continues to evolve the New Project interface from version to version is that the developers are chasing some x factor that has been quite difficult for them to hone in on. But it's also that they are continually willing to reinvent something that doesn't quite work perfectly. The goal of a dialog box like this one is to present a wizard-like, one-click interface that answers the following question: "What specific list of choices can we present to the user that will satisfy every possible desire that a person launching GarageBand might have?" The New Project interface in GarageBand '09 has so far come the closest to hitting that mark.

The main thing to realize when navigating this window is that these choices trigger predetermined setups of the GarageBand interface and are designed to get you recording quickly. There are at least a dozen panels, control strips, and browser windows that are optionally shown or hidden within the GarageBand interface, based on what your end goal is. This selection process allows you to begin working on a recording or composition project with a minimal amount of interface fiddling. The underlying truth here, however, is that you could conceivably open up any one of the new project types in this window and, with four or five menu selections or display-button clicks, be working in any of the other new project types. They are all just variations on a theme. GarageBand version 1 opened up with a blank slate. Nothing but a GarageBand window in front of you and a Software Instrument track set to trigger a grand piano sound, armed and ready for recording. Users who had no desire to record a MIDI piano track likely grew tired of creating a Real Instrument track and deleting the Software Instrument grand piano track, just to get tracking something through a connected microphone. In response to user feedback, it can be supposed, Apple decided to start with a window that asks you, "What would you like to do?"

The New Project interface in GarageBand '09 is their latest best idea. I think it works really well. There are six categories in the left column—yet another migration of one of the Apple interfaces toward the iTunes model of sources or categories on the left, which, when clicked, populate the right-hand portion of the window with all of the options in that category. I'll go through all of the options in each of the six categories one by one.

New Project

This option presents nine possibilities for project creation. Although they may seem very different from one another in terms of intent, they are all project presets that provide you with certain panels shown and others hidden, and often several pre-created audio tracks with different instruments and effects set up to help make it easy to embark on a recording project of that type (see Figure 2.2).

Figure 2.2 The New Project interface in GarageBand '09, displaying the nine default project types.

When you would like to create one of the projects listed in the New Project window, you can click on one of them and click the Choose button, or you can simply double-click on any of the New Project type icons. Once you choose one, you will be prompted to save your project and name it, and you have the option of setting the tempo, the signature, and/or the key or leaving them set to their defaults if you don't know what you would like to set them to. These can always be changed later. We'll go through exactly what tempo, signature, and key are later in this chapter. In Chapters 4, 5, and 6, respectively, we'll be covering in great detail the principles involved in working with tracks and recording Real Instruments and Software Instruments.

Piano

Selecting Piano from the New Project category creates a GarageBand project that most closely resembles the Software Instrument project choice in GarageBand '08. You have one Software Instrument track created for you, set to Grand Piano, and your Loop Browser window open. This is the project type you would want to choose if your goal were to simply use your computer, a MIDI controller, and GarageBand to play some piano. The piano is one of the songwriter's most versatile tools, and sometimes you just want to tap out some notes. The New Piano Project setting is the quickest way to begin playing some notes (see Figure 2.3).

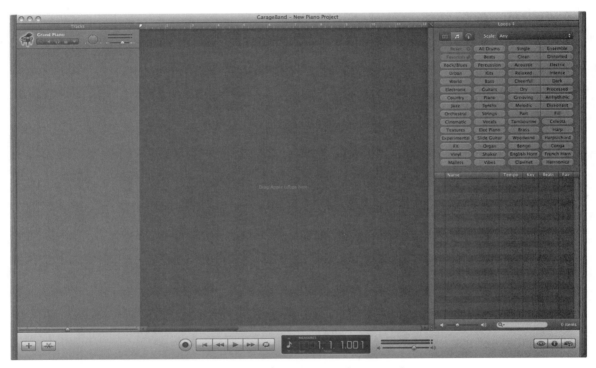

Figure 2.3 A GarageBand project opened as a new piano project.

Electric Guitar

Selecting Electric Guitar from the New Project category creates a GarageBand project that is ready to receive an electric guitar signal and begin recording. A Guitar Track is set up, and a Clean Combo amp model is selected. Sustain and Delay Effects Stomp Boxes are ready for use. It's easy to use an Electric Guitar Track in GarageBand to simply plug your guitar in and play in headphones or through speakers, or to start recording tracks. I think of the Piano and Electric Guitar selections in the New Project window as the ones to choose if you would just like to play. See Figure 2.4.

Voice

Selecting Voice from the New Project window creates a GarageBand project with two Real Instrument tracks set up and named Male Basic and Female Basic. Both are

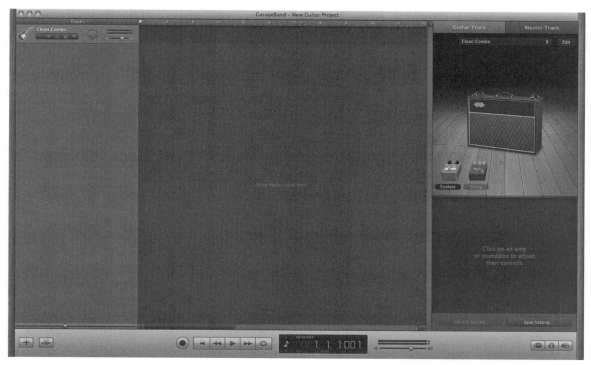

Figure 2.4 A GarageBand project opened as a new electric guitar project.

preconfigured to use the Male Basic and Female Basic effects settings, which include
presets such as Gate, Compressor, and Visual EQ. These settings are just starting places and can be immediately customized to your liking. This is the project type to use if
you are planning to do some singing or you need a shortcut to having two Real Instrument tracks up and ready to go. See Figure 2.5.

Loops

Selecting Loops from the New Project window creates a GarageBand project with the
Loop Browser opened and an empty main project window. By dragging and dropping
loops into the main window, tracks are created on the fly. If the loop is MIDI, a Software Instrument track is created for it, and if the loop is regular audio, a Real Instrument track is created. The difference between these two will be discussed at length in
Chapters 5 and 6, "Real Instruments and Electric Guitar Tracks" and "Software
Instruments" (see Figure 2.6).

Keyboard Collection

Selecting Keyboard Collection from the New Project window creates a GarageBand
project with seven Software Instrument tracks set up, with a variety of different keyboard Software Instrument selected and configured with various effects and EQ settings designed to get you up and running very quickly to start playing all kinds of
synths and keyboards. The tracks in the preset are Grand Piano, Electric Piano, Classic
Organ, Smokey Clav, Solo Star, Falling Star, and Synchro Nice (see Figure 2.7).

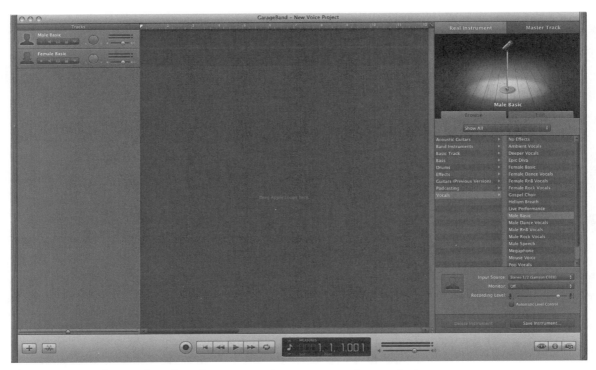

Figure 2.5   A GarageBand project opened as a new voice project.

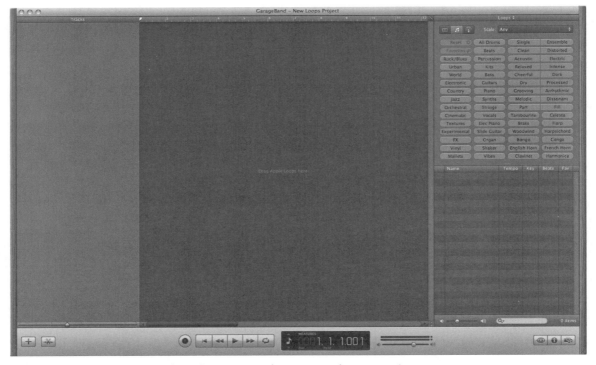

Figure 2.6   A GarageBand project opened as a new loops project.

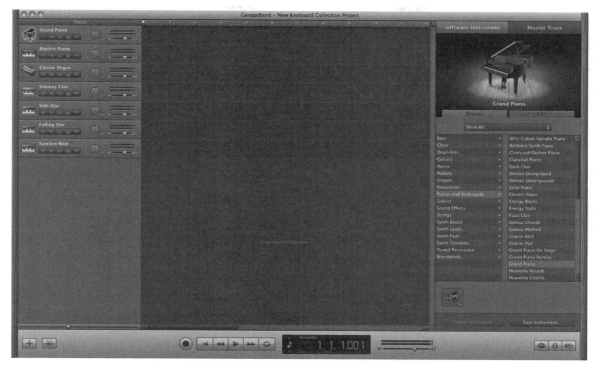

Figure 2.7 A GarageBand project opened as a new keyboard collection project.

Acoustic Instrument

Selecting Acoustic Instrument from the New Project window creates a GarageBand project with a single Real Instrument track armed and ready to record through a microphone. The purpose of a lot of these project choices is to get you going immediately. If you're someone who has a microphone connected to your computer at all times, and you have an acoustic guitar, a violin, or some other acoustic instrument sitting near your computer, all you need to do is launch GarageBand, click Acoustic Instrument from the New Project window, press Record, and you're off and running with tracking your acoustic instrument (see Figure 2.8).

Songwriting

Selecting Songwriting from the New Project window creates a GarageBand project with tracks for Voice, Acoustic Guitar, Piano, Muted Bass, and Drums. The Voice and Acoustic Guitar tracks are Real Instrument tracks and can be recorded into with a mic or guitar plugged into your computer. The Piano and Muted Bass tracks are preconfigured as Software Instrument tracks, and you can use your MIDI controller to write piano and bass parts in your new song. The Drums track is a Real Instrument track and already has a drum loop in the track, ready to keep the beat as you write your new song (see Figure 2.9).

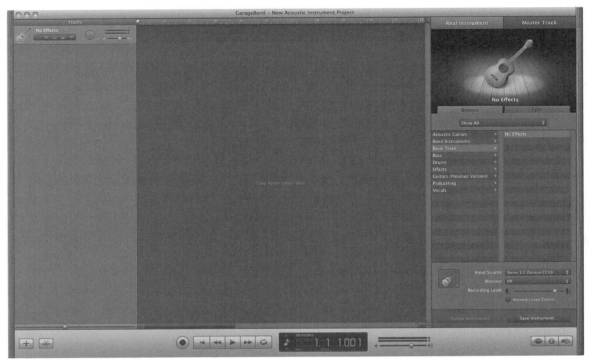

Figure 2.8 A GarageBand project opened as a new acoustic instrument project.

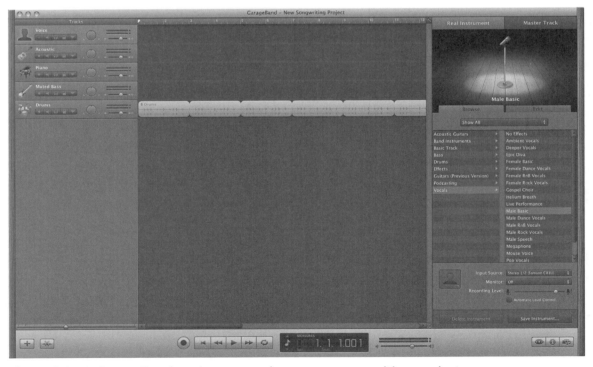

Figure 2.9 A GarageBand project opened as a new songwriting project.

Podcast

Selecting Podcast from the New Project window creates a GarageBand podcast episode project. As mentioned earlier, these are similar to regular GarageBand music projects, but they utilize some additional specific tools, tracks, and windows that are set to show by default in your GarageBand project window and that aid in the creation of a podcast. Working with podcast episodes is covered in depth in Chapter 10, "Podcasting" (see Figure 2.10).

Figure 2.10   A GarageBand project opened as a new podcast project.

Movie

Selecting Movie from the New Project window creates a GarageBand project that is ready for scoring a video. When the GarageBand project template opens, the Video Track is enabled, the Media Browser is open and pointing to your Movies directory on your hard drive, and the Track Editor is showing the Movie Markers panel (see Figure 2.11).

A movie score is a GarageBand project file that allows you to drag a movie file (presumably something you've edited in a video editing application, such as iMovie or Final Cut Pro) into the main timeline. As a result, GarageBand displays a filmstrip of thumbnail images from your movie along the timeline horizontally, dynamically created at intervals of the movie that are relative to the level of zoom at which you are viewing the timeline and the current position of the playhead.

The benefit of creating a new movie project is that you can record music or voiceover while watching a movie play back inside your GarageBand window, and your audio

Figure 2.11 A GarageBand project opened as a new movie project.

and the frames of the movie are always kept in synchronization with one another. This will allow you to react to things in the movie that you might want to accentuate in your performance. GarageBand also makes it very easy to export the finished product directly to iDVD or to just output the final mix as an AIF audio file. See Figure 2.12.

Creating Your Own New Project Templates

Perhaps the only thing lacking in the New Project interface in GarageBand '09 is a simple button for creating your own templates. Luckily, it's very easy to do. Simply create a new project of any type you like and make all of the configurations and choices you would like to be able to use for your starting point. Then choose File > Save As. Name the file with the name you'd like to use—for example, Todd's Project.band—and save the file to your desktop temporarily. Next, open up a new Finder window by double-clicking your hard drive icon on the desktop or pressing Command+Shift+N and navigate to /Library/Application Support/GarageBand/ Templates/Projects. Notice that you will see the other nine New Project template files. Notice how they are named; this will come into play in a moment.

Copy or move the project file you just saved to the desktop into this folder and add a number to the beginning of the filename that is one higher than all the others. Follow the same file-naming format of the other template files you see in the Templates folder. For example, in this case, I will use 10. Todd's Project.band as the filename of my new project template. If you launch GarageBand, you will see your new project file available for the choosing in the New Project interface—but it has the default GarageBand

Figure 2.12   A GarageBand movie score with a movie added to the Movie Track from the Media Browser.

document page icon, which is a little out of place within the slick window with the black background. If you want to use one of the other icons, such as the guitar or keyboard, right-click on the file in the Projects folder and choose Show Package Contents from the menu, and a new Finder window will open up. Inside the Contents folder is a file called ProjectIcon.tif, which can be copied. (You can use copy and paste or Option-click and drag the file to your desktop.) Right-click your custom project file, choose Show Package Contents, and paste (or move a duplicate of) the ProjectIcon.tif file into your Contents folder. You could conceivably create your own transparent .tif file—or edit one of Apple's—to create your own custom icon (see Figure 2.13).

Learn to Play

The Learn to Play option opens up an exciting new feature introduced in GarageBand '09. Learn to Play is a great new way for beginning musicians to learn how to play the piano or the guitar—right inside of GarageBand. Are you interesting in learning more about music? Always wanted to play but never got around to taking lessons? Have you had a lot of fun building songs in GarageBand with Apple Loops, and you are ready to start getting better at playing the keyboard? A whole world of possibilities is opened up by this new paradigm called Learn to Play (see Figure 2.14).

It is a video-based, interactive music lesson, where you are guided by visual cues and fingerboard and keyboard layouts with clear indicators showing you where to put your fingers. There's even a friendly instructor named Tim to take you through the process (see Figure 2.15).

Figure 2.13 The New Project interface with Todd's Project (utilizing the Loops ProjectIcon.tif) available for use.

Figure 2.14 The Learn to Play category of the New Project window selected, with some Basic Lessons and Artist Lessons available for use.

Figure 2.15 Piano Lesson 1: Intro to Piano with Tim, your instructor.

As of this printing, there are nine lessons in the Intro to Piano series and nine lessons in the Intro to Guitar series. These are all designed for people who are brand new to the instruments.

The thing that is most exciting to me in the long run about Learn to Play is that the engine is now in place, and the fact that GarageBand connects to the Lesson Store to download the lessons means that if this is successful and users enjoy the lessons, this can be a whole new way for people to learn to play an instrument. And this is something that I think everyone should do at some point in their life! We will cover Learn to Play in depth in Chapter 13, "GarageBand Learn to Play Music Lessons."

Piano Lesson 1: Intro to Piano

The first nine lessons in Intro to Piano are free to download, and only Lesson 1 comes installed with GarageBand. You will need to choose Lesson Store and download free Lessons 2 through 9. Once you have lessons downloaded, they will always be located here, in the Learn to Play section of the New Project window. Double-click the lesson to watch it.

Guitar Lesson 1: Intro to Guitar

The first nine lessons in Intro to Guitar are free to download, and only Lesson 1 comes installed with GarageBand. You will need to choose Lesson Store and download free Lessons 2 through 9. Once you have lessons downloaded, they will always be located here, in the Learn to Play section of the New Project window. Double-click the lesson to watch it (see Figure 2.16).

Lesson Store: Basic Lessons

The GarageBand Lesson Store connects to Apple's servers and allows you to download Learn to Play lessons to your computer and use them in GarageBand. You will need to be connected to the Internet to download lessons, but once they are downloaded, you

Figure 2.16 Guitar Lesson 1: Intro to Guitar with Tim, your instructor.

can use them any number of times, regardless of whether you are online. On the right side there are two tabs labeled Basic Lessons and Artist Lessons. Basic Lessons will display all of the basic lessons available. At the time of this printing, there are a total of nine piano lessons and nine guitar lessons. You can download them all at once and use them at your leisure, or download them when you are ready for each new one (see Figure 2.17).

Figure 2.17 All of the piano and guitar lessons available for download in the Basic Lessons tab under the Lesson Store.

Piano Lessons

All of the basic piano lessons available for download are listed here. Click the Download button to begin downloading the lesson. Each is roughly 200 MB in size, so they may take a few minutes to download and install, depending on your connection speed and network traffic. Once Learn to Play lessons are downloaded, they will be available in the Learn to Play category of the New Project window.

Guitar Lessons

All of the basic guitar lessons available for download are listed here. Click the Download button to begin downloading the lesson. Each is roughly 200 MB in size, so they may take a few minutes to download and install, depending on your connection speed and network traffic.

Lesson Store: Artist Lessons

This option connects you to the Lesson Store, where you can preview and purchase GarageBand Artist Lessons. For $4.99 each, you can download an interactive video-based lesson where the artist will teach you how to play one of his or her songs on the guitar or piano. Click the Add to Cart button to add lessons to your cart from the Artist Lessons menu and then click Checkout to be taken to the Apple Store online to sign in with your existing Apple account or to create a new account and use a credit card. Then you will be able to download the lessons to your computer. You can remove Artist Lessons from your cart before checking out by clicking the Remove button on the lesson. Once downloaded, you will not need to be connected to the Internet to watch the Artist Lessons. (See Figure 2.18.)

Figure 2.18 The Artist Lessons tab under the Lesson Store category in the New Project window.

While it can be presumed that Apple will continue to produce and release new Artist Lessons, the complete list of Artist Lessons available in GarageBand '09 as of this printing is as follows:

- Ben Folds: "Brick" (Piano, Advanced)

- Fall Out Boy: "I Don't Care" (Guitar, Medium)

- Fall Out Boy: "Sugar, We're Goin' Down" (Guitar, Advanced)

- Norah Jones: "Thinking About You" (Piano, Advanced)

- Sara Bareilles: "Love Song" (Piano, Medium)

- Colbie Caillat: "Bubbly" (Guitar, Easy)

- John Fogerty: "Proud Mary" (Guitar, Easy)

- John Fogerty: "Fortunate Son" (Guitar, Medium)

- OneRepublic: "Apologize" (Piano, Advanced)

- Sting: "Roxanne" (Guitar, Easy)

Artist Lessons are somewhere between 350 and 800 MB in file size and will take several minutes to download. These are pretty large files, so if you purchase a lot of Artist Lessons, be sure to keep an eye on your hard drive capacity. While downloading, there is a progress bar indicating what percentage of the file has transferred to your computer, and any Artist Lessons that are in the queue to download are listed as pending in the New Project interface. Many of the Artist Lessons include instructions for playing an easy version of the chords or strums of the song, while also including more information about the way the artist actually performed the song. The lessons themselves are done in a live video and instructional combination that really works for learning the songs quickly for those who already have some background on the instrument in question, while remaining completely understandable and accessible for people who are approaching guitar and piano for the first time. We will cover Artist Lessons and the GarageBand Lesson Store more in Chapter 13, "GarageBand Learn to Play Music Lessons."

Magic GarageBand

The Magic GarageBand selection in the New Project interface provides you with a list of song genres. These are Blues, Rock, Jazz, Country, Reggae, Funk, Latin, Roots Rock, and Slow Blues. Each song genre icon reveals a Preview button when you move your mouse over the icon. Click Preview to hear a snippet of the song to get an idea of the general sound of the piece, and click it again to stop the preview (see Figure 2.19).

The Magic GarageBand project type lets you audition different instruments playing any of the different premade parts of the song in real time or jam along with the band on an instrument (Real Instrument or Software Instrument) of your choice. Once you've chosen the instruments for the band to play, you can convert the whole project into a full-blown, editable GarageBand project and begin recording additional elements over the top of the Magic GarageBand tracks to create your

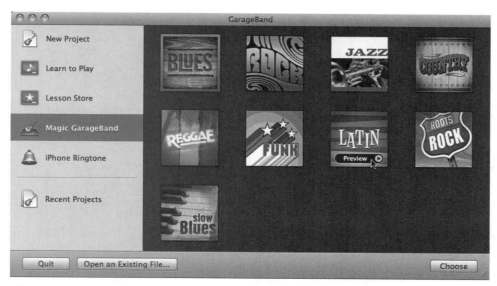

Figure 2.19 The Magic GarageBand category in the New Project window.

own version of the song. You can click and drag sections of the song around to rearrange things or duplicate and even delete the premade sections of the song. Magic GarageBand is covered in depth in Chapter 8, "Magic GarageBand Jam Walkthrough."

iPhone Ringtone

A ringtone is an audio file that is 40 seconds in length or fewer and that can be exported to iTunes and uploaded to an iPhone for use as a custom ringing sound. The only difference between a ringtone GarageBand project and a regular music project is that the Cycle function is activated. The cycle region bar is how you designate what segment of a given GarageBand song file will be exported as a ringtone. We will be discussing the cycle region and its multifaceted functionality in Chapters 5 and 6, when we look at recording multiple takes and building drum beats using the Cycle Record function.

Example Ringtone

This option opens up a GarageBand project with cycle region activated and one Real Instrument track called Jingles, with the podcast Jingles library opened up in the Media Browser. See Figure 2.20.

Loops

This option opens up a GarageBand project with cycle region activated, the Loop Browser opened, and a few tracks of loops in place, demonstrating how you can create your own ringtones using Apple Loops. See Figure 2.21.

Voice

This option opens up a GarageBand project with cycle region activated, one Real Instrument track called Voice, and the Voice Effects tab opened in the Effects panel,

Figure 2.20   The Example Ringtone project template.

Figure 2.21   The Loops Ringtone project template.

and is ready to record anything that is coming through a microphone into the Ringtone example project. All of these ringtone projects are simply short-form song projects, with cycle region activated. See Figure 2.22.

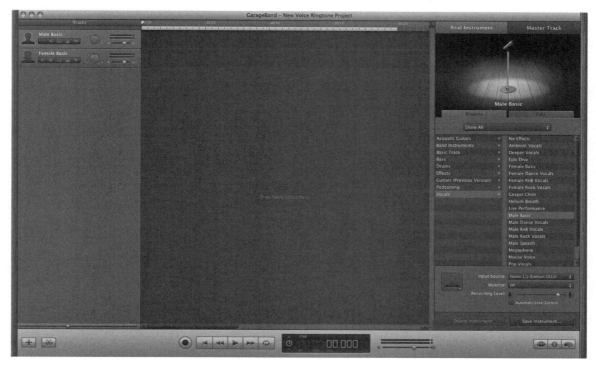

Figure 2.22   The Voice Ringtone project template.

You can create a ringtone out of any project that you like by activating cycle region, using it to specify which portion of the song you'd like to use, and choosing Send Ringtone to iTunes from the Share menu. We will cover this process in great detail in Chapter 12, "Sharing and Archiving Your GarageBand Projects."

Open an Existing File

At the bottom left of the New Project interface is a button for opening an existing GarageBand file. This option brings you to a standard Open dialog box that allows you to locate an existing GarageBand project on your hard drive and open it. The idea behind providing you with a way to open existing GarageBand files from the New Project window is that you'll only ever have to concern yourself with launching the GarageBand application itself, whether you want to create a new project from scratch or open an existing one. By default, GarageBand stores your project files in the Home directory on your main hard drive, inside your Music folder, inside a subfolder called GarageBand (Home/Music/GarageBand/). When you click Open an Existing File, you are automatically taken to this directory, making the whole process a two-click affair. Although it is ultimately your decision where projects are stored, if you allow GarageBand to store your projects in its default directory, then the Save As and Open processes will always be very straightforward, requiring the fewest number of clicks to save or open your projects. If you don't have some particular reason for wanting to store your projects somewhere else—such as a workflow methodology that dictates that you save all projects and documents on an external media drive, for example— then I recommend saving projects to your Home/Music/GarageBand folder for easy access. For most users, this arrangement will be just fine. See Figure 2.23.

Figure 2.23 The Open dialog box for opening an existing GarageBand project file. Select a file and click Open or double-click the file.

Quit

The Quit button will quit GarageBand on the spot and return you to the Mac OS X Finder. If you have any unsaved changes, you will be asked to click Save before the application quits.

Anytime you close your GarageBand project by clicking the Close button in the upper-left corner of your project window (the little circular colored button that displays an X when you hover your mouse over it), GarageBand will return you to the New Project interface. If you are working on a project and GarageBand is running, and you're ready to close it and work on something else, simply save your project, click the Close button at the upper-left to close the window (or press Command+W), and then select your next project type—or open an existing project—from the New Project interface. If you click the Close button and have any unsaved changes, you will have the opportunity to click Save before GarageBand takes you back to the New Project interface.

An In-Depth Look at Project Types in GarageBand

GarageBand is an application with a fairly deep feature set structured around a very simple interface. One of the ways Apple has accomplished this is through the showing and hiding of its various panels, views, tracks, and browsers—making them visible and available only when you need them. This maintains a clean interface and a non-cluttered working area, but it sometimes leaves the user with the inevitable egg hunt. Many new users of GarageBand don't realize the depth of its feature set simply because so many of GarageBand's features are not thrown into your lap when you first launch the application. When you look at the New Project interface, GarageBand appears to have a dozen different project types, and this really is not the case. A GarageBand project is an audio project. That audio project may or may not have certain attributes that make it seem like something entirely different. One example might be a movie project in GarageBand, which is actually nothing more than an audio project that has had a video file imported into it so the user can create his or her audio synchronized with something seemingly external—in this case, a video. The truth is the GarageBand New Project interface is nothing more than a group of project presets.

In this context, when we are discussing projects, we are talking about purposes. What is it that you're ultimately doing with GarageBand? Generally speaking, there are three different types of projects you can create in GarageBand '09: music projects for creating songs (which may include any number of Real Instrument or Software Instrument tracks), podcast projects for creating podcast episodes, and Magic GarageBand projects for jamming with a prebuilt band or using genre-based example songs as a jumping-off point for creating your own song. This section will provide a breakdown and an in-depth look at all three, illustrate the distinctions between them, and provide a foundation for you to begin thinking about each of these project types as I take you through all of them in even greater detail throughout the rest of this book.

Music Project

A music project is one in which you intend to record audio elements and performances for the purpose of making a song. These terms are a little loose, of course, in that you could easily decide to create a "music project" by GarageBand's standards and just talk into the mic for 20 minutes, export your finished sound file as an MP3, upload it to your website, add it to your RSS feed, and create a podcast. Why, then, does Apple call this a music project? The idea with GarageBand is to make recording music and audio easy, and in all of these different project types and preset templates, the Garage-Band interface is set up a little bit differently, revealing features that are more relevant to doing each particular task and hiding those that are less so.

The software designers at Apple have decided that GarageBand is best suited as a tool for recording songs and podcasts (as opposed to audio books, live interviews, film dialogue, and so on), most likely based on some amount of customer research where it was determined that these are the things most users are doing regularly. This has driven them to present us with these particular options. The fact is that you could utilize the power of GarageBand to record any of these types of projects. The intent of the New Project interface's various choices is to get you started quickly and easily so you're off and running on creating something, rather than spending

15 minutes working with settings, configurations, or window and interface setup. That deep, under-the-hood approach is just not where GarageBand is coming from. The application is designed to be simple and quick to get rolling. From that perspective, I believe it is one of the best-designed interfaces, in terms of approachability and ease of use, of the audio applications on the market today at *any* price point. Think of GarageBand's various project types as project templates. They are starting places, not limitations or restrictions.

If you ever need to create an out-of-the-ordinary GarageBand project in terms of the type of project you want to make, and you aren't sure which project type to select, you can just select New Project > Piano if you want to record or play some MIDI, choose New Project > Voice if you want to record something with a microphone connected, choose New Project > Guitar if you want to record or play your guitar, or choose New Project > Loops if you want to create a song using loops from the Apple Loop library. You will end up with a generic GarageBand window, ready for you to do anything you want. Just remember that these project types are window and tool configurations only—they do not enable certain features or disable others. In fact, to prove my point, you could select any project from the dialog box, and within about four or five menu choices and button clicks, you could set up the project file exactly the way GarageBand would have set it up automatically if you had chosen to create a new podcast episode. These are simply predetermined, convenient GarageBand window and panel arrangements.

There is, however, one other distinct step to discuss. Whenever you select any new project, you will be presented with a Save As dialog box before getting the main

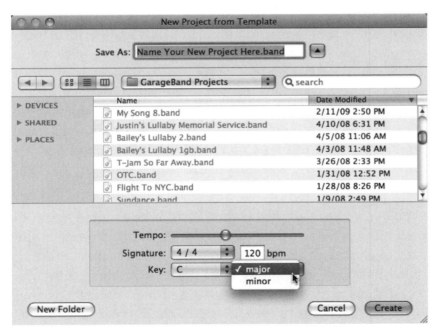

Figure 2.24 The Save As dialog box for the Create New Music Project option with tempo, signature, and key options.

GarageBand window. The distinction is that in addition to being asked to name the file and save it somewhere (which is important to do conscientiously), you will be prompted to choose a tempo, signature, and key (see Figure 2.24).

Tempo

You set the tempo of your song—the speed or pace of the song—in the initial Save As dialog box for the Create New Music Project option by either dragging the Tempo slider left and right or typing in a number to represent a certain number of beats per minute. You can also change your tempo after you start working on the project. So you can consider this step a starting point. If you haven't yet decided what tempo you want to use for a particular song project, don't worry too much about setting it in the Save As dialog box. You can leave it at its default of 120 beats per minute and adjust it once you start working on your song.

> **Tempo:** Tempo is defined as "the speed of the rhythm of a composition. Tempo is measured according to beats per minute. A very fast tempo, prestissimo, has between 200 and 208 beats per minute; presto has 168 to 200 beats per minute; allegro has between 120 and 168 beats per minute; moderato has between 108 and 120 beats per minute; andante has 76 to 108; adagio has 66 to 76; larghetto has 60 to 66; and largo, the slowest tempo, has between 40 to 60 beats per minute."
>
> —The Virginia Tech Multimedia Music Dictionary (www.music.vt.edu/musicdictionary)

Signature

In musical terminology, signature can refer to either a key signature or a time signature. In GarageBand, key signature is simply called *key* and is explained in the next section. For the purposes of the Create New Music Project Save As dialog box, signature refers to time signature. In GarageBand '09, you can choose from 2/2, 2/4, 3/4, 4/4, 5/4, 7/4, 6/8, 7/8, 9/8, and 12/8.

> **Signature:** The Virginia Tech Multimedia Music Dictionary defines time signature as "a symbol placed at the beginning of the staff, indicating the meter of the composition. A time signature consists of two numbers; the top number indicates the number of beats in each measure, and the bottom number indicates the kind of note that is counted as one beat (e.g., a time signature of 3/4 would indicate that there are three beats to each measure, and that a quarter note is one beat)."
>
> —The Virginia Tech Multimedia Music Dictionary (www.music.vt.edu/musicdictionary)

Key

Setting the key of your song in GarageBand is important if you are planning to use any of the Apple Loops that come with GarageBand or in the many available Jam Packs. Many of the Apple Loops are actual recorded samples of a real musical instrument playing a musical riff or beat and then trimmed down to work as a loop in GarageBand. Each was originally recorded in a particular key, which means the loops themselves will sound best if your song is in the key in which the loop was recorded or a key quite near it. The Software Instrument Apple Loops (we'll cover these in depth in Chapter 7, "Working with Apple Loops") will automatically transpose (change key) if necessary to match the key of the project. This is the other case in which choosing the key is important: GarageBand is smart enough to transpose Software Instrument and MIDI-based loops into the key of your song project when you add one of these loops to your song. If you don't know what key you want or what key your song is in, you can leave the default key of C selected.

Key: Key is defined as "a specific scale or series of notes defining a particular tonality. Keys may be defined as major or minor, and are named after their tonic or keynote. Thus the series of notes with intervals defining a major tonality and based on the key of C is the key of C major."

—The Virginia Tech Multimedia Music Dictionary (www.music.vt.edu/musicdictionary)

Each time you create a new project, GarageBand presents you with a Save As dialog box and automatically fills in a default filename of My Song.band. The next time you create a project, GarageBand will suggest My Song 2.band, then My Song 3.band, and so on.

You should probably change this default name. I recommend always naming your project files something descriptive—preferably with the name of the song itself. Include a version number after the song name if you have multiple versions (such as Rockin' Song 03, Rockin' Song 04, and so on). If the Hide/View File Extension check box is on, you will see the .band file extension displayed in the Name field. If you have the check box set to Hide, you don't need to worry about typing the .band part of the name; Mac OS X will do it for you. If you have the Extension check box set to Show, be sure to keep that part of the filename intact when you are renaming. It's very easy to accidentally erase the extension when naming your files.

After you have selected a tempo, signature, and key, and you have given your project a name and pointed GarageBand's Save As dialog box at your Home/Music/GarageBand folder or other suitable location for saving GarageBand project files, you can click OK, and your file will be saved. You will then be taken to the default GarageBand music project window arrangement for the new project type you chose (see Figure 2.25).

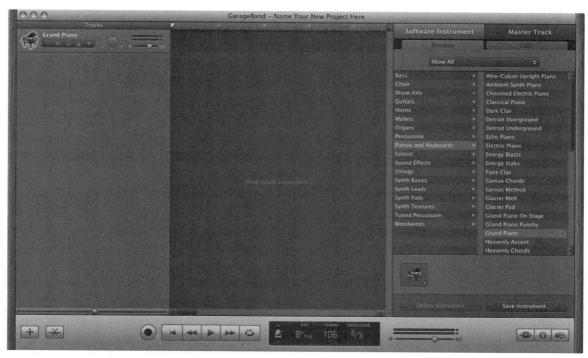

Figure 2.25   A new project in GarageBand '09.

Podcast

Describing what a GarageBand podcast project is all about would undoubtedly require a fairly definitive statement about what a podcast *is*. Wikipedia.org (as per usual—especially in the technology sector) has a few good words to say on the subject.

Podcast: A podcast is a digital media file, or a related collection of such files, which is distributed over the Internet using syndication feeds for playback on portable media players and personal computers. The term, like "radio," can refer either to the content itself or to the method by which it is syndicated; the latter is also termed *podcasting*. The host or author of a podcast is often called a *podcaster*. The term "podcast" is a portmanteau of the words "iPod" and "broadcast," the Apple iPod being the brand of portable media player for which the first podcasting scripts were developed. These scripts allow podcasts to be automatically transferred to a mobile device after they are downloaded. Though podcasters' websites may also offer direct download or streaming of their content, a podcast is distinguished from other digital media formats by its ability to be syndicated, subscribed to, and downloaded automatically when new content is added, using an aggregator or feed reader capable of reading feed formats such as RSS or Atom.

—Wikipedia (en.wikipedia.org/wiki/Podcast)

Recently, there has been a fairly consistent leaning on the part of podcasters and journalists alike to drift away from the word "podcast" in favor of referring to the entire genre as "new media." I personally support this move, but it's tough to say whether we'll see Apple let go of the term anytime soon. What a coup to end up with part of one of your product names combined with another term and see it re-materialize into yet another household word! "Podcast" is indeed becoming a household word, the way "blog" did in 2008. Now everyone knows what a blog is, and my view is that public awareness of podcasting and other forms of new media is hot on its heels.

The beauty of podcasting is the syndication part. This method of distribution is "opt in," it's almost always free (but it certainly is not free by definition), it has a subject and a topic base literally as wide as the whole of humanity, and it presents huge opportunities for educational institutions, content providers, entertainment outlets, or anyone with an idea and a desire to package that idea as audio or video content and distribute it globally. It certainly seems that podcasting, such as it is today, represents the initial stage of a creative content revolution.

When you choose to create a new podcast project in GarageBand, you are given a regular GarageBand production window, just like with all project types, but several features that were hidden in other project types by default are now visible (see Figure 2.26).

Figure 2.26 A new podcast project file in GarageBand '09.

These features include the Podcast Track, which is a special linear track in Garage-Band for setting chapter markers, assigning various parameters to those markers, and viewing podcast artwork, which are still images that you can import and set to be shown at custom intervals throughout your timeline. The Track Editor is set to display even more detailed information about your Podcast Track, such as marker times, thumbnails of your artwork, and methods for assigning hyperlink URLs to specific markers in your track. (These elements will all be covered in depth in Chapter 10, "Podcasting.")

Magic GarageBand

Magic GarageBand is an incredibly fun tool for creating a sound, a song, a band, and ultimately a bed of tracks to use as a starting point for creating a new song. To me, it's almost like GarageBand: The Video Game. It's built for jamming along with the band, and in GarageBand '09 a new full-screen mode has been added. You begin a Magic GarageBand session by choosing from a list of nine different music styles. Blues, rock, jazz, country, reggae, funk, Latin, roots rock, and slow blues are the choices available in GarageBand '09—a list which, sadly, has not changed since GarageBand '08, but one might assume there will be more song styles added somewhere down the road. You can click on each style button once to preview a snippet of the song in that style. These styles and songs are somewhat generic and seem to be best suited to jamming, practicing, experimenting with mixing and recording, and perhaps best for working on your soloing chops.

Once you've selected a style to play, double-click that style to begin. A band of disembodied instruments on a lighted stage will be revealed to you. By default, Magic GarageBand starts in full-screen mode, but you can click easily the double-headed arrow screen-size icon in the lower right to step out of full-screen. Each instrument plays a part in the song that you hear, and you can switch between styles of playing and instrument sounds for each part in the band. Then you choose an instrument to play yourself, and you can jam along with the band. Everything is customizable at this point except the structure of the song itself that Magic GarageBand plays for each musical style that you choose. See Figure 2.27.

When you have decided which band setup you like best, and perhaps have even made some adjustments to the relative volumes of each of the players, you create your project by clicking Open in GarageBand. A GarageBand file is set up for you with a track for each instrument in the band, and their audio tracks are all in place. You can then begin to monkey around with the song's form by dragging and dropping or even cutting, copying, and pasting sections of the song, such as the verse, the chorus, the bridge, the intro, or the ending, and moving them around to build the structure of the song as you like. These tracks are all made up of Apple Loops, so you can't edit the actual notes the instruments play, but you can change the order of the sections and decide which instruments play at what times. In other words, you can mix, record, and

Figure 2.27   Choose which sounds to use for each "member" of the band, and choose your own instrument to play.

play along with the song to your heart's content, but it's not going to be an original song that you create from scratch. With a little creativity and some added original parts, you will be able to make Magic GarageBand's songs quite different from the way they started. See Figure 2.28.

You can invent original parts to play or sing over it—for example, you can make up some funny lyrics and do it up as a birthday present for your significant other—but you didn't really "write" the song. What I'm trying to say here is that it's a little like karaoke, but with songs you don't know. The basic song is there, but you do what you want on top of it. Magic GarageBand lets you take it further than karaoke in that you have the ability to change instruments, scramble the song form arrangement, record your own overdubbed parts, and create your own mix, but as you'll see when you start playing with it, there is a particular aspect—the patterns, rhythms, licks, and grooves themselves—that you cannot substantially alter. Apple provides this music royalty-free, so you can use it any way you want—you can even post it on your website or charge money for a CD that you produce—but it won't be long before the songs in the Magic GarageBand tool start sounding pretty familiar to anyone who has used GarageBand for this purpose. That said, it's a blast to play around with for seasoned musicians and novices alike.

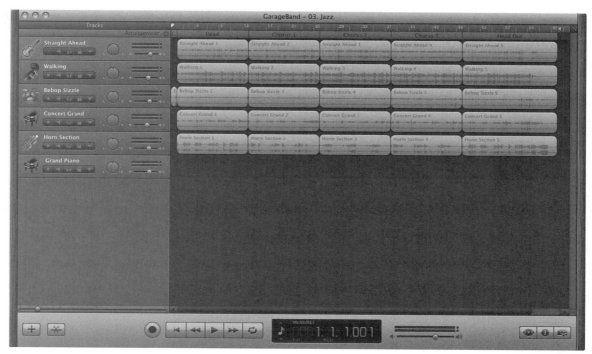

Figure 2.28 A Magic GarageBand project opened in GarageBand. Now you can begin to edit and mix your song, add parts, and change the form.

I think Magic GarageBand will be most interesting to people who are not necessarily songwriters or interested in recording original music from scratch, but who would like to experiment, practice, and experience what it's like to mix a band. You can use this tool to choose parts that go well together, mix and match styles, and even build your mix by trying different combinations of instruments at different times. Also, for people who like to create their own lyrics and sing along with someone else's music, Magic GarageBand can be an awful lot of fun, and it's so easy to set up a project that you can be off and running in a matter of seconds.

What's Next?

In the next chapter, we'll take an extensive walk through all of GarageBand's Preferences settings, as well as the user interface itself, all of its functions, and GarageBand's menus. It will serve as a good reference for you and might shed some light on any additional setup you may still need to do to finalize your recording setup. It is also the type of detailed view that could help you troubleshoot any issues you might still be having in terms of setup and configuration of GarageBand for recording real instruments and MIDI tracks. Launch GarageBand '09 and follow along if you like—I will take you through each and every component of the application and give you a brief overview of what everything you can see, click, or interact with actually does in practice. Then, in later chapters, we will explore all of these features and functions in full detail.

3 GarageBand Preferences and the User Interface

Now that you've learned how to install your iLife '09 with GarageBand '09 software and you've gotten your hardware devices connected, learned about the different project types you can create, and discovered some leads on additional troubleshooting resources on the Internet, it's time to start digging into the nuts and bolts of this powerful creative tool we call GarageBand.

GarageBand's Preferences Window

One of the ways in which you can alter GarageBand's behaviors and configurations is through the Preferences window. I always recommend to new users of a software application that they explore the application's preferences. As with any of the Apple software applications (and a large number of other Mac OS X applications as well), pressing Command+, (comma) will always bring up the user-configurable preferences for the current active application. Launch GarageBand and bring up the Preferences window to explore your options there. Let's go through them one by one.

The GarageBand Preferences window is set up like many preferences windows you may have seen in the past. It has a series of tabs running along the top, which function as categories or areas of interest. When you click on each of the icons, the details and options for that category are displayed in the lower portion of the pane, and you can set the specific parameters of each item the way you like. Then, you simply close the Preferences window when you are finished to save your changes.

Preferences: General

The first category in GarageBand's Preferences window is General. In General, you can set preferences for Metronome, Cycle Recording, and Audio Preview (see Figure 3.1).

Metronome

A *metronome* is a device that produces a steady clicking sound at a certain predefined tempo. In GarageBand, the metronome can be turned on or off at will and will click to your current tempo. Using the tempo automation feature in the Master Track allows you to have the tempo of your project vary at will, and the metronome will click the tempo for you and follow along with your changes.

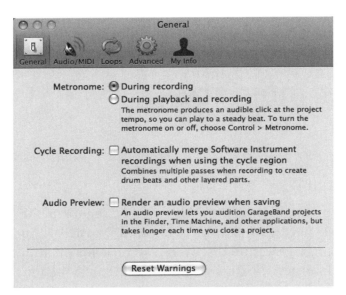

Figure 3.1 The GarageBand '09 Preferences window: General.

This device allows musicians to perform a musical part along with an audible guiding pulse, helping to keep them in time, on track, and in the groove, so to speak. It's almost like an electronic conductor, beating time for you while you play. Many musicians find it helpful to practice music with a metronome, and doing so helps many beginning musicians develop a better internal sense of time. Playing along with a so-called click while practicing can help individuals who have a tendency to rush or drag the tempo of performances. Musicians who are said to have "really good time" are those who seem to play to some tight, reliable inner metronome. These individuals make excellent additions to any rhythm section.

You might have seen the old-style metronomes, which look like an upside-down pendulum—they consist of a metal or plastic rod pointing upward from a solid base, with a slidable weight marker that you use to set the tempo, and there is a key on the base for winding the device. When you turn it on by sliding the tip of the pendulum out of its clasp, it begins to rock back and forth, producing a very steady tick-tock pattern, and you can perform music along with it, being mindful of staying with the tempo that the metronome is counting out for you.

In the studio recording process, the metronome performs another regulatory function. It helps to keep the different musical parts of a piece in sync with one another by giving each performer a common beat to play to. If the drummer records along with the metronome (often just referred to as playing to the click or the *click track*), which has been recorded to one of your available tracks, then another musician (the bass player, for example) can also play to that same click. The idea is that a solid rhythm is established so that everyone can easily remain in sync with one another once the metronome track is muted or removed.

The metronome, or click, is an entirely optional function—it's not required that you use a metronome to successfully record. In fact, some musicians and groups of musicians feel that the metronome stifles them and would much rather take an organic "see what happens" approach to keeping in time with each other while recording multiple parts of a song. (In this case, by "parts" I'm referring to the individual performances that make up the whole of the piece, such as the drums, bass, guitar, and vocals.)

I think it's important to point out that multi-part, multi-instrumentalist musical pieces can be recorded with a number of different approaches. Some that come to mind are as follows:

- All musicians are in the same room, all watching and listening to one another record their individual parts on the song, one by one, one musician at a time. When one part is finished, the next musician starts recording her part while listening, usually on headphones, to the part(s) that were recorded before her—a process known as *overdubbing*.

- All musicians are in the same room, and several (but not all) of them perform some of the parts of the song (for instance, the drummer and bass player might decide to track their rhythm parts simultaneously), and then another musician (or musicians) overdub more parts on top of the rhythm section's parts, and so on.

- Musicians are in different rooms, perhaps not even in the same location, and each records his part and then sends the tapes, files, or GarageBand project to the next musician, who then overdubs his part and moves the project files forward to the next band member, and so on.

- All musicians are in the same recording session, all wired in or set up at a microphone, and many or all have headphones so they can hear one another and the click track if there is one. They play the song all the way through, together, and each part gets recorded—sometimes to an individual track in the recording system and sometimes all mashed together in one stereo "mix." This is often called *tracking it live*, meaning the performers played the piece live, and it was recorded all at once. Whether the song is recorded to a two-track stereo recorder, yielding a mix ready for mastering and release, or the parts of the song are each recorded to discrete tracks within a multitrack system is entirely a matter of preference and the goals and/or requirements of the recording.

There are certainly other combinations of performers, tracks, and approaches to recording, but these are some of the most common configurations that might exist while recording a piece of music. My point here is to demonstrate that these many possible configurations and approaches all require different levels of adherence to a sort of "umbrella" or "global" rhythmic alignment. Everyone needs to play together (together meaning in sync, not simultaneously) in order for the song to sound pleasing to a listener, whose sensibilities might be informed by past enjoyment of listening to bands that one might refer to as "tight." The metronome, in its various uses, can play a major role in achieving that goal. This is, of course, only one particular sensibility. I know artists who thrive on decidedly *not* playing in time. In their case, a metronome is a complete waste of time and a stifling shackle on their creative expression.

Another way a metronome can be helpful is when you compose a piece and decide through experimentation, improvisation, or good old-fashioned trial and error what you want the tempo of the song to be. A song's tempo is measured in beats per minute, or bpm. The cool thing about using a metronome to aid you in making this decision is that you can now communicate to another musician what the tempo of your song ought to be. This could be in the case of a composer such as Beethoven, who was known to indicate metronome settings in his music—it's a method of telling future performers of your piece what tempo ought to be used. Of course, this is not a hard-and-fast rule because any performer could opt to play a song at any tempo he likes, but if you truly wanted to know what tempo Ludwig himself wanted you to play at, you could.

Likewise, if I created a song on my guitar and found that I really liked playing it at 104 bpm, I could call my friend who is a drummer and ask him to record me some drum beats at 104 bpm. He could send them to me in a GarageBand project file, and I could then open up the project and play my guitar song along with his drum beat, and the tempo would be precisely to my creative specification. As you can see, the tempo (in beats per minute) and the metronome (as a tool for deciding, communicating, and hearing that tempo) can be invaluable features of any audio recording software package.

GarageBand's Metronome function can be set to a tempo when you first create a project (covered in Chapter 2), or you can adjust it anytime a project file is open (as we will cover later in this chapter in "The LCD Display" section). Once the tempo is set, you can use the General tab of the GarageBand Preferences to determine where and when the click is heard as a global setting for the GarageBand application. Your two choices are During Recording and During Playback and Recording. If you set it to During Recording, then you will only hear the metronome clicking while you are actually recording a track. If you set it to During Playback and Recording, you'll hear the click when you are recording a track or listening back to recorded tracks. When I am using a metronome for a project, my personal preference usually ends up being to only hear the metronome during recording.

On an as-needed basis, you can toggle (with an on/off check mark) the Metronome option in the Control menu. If you simply want to turn the metronome off, make sure there is no check mark in the menu, and if you want it on, go to the menu again and choose Metronome to toggle the check mark on. The keyboard shortcut for toggling the metronome on and off is Command+U (see Figure 3.2).

Cycle Recording

The Cycle Recording option will require some general explanation about how GarageBand records normally. GarageBand has tracks, as you saw in some of the

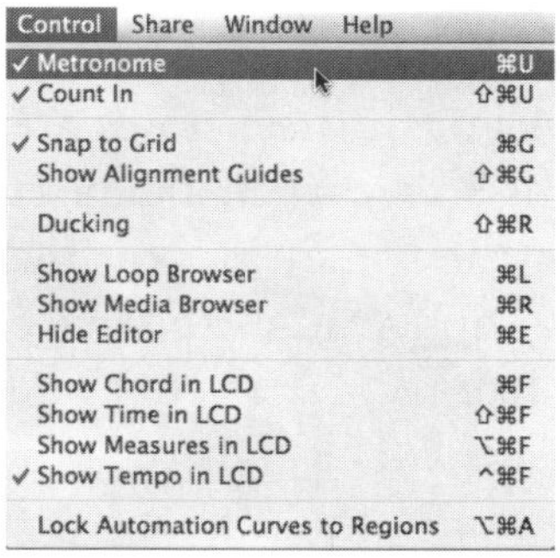

Figure 3.2 Toggle the check mark next to Metronome in the Control menu to turn the metronome on and off.

previous screenshots of the application in Chapter 2. There can only be one track selected at a time. You can select a track by simply clicking on the track once (which we will go over in detail in Chapter 4, "Working with Tracks").

There is also something called the *playhead* (which is another major concept we'll explore in Chapter 4). The playhead is the thin vertical line topped with a downward-pointing triangle that spans all tracks in the Timeline window. This playhead indicates where you are in the song. Suppose you are listening to your song, and at 1:27 into the song, you press Pause. The playhead is now frozen, sitting at 1:27. If you press Play, the song resumes playing from wherever the playhead was when you pressed Play. When you paused the song at 1:27, if you manually clicked and dragged the playhead out to 3:12 and then pressed Play, the song would resume playing from 3:12 forward. There are also easy keyboard shortcuts for moving the playhead to the beginning of the timeline (the Home key) or the end of the timeline (the End key).

The only time the playhead does anything that departs from these ideas is when you engage the Cycle function. Although I'll explain all of these functions in depth in Chapter 4, it's helpful to know that engaging the Cycle function allows you to mark and specify a certain portion of the timeline, and once that is done, the playhead will always start at the beginning of the specified region of the timeline. When it reaches the end, it automatically goes back to the beginning of the region and continues playing from the start of the region once again.

This brings us to the distinction of cycle recording. When you press Record in GarageBand, the default behavior of the application is that it starts to record in the selected track at the point where the playhead marker happens to be located. This goes for recording voice or real instruments, as well as recording MIDI-controlled software instruments. GarageBand then records in a linear fashion until you press Stop. With the Cycle Recording check box checked in the General Preferences tab, you can establish what is known as a *cycle region*, which is sort of a recording loop. With a cycle region activated, the first thing that happens when you are recording a software instrument, for example, is that GarageBand will allow you to record one pass. Then the playhead automatically returns to the beginning of the cycle region, and you immediately begin recording a second pass, and while you record each new pass, you can hear your previous passes as you add new notes each time. All of the new notes are superimposed onto the original notes that were recorded into the software instrument recording region, almost as though you had played them all at the same time on the first pass—if you had more than two hands, that is! You can loop through the cycle region, recording as you go, until you've hit all the notes you'd like to play in that one region or track. Once you press Stop, you can edit your notes as much as you like, removing mistakes, moving things around, adding a few more notes, and so on.

We will cover cycle recording in depth in Chapter 5, "Real Instruments and Electric Guitar Tracks," and Chapter 6, "Software Instruments," but I want to mention that it might be particularly helpful to engage this check box if your intent is to create a drum beat, for example. Suppose you dial up a rock drum-kit software instrument from GarageBand's library. You go to General Preferences and click the Cycle Recording check box. Then you click and drag a cycle region and start recording, and you just press the key for hi-hat and lay down that part. Then the cycle returns to the beginning, and you start playing a kick drum—while you're hearing the hi-hat play. On the third pass, you add a snare drum, and the fourth time, you play a tambourine part. Now you've got one single MIDI recorded region that has hi-hat, kick, snare, and tambourine, and you can loop that, edit it, add to it, delete from it—but it's all one solid region. I'll explain this method's counterpart procedure, multi-take recording, in Chapter 5, in the section called "Recording Multiple Takes," but suffice it to say that the normal behavior for cycle recording when the Cycle Recording preference is not set is that each pass (hi-hat, kick drum, and so on) gets saved and stored to its own unique region—each region being saved as its own "take"—and it takes a lot more manual clicking, dragging, cutting, copying, and pasting than just setting things up with the Cycle Recording check box turned on to start to create a clean, merged performance.

Audio Preview

The Audio Preview check box tells GarageBand to perform an "audio thumbnail" generation step. If this option is checked, it will add a few minutes of time to the closing of any project in GarageBand. It's just long enough that if you don't need the supposed benefit of doing so, it's about 10 times longer than you want to wait to save and close your application. Chances are, you're closing GarageBand because you have to go do something else, and you don't have time to wait three minutes for it to quit. However, if you are interested in the benefit, it's a short enough time that it's really no big deal.

What am I talking about here? Audio Preview is a function that allows GarageBand to play nicely with all of your other iLife applications. It also provides for previewing your GarageBand projects as playable "audio files" within the Finder and Quick Look in Mac OS X Leopard, much like MP3s and QuickTime files can be clicked and previewed in the Finder. When you are using iMovie, iDVD, iWeb, or iPhoto, there are times when you want access to the media created by another iLife app. (The same goes for GarageBand looking *to* those other apps.) For instance, suppose you are in iPhoto and you create a slideshow. One of the features of a slideshow is that you can add music to it. The Media Browser in iPhoto lets you browse through your iTunes library and also your GarageBand folder. Browsing these libraries is only really effective if you can preview the files that you think you might want to use. If your GarageBand files were not saved with the Audio Preview option checked in the General Preferences, then you will not be able to play the songs from iPhoto in the Media Browser, and unless you have all of the names of all of your files memorized, this may become frustrating. See Figure 3.3.

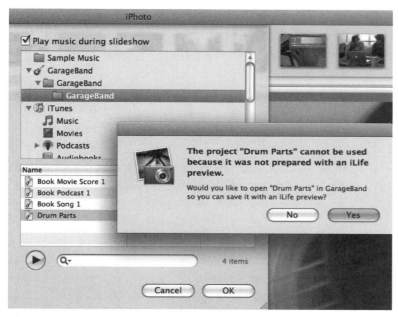

Figure 3.3 iPhoto unable to preview the GarageBand song file because no Audio Preview has been saved.

If you *did* save your files with Audio Preview, you will be able to preview them, which means you can select them from the Browser and click Play to hear the file. You will know whether a song has been saved with an Audio Preview in one of the other iLife applications by the icon of the file as it is listed in the browser window. A document style icon with the GarageBand logo on it is a file with no preview, whereas a file with the GarageBand icon standing alone (not on a document) can be previewed in the iLife app at hand. See Figure 3.4.

It should be noted that the GarageBand Audio Preview setting also has the same effect on whether you can preview a GarageBand song file when you are browsing back in Time Machine, Leopard's (Mac OS X 10.5) backup/restore application.

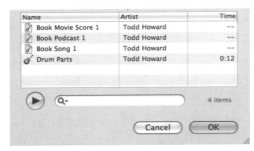

Figure 3.4 The document/GarageBand icon means no preview is available, whereas a standard GarageBand icon means you can press the Play button and preview your GarageBand song file.

If you have one of the newer, faster Macs, it won't take very much time at all to save the Audio Preview, and I recommend you leave this preference on unless you do not use *any* of the other iLife applications. In that case, there is no reason for you to use it unless you would, in fact, like to be able to preview GarageBand files in Time Machine, Quick Look, or the Mac OS X Finder.

Preferences: Audio/MIDI

The second tab in the GarageBand Preferences is the Audio/MIDI Preferences category. This tab is all about getting sound into and out of GarageBand. The System Preferences application for Mac OS X (discussed in Chapter 1) is where you edit your configuration for getting sound into and out of your Mac at large. The two options are not necessarily set to the same devices, although they can (and may) be. See Figure 3.5.

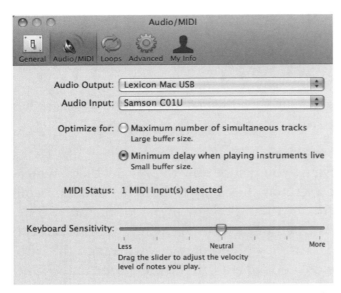

Figure 3.5 The GarageBand '09 Preferences window: Audio/MIDI.

Whenever people ask me why they can't get any sound, I always start by taking them to the System Preferences > Sound control panel (as covered in Chapter 1) and the

GarageBand Preferences > Audio/MIDI pane. Nine times out of ten, we get things resolved in a few seconds. If there were a basic "using computers" tenet, I would elect to have printed on a red sticker and smacked on the front of every computer box that gets shipped with something like, "Preferences are your friends. Visit them early and go back often." If new computer users visited their System Preferences application and the preferences for their favorite applications once a day—or even once a week—for the first three months of having their new computer, the call centers would see a marked drop in call volume. This is my assertion, and I'm sticking to it. Computer users seem to think preferences are for setting once and forgetting about. Although this can, in fact, be the case, if you alter your settings regularly, not only do you become intimately familiar with what *can be changed*, but you also become familiar with which off-the-cuff changes might benefit you at the moment, and you'll just go make them. May the cry, "I didn't know I could do that," be heard no more from computer users! Browse your preferences!

Audio Output and Audio Input

These two drop-down menus will give you the same input and output options that you had in Mac OS X's System Preferences application, and this is where you tell Garage-Band which device you'd like to send sound out to (your Audio Output choice) and which device you want to use to bring audio in (your Audio Input choice). As a sort of default, I usually leave my Audio Output set to my Lexicon (my third-party digital audio interface), so that my GarageBand sound travels out to my main speakers, which are two powered speakers that are connected to the Lexicon's outputs. If I need to use headphones, I turn off my speakers and plug headphones into the headphone jack on the front of the Lexicon, or if I want, I can plug my headphones into the headphone jack on my computer and change the Audio Output drop-down menu to Built-in Output. Alternatively, you can set these two menus to automatically configure themselves to be the same as whatever settings you have configured in the main System Preferences Sound control panel by choosing System Setting from both.

My usual default for Audio Input when I'm using GarageBand is a Samson C01U USB condenser mic, which is a decent-sounding, if somewhat lower-end, mic. I use it for voiceover and quick songwriting demos of new material, and it has a pretty decent sound for a mic that costs less than $100. If I am doing more serious recording, I usually set up a large-diaphragm condenser mic (such as my Audio-Technica 4050), which requires an external power source (48-volt phantom power, supplied by many mixing boards and audio interfaces, such as my Lexicon Omega), and I connect that mic via XLR jack to one of my Lexicon's microphone inputs, and then I set my GarageBand Audio/MIDI preference for Audio Input to the Lexicon temporarily. When I'm finished with my session and I put the "good" mic away, I usually come back into this Preferences window and reset it back to my Samson so that my "default" setting is back the way it should be, in case I get some middle-of-the-night inspiration and need to fire up GarageBand and start recording something right away.

Optimize For

You have two choices for optimization here. They each affect your computer's processor, and that's why they are described as Maximum Number of Simultaneous Tracks (Large Buffer Size) and Minimum Delay When Playing Instruments Live (Small Buffer Size). Essentially, these two choices represent opposing, mutually exclusive options. You're deciding whether to give GarageBand a large buffer or a small buffer, and each option has a tradeoff. Buffer size refers to the size (in bits) and frequency of the data packets that your analog-to-digital converter in your audio interface sends through GarageBand and into your hard drive. Lower buffer size means smaller data packets and higher frequency, which is more intensive for the CPU since they are coming in more often. This setting also affects the way in which GarageBand uses RAM in your Mac and therefore also has an effect on the CPU speed and the latency of the system. The more buffer you give GarageBand to use, the more simultaneous tracks you can record, but there will be a mild, if somewhat noticeable, delay between the moment you pluck that note on your guitar and the moment you hear that note played back in your headphones. This is usually a small interval of time, often measured in milliseconds (thousandths of a second).

This delay, or *latency*, is disconcerting to some musicians, and if you are one of these or you are working with others who may be turned off by this factor, your tradeoff is to choose the second radio button for minimum delay when playing instruments live. The downside is that you'll be limited in the number of simultaneous tracks you can record.

As sophisticated as GarageBand is—and it is head and shoulders above any other product in its class—it does have some limitations, and this is one of them. If you want zero latency and huge numbers of simultaneous record tracks running, you might need to contemplate moving up to a product like Logic Pro and investing in a high-end audio interface, a super-fast computer, and the maximum amount of RAM.

I tend to keep this set to minimum delay when playing instruments live, because I don't have many occasions when I need to record several musicians at once with multiple headphone outs running. You'll have to experiment with each and decide where your own comfort zone is when using GarageBand.

MIDI Status

Next to MIDI Status, GarageBand reports to you how many MIDI input devices it's currently detecting. If the number is not what you're expecting, try quitting GarageBand, shutting down your computer (or logging out and logging back in), and powering off your MIDI devices. Wait a few moments and then power up the MIDI devices again, start up your computer, launch GarageBand, and return to this Preferences window to see whether the number updated.

Keyboard Sensitivity

You can drag this slider left or right to adjust the relative velocity level (the hardness of the key press) of notes you play on your MIDI keyboard or device. If you find your MIDI notes are always coming up as either too loud or too soft, you can adjust GarageBand's sensitivity to your controller here. To the left is less sensitive; the middle is as-is, or neutral; and to the right is more sensitive.

Preferences: Loops

The third tab of GarageBand's Preferences is Loops. This Preferences window lets you make a few adjustments to the way GarageBand handles Apple Loops (see Figure 3.6).

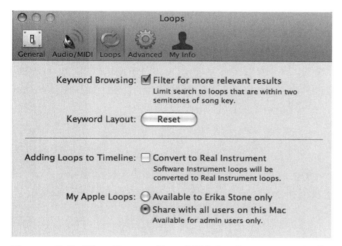

Figure 3.6 The GarageBand '09 Preferences window: Loops.

Keyword Browsing

In GarageBand, there is a Loop Browser where you can sift through, search, and preview loops that you might be considering using in your project. There are category, style, instrument, and genre buttons that you can press to "filter down" the rather gargantuan list of loops. The Keyword Browsing check box will filter for more relevant results. GarageBand describes this relevance as "loops that are within two semitones of the song key." If you are creating a song in GarageBand that is in the key of D, this setting will reveal only those Apple Loops that are in the keys of C, C#/D♭, D, D#/E♭, or E—and all minor or major keys thereof. A semitone is a half-step on the piano. D to D# is one semitone. Two semitones, therefore, are also known as a *whole step*, and in the case of this filter, you can think of it as loops that are either in the key of your song or within one whole-step key in either direction.

The reason why it is desirable to only use loops that are within two semitones of your song is that GarageBand automatically transposes Apple Loops into the current key of the song they are being added to, and the more severely GarageBand has to "bend" the key of the loop to fit your song, the more noticeable the transposition will be. This will manifest as a degradation of the sound quality of the loop. An extreme example to underscore the point would be if you increased the pitch of yourself singing way too far up the scale. You know how it starts to sound inhuman when voices are sped up? Almost like a chipmunk? Well, if your desire is for your GarageBand song to sound as professional and polished as possible, then you might want to use loops that were created and recorded in a key that is very close to your song so they do not have characteristics of chipmunks on Red Bull or the like. Conversely, if there is a loop you simply must use, then you will want to consider doing your whole song in that key—or perhaps a few semitones (maximum!) in either direction. All of the loops in GarageBand have their keys listed next to them.

This only applies to Apple Loops that are recorded tracks (the blue ones in the Loop Browser, known as *Real Instrument loops*); it does not apply to Software Instrument loops (the green ones in the Loop Browser). Software Instrument loops can be transposed to any key and any tempo because they are MIDI data, not actual recorded sound files. We will cover Apple Loops extensively in Chapter 7.

Keyword Layout

The keyword buttons used to filter your loops can be moved around, customized, and added to favorites. The Keyword Layout Reset button returns those alterations to their preset factory defaults.

Adding Loops to Timeline

The Adding Loops to Timeline check box will convert Software Instrument loops into Real Instrument audio files. Once this is done, the loop becomes an actual audio file— essentially, a recording of itself—and no longer can be manipulated in the same ways that MIDI loops can. Real Instrument (or actual audio) regions—whether they be loops or regular recordings—require far less processor power on playback, so if your computer will have a difficult time adding several more tracks, yet you want to add some more Software Instrument loops, you can convert them into Real Instrument loops on the fly and save the processor for the things you really need it for, such as processing effects or other MIDI tracks that you have performed and would like to leave as native, editable MIDI tracks.

My Apple Loops

You can click the bottom My Apple Loops radio button to choose to share your Apple Loops with all user accounts on your machine. Also, if you have several different accounts set up on your Mac for yourself to use, you will want to share your loops here. You will only be able to set the My Apple Loops preferences if you are logged in as the admin user of your machine.

Preferences: Advanced

The fourth tab is Advanced Preferences. This is where you will have some access to the under-the-hood digital settings as they pertain to your audio recordings, your bit rates, and more. See Figure 3.7.

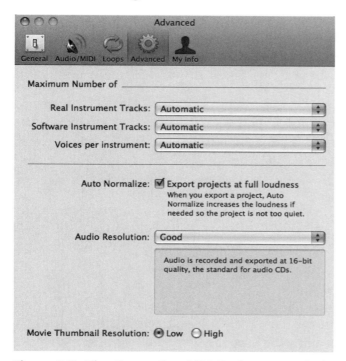

Figure 3.7   The GarageBand '09 Preferences window: Advanced.

You can allow GarageBand to automatically determine the maximum number of Real Instrument tracks, Software Instrument tracks, and voices per instrument by selecting Automatic from the top three drop-down menus, or you can set them to your desired number of 8, 16, 32, and so on. The Voices Per Instrument setting refers to the polyphony of a given software instrument sound. *Polyphony* means the number of pressed notes that can be producing sound at the same time within a given software instrument. You can choose a range from 10 Sampled Voices/5 Other Voices, all the way up to 64 Sampled Voices/Max Other Voices. I recommend choosing Automatic on all of these settings and allowing GarageBand to determine these maximums based directly on your processor and RAM.

The Auto Normalize check box will increase the loudness of a project when exporting it if needed, so the project is not unintentionally too quiet. Full loudness is essentially as loud as GarageBand can make your song without distorting. I usually don't keep this turned on, but that's because I have some experience with mixing and usually make sure of this fact manually. However, if you are new to the process of digital recording, you may want to keep this turned on for the time being. With settings like this one, I encourage users to experiment. Make a song, export it with Auto

Normalize on and then again with Auto Normalize off, share both versions out to iTunes, burn the two tracks to a CD, and go for a drive in the car. See what they sound like compared to one another.

Audio Resolution is a drop-down menu in which you set the recording quality of GarageBand's Real Instrument and Guitar Track recording function. The first choice is Good, which records and exports audio at 16-bit resolution. This is what is known as *CD quality*. Don't let that phrase fool you; CD quality is considered to be substandard for recording raw original tracks these days, especially within the professional audio recording community.

Choosing Better will give you 24-bit recording, which is very good, but then exports at 16-bit. If your plan is to record things at as high a quality setting as you can get, but you are still going to just burn CDs and make MP3s of your audio, then this setting will suit you fine. It will take up approximately 50 percent more hard drive space for your project file than the Good setting does.

Finally, Best gives you 24-bit recording and 24-bit exporting. This is the highest quality setting available in GarageBand, and this is where I keep my GarageBand Advanced preferences for audio resolution set to. That way, no matter what I am doing, even if I am planning to send my file to a professional mastering firm for final prep for duplication, I know that I can export and send them a 24-bit master. This would be far superior to the 16-bit master that a project recorded at Better or Good would yield. If you have plenty of hard drive space, I would not hesitate to use Best. If you have somewhat limited storage space, then you may want to visit this Preferences window at the start of each project and lower the quality for projects that don't require as high of a bit rate. The other thing to consider is that higher bit rates are more taxing on your CPU and depending on the limitations of your system, using Best may cause you to trade off with fewer tracks overall.

Lastly, select a Low or High setting for the resolution of your movie thumbnails. I keep this on Low. If you ever feel that you need to be getting more resolution out of your movie thumbnails, you can set this to High. Keep in mind that it will add more file size to your project file. My feeling is that hard drives are so inexpensive nowadays that I like to do all of my creative projects on my Mac at the highest resolution possible, across the board. I can always buy another hard drive. I can't, however, go back and re-record that magical performance at a higher resolution after the fact.

Preferences: My Info

My Info is the final tab in the GarageBand Preferences window (see Figure 3.8). It is, quite simply, a place for you to enter what amounts to four pieces of metadata that get plugged into all files that you export to iTunes via the Share > Send Song to iTunes menu selection. You can name the iTunes playlist to which your files get exported in the first field (see Figure 3.8).

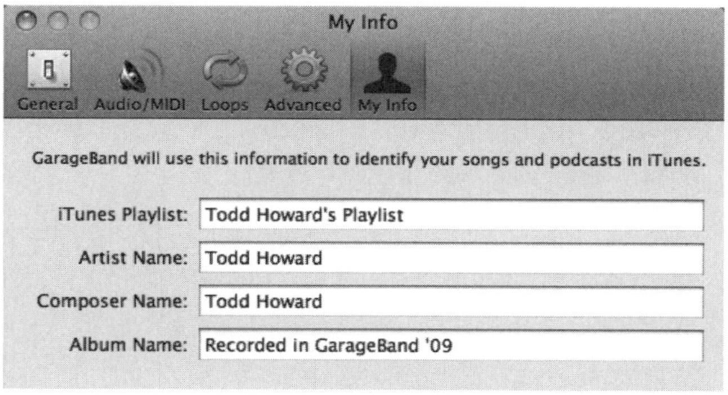

Figure 3.8 The GarageBand '09 Preferences window: My Info.

The second and third fields are for the artist name and composer name that you'd like associated with your exported files. GarageBand fills these in with the name of the admin user for your computer by default, but you can edit them as you can any text field. You can also change these on an ad hoc basis or for each project you're working on, if you'd like. Just bring up GarageBand's preferences and make the change for the project you have open.

The last field is for the name of the album that the song is part of. I tend to leave these fairly general, and if I care to make specific choices about the metadata for my song files, I just edit them fully in iTunes after I've shared the files over to iTunes from GarageBand. I see the My Info Preferences tab as kind of a throwaway, but you may find it valuable. Overall, I do like that you can set the playlist to which Garage-Band exports show up; it makes the song files easier to find in iTunes.

The GarageBand '09 Menus

In the next several chapters, we will be exploring all of the functions and features of GarageBand '09. The purpose of this section, however, is to take a quick tour through the interface and the menus and shed a little light on everything you see when you look at the application. This section will serve as a reference; it is not meant to be exhaustive from an explanatory standpoint. Given that references are often placed at the end of books, as appendixes, you might wonder why I've chosen not to do that here. The reason why is that I believe it is important to offer an up-front nickel tour, if you will, of the entire application and all of its menus. The purpose is to establish some vocabulary for moving forward and to act as a friendly nudge to get you exploring the application yourself. GarageBand is really quite straightforward, and although it is very powerful and feature-rich, almost everything is right on the surface and incredibly easy to understand.

Let's walk through each of the menus in GarageBand '09, and I'll provide a brief description of each menu item, its keyboard shortcut (if any), and what its basic function is. After that, we'll take a look at the interface itself.

The GarageBand Menu

The GarageBand menu serves some administrative functions and contains some of the features standard to every program on the Mac, such as Quit. Following is a list of all the items in the GarageBand menu and what they do (see Figure 3.9).

Figure 3.9 The GarageBand menu.

- **About GarageBand.** This is the easiest place to see the version of GarageBand that you have installed and to read the fine-print copyright of the software. See Figure 3.10.

Figure 3.10 The About GarageBand window.

- **Preferences.** This opens the main GarageBand Preferences window.

- **Shop for GarageBand Products.** This menu choice connects you to the Apple Online Store. You will need to be connected to the Internet to use this menu option. Apple put together an online GarageBand accessories shopping page with software, audio devices, and speakers, as well as any new Jam Packs that may be released in the future and all of those currently available.

- **Provide GarageBand Feedback.** This connects you to a page on the Apple.com website that has a form for submitting comments and suggestions about Garage-Band. Have an idea for how GarageBand could be better? Submit it here!

- **Register GarageBand.** This takes you to a page on the Apple.com website for registering your software.

- **Check for Updates.** This option looks to Apple's servers to see whether the version of GarageBand that you are currently running is the most current one.

- **Learn about Jam Packs.** This menu choice takes you to a page on Apple.com with detailed information about the GarageBand Jam Packs.

- **Services.** This is a standard submenu in your operating system and is not unique to GarageBand. It always appears in the application menu (the menu on the left, next to the Apple menu, that is named for the application that is currently in the foreground), no matter which application you are using. Services are programs or scripts that accept input from a user text selection. You select some text and then choose something from the Services menu, such as Format > Remove Extra Spaces, Look up in Dictionary, or ChineseTextConverter > Convert Selected Simplified Chinese Text, just to name a few.

- **Hide GarageBand.** This option makes all of your GarageBand-related windows disappear temporarily. You can call GarageBand back to the foreground by either clicking the GarageBand icon in the Dock again or pressing Command+Tab to cycle through your open applications until you come to GarageBand.

- **Hide Others.** This keeps GarageBand open and in the foreground and hides every other application and window you currently have open.

- **Show All.** This brings all windows back into view.

- **Quit GarageBand.** This option closes and quits the GarageBand application. If you have any unsaved changes in your project, GarageBand will prompt you to save them before quitting.

The File Menu

The main File menu in GarageBand gives you access to menu choices having to do with using documents, opening and closing projects, printing, and more. See Figure 3.11.

- **New.** This option closes your current GarageBand project, prompting you to save if you have any unsaved changes, and then takes you back to the project type selection screen so you can create a new project.

- **Open.** This option closes your current GarageBand project, prompting you to save if you have any unsaved changes, and then takes you to an Open File dialog box, as if you had clicked Open Existing Project from the project type selection screen.

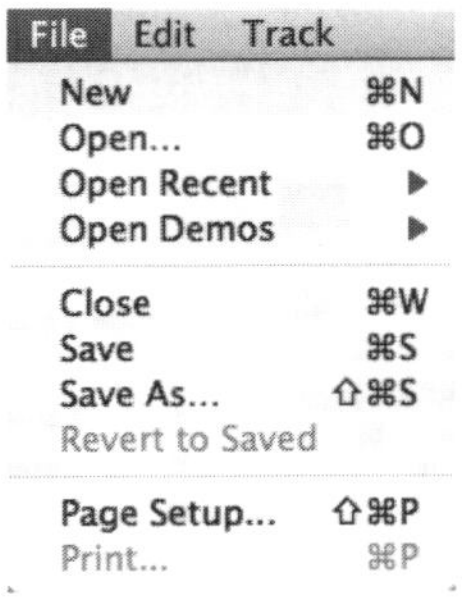

```
File  Edit   Track
New                ⌘N
Open...            ⌘O
Open Recent        ▶
Open Demos         ▶

Close              ⌘W
Save               ⌘S
Save As...        ⇧⌘S
Revert to Saved

Page Setup...     ⇧⌘P
Print...           ⌘P
```

Figure 3.11 The File menu.

- **Open Recent.** This contains a submenu listing of the last 10 GarageBand projects you had open, allowing you to quickly move between several projects that you may be working on concurrently. The bottom choice in the Open Recent submenu allows you to clear the list of all entries at once.

- **Open Demos.** This contains a submenu listing of the two demo songs that come with GarageBand '09. They are called "Dawn After Storm" and "In Paradisium." These two choices open up GarageBand projects with four or five tracks each of prerecorded MIDI parts from the GarageBand Software Instrument library. A demo song is a good place to start if you want to pull up a project with a few tracks already established to experiment with a sound, effect, or mixing technique or investigate the way in which Apple suggests setting up tracks within a song project.

- **Close.** This prompts you to save any unsaved changes and takes you back to the project type selection screen.

- **Save.** If you are working on a document that has already been saved at least once and that has unsaved changes, this option saves them.

- **Save As.** This option allows you to save the current state of the project off to your hard drive and lets you specify a name on the way out.

- **Revert to Saved.** This reverts the currently open document, which has new changes, back to the state it was in the last time you saved it or when you opened it. This menu choice only becomes available once you've saved your project for the first time and then make additional changes.

- **Page Setup.** This option allows you to make printing choices. These choices will depend on the printer that you have connected to your computer. These choices might include formatting, printer paper size, landscape or portrait orientation, and scale. This pertains to printing sheet music from GarageBand.

- **Print.** This option is only active in musical notation mode, allowing you to print sheet music that you have created using software instruments and MIDI to produce notes.

The Edit Menu

The Edit menu presents a series of choices that allow you to edit specific objects, copy and paste, and even have access to the Special Characters palette for enhancing your scores. See Figure 3.12.

Figure 3.12   The Edit menu.

- **Undo.** As in most software applications, the Undo option retraces your steps, one step at a time. GarageBand has unlimited levels of undo.

- **Redo.** This option re-executes any step, task, or edit that you have just undone with an Undo command. If Undo is backward in process, Redo goes forward again. As soon as you make one alteration in GarageBand's Edit or Arrange window, you will reset the Undo/Redo cycle. This is not a "history" function.

- **Cut.** This removes highlighted/selected text or an object from GarageBand and places it in buffer memory, or cache.

- **Copy.** This option copies highlighted/selected text or an object into buffer memory, or cache.

- **Paste.** This option places any text or object that is in buffer memory, or cache, into the selected or highlighted field, area, box, or region in GarageBand.

- **Delete.** This option removes the highlighted/selected text or object from GarageBand. If you select Undo immediately, the text or object will come back, but as soon as you click once somewhere else, you have lost the deleted text or object forever.

- **Delete and Move.** This is also known as *ripple delete* in some applications. The option deletes a selected region, and if there are any regions to the right of the deleted region, the ones to the right move left—or back in time—to fill in the newly vacated space.

- **Select All.** This option selects everything available to be selected within the active window.

- **Add Marker.** This adds a marker to a podcast or a movie at the current position of the playhead. You need markers in podcasts, for example, to add URLs, chapters, or chapter artwork.

- **Split.** This option cuts a region at the position of the playhead, yielding two individual regions. This is like cutting the audio region with a razorblade and allows you to make edits in your regions.

- **Join.** This option joins multiple regions into one.

- **Add to Loop Library.** You can add loops to the loop library at any time by dragging and dropping them into the Loop Browser. If you'd rather use the menu and point to a folder of loops or an individual loop to add loops, then this is your solution.

- **Special Characters.** This option opens up a font browser, allowing you to use special characters, such as notation, dingbats, and other font/text character elements. It is useful for marking up a score or sheet music.

The Track Menu

The Track menu is all about the visibility of all of your different kinds of tracks in GarageBand. See Figure 3.13.

Track	Control	Share	
Show Track Info			⌘I
Hide Arrange Track			⇧⌘A
Show Master Track			⌘B
Show Podcast Track			⇧⌘B
Show Movie Track			⌥⌘B
New Track...			⌥⌘N
Delete Track			⌘⌫
Duplicate Track			⌘D
New Basic Track			⇧⌘N
Fade Out			

Figure 3.13 The Track menu.

- **Hide/Show Track Info.** This is a toggle menu option (using the check-mark motif) that will hide or show the Track Info panel depending on its current state. The Track Info panel gives you access to all your effects, sounds, and options for each individual track.

- **Hide/Show Arrange Track.** This is a toggle menu option (using the check-mark motif) that will hide or show the Arrange Track depending on its current state. You specify content regions in the Arrange Track, such as verse, chorus, intro, outro, and so on.

- **Hide/Show Master Track.** This is a toggle menu option (using the check-mark motif) that will hide or show the Master Track depending on its current state. The

Master Track is for storing volume or effect settings and automation information that apply to your entire mix.

- **Hide/Show Podcast Track.** This is a toggle menu option (using the check-mark motif) that will hide or show the Podcast Track depending on its current state.

- **Hide/Show Movie Track.** This is a toggle menu option (using the check-mark motif) that will hide or show the Movie Track depending on its current state.

- **New Track.** This option creates a new track in GarageBand's Arrange window and allows you to specify whether you want it to be a Real Instrument track or a Software Instrument track.

- **Delete Track.** This deletes the currently selected track from the Arrange window.

- **Duplicate Track.** This duplicates the currently selected track in the Arrange window, maintaining all settings, effects, sounds, and automation. The Duplicate Track option does not duplicate the contents of the source track, only the container and its settings.

- **New Basic Track.** This option provides for a one-keyboard-shortcut method for creating a new Real Instrument track in the Arrange window. If you are recording vocals, guitars, and so on and you just need another track, use this selection.

- **Fade Out.** This option creates a 10-second fade-out at the end of your project and applies it to the Master Track. You can then edit the fade by showing the Master Track and adjusting the fade-out properties. We will cover this in more detail in Chapter 11, "Mixing and Automation."

The Control Menu

The Control menu give you access to things such as panel visibility, metronome, count in, grid-snapping, the ducking function, and more. See Figure 3.14.

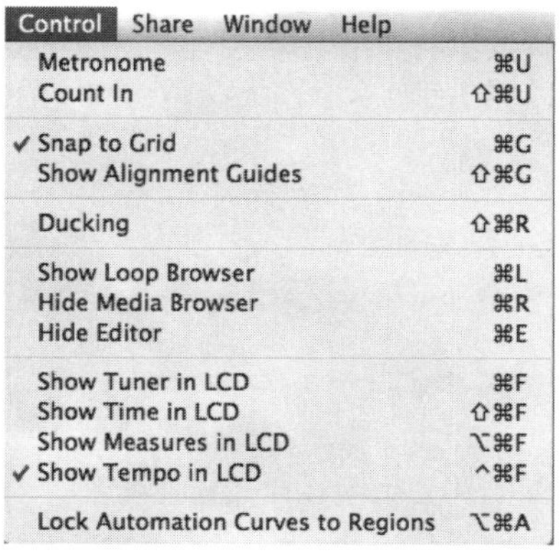

Figure 3.14 The Control menu.

- **Metronome.** This option toggles the metronome on or off.

- **Count In.** If this option is checked, every time you press Record, GarageBand will make the metronome sound for one full measure before playing the track and beginning to record, allowing you to press the Record button and then take a moment to get ready before you begin performing. A count in is like when the band director goes "and-a-one, and-a-two" and then the band starts playing.

- **Snap to Grid.** We will cover how to set the resolution of the grid in Chapter 4, "Working with Tracks," but this menu choice toggles snapping on and off, which helps you move things around in the timeline with more accuracy, always "magnetically snapping" them to a predetermined "grid" framework.

- **Show Alignment Guides.** With this selection toggled on, graphic representations of your "alignments" will show up while you move items around in the timeline, helping you to see across the tracks where something will be falling. This is particularly useful for *spotting*, a process of manually positioning audio elements in time to match up with other elements—often dialogue or sound effects, but it can also be music.

- **Ducking.** Ducking is a function that allows you to set a ducking priority level for each track. When there are tracks that start and stop, sometimes playing at the same time as one another in your mix, those tracks that have ducking seniority stay loud, those that have no designation don't change at all, and those that are subordinate get quieter. This is very useful in a case where you might have music playing and then a voiceover comes in a few seconds later. If you activate Ducking on the voice track as senior and Ducking on the music track as subordinate, the music will automatically get a lot quieter when the voiceover begins—thus "ducking" down behind the voiceover track.

- **Hide/Show Loop Browser.** This is a toggle menu option (using the check-mark motif) that will hide or show the Loop Browser panel depending on its current state. This is where you can browse and preview all of your stored loops. You can then click and drag them from the Loop Browser into your project.

- **Hide/Show Media Browser.** This is a toggle menu option (using the check-mark motif) that will hide or show the Media Browser panel depending on its current state. This is where you can browse and preview all of media elements in iPhoto, iMovie, and so on to consider and preview them for inclusion in your project. You can then click and drag them from the Media Browser into your project.

- **Hide/Show Editor.** This is a toggle menu option (using the check-mark motif) that will hide or show the Audio or MIDI Track Editor panel depending on its current state. This is where you can zoom in on audio or MIDI information and make precise edits or analyses of the regions in question.

- **Show Chord/Tuner in LCD.** This option switches to the Chord or Tuner panel in the LCD display. If you have selected a Software Instrument track, the Chord display will show chord symbols as you play them. With a Real Instrument or Guitar track selected, the Tuner will allow you to tune your instrument. You can tune an analog instrument that is connected via line in or coming in over an open microphone with this sensitive, chromatic, pitch-based tuner.

- **Show Time in LCD.** This option switches to the Absolute Time panel in the LCD display. Here you can see your current position in the timeline represented in hours, minutes, and seconds.

- **Show Measures in LCD.** This option switches to the Musical Time panel in the LCD display, where you can see your current bar and beat.

- **Show Tempo in LCD.** This option switches to the Project panel in the LCD display, where you can see your key, tempo, and signature.

- **Lock Automation Curves to Regions.** With this option toggled on, for any regions that have automation information created (we will cover this in Chapter 11), the automation nodes will remain "with" their region when the region is moved, as if the automation moves were glued to the region itself. Without this toggled on, the automation information stays locked in real time to the track position, and the regions within that track can be freely moved independent of those automation nodes and moves.

The Share Menu

The Share menu will help you whenever you want to get audio out of GarageBand and share it with another person or application. See Figure 3.15.

Figure 3.15 The Share menu.

- **Send Song/Movie/Podcast to iTunes.** This option exports the current project to iTunes. You are given an opportunity to edit the metadata for that file and adjust its compression settings before it begins to export. This process may take a few minutes, depending on the length of your project.

- **Send Ringtone to iTunes.** This option exports a designated cycle region of up to 40 seconds in length to iTunes for use as an iPhone ringtone.

- **Send Song/Movie/Podcast to iWeb.** This option exports the current project to iWeb for publishing to the web. You are given an opportunity to adjust the file's compression settings before it begins to export. This process may take a few minutes, depending on the length of your project.

- **Send Movie to iDVD.** Once you have finished editing your movie score, if you'd like to export the finished movie with its new soundtrack to iDVD for burning, you can choose this menu item.

- **Export Song/Movie/Podcast to Disk.** Use this option if what you are looking for is to simply export the project; "mix it down," so to speak; and save it to your hard drive for later use.

- **Burn Song to CD.** This option readies the CD-ROM burner in your computer for an audio burn of the song project you currently have open. Insert a blank CD, and within a few minutes you can take your masterpiece to the car or give it to someone to listen to.

The Window Menu

The Window menu allows you to minimize your main window, see the name of the window you are in, and open up the mini keyboard and musical typing functions. See Figure 3.16.

Figure 3.16 The Window menu.

- **Minimize.** This option hides the GarageBand window by placing it on the Dock. You can open it again by clicking once on it in the Dock or choosing it from the application switcher using Command+Tab. This is the equivalent of clicking the minus bubble at the top-left of your GarageBand window.

- **Zoom.** This option makes GarageBand fill your display. If it already is filling your display, Zoom will make it a bit smaller. This is the equivalent of clicking the plus bubble in the upper-right of your GarageBand window.

- **Keyboard.** This option brings up a miniature piano keyboard, allowing you to click notes and hear them. This will only work if you have a Software Instrument track selected.

- **Musical Typing.** This option brings up a graphical representation of your computer keyboard, with piano-style arrangement of keys highlighted, instructing you how to press keys on your typing keyboard to get polyphonic (multi-note) sounds out of it. Again, you'll need a Software Instrument track created and ready to go before this will work.

- **Project Name.band.** This will show the GarageBand window for the project that is currently open and active.

- **Podcast Preview.** This option is only displayed when you are working on a podcast episode and you have clicked on the preview icon in the Podcast Track's header.

The Help Menu

The Help menu will help you out when you are looking for a tip. See Figure 3.17.

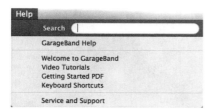

Figure 3.17 The Help menu.

- **Search.** Type in some text to search, and your results list will auto filter similar to how Spotlight works in Mac OS X, and you'll see some possible results before you even open the GarageBand help utility.

- **GarageBand Help.** This option provides fully searchable access to the GarageBand online manual. It's a hyperlinked document with all the help you could need with GarageBand, straight from Apple's documentation department.

- **Welcome to GarageBand.** This option opens an interactive browser, giving you direct access to Apple.com's online resources for GarageBand.

- **Video Tutorials.** This option opens an interactive browser, giving you direct access to Apple.com's online video tutorials for GarageBand.

- **Getting Started PDF.** This option opens a PDF file that will help you get started.

- **Keyboard Shortcuts.** This option provides a complete list of all the keyboard shortcuts in GarageBand.

- **Service and Support.** This option opens Safari and takes you to Apple's GarageBand support page on their website.

The GarageBand '09 Application Interface

For a large view of GarageBand's complete interface, see Figure 3.18.

The Arrange Window

This is the main area of GarageBand, shown in Figure 3.19. Here you have access to all of your regions. This is the main area where you compose your arrangement of audio elements to make your finished project. This is the timeline, and it's also the

Figure 3.18 The GarageBand '09 interface.

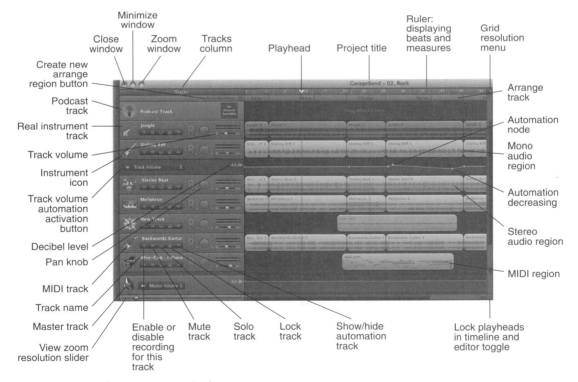

Figure 3.19 The Arrange window.

mixer. This is where your audio gets recorded to and where you see everything laid out. This is the big-picture view.

The Transport Controls

The Transport is essentially your play, stop, rewind, fast-forward control center. You also can create a new track from here by clicking the plus icon. You can show or hide your Track Editor window from here, refer to your LCD panel, and change the LCD view by clicking the arrows above and below the LCD display icon. I discuss the LCD panel in depth near the end of this chapter, in the section called "The LCD Display." Herein also lies your master volume fader, master mix clip indicators, and buttons to open your Loop Browser, Track Information, and Media Browser panels. See Figure 3.20.

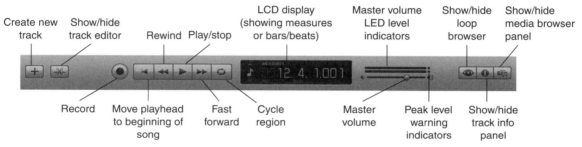

Figure 3.20 The Transport controls.

The Track Editor

This is the window where you'll do all of your fine edits on audio and MIDI regions. Here you can name or rename your regions, adjust the pitch, and enhance your tuning. Also, you can enhance the timing of your Real Instrument audio parts to get that drummer back in line—sometimes called *quantizing*, which can be especially effective when dealing with MIDI regions. In the Track Editor you can also cut and reposition regions in time. It's often far easier to make a very specific selection in the Track Editor than it is to do so in the Arrange window, because you are effectively zoomed in and able to more easily identify characteristic waveforms that may guide you visually in choosing exactly where to split your region or knowing how two disparate regions may come together. See Figure 3.21.

When editing a Software Instrument track in the Editor or a musical notation score, you have direct access to MIDI notes and can alter their characteristics, such as sustain, velocity, and even the note value itself. We will cover this in more detail in Chapter 6 "Software Instruments."

The Loop Browser

In GarageBand '09, the Loop Browser has moved from the lower third of the Garage-Band interface into the family of panels on the right side. Clicking the Loop Browser icon in the lower right reveals the panel (refer back to Figure 3.19). From the Loop

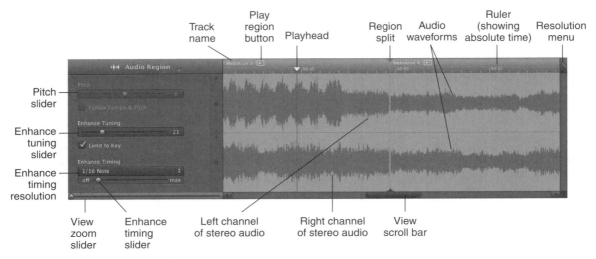

Figure 3.21 The Track Editor.

Browser, you can sort and preview all of your loops, Jam Packs, and custom loops. You can customize the view options here, search by keyword, adjust preview volume, and filter by key or scale. From this window, you drag loops to the stage for use in your song. See Figure 3.22.

Track Info Panel

This is the panel where you make decisions about effects on Real Instrument tracks and sounds for your Software Instruments. You also access settings and effects for your Master Track from here. Click on the Browse tab to see all the available effects or sounds available to you, and click the Edit tab to make changes to the parameters of the effects and sounds once you have selected them. See Figure 3.23 and Figure 3.24.

If you are working on a podcast, and you select the Podcast Track, the Track Info panel will allow you to edit the metadata for your episode. This includes title, artist, composer, parental advisory, and description. See Figure 3.25.

The Media Browser: Audio

From here you have access to all of your GarageBand and iTunes music for inclusion in your project. You can search, sort, and filter your audio files and drag them from the Browser into your project. The song file list has columns for name, artist, and the running time of the song file, and you have access to all of your playlists, smart playlists, podcasts, and movies within your iTunes library as well. You can play any audio file in your iTunes library from the Media Browser's Audio panel just by clicking on a song and pressing the Play button at the bottom of the panel. See Figure 3.26.

The Media Browser: Photos

This panel gives you access to your entire iPhoto library. It shows all the searchable groups and items normally seen in iPhoto's left source column, including events, all

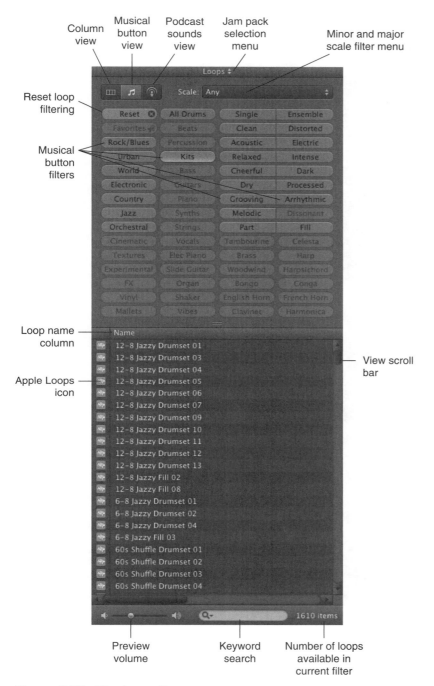

Figure 3.22 The Loop Browser.

photos, last import, flagged photos, all of your albums and galleries, and also all the pictures you have taken with Photo Booth. These can be dragged and dropped into podcasts to be used as artwork track elements. You can also search by keyword and other metadata in the Spotlight-style search field at the bottom of the panel. See Figure 3.27.

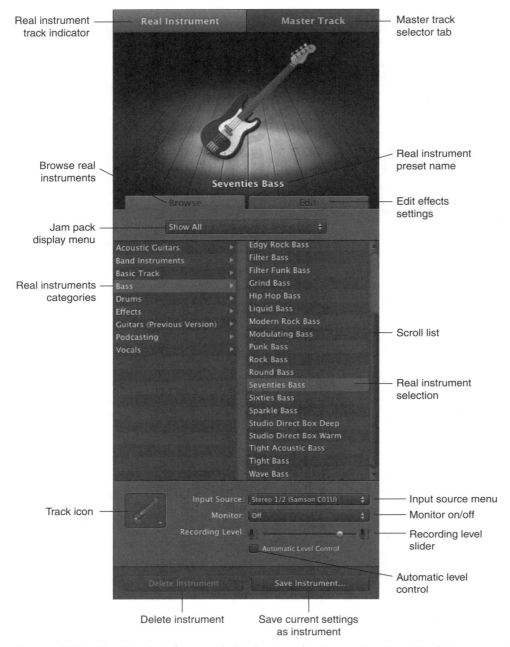

Real instrument track indicator
Master track selector tab
Browse real instruments
Real instrument preset name
Jam pack display menu
Edit effects settings
Real instruments categories
Scroll list
Real instrument selection
Track icon
Input source menu
Monitor on/off
Recording level slider
Automatic level control
Delete instrument
Save current settings as instrument

Figure 3.23 The Track Info panel displaying the Seventies Bass Real Instrument preset.

The Media Browser: Movies

This panel gives you access to your movies directory in your home folder, as well as iTunes movies, iMovie movies, video podcasts, and any video clips you've created in Photo Booth. You can search using keywords in the field at the bottom, and you can preview your movies here before dragging them into a Movie Track in GarageBand. See Figure 3.28.

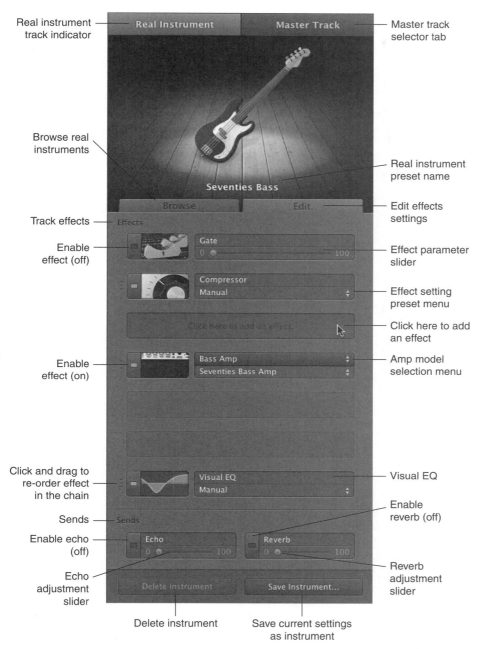

Real instrument track indicator

Master track selector tab

Browse real instruments

Real instrument preset name

Track effects

Edit effects settings

Enable effect (off)

Effect parameter slider

Effect setting preset menu

Click here to add an effect

Enable effect (on)

Amp model selection menu

Click and drag to re-order effect in the chain

Visual EQ

Enable reverb (off)

Sends

Enable echo (off)

Reverb adjustment slider

Echo adjustment slider

Delete instrument

Save current settings as instrument

Figure 3.24 The Track Info panel displaying the Seventies Bass Real Instrument with the Effects Edit tab selected.

The LCD Display

At the bottom of the GarageBand interface, next to the Transport controls, is the LCD. It's not a real LCD (*liquid crystal display*) of course—although if you are using GarageBand on a computer with an LCD flat panel, you could get into an interesting debate about that statement—but the idea is it's designed to look and behave like a standard LCD display you might find on a hardware recording console or a multitrack

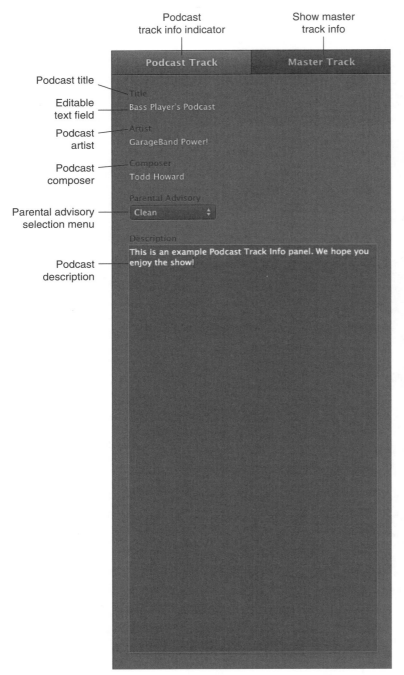

Figure 3.25 The Track Info panel displaying information for the Podcast Track.

recording deck. It's a readout, updated in real time, that can give you various information about where you are in your project. The GarageBand LCD also has some additional information and functionality that we'll explore in this section. The two main ways you can see where you are in your project are the Time view, shown in Figure 3.29, and the Measures view, shown in Figure 3.30.

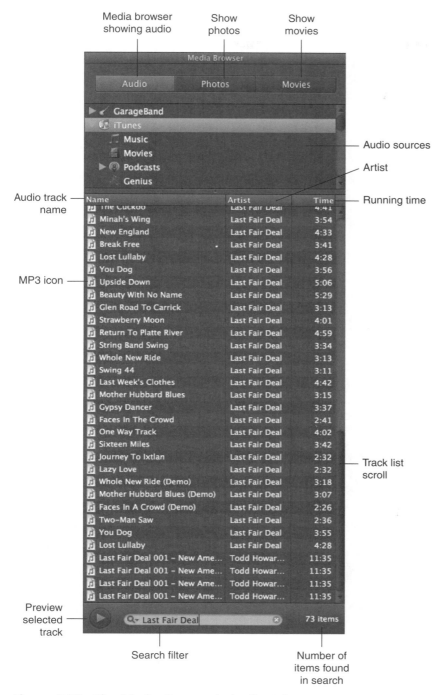

Figure 3.26   The Media Browser's Audio tab.

Time View

Time view represents absolute time. Wherever the playhead is in your project at any given second—millisecond, actually—the Time view reflects that position by telling you the hour, minute, second, and millisecond of its current position. When your

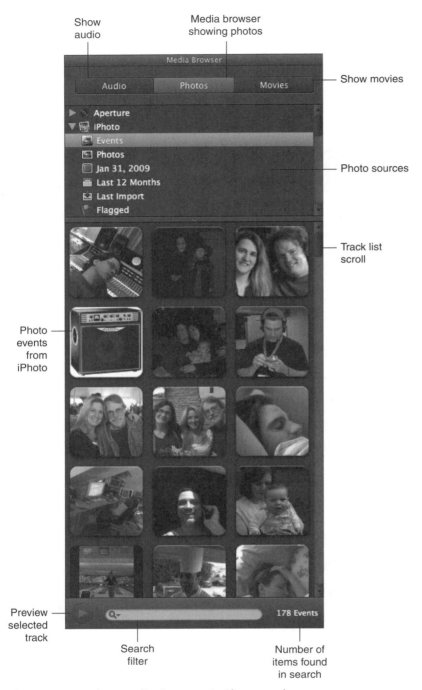

Figure 3.27 The Media Browser's Photos tab.

song is playing, the Time view LCD counts along with you in real time, displaying minutes and seconds, and you can quickly move to a certain number of minutes and seconds within the song by manually moving the playhead by clicking and dragging with your mouse. Move the playhead until the LCD reads the time to which you'd like to move.

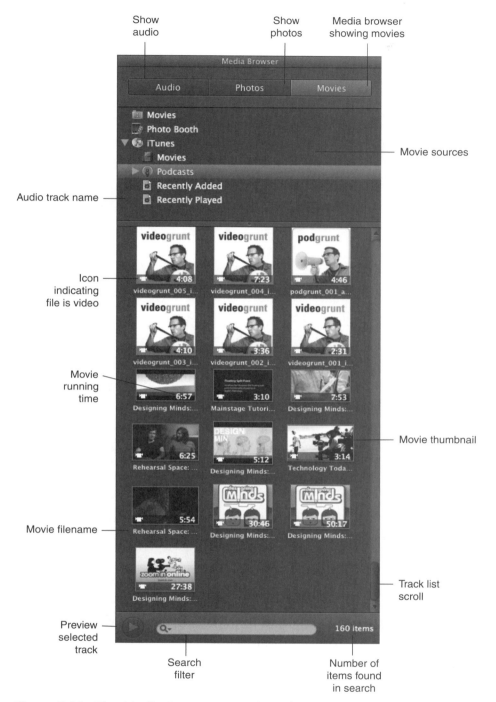

Figure 3.28 The Media Browser's Movies tab.

Figure 3.29 The LCD display set to Time view.

Another way to move the playhead to a specific place in your song is to double-click on the hours, minutes, seconds, or milliseconds portion of the readout and just type in the number of where you want to go and then hit Return (or Enter on your extended number keypad). For example, if your playhead was at the beginning of the song (00:00:00.000, which is to be read hours:minutes:seconds.milliseconds) and you wanted to go to the two-minute mark in the song, you'd only have to double-click on the minutes column (00:00:00.000), type the number 2 on your keyboard, and press Return or Enter. The playhead would then zoom ahead to exactly the two-minute mark. I like using the number keypad for these types of moves because the number keys are all right there and easy to access and type quickly, and then I press the Enter key from there as well.

Measures View

The other way to visualize your location in the song in the LCD display is Measures view, also known as *musical time*. Instead of minutes and seconds, this display shows you measures or bars and beats, as shown in Figure 3.30. We covered some of these ideas in Chapter 2, in the section about time signature.

Figure 3.30 The LCD display set to Measures view.

If you are in 4/4 time, there are four beats in a measure. So if you watched the Measures view of the LCD counting away while your song was playing, you'd see it say bar 1/beat 1, bar 1/beat 2, bar 1/beat 3, bar 1/beat 4, bar 2/beat 1, and so on. Again, as with the Time view, you can move around by double-clicking on the bar area of the display (or the beat area), typing in your desired number, and pressing Return or Enter on your extended number keypad. The playhead will zoom ahead or back in your song to the specified measure and beat.

If you are not adhering to a particular tempo in your song and you are not using the metronome, you might want to keep the LCD set to Time view mode, because it is completely viable to create a project that is free of bars and beats (for example, a spoken-word piece, a podcast, or an improvisational song, to name a few possibilities). Time view is probably the most beneficial LCD view in any of those circumstances.

There are three other view options in the LCD display, and they are used for purposes other than marking where you are within your song project.

Tuner View

The Tuner view in the LCD display will show you the pitch of the note you are playing or singing, if you have selected a Real Instrument track. (We will cover Real Instruments in depth in Chapters 4 and 5.) This can help you to tune an instrument, such as a guitar or a bass. The Tuner in the LCD functions much like any electronic tuner you may have seen or used in the real world. You plug your guitar into the line in on your audio interface or into your computer, and you create a track for it, arm the Record button (we will go through this in detail in Chapter 5, in the "Recording" section), and strike a note. The Tuner reflects the note you played. It will display the note you are closest to and then become red and highlight an area of the spectrum to the left (flat) or right (sharp) to indicate which direction you will need to tune to reach the right pitch. The example in Figure 3.31 shows a D note that is reading slightly flat, so I would need to twist my tuning knobs (or machine heads) on my instrument to make the note go higher, until that little red, bold line on the spectrum reaches dead center and the display goes cool blue.

Figure 3.31 The LCD display set to Tuner view.

Chord View

If you are using a Software Instrument instead of a Real Instrument, the Tuner view becomes the Chord view (see Figure 3.32). This will reflect back to you whatever chord you play on your MIDI keyboard controller. If you play a B flat sus2 chord, the Chord view of the LCD display will read B flat sus2.

Figure 3.32 The LCD display set to Chord view.

Project View

The final mode of the LCD display is the Project view. This view shows you the key, tempo, and time signature of your current project. These are the settings that you chose when you first created your project. See Figure 3.33.

Figure 3.33 The LCD display set to Project view.

At any time, you can alter your tempo, key, or signature by editing the areas in this LCD display. Click and hold on the key, tempo, or signature, and you will be able to edit the value in the menu or the slider that pops up.

Let's Make Tracks

Now that you've had an overview of where things are and what they do, it's time to get down to it. You're ready to start learning how to create tracks and then record audio or MIDI information into them using Real Instruments and Software

Instruments. Creating songs using a combination of three track types (Real Instrument tracks, Software Instrument tracks, and new in GarageBand '09, a unique kind of Real Instrument track called an *Electric Guitar track*), plus the power of Apple Loops and the huge effects and sound libraries at your fingertips, is where all the fun begins. In the next chapter, we're going to take a much closer look at how tracks function and how to work with them, as well as how to gain proficiency with the techniques required to create in the timeline.

4 Working with Tracks

Now that you've been exposed to all the various starting points for creating new GarageBand projects, we're going to put Learn to Play music lessons off to the side (to be covered in Chapter 13, "GarageBand Learn to Play Music Lessons") and focus on GarageBand's most powerful and fundamental function: recording audio. The first thing we'll be exploring is the most basic element of any GarageBand project—the *track*. In this chapter, we'll look at what constitutes a track, how you can create and delete tracks, and how to record audio into specific selected tracks using both Real Instruments and Software Instruments. We'll also dig into working in the timeline, which is the main "project space" where you will likely spend most of your time while using GarageBand. And, we'll look at using the controls you will use while mixing your tracks.

Mixing is the process of adjusting the individual volume level of each of your tracks—to your taste—thereby creating a specific balance between all of the individual recorded elements of your piece, from both the aesthetic and the technical perspectives. We will get more into mixing and using effects and post-processing in later chapters, but this chapter will focus on the interface itself, the controls you will use to execute your creative whims, the basics of playback, and generally working with GarageBand, the software application itself. If you haven't used GarageBand before, this chapter will give you a complete lay of the land. See Figure 4.1 for a visual of a track in GarageBand.

Figure 4.1 A typical GarageBand track.

What Is a Track?

A track is the unique, singular, individual building block of an audio project. It is one lane, channel, strip, or row of a given project file, and it almost always will contain at least one discrete element or sound (known as a *region*) within a larger tapestry of elements or sounds. This so-called tapestry would be a group of tracks, each containing its own discrete elements or sounds.

Tracks contain one or more regions of sound. A region can be either an audio region or a MIDI region in GarageBand, and so-called tracks are always of one type or the other—the two types are mutually exclusive. You can't have an audio track (called a *Real Instrument track* in GarageBand) that holds MIDI regions (called *Software Instruments* in GarageBand) or vice versa. To speak of tracks in terms of a song, think about a song with which most of us probably are familiar: "Let It Be" by The Beatles. If you have access to that song, throw it on right now and listen to it while you read the next section. If not, just follow along and imagine the song's constituent parts as I lay them out here.

This classic song begins with only piano, and then Paul McCartney's vocal comes in. For the entire first verse, it's just piano and Paul. This verse would be said to have two tracks: a piano track and a vocal track. Now, in the case of "Let It Be" specifically, it's possible (even probable) that these two elements—piano and voice—were recorded simultaneously. It is likely that Sir Paul sat at the grand piano at Apple Studio, in the basement of The Beatles' Apple Headquarters at 3 Savile Row in London back in late January of 1969, and George Martin, The Beatles' career-long producer, probably had Phil McDonald, the engineer on the session, put a microphone on the piano and a second mic up for Paul to sing lead into. If that was in fact how it was done, Paul likely performed the song all the way through to the end, and the recording engineers recorded audio—piano and voice respectively—onto two discrete tracks on the multi-track tape machine.

Then, they rewound the tape and set up some new tracks, one by one, and added other elements to the song while listening to the prerecorded Paul and piano tracks—a process known as *overdubbing*. Overdubbing is recording a new track (or tracks) on top of an already existing track or tracks, and it is most often performed while simultaneously listening to the original tracks and playing along with them. In the late '60s, overdubbing was often achieved by playing the original tracks out of one tape machine and recording those tracks onto another tape machine, while simultaneously adding new tracks during that re-recording process. Throughout the rest of the song "Let It Be," you can hear each of the individual tracks that was overdubbed. They added organ (played by the incomparable Billy Preston) and backing vocals (including Linda McCartney and George Harrison), both of which start at the first singing of "Let it be, let it be…" and carry us out to the end of that first chorus.

Next, on the second verse, Ringo's hi-hat comes in on its own track, and a little further in you can hear the bass guitar come in on its own track. The piano and vocal are still perfectly audible, and after a bit even the harmony vocals and the organ come back in once again. On the organ and backing vocal tracks, for the time that elapses between when the harmonies first sang out and the second time they appear, that track has nothing but silence on it. If you were to listen to that track in isolation (a process called *soloing* the track), you'd hear the choirlike backing vocals sing their last lyric and then grow silent. A minute or more with no sound at all would elapse, and then they'd come back in again at full force.

Finally, we get a full drum kit part, a horn section, and then there is an electric guitar track for the solo. (Some sources say Harrison played the part, but others assert that it was in fact John Lennon.) In the last verse, we even get one final new track, a maraca—that shaker part you hear playing in a nice rhythm with the tom-tom drum part—likely still on the same physical track the drums were already on, but it could just as easily have been on its own track.

Occasionally, people in the music business use the word "track" to mean "song." For example, someone might say, "There's a really great mood on the last track on Abigail Washburn's first record." Other times, songs are even referred to as *cuts*, as in, "The first cut on Toad the Wet Sprocket's *Coil* album is fantastic." In terms of this discussion and to get specific for our purposes, a track in GarageBand is what we will call those discrete "places" into which we will record audio regions or MIDI performances. After we have several tracks recorded, we will talk about mixing those tracks together. A track in GarageBand is one horizontal row in the timeline area of the main window, where recorded audio regions are stored and where they are manipulated. (Refer to Figure 4.1.) When we talk about creating a new track, we will use the Create New Track function, and we will be asked to decide each time we create a new track whether we want it to be a Real Instrument track or a Software Instrument track.

Real Instrument Tracks and Software Instrument Tracks

As we move forward—specifically in Chapters 5 and 6—we will explore the distinct differences between Real Instrument tracks and Software Instrument tracks. For now, you can think of them in terms of the following. Real Instrument tracks are used to record live audio, such as guitars, voices, basses, and so on. Software Instrument tracks are used to record audio that is played on a MIDI controller—such as a MIDI piano keyboard—the sounds of which are manually selected from of the vast library of Software Instruments available in GarageBand and in its many Jam Pack software add-ons. In GarageBand '09, you can choose between a Real Instrument track, a Software Instrument track, and an Electric Guitar track when creating a new track, and while Electric Guitar tracks have guitar-specific effects, stomp boxes, and amplifier models preconfigured for your use in the track, they are still just Real Instrument tracks but are optimized for tracking electric guitar parts. We will discuss Electric Guitar tracks and their distinctions throughout the next few chapters, but it's important to remember that at the end of the day, they are still Real Instrument tracks.

An example of a Software Instrument track would be if you used your MIDI keyboard to play some drum parts using the Edgy Drums sound in GarageBand's Software

Instrument library. At a later time, you could simply decide you didn't want Edgy Drums anymore and change the Software Instrument setting for that track to Jazz Drums. The sounds and tones of each individual drum in your part would change instantly, but the timing, velocity, and rhythm of the performance that you played on your MIDI keyboard would remain unaltered. You can't do this with a Real Instrument track. If you record yourself playing five-string acoustic bass onto a Real Instrument track, you can't decide later to change the bass sound to a clarinet sound. That only works with Software Instrument MIDI tracks. MIDI tracks are virtual, whereas audio tracks are real or physical. To reiterate this very important distinction: Software Instrument tracks are for recording MIDI performances, and Real Instrument tracks are for recording real instruments being played live into a microphone or through a direct line connected to your computer or audio interface.

Creating and Naming New Tracks

Whether you are going to create a Real Instrument track or a Software Instrument track, the process for creating and naming it is the same. Let's look at that process now. It's almost like naming a file in the Finder on the Mac.

Creating a New Track

When you are ready to begin recording a new track, you'll have to create a new track to record into. Every GarageBand project starts out with at least one track. Garage-Band's default behavior when you create a new piano project, for example, is to present you with one Software Instrument track when you start, with its sound set to Grand Piano. This is a fine place to start if you're someone who has a MIDI keyboard set up all the time, and you just want to try an idea that came into your head. You launch GarageBand, you create a new piano project, name it anything you like, and begin playing piano. This is nice especially when all you want do is to use GarageBand to play something, not to record something. It's just a matter of using your computer and your MIDI keyboard as an instrument. This is akin to having a real piano in the room, walking over to it, and pecking out some notes—playing anything you like without focusing on recording. I feel this is an important point to make: GarageBand can just as easily be used as a music performance tool (to simply play music) as it can to record, edit, and mix music.

When you do want to create a new track in your project, you simply click the plus button in the lower-left corner of the GarageBand interface (see Figure 4.2). Alternatively, you can select New Track from the Track menu, or just press Option+ Command+N. You will be presented with a dialog box with three radio buttons from which you can select what type of track you'd like to create. The first radio button

Figure 4.2 The Create New Track button.

is for creating a Software Instrument track, the second is for creating a Real Instrument track, and the third is for creating an Electric Guitar track.

This dialog box describes a Software Instrument track as being used "for instrument sounds created by GarageBand and playable using a USB, MIDI, or onscreen keyboard." The dialog box describes a Real Instrument track as being used "for audio recordings such as voice, guitar, bass, or any instrument that can be captured by a microphone." The dialog box describes an Electric Guitar track as being used "for audio recordings of electric guitar using built-in GarageBand amps and effects." Simply make your selection by clicking one of the radio buttons and then click the Create button in the lower-right corner (see Figure 4.3). To cancel the creation of a new track, simply click the Cancel button.

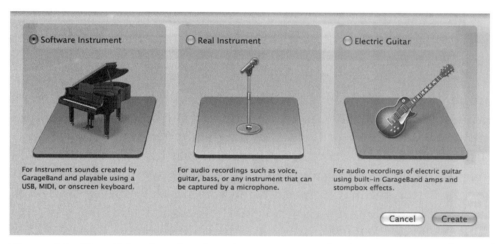

Figure 4.3 The dialog box for choosing to create a Real Instrument track, a Software Instrument track, or an Electric Guitar Track.

Editing a Track's Name

Whenever you create a Software Instrument track, you will get a default Grand Piano track. The default track is named Grand Piano because that is the preset Software Instrument it is assigned to. As soon as you change the Software Instrument preset for the track, the name of the track and its icon will change accordingly. When you create a new Real Instrument track, you get a basic blank track with no effects presets loaded, which is why the track is named No Effects. This refers to the fact that it is a naked track, with no audio processing effects yet assigned.

Chances are good that you will want to edit these default names. Naming your tracks can help with organization and recognition, especially when you start to have a large number of tracks. Good track naming will always save your neck in the long run—trust me. Take the three seconds or fewer required to name each track as you create them. You can always change the names later. Truth be told, you'll often want to once your projects start to take shape. Besides, whenever you change the Software Instrument sound or load a new audio effects preset onto a track, the name will change automatically to this new name. If you still want the track to be named My Great Solo, you'll have to change it back manually each time you select a new Software Instrument or a new effects preset on the track.

To edit a track's name, simply double-click on the text of the existing track name and wait about a second. The text will be highlighted, just like when you are naming a file or a folder in the Finder on your Mac (see Figure 4.4). You don't need to press Delete or Backspace; you can just begin typing, and your new text will replace the highlighted text that was there before. When you are finished, press Return. Now your track has a new name. Double-click, type the name, and press Return.

Figure 4.4 Rename your default tracks.

As I mentioned before, one thing to keep in mind is that when you use any of the preset effects on your tracks, GarageBand likes to rename your tracks to the name of the effect. Suppose you create a new Real Instrument track, and right after creating it, you change its name to Guitar Break. Then you record some guitar on that track. Later, when you are mixing and editing, you decide you want to add some effects, so you choose Eighties Power Chords from the Effects menu. GarageBand will automatically change your track name from Guitar Break to Eighties Power Chords. I think this is a rather annoying function, but luckily, it's easy to edit the name and change it back to Guitar Break if that's really what you want to call it. You can also feel free to leave it as Eighties Power Chords if that suits you, of course. I believe this feature was created to guard against ending up with tons of tracks all named "untitled 1" in the GarageBand projects of those users who don't bother with naming things—essentially trying to help them out with a little automatic organization. As an obsessive file- and track-namer myself, I see this feature as one whose heart is in the right place, but still, I'd rather not have my software do too much creative decision-making on my behalf.

Duplicating and Deleting Tracks

One distinction that the idea of duplicating and deleting tracks brings up is the difference between a track and the audio or MIDI information recorded onto that track. The track is the container, and the audio or MIDI information—called an *audio region* or a *MIDI region*—is the audio or MIDI information actually recorded into the track. Deleting all of the regions in a particular track does not delete the track itself—it just empties it out. Similarly, duplicating a track only duplicates the container, not the contents. If you want to duplicate a track and its contents, you can do that, but it takes two steps.

Duplicating a Track

One of the most common reasons to duplicate a track is if you really like the sounds, presets, or effects you have selected and adjusted within a certain track, and you want to record more parts with that same instrument or a variation on it. An example might be if you recorded a backup singer on your song, and that person sang a harmony part. After the singer recorded the part, suppose you took some time to adjust the EQ of the sound, added some reverb or delay, or maybe did both. Then you got the idea that you wanted to record five additional backup parts with the same singer and layer those parts together. If you are really happy with the sound that you created through the use of effects on the original backup vocal track, you don't want to have to take the time to create five fresh tracks, manually configure all of those settings, and click back and forth to refer to the original one and then make the adjustments in the new ones. This method might yield the same results, but it will most definitely take longer, and it leaves you open to making a mistake. If you select the track and duplicate it five more times, the effects and EQ settings from the original track will travel with the duplicates, and you will be able to record new vocals into each of those tracks and be guaranteed to have the same settings in each. (Don't forget to name each track uniquely!)

To duplicate a track, select it by clicking once on the track from the list of tracks on the left of your main GarageBand window, and then choose Duplicate from the Track menu. Alternatively, you can select a track and press Command+D. It's best to try to click over on the left, on the icon for the track, rather than to try to click where all the little buttons are. If you click where all the little buttons are, you might accidentally click one of the buttons, rather than actually selecting the track. Click on some of the gray space—or background area, often called the *chrome* of an application's interface—and once the track is highlighted with a green or blue color, you'll know that it has been selected.

One more note on this subject: If you want to duplicate audio regions (individual audio objects), you can treat them just like text in a word processor. You can select them and copy, cut, and paste to your heart's delight. Be careful when pasting your duplicated regions—if you want them to line up perfectly, you'll have to zoom in and paste them. Be prepared to have to click and drag the region once you've pasted it to position it exactly where you'd like it to be.

Deleting a Track

Deleting a track is just as straightforward as duplicating one. Select the track you want to delete and select Delete from the Track menu. Or, press Command+Delete. If you accidentally delete a track that you wanted to keep, you can select Undo from the Edit menu or press Command+Z. Be cautious when deleting audio regions (the actual audio elements that are inside of a track), because once they are gone, there is no place from which to retrieve them, as there is with many higher-end audio-production software applications. There is no repository of the recorded audio files from which to restore a take. Once they're gone in GarageBand, they are gone. You can use Undo, of course, but then you have to watch for all of the other things that a long series of Undo actions might restore to your project as well.

Reordering Your Tracks

Sometimes it's convenient to move tracks upward or/and downward in the track list to reorder them. For example, you might want to have all three vocal parts right next to each other at the top of the track list while you do some vocal editing, mixing, or recording. Or maybe you don't need to see the bass guitar part for the moment, so you decide to move it all the way to the bottom of the list. This is your workspace; by all means, set it up as you see fit.

You can move a track simply by clicking and dragging it up and down within the track list. Be sure to click on a non-active area of the track object itself—the solid blue (for Real Instrument tracks or Guitar tracks) or solid green (for Software Instrument tracks)—and drag from there.

You don't want to click on the volume control and drag, for example, because that would just change the volume setting. I think you get the picture. Find somewhere in the track object to click that isn't a function or a button, and you can move it around easily. See Figure 4.5.

Figure 4.5 Click and drag from the icon of a track to change its vertical position in the track list.

Working in the Timeline

The main window of your project in GarageBand is a graphical representation of time, moving from left to right. To the left is the beginning of the song, and to the right is the end of the song—further along in time. You can use the playback Transport controls at the bottom of the interface, which behave much like the controls of a traditional tape recorder in that there are buttons to stop, play, pause, record, rewind, fast-forward, and rewind to the beginning. See Figure 4.6.

Figure 4.6 The Transport controls.

However, these so-called *Transport controls* are almost too clunky for any level of efficient use. There are times when pressing these buttons will feel like the natural choice, and when it does, feel free to use them. However, I encourage you to consider a click-and-drag-plus-keyboard-shortcut approach to general playback in GarageBand. It's much faster and more easily accessible to simply click (or drag) the playhead into position and press the spacebar to play.

Playback Control

One of the most basic things you will do repeatedly in GarageBand is play—or listen to—your previously recorded audio. The playback function in GarageBand is the method by which you begin listening to particular pieces of audio from a certain point in time and then stop listening at some other point in time. You can specify on the fly whether you want to hear all the tracks of audio or just certain ones. You can even specify whether you want to hear everything *except* certain other tracks. In other words, you can approach these decisions from an inclusive or exclusive perspective depending on your need at the moment.

A cool feature of GarageBand, as well as many other digital audio software applications, is that you are not locked down to the linear passage of time as you are with linear analog tape. In a tape-based recording system, for example, to listen to Verse 3 of your song, you'd have to fast-forward, hunt around a bit to find your place, and then press Play. Some analog systems do have markers and memory points, but even those are often limited to one or maybe a few memory registers. They also take time to "seek," and you aren't afforded the ability to simply decide on a whim and a dime to play from Chorus 2 onward, for example.

Life is indeed much easier in the digital age! With a digital audio system, choosing a start point is a simple click or key press, and rewinding and fast-forwarding don't really exist. Because digital is nonlinear, you can be at any desired point in time in an instant. You aren't required to endure the long journey from here to there; you just click where you want to be, and there you are.

The Playhead and the Timeline Grid

The playhead is the triangular marker with the thin red hairline extending down the length of your GarageBand window. See Figure 4.7. The playhead in GarageBand is a metaphor for the old analog tape machines, where there was a fixed playhead, and the tape was on reels. The motors of the tape machine rolled the reels, dragging the tape across the magnetic surface of the playhead, producing audible sound from the speakers. The difference here in GarageBand is that your audio regions (meaning the individual audio elements you have recorded into tracks in the timeline) are fixed in position, and the playhead moves across them. So in a sense, it's the exact opposite of the old analog model. With analog tape decks, the audio moved across the

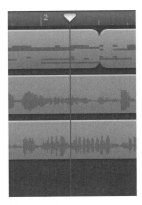

Figure 4.7   The playhead.

stationary playhead, and in digital audio software such as GarageBand, the playhead moves across the stationary audio regions.

Across the top of the GarageBand window, there is a multifunctional ruler. This ruler measures time and/or space, depending on the way you have it set. If you have the LED view set to Time, you will see the ruler as it looks in Figure 4.8. If you have the LED view set to Measures or any of the other views, you will see the ruler as it looks in Figure 4.9.

Figure 4.8   The GarageBand ruler displaying time.

Figure 4.9   The GarageBand ruler displaying measures and beats.

At the far right of the ruler is a tiny square ruler icon, which is actually a click-and-hold drop-down menu that allows you to set the snapping resolution of the playhead. This drop-down menu suggests that you click to choose a value for the timeline grid. This means you can set the playhead to snap whenever you move it to each bar or measure (1/1), half note (1/2), quarter note (1/4), and so on, and you can even have it snap to triplet and swing-feel intervals. See Figure 4.10.

You can click and drag the triangle at the top of the playhead to any new position. If you click and drag the playhead, and the setting in your ruler drop-down is set to quarter note (listed as 1/4), then the playhead will snap—or gently stick—at every quarter note you pass while dragging it.

An interesting feature of clicking and dragging the playhead is that you don't have to actually click *on* the playhead's triangle to move it—you can click anywhere in the

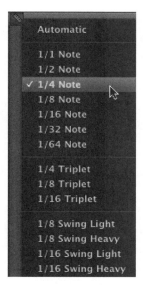

Figure 4.10 The Timeline Grid Value menu under the ruler icon at the top-right of the timeline.

ruler, and the playhead will instantly jump to your cursor so you can begin dragging from *any* point of your choosing, not just from the location where the playhead happens to be. So save yourself the moment's anguish of trying to click exactly on the tiny triangle, and just click in the ruler somewhere and begin to drag the playhead to where you want it. When you are at the desired location, you can release your mouse and press the spacebar to begin playing. When GarageBand is playing, the spacebar will pause playback. Whenever you want audio to start or stop, just press the spacebar. Taking the two or three extra seconds to mouse over and click that little Play button in the Transport controls area seems like a waste of time to me.

You can use the right and left arrow keys on your keyboard to step forward and back along your timeline, at the snap interval set in the Timeline Grid Value drop-down menu (or one notch more fine or more coarse, depending on how closely you are zoomed in or out on the timeline), as well. If you press and hold the right or left arrow key down, the playhead will move quickly along the timeline at that same snap interval. The right and left arrows are almost like fast-forward and rewind keys. If you want to rewind a bit and then play, you can press and hold the left arrow key, keeping an eye on the timeline until the playhead gets back to the area from which you'd like to play, then release the arrow key and press the spacebar. If you are currently playing your tracks back, you can simply press and hold the right or left arrow key for a bit and then release it to go back or forward and immediately begin playing. If you want to move ahead a bit in the song that you are listening to, just hold the right arrow for a second or two to move ahead. The resolution you have set in your Timeline Grid Value menu will determine how fast or slow this rewind or fast-forward function appears to behave.

Quick Tip: Double-click in the ruler to instantly begin playing at a certain spot. If you are already in playback mode, double-clicking in the ruler will pause playback and keep the playhead at the location you double-clicked, awaiting the next instruction.

Another helpful feature of the playhead is that the color of the triangle can communicate to you how hard you are hitting the processor of your computer. The older your machine is, or the slower your processor, the more likely you will run into situations where the color of the triangle changes due to increased strain on the CPU. The playhead's triangle experiences a color shift from clear and gray all the way through yellow and orange to deep red. The closer to red you get, the more GarageBand is taxing your computer's processor. If the playhead goes completely red, your playback will stop automatically. This can be the result of having too many tracks playing at the same time. Another possibility is that you may have more real-time effects being processed on individual tracks than your computer can handle. If you see a lot of yellow and orange, then you know it's time to consider either muting some tracks that you don't necessarily need to be hearing right at that moment or locking some of your tracks, causing GarageBand to temporarily freeze the track in its current configuration and with all of its post-processing plug-ins, EQs, and effects. The act of locking a track effectively renders all of its distinct audio regions and their effects settings to one solid file on the hard drive, requiring GarageBand to do nothing more than play back an audio region. Locking sort of tricks GarageBand into thinking that the track has no real-time effects applied to it at all, because it has "baked" those effects into the track temporarily, reducing strain on the CPU. You can always change the effects, automation, and other settings of that track in the future, but you'll have to unlock the track first. I will cover the locking and unlocking feature in more depth in Chapter 11, "Mixing and Automation."

Scrolling and Zooming

There are some additional ways to move around your project. One is the old computer-window staple: scrolling. There are scroll bars on the right side and the bottom of your main Timeline window, and you can use the arrows or click and drag the scroll position indicator side to side or up and down to move around the window.

The scrolling resolution is tied to your zoom level. Zoom level is how close to—or far away from—your audio regions you are. In other words, when you are zoomed all the way in, you might be seeing only one measure or less in your entire field of view, and when you are zoomed all the way out, you will be able to see 100 or more measures at once in your view. Zooming in allows you to get really close to your audio elements and adjust them with fine detail—it's almost like blowing up a photograph 600 times and being able to edit all the little pixels one by one. Sometimes you will need that level of control to achieve your objective. Other times, you will find that a medium-scale zoom or even zoomed all the way out will be sufficient to accomplish your goal.

Your zoom slider is in the mid-lower left of your GarageBand interface, right below all of your tracks. Sliding the needle all the way to the left zooms all the way out, and sliding it all the way to the right zooms all the way in. I find myself adjusting this slider all the time to give me just the right view for whatever it is I want to do. The keyboard shortcut for zooming in is Control+right arrow, and the shortcut for zooming out is Control+left arrow. Often, zooming in and zooming out require an adjustment in your field of view after zooming, which you can achieve by scrolling left or right using the scroll bar at the bottom of the Timeline window, under all of your tracks. See Figure 4.11.

Figure 4.11 The zoom slider.

Trimming and Looping Audio

Every time you press Record, play something into GarageBand, and then press Stop, you are creating an audio region. See Figure 4.12 for a look at three audio regions. Each audio region is an individual, movable audio object within the timeline grid. You can copy and paste audio regions. You select them by clicking on them (you can select multiple audio regions by holding down the Shift key while you click several regions or by clicking and dragging a marquee selection box around a group of audio regions; see Figure 4.13), and then you can move them around with a click and drag within the Timeline window. Once they are selected, you can delete regions by simply pressing the Delete or Backspace key on your keyboard or choosing Delete from the Edit menu.

Figure 4.12 Three audio regions with the middle one selected.

Figure 4.13 Click and drag the marquee selection box to select two of the three audio regions.

I'd like to discuss in more detail some additional things you can do with existing audio regions in your timeline. In the next chapter, we will cover the ins and outs of actually recording an audio region, and I'm hoping that the presence of these instructions before covering recording doesn't feel out of order to you. The reason why I want to cover these basics before covering recording is that all of the recording processes coming up in Chapters 5 and 6 (the chapters on recording Real Instruments and

Software Instruments, respectively) depend on you having some basic knowledge about interacting with tracks and audio regions, and they assume you already know how to make your way around the main Timeline window. If you're working through this book in order, and you have GarageBand open and would like to have an audio region in your timeline to work with, see the following tip for quickly getting an audio region into your timeline.

Creating an Audio Region: The quickest method for getting a fresh audio region into your timeline so you can practice copying and pasting, moving, trimming, and looping is to record a little bit of audio. You can use either a built-in microphone if you have one or a mic that you may have connected through your audio interface. (Both of these options were covered in previous chapters.)

Click the plus icon at the bottom of your track list to create a new track, click the radio button for Real Instrument, and click Create. A new track, called No Effects, will appear in the track list, and you'll notice the little red record light is on, indicating that the track is armed for recording. Next, press the R key to begin recording or click the circular red button near the Transport controls at the bottom of the interface. Say, "One…two…three…four…five…," into your mic and then press the spacebar to stop the recording. You now have an audio region in the timeline.

If you don't have a mic, the quickest method would be to just open up the Loop Browser, drag any loop into the Timeline window, and use that to mess around with.

Now that you have an audio region, we can look at trimming and looping audio regions. You might be asking, "When would I want to trim or loop an audio region?" In the following chapters, we will go through various song creation techniques and discuss the reasons for using these techniques in the context of actually creating songs, but for now I'd like to illustrate the use of the functions themselves. Let's look at an audio region for a moment. It might be beneficial to be at a medium zoom level. Make sure you can see both the beginning and the end of your audio region in your Timeline window, and be sure to have some empty gray background space on either side of it.

First click on the region and then click on the gray background of the timeline area. Clicking on the region selects it, and clicking "off" the region (meaning on some empty background space) deselects it. Notice that the region appears slightly faded when it is not selected and comes into full, intense color when it *is* selected. Tucked in at the top left of the region, you will see the name of the region, which is based on the name of the track you are recording into at the time of recording the region by default. If you edit the name of a track after recording a region into the track, you'll see that the audio region keeps its name, because a region's name is based on the name the track had when the region was originally recorded. You can edit region names after they have been recorded by double-clicking on the region to open it in the Editor, then clicking once on the region name in the upper-left corner of the region, typing in a new name, and pressing Return.

You can also see the audio waveform (the scribbly black lines within the audio region itself). If you recorded a stereo track, there will be a pair of matching lines, and if you recorded a mono (monaural) track, there will be only one line representing the audio waveform. We will cover how to choose whether to record a stereo or a mono track in the next chapter, in the section called "Input Source." See Figure 4.14.

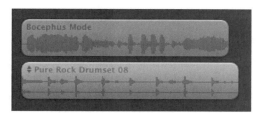

Figure 4.14 A mono (one-channel) audio region and a stereo (two-channel/left and right) audio region.

The last thing I want to look at before moving on is something fairly subtle—trimming and looping regions. These actions depend on recognizing a subtle change in the appearance of your cursor when you position your mouse in relation to the audio region itself. If you place your cursor over the middle—I like to say the *heart*—of the audio region, your cursor behaves normally (see Figure 4.15). It remains a standard cursor arrow, and this arrow indicates that you can click to select the region.

Figure 4.15 Normal selection cursor.

There are three distinct areas of each audio region that will trigger your cursor to *change* its appearance, indicating a different function—all three of which require a click and drag to perform the function. The first such area triggers the trimming function. Trimming means adding or removing material from either the beginning or the ending of a region. Said another way, it's altering where a region begins and ends, down to very accurate increments. If you position your cursor precisely at the bottom-left or bottom-right corner of the audio region itself, you will notice that your cursor changes into the trim cursor. It looks like a double arrowhead pointing left and right, surrounding a bracket—the bottom-left corner of an audio region displays the left bracket, and the bottom-right corner of an audio region displays the right bracket. See Figure 4.16 and Figure 4.17. This is to indicate which end of the region you are on or which end of the region you will be trimming if you click and drag the mouse. (The beginning is called the *head* of the region, and the end is called the *tail* of the region.)

Figure 4.16 The Trim Left cursor at the head of the audio region.

Figure 4.17 The Trim Right cursor at the tail of the audio region.

By way of example, suppose the audio region you recorded is your voice, counting from one to five. So the region contains the sound of your voice saying, "One… two…three…four…five…." If you wanted to remove the "one" from the head of the region, so that you'd only be saying, "Two…three…four…five…," you could trim the head of the region to the point between the "one" and the "two." To do so, you would click and drag the lower-left corner of the region toward the right, effectively eliminating the part of the region where you said "one." In fact, if you look closely, you should be able to actually see the waveforms representing the five spoken words—they might look like five blobs somewhat evenly spaced out from one another. Trim the head visually by dragging the head to the right until you see that you are past the first waveform, and then release your mouse. Now, click within the play-head ruler to position the playhead to the left of the trimmed audio region and press the spacebar to play. You should hear, "Two…three…four…five…."

Similarly, you can trim the "five…" off the tail by clicking the lower-right corner of the audio region and dragging it to the left, to a place before the word "five…" is uttered. Trial and error in trimming is normal and should be considered the appropriate method of getting it just right. Trim the head or tail, and then press Play. If it's not quite right, adjust the trim and play again. Remember, you can zoom in closer to refine your movement. If you really need to be precise, you can use the Track Editor window, which you can access by double-clicking any audio or MIDI region in the timeline. This will automatically open up a zoomed-in view of the region you double-clicked and give you a much finer degree of control over positioning the playhead, trimming your region, deciding where to split your regions, and so on. You can perform most basic trims right in the timeline, using the trim function with the cursor in the lower-right or lower-left area of the audio region.

It's important to note that once you have trimmed an audio region, you can always un-trim it, so to speak. GarageBand and all of its peers in the world of digital audio and video editing are known as *nondestructive* editors. This means that in most cases, you can get back what you've taken away—and I'm not referring to using Undo. Somewhere within the system—on the hard drive or, in GarageBand's case, saved in the data package structure of the GarageBand project file itself—is your original recording, untouched. Using certain techniques (such as the notion of un-trimming in this example), you can restore the old data that you trimmed away just by clicking and dragging the head trim cursor to the left or the tail trim cursor to the right. See Figure 4.18. You can only un-trim as far backward or forward as there was original recorded audio media. GarageBand will stop the trim cursor from going any farther than wherever you started or stopped recording initially. As mentioned earlier, a deleted region cannot be reclaimed, except by using Undo. As soon as you quit GarageBand and relaunch, the region will be gone forever.

Figure 4.18 Click and drag the tail cursor to the right to reveal portions of the audio region you may have trimmed off earlier.

Back to our example. Now that you have an audio region that has you speaking, "Two…three…four…," what if you wanted to loop that audio so that you say, "Two…three…four…two…three…four…two…three…four…?" Position your cursor at the top-right corner of the audio region to see yet another cursor type: the looping cursor. This is a circular arrow and indicates that if you click and drag that top-right corner of the audio region to the right, the region will be played over and over to the extent to which you drag it out into your timeline. See Figure 4.19 and Figure 4.20.

Figure 4.19 The looping cursor.

Figure 4.20 Click and drag the looping cursor to the right to loop the audio region as many times as you want.

You could make it repeat for several minutes, if you so desired, just by extending the drag of your loop out as far as you like. You'll notice that the graphic representation of the loop looks the same as a regular audio region, but at the moment where the loop cycles (meaning the point where it starts anew), there is a little dimple in the region on the top and bottom. The looping function only works on the top-right corner of the region. The top-left corner of the region does not trigger any functions, and it's important to know that you can't loop something backward in time, but only forward. If you want your loop to begin earlier, just click and drag the region to the left and position it to start where you want it to start, and then use the looping cursor to click and drag out to the right to the point where you want it to end.

Looping is a terrific technique for creating beats because you can play a short segment of rhythm (such as four bars of a percussion part, for example) and then loop that out across a long piece. This prevents you from having to perform a long take of drumming, and it lets you trim yourself one really hot performance of those four bars and then reuse that performance throughout your song. This is a technique used by countless artists and music producers in the professional sphere.

Tracks and Track Mixer Controls

In the previous chapter, we breezed over what all of the buttons and sliders in the Track Mixer are called in the section called "The Arrange Window," and in this section, I'd like to spend a moment with each function and feature to explain what it actually does. See Figure 4.21 for a detailed view of the Track Mixer controls.

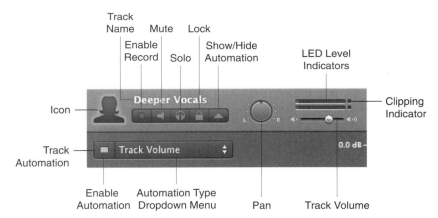

Figure 4.21 Track Mixer controls.

When you're recording onto one of your tracks, many of the functions in the Track Mixer are not terribly relevant. Many of them control how you hear a track after it has been recorded. Some of the functions, such as pan and volume, do have an effect on how you hear your performance while performing it, but they do not determine the volume or panning of what's actually getting recorded—they perform more of what's called a *monitoring* function when used in this way. The Track Mixer controls are all about what you're hearing in the speakers or headphones, each track being relative to all the other tracks.

To put a fine point on this, suppose you have guitar and bass recorded on Tracks 1 and 2, and you are preparing to add vocals onto Track 3. You set an input level (which we'll cover in Chapter 5, "Real Instruments and Electric Guitar Tracks"), you perform a couple of takes, and things aren't really working for you. You start to realize that you wish you could hear your live vocal a little louder in relation to the guitar and bass parts. All you have to do is raise the volume of Track 3 in the Track Mixer, and your live voice will sound louder in your headphones while you sing. Doing this does not change the input level you set and has no impact whatsoever on the audio file that is getting saved to your hard drive. The same example could be made if what you wished was to hear less vocals or perhaps more of the guitar track.

While recording, the Track Mixer controls the relative volumes of the existing tracks in relation to the current performance—and one another. Take the time you need to get that headphone or speaker mix just the way you want it so that you feel *on* when recording your performances. Don't let anyone tell you that you are being demanding or a prima donna if you want to tweak your headphone mix again. Great performances come down to many things, chief of which is having a sweet mix to perform to. Tweak your mix, nail your part, and be sure to buy a round for those who did the tweaking if you have anyone other than yourself to thank for spending the time to make you comfortable. If you're your own engineer, then I encourage you to remember that if things in your headphone mix don't feel right, change them. It's that simple.

Track Volume and the LED Level/Clipping Indicators

The track volume slider controls how loud the track is. Clicking and dragging to the left on the volume slider makes it quieter—all the way down, and it will appear to be off. Clicking and dragging to the right on the volume slider will make the track louder, and if you go all the way, your audio will very often clip or distort.

The LED level meters show you how loud the audio is relative to clipping. Green LED lights are good. The occasional orange LED lights are fine and are at the very top range of sounding good. Red LED lights are bad, and you have clipped. If the audio does in fact clip or peak, the little red clipping indicator light will light up and stay lit up until you reset it by clicking on it to turn it off, essentially resetting the clipping indicator. This is a valuable feature because you might not actually be staring at the LED indicators on that track 100 percent of the time, and you might not notice some little moment where the sound spiked for a split second, clipping the track. This light tells you, "Hey, somewhere in the recent past (since the last time you reset the clipping indicator), something on this track peaked and the meter clipped. You might want to look into it." There are many ways to deal with volume spikes like these. For now,

I want you to know what that red light means and that clicking it resets it, allowing it to stand at the ready, waiting to find and indicate the next offending moment for you.

When an audio signal clips (also called *peaking* or *spiking*) in a digital environment, it's very different than when an audio signal peaks in an analog environment. Both are undesirable in most cases, but the salient detail here about digital distortion caused by peaking levels is that you actually lose data when digital information clips. Some of the sound that you recorded is potentially lost or damaged. This can introduce unpleasing sound anomalies—buzzes, chirps, scratches, and fuzziness—to your track. In Chapter 5, you'll read about setting your input levels and using the clipping indicator to adjust while you do your takes.

If you Option-click the volume slider, it will automatically reset to 0.0 dB (zero decibels), also known as *unity gain*. This means that GarageBand is not adding gain (making it louder) or subtracting gain (making it softer), but you are hearing the audio track at "flat" volume, meaning an exact reproduction of what you recorded at the level you recorded it at. When you move the volume slider up or down, watch for the floating yellow tooltip to appear, indicating how much gain you are adding to or subtracting from your track. A quick way to reset all of your volume sliders on all of your tracks to flat is to hold down the Option key and click all of your volume sliders on all of your tracks.

Panning

You twist the pan knob (from the word *panorama*) left or right to move the sound of a particular track into the left or right portion of the stereo space. You can click and drag down on the pan knob to move the sound to the left; a slight move might give the aural impression of the instrument or voice being slightly to your left, whereas moving all the way to the left will result in a sound starkly to the left of you. Clicking and dragging up on the pan knob places the sound to the right. Usually, a slight move of between –20 and +20 (watch for the little yellow tooltip indicating how far you've moved away from center as you twist the knob) is all that's required to help a particular sound within your piece appear to "sit" in the mix better than if all of your sounds are panned center. Sometimes a little goes a long way. For a drastic effect, go even further with it.

Panning is very subjective, as are many of the mixing techniques you will use in GarageBand. So use your ears and don't try to mix by the numbers. You should always go with what sounds good to you. Try to set up your listening and recording station as well as you can in terms of speaker position, lack of outside noise, and so on, and then just start listening.

Enable Recording

To record a new performance to a track, you will have to enable recording by clicking the little red light so that it lights up. To disable recording, click the light off. When you create a new track, by default GarageBand enables recording, assuming that you want to record when you make the new track. If this is not the case, simply disable recording. Enabling recording is sometimes referred to as *arming the track*.

Mute

The button with the speaker icon is the Mute button. Clicking Mute makes a track temporarily inaudible. Suppose you were working on a guitar solo but you didn't want to hear the horn part. You could mute the horn part by clicking its Mute button.

Solo

The button with the headphones icon is the Solo button. When you click it, you will only hear that one track. You can click the Solo button on more than one track. All tracks that have their Solo buttons clicked on will be audible during playback, and those without the Solo button on will not be audible. If no tracks have the Solo button enabled, then all tracks will be audible, except those that are muted. A track cannot be muted and soloed at the same time. If the Solo button is enabled and you click the Mute button, the Solo button will be disabled at the moment the Mute button becomes enabled.

Lock

You can click the padlock button to lock or unlock the track. Locking a track protects regions from being edited and renders the track to the hard drive, freeing up processing power and memory. Once you have locked a track, you always need to unlock it again before you can edit it. Unlocking a track will reclaim all of the system resources that were required to play it before it was locked. Some other audio applications, such as Logic Pro, refer to this process of rendering the audio regions and freeing up system resources as *freezing the track*. Additionally, Logic allows you to protect the track from editing without freezing it (and vice versa), which means the system resources are still required to play the track, but it is protected from further editing. In Garage-Band, protecting and freezing go hand in hand in a singular function called *locking*.

View/Hide Track Automation

This triangular Show/Hide Automation button will reveal the track automation area for any individual track. Click it again to hide the automation area for the track. In Mac OS X, this type of button is often called a *disclosure triangle*.

Track Automation

We will cover automation extensively in Chapter 11, but it's important to know that you have this very powerful feature at your fingertips in GarageBand. In digital recording, *automation* refers to anytime you want settings of any kind to change gradually over time or instantly at any specific point in your song. A good example might be a fade-out at the end of a song. Fading out is the process of all of the tracks simultaneously getting quieter until they are no longer audible. Many pop and rock songs end this way. Even songs that have a definite end in terms of the composition still have that five- to ten-second tail at the end where all the instruments hang there on the final chord and then fade out.

Creating automation is a simple node-based (or keyframe-based) function. All this means is that for a given parameter—let's say volume—you can say at a certain point in time that you want the volume to be set a particular way and then at a later time you want the volume to be set another way. GarageBand knows how to smoothly make the change for you over time; all you have to do is set the two points. Likewise, you can set a series of points over time, having an effect on the volume of your own design at each point in time represented by a node. GarageBand will smoothly transition between each node you create over the time that is represented by the horizontal distance between each of the nodes.

Briefly, let's talk about fading out one track. Click the Track Automation button and then open the drop-down menu and choose Track Volume. Then click the indicator light to the left of the drop-down menu, and it will glow blue. When it's on, GarageBand is reading your automation settings. You can remove the automation without losing the work you did in refining it simply by clicking the blue light off. See Figure 4.22.

Figure 4.22 A track with volume automation nodes drawn in to create a fade-out of the track.

To create automation in your song, you must add nodes (sometimes called *keyframes*) to the automation track. These designate specific moments in your song where something is so. Simply click on the line that is currently set by default to the level you have set in your volume slider for the track. For example, suppose you wanted to click the line at 10 bars into your song and then click the line again at 15 bars into your song. At the 10-bar mark, click and drag the node downward slightly and lower it a couple of dB. (Watch the floating yellow indicator box as you drag.) Then, at 15 bars, raise it a couple of dB. Now, at 10 bars in, your level is at –4 dB, and at 15 bars in, your level is at +4 dB. GarageBand will smoothly fade the level a total of 8 dB louder over the course of those five bars. It will appear as though the instrument or voice on that track gets louder and louder until it is prominently featured.

You can create all kinds of wonderful artistic effects with automation. Again, let your ears be the judge. If you want something to get softer during a certain passage, just create four nodes. The first is normal (or where you are coming *from*), the second is down a bit (the new level you want the sound to be at), the third is still down (presumably in the same position as the second node, but it doesn't have to be!), and the fourth is back to normal. This will "duck" that audio down for a bit, and then raise it back up to where it was.

You can change both volume and panning with automation, and you can also add automation for EQ, echo, and reverb, as well as any other effects that you may have assigned to your track. This is particularly effective for creating different-sounding sections of your song and will make your mixes much more professional. In Chapter 11, this topic will be covered in depth, and I will show you how you can automate many hundreds of different parameters within specific audio effects and Software Instruments, taking things far beyond the basic automation available in previous versions of GarageBand!

The Master Track

Pressing Command+B will reveal and conceal the Master Track. The Master Track allows you to make settings (including automation) that will affect your entire mix at the same time. If you want to create a master fade-out at the end of your song, this is where to do it. If you want to add some compression to your overall mix or some EQ or other mastering effects, the Master Track is the place to do it. The Master Track even has the ability to change tempo throughout your song, along with specific settings such as timing and repeat for echo, and even allows you to add varying degrees of pitch adjustment to your whole mix. See Figure 4.23.

Figure 4.23 The Master Track with volume automation enabled.

The Ducking Function

Ducking is an automated way to prioritize one track over another, and it allows the audio content of the tracks to drive the function itself. Ducking just means lowering the volume of one thing relative to another—effectively ducking one behind the other. A good example of this is an announcer who might be featured at the beginning of a radio program. The music cranks up at the beginning, and then when the announcer starts talking a few seconds in, the music ducks down to make room for the announcer in the audio space. When the announcer stops talking or takes a little break between thoughts, the music raises back up again for a moment and then ducks back down when the voiceover resumes. This is fairly easy to achieve manually with automation nodes and volume, but it's tedious. GarageBand includes an automated ducking feature that makes it all a simple matter.

To see the ducking controls, choose Ducking from the Control menu or press Shift+ Command+R. The ducking function consists of two clickable buttons, one pointing up and the other pointing down. There are three possible settings for ducking. Click the top arrow, which will glow yellow, to make the track force other tracks to duck.

Click the bottom arrow, which will glow blue, to make the track duck relative to any tracks that have the yellow ducking arrow enabled. Click both arrows off, which will look plain gray, to leave the track out of the equation all together—it will remain constant at whatever volume level you have it set to. See Figure 4.24.

Figure 4.24 Three tracks with the three different ducking priorities enabled.

If you have a voice track on Track 1 and a music track on Track 2, and you want the music to duck down behind the voice whenever it is present, click the up arrow on Track 1 and the down arrow on Track 2. Track 2 will duck behind Track 1. If you have a sound effect that you want to come in at a certain time, but you want to be able to set its level yourself and not have it impacted by your decisions about ducking, you can leave both ducking arrows deactivated, and the track will simply play at the level at which you mixed it on playback.

Track Info

As mentioned in Chapter 3, the Track Info panel is where you make decisions about post-processing effects that you will apply to Real Instrument tracks. It is also where you select and customize the sounds of your Software Instruments. The mechanics of using the Track Info panel are quite simple. Choose a Real Instrument track on the left by clicking on it and then open the Track Info panel by clicking the button in the lower-right corner of the GarageBand interface (the button with an "i" on it). Click the Browse tab and click on a settings group, such as drums, effects, or vocals, and within each group you can click from the list of settings. Once you have clicked on a setting, click the Edit tab to the right of Browse to access all the effects processors that are employed to generate the preset sound setting. You can customize the settings, add new ones if you like, delete others, and then save your custom configuration as a "new instrument" with the Save Instrument button at the bottom of the Track Info panel, name your New Instrument, and recall it from the Browse tab at any time in the future. See Figure 4.25.

If you select a Software Instrument track from your track list on the left, the Track Info panel will display a Browse tab filled with a vast library of instrument sounds from which to choose, broken into groups such as guitars, strings, and woodwinds. Click on a group and explore the sounds available in that group by clicking a Software Instrument from the column on the right. When you have done so, you will be able to press keys on your MIDI controller to hear what they sound like and record them.

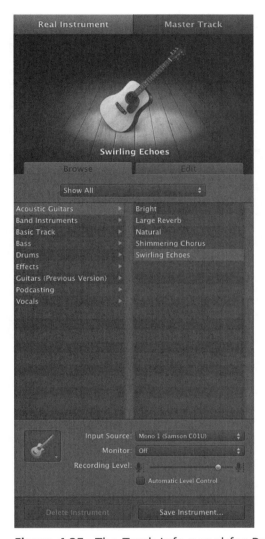

Figure 4.25 The Track Info panel for Real Instruments.

If you want to customize the parameters of a given Software Instrument, just click the Edit tab on the right of the Track Info panel and then click the on any of the icons along the right side of the list to edit the individual parameters of either the sound generator or any of the individual effects modules that may be assigned to the Software Instrument. You can even change the instrument generator itself here to create your own new sound from scratch. Notice the drop-down menus in each generator or effect. You can choose alternate generators or effects from these menus to utterly change the sound modules you are working with. Just click Save Instrument at the bottom right of the Track Info panel to save your settings once you've customized them. To delete an instrument you created, choose it in the Browse tab area of the Track Info panel and then click the Delete Instrument button at the bottom left of the Track Info panel. See Figure 4.26.

Figure 4.26 The Track Info panel for Software Instruments.

It's Time to Do Some Recording

Now that you know what all of the functions in the main Track window do and how to work with tracks and audio regions, it's time to start actually making some music and working with the audio regions and MIDI recordings. The next two chapters will deal with recording Real Instruments and Electric Guitar Tracks (Chapter 5) and Software Instruments (Chapter 6) and editing those performances to your liking. I will be getting fairly in depth, and you can follow along by getting GarageBand up and running and recording some audio and MIDI so that you can work along with me and try out some examples yourself.

5 Real Instruments and Electric Guitar Tracks

We discussed some of the aspects of Real Instrument tracks in previous chapters, but to sum it up briefly: Real Instruments are those real-world instruments you can make sounds with out in the air, in your studio or recording space, and a Real Instrument track is the track type that allows you to record those physical real-world sounds digitally into GarageBand. An Electric Guitar track is a Real Instrument track that is preconfigured with electric guitar amps and effect stompboxes. Think of Electric Guitar tracks as perhaps the most common type of Real Instrument track that one might choose to record in GarageBand, but that also has some specific requirements/benefits that made Apple decide to create a specially designed Real Instrument track preset for recording electric guitars.

To record a Real Instrument, you need to create a Real Instrument track in your GarageBand project. As we covered in Chapter 4, click the plus button at the bottom of the GarageBand interface. Alternatively, you can choose New Track from the Track menu or press Option+Command+N. Then, click the Real Instrument track radio button in the overlay window that pops up and click Create. You now have a Real Instrument track, armed and ready to be recorded onto. If you have a microphone connected and properly configured or you have an instrument plugged into your Line In on your audio interface or the Audio In on your computer, you should see the LED level indicators in the mixer controls for that new track responding to you talking into the mic or producing a sound on your instrument. If you aren't getting any levels, check the next section for a sound preferences refresher.

Check Those Sound Prefs!

If you aren't getting any sound input level, it's always worth a visit to the System Preferences application and the Audio/MIDI tab in the GarageBand Preferences window.

System Preferences Check

Open System Preferences from the Dock or choose System Preferences from the Apple menu and click on Sound in the Hardware category. In the Sound Preferences pane, choose Input and be sure your desired input device is selected from the list.

You should be able to make a sound and see the level meter move. Set your input level nice and high, but be sure that it's not peaking. (Your setting might end up being between 70 and 85 percent.) If you can't move your level input slider or if this does not work, you might want to restart your computer. Choose Restart from the Apple menu and return to the System Preferences application to set your input. It's also good to remember that some hardware audio interfaces "hijack" the input slider control in the Sound control panel. However, in that case, you should still see level coming through if your interface is connected properly and powered up. Be sure to try unplugging the connectors of the audio interface and reconnecting them, or restarting your computer after making sure everything is seated—or connected—properly and that your computer has recognized the interface on startup. See Figure 5.1.

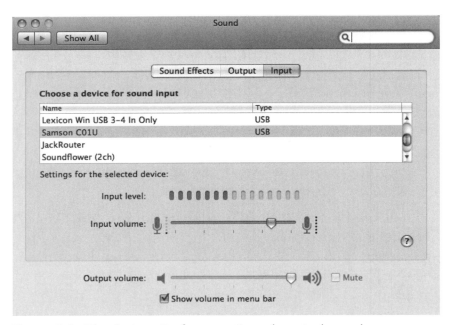

Figure 5.1 The System Preferences Sound control panel.

GarageBand Preferences Audio/MIDI Check

Back in GarageBand, choose Preferences from the application menu and click Audio/ MIDI. Be sure your desired input device is selected here. Then return to GarageBand, arm your track by clicking the red-light record indicator on the left in your track controls, and test your level indicators to be sure you're getting an input signal. See Figure 5.2.

Setting Up the Input Source, Monitor, and Recording Level

Next you want to be sure you're getting the correct input device routed to this new track, choose between stereo and mono, choose between monitoring on and off, and set your actual input level. In the Track Info panel of the GarageBand interface, you will find the Input Source, Monitor, and Recording Level settings. These settings apply directly to the current track you have selected on the left in your track list. Access the

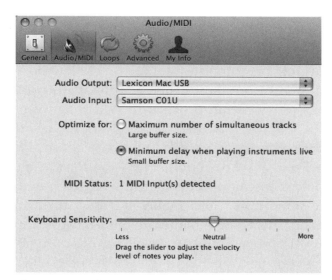

Figure 5.2 The GarageBand Preferences Audio/MIDI pane.

Track Info panel by clicking the "i" icon in the lower-right of the GarageBand interface or by pressing Command+I. See Figure 5.3.

Figure 5.3 The icon for accessing the Track Info panel.

Input Source

Your specific audio configuration (meaning your particular audio interface, number of inputs, microphones, and so on) will largely determine what options will show up in the Input Source drop-down menu. You'll often have multiple listings—some will say Stereo after the name of the input source, and some will say Mono. You'll have to choose. If your signal is a mono source (such as a direct guitar or bass line in or a single microphone), you'll want to choose one of the settings that says Mono. If you have a keyboard or another instrument or piece of outboard gear (such as a sound processor or a mixer) that has a stereo output, you'll want to choose one of the settings that says Stereo. See Figure 5.4 for a look at the Input Source, Monitor, and Recording Level controls.

Figure 5.4 The Input Source, Monitor, and Recording Level controls.

Monitor

A word of warning before we get too far into this section: In most configurations of computer, speakers, and microphone, turning the Monitor setting on will almost always produce feedback if your speakers are turned on and your microphone is connected to a track that is enabled for recording. Before you start switching your Monitor setting, you might want to adjust your volume to a fairly low level while you set it up to avoid feedback while experimenting with levels. Your choices in the Monitor menu are Off, On, and On with Feedback Protection. The Monitor setting applies to whether you want to hear the sound that is coming through your input source come out of your speakers at the same time. This makes it easier to hear what you're playing or singing, to ensure a better performance. If you have headphones plugged in, and your speakers are off, you will likely want to choose On so you can hear yourself singing or performing your instrument along with the mix while you record a track.

If you leave monitoring on and also have your speakers on, you will probably get some amount of feedback, which is that terribly screechy, echo-y sound that builds up to a deafening roar that could damage your speakers and/or your ears. Also, remember that if you have the Monitor setting on and your speakers on (even with feedback protection on), if you are running GarageBand's metronome to play along with, you will be "recording" that metronome click back into the open microphone. Later, while mixing, you will likely turn off the metronome setting in GarageBand, but you'll still hear it quietly in the background because you recorded it *with* your voice—onto the vocal track, for example. There is no way to remove that click after the fact. If you are recording with the metronome on, you will want to consider going with the Monitor setting on, your speakers turned off or volume completely down, and your headphones plugged in. Be sure Built-In is selected in your Output settings under GarageBand Preferences Audio/MIDI, or whichever device you are connecting headphones to.

Recording Level

The Recording Level control is a slider that allows you to adjust the input level of the source you are recording. Adjust this slider back and forth while strumming or singing (you might need to strum, then adjust, then strum, then adjust, and so on if you are alone) and try to get the LED level indicators on the track to be fairly high, but only just flirting with the orange every once in a great while. Selecting the Automatic Level Control option will tell GarageBand to adjust the level for you. I sometimes use the Automatic Level Control option to set my level—I select Automatic Level Control and then begin singing or strumming like I plan to in the final performance, and I watch as GarageBand sets the level for me. When I'm satisfied, I quickly reach over and click off the Automatic Level Control check box, and then the level stays put. Otherwise, it will continue to change while I am performing, which may produce an unnatural-sounding recording. Remember not to let your audio levels get too high and clip! I can't emphasize that enough for people who are new to the recording process—it's one of the most common pitfalls to ruin a good performance by having your levels cranked up too high and having that distort and ruin the recording of your track.

Effects

You don't have to use effects while tracking, but often you might want to have a little EQ or reverb on your voice so it sounds better to you in your headphones while performing. In this case, "better" means "more in the mix"—more blended into the actual recording, better in the sense that it might make you more comfortable performing. This can also be helpful when you're tracking an electric guitar part that needs some stompbox effects on it to sound something like you might want it to sound in your final song. While you are recording, you might want to make the part you are tracking sound something like what it will sound like later, so that it feels more fitting and natural to the performer during his take.

The brilliant thing about digital effects in a digital recording environment such as GarageBand is that you can track your part with effects on, and those effects don't get recorded as part of the track—they are always handled as separate post-processes to the recording of the audio. This is what's knows as a *nondestructive* process. Your original, pristine recorded performance will always be available to you if you want to get back to it. All you have to do is disable all of the effects you have on it.

In the Track Info panel, with Real Instrument selected and the Browse tab active, in the left column click on the type of Real Instrument that you plan to have on this track, such as vocals, for example. Then, you will be able to choose from one of the GarageBand presets that come with the stock application. Click on any of the vocals effects that you see in the right column and play your track to hear what they sound like. (You may need to record something into this new vocal track to have anything to play back while you audition the various sounds.) There are additional effects available if you purchase some of the GarageBand Jam Packs. Many of the Jam Packs come with dozens of new effects presets.

The presets themselves are very well designed, but often they may not quite sound like what you have in mind right out of the box. If this is the case, you can click the Edit tab on the right side of the Track Info panel to open up the specific effects and gain access to the parameters that make up each effect. You can change any of the settings you want and even save the result as a new effect. (GarageBand calls your new saved effects settings *instruments*.) Name the new effect something like My New Vocal Sound. This way, you can call up the new, customized effect at any time in the future by selecting the Vocals category under Browse in the Track Info panel and clicking on My New Vocal Sound in the right column to apply it to any track you like. Click Save Instrument at the bottom of the Track Info panel and name your new Real Instrument effects preset to save it for future use. See Figure 5.5.

Figure 5.5 The Track Info panel with the Real Instrument Browse tab active. Note the Save Instrument button at the bottom right.

To adjust any of the parameters of the preset effects, you will need to be in the Edit tab of the Track Info panel. You will use the check boxes on the left to activate or deactivate any of the effects. Some of them are straight-up one-function effects, such Gate, Echo, and Reverb, and they can be activated and deactivated at will. If they are active, you'll need to slide the parameter slider from 0 to 100 to adjust the amount of the effect you want to hear. Gate is at the top of the list because Gate is all about limiting the extraneous sound that comes into the effects processing chain to begin with.

The Echo and Reverb sends at the bottom of the list are meant to sprinkle a little echo (delay) or reverb, respectively, onto your whole effect setting at large. The idea of an effect send in the real world is that you are taking your signal as-is and sending it out of a particular channel into a piece of outboard gear (a separate reverb unit, for example) and adding processing to that sound. That newly processed sound (the track as it was originally, plus the reverb effect from the outboard unit it was sent to) comes back into your mixing console through a *return*. At that point, you are hearing a combination of the original sound plus the reverb. This new, composite sound is the sound that is headed to your mix.

In GarageBand, by default you have an echo (or delay unit) and a reverb unit available to you at all times, and that's why I used the word "sprinkle" earlier. You can simply mix in as much echo or reverb as you'd like on any of your tracks. If you click Master Track at the top of the Track Info panel, you'll see down at the bottom that there is yet another echo and reverb that you can apply onto the entire mix as a whole. These effects are best used judiciously, as they can very quickly compound one another and create an extremely muddy overall sound. Experiment with what sounds good to your ears, but believe me when I tell you that a little can go a very long way.

It's helpful to think of this Effects Edit portion of the Track Info panel as a signal path, running from top to bottom, with each effect in the series compounding the results of all of the preceding effects. Think of each step along the path, or chain, as a brand-new sound that is then being fed into the next effect in the chain, and so on.

The Edit tab features seven slots for effects and has two sends at the bottom, as mentioned, for Echo and Reverb. All seven of the slots under Effects can be potentially filled with effects of your choosing or those that come as part of any given instrument or effects preset you may have chosen from the Browse tab. Empty Effects selectors display the text "Click here to add an effect" if you position your mouse over them, and when you click and hold, a menu appears, allowing you to choose an effect preset to either use out of the box or begin customizing.

The Effects drop-down menu will be populated by any and all digital effects you have installed on your system. This could include GarageBand Jam Pack effects, as well as effects plug-ins you may have installed in another audio application, such as Apple's Logic Pro 8. These must be AU (Audio Unit) plug-ins for them to show up in GarageBand. If you investigate the drop-down menu, you will see the list divided into GarageBand Effects and Audio Unit Effects. I also have Logic Pro 8 installed on the computer on which these screenshots were created, and Logic installs a number of AU effects, so you can see them listed in the grouping underneath GarageBand Effects. If you don't have any AU effects installed, you won't see the second list. If you have any additional effects installed, you will see them displayed in this menu as well. See Figure 5.6.

It's very easy (and often makes for good experimentation!) to position your effects within the effects chain into a different order. Any effect that has a little "grippy" texture on the left edge is able to be clicked and dragged to another position in the list to change the order of the signal-processing chain. Each effect has five components:

Figure 5.6 An Effects drop-down menu in the Edit tab of the Track Info panel.

the three grip dots on the left edge for positioning; the clickable blue light on the left for enabling and disabling the effect; the colorful icon image, which can be clicked to access parameters for the effect; the top drop-down menu for reassigning the effect altogether; and the bottom drop-down menu for selecting a preset for a specific effect. Choose None from the top drop-down if you don't want any effect to load on a particular step of the chain or you want to delete one that you currently have assigned. You might be surprised at the widely varying results of having certain effects come either before or after others in the chain.

Some of the effects that you choose will only have manual configurations, and if you click the color image icon to access the editing of parameters on the left side of any effect, the effect plug-in will open in a separate floating window, and you will be able to adjust its parameters manually. You can do this and play your track at the same time, so you can preview your parameter adjustments in real time. Some effects, such as the Speech Enhancer, have a number of presets that come with them. In addition to being able to adjust their parameters manually by clicking the icon (Edit Parameters) button, you can choose from the secondary drop-down menu to access all of the presets in one click. I like to select presets to get a starting place and then edit the presets' parameters manually. It's a good exercise for seeing how the sounds were created in the first place by looking at the parameters that make certain presets sound the way they do and then messing them up! You can always save your work by clicking Save Instrument at the bottom and giving it a name. Choose Manual from the presets menu, and a default set of parameters for the effect will be loaded, allowing you to sculpt the sound from scratch, and then you can save and name your new effects preset. Now you can choose to use it or edit it further in the future from the Browse tab. See Figure 5.7.

Figure 5.7 The Speech Enhancer preset's drop-down menu.

Often, these presets are available from within the plug-in as well, so if you click the Edit Parameters icon, you will have access to a drop-down menu within the plug-in interface that contains all of them. Take a look at the effect parameters window of the plug-in for Speech Enhancer in Figure 5.8.

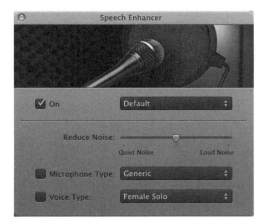

Figure 5.8 The Speech Enhancer effects plug-in.

I encourage you to experiment heavily in this area of the application, because these effects that are available in GarageBand are topnotch pro-level audio effects, and many of them are the very same effects that come stock in Apple's pro audio application, Logic Pro 8. Apple did not skimp on or dumb down these effects. In fact, the audio quality, fidelity, and resolution of all of GarageBand's sound processors are professional-grade across the board.

Make no mistake, full broadcast-quality sound productions can come out of Garage-Band. It's no toy, and these effects really prove it. I only showed you a few ideas about customizing Speech Enhancer, but there are amplifier models, noise gates and limiters, compressors, reverbs, EQ, notch filters, chorus, flanger, boosters, reducers, and a bit crusher, not to mention the wide variety of stompbox effects for electric guitar that have been added in GarageBand '09—almost anything you can think of. And keep in mind that you can add your own effects to GarageBand by purchasing third-party AU plug-ins and installing them on your Mac. Follow the developer's instructions for installing the plug-ins, and they will show up in these menus the next time you launch GarageBand.

For a complete rundown of all of the audio effects available in GarageBand and some specifics about working with each of them, see Chapter 11, "Mixing and Automation," specifically the section called "Using Effects and Post-Processing."

Electric Guitar Amps

In GarageBand '09, Apple has delivered a whole new level of flexibility and functionality for electric guitar players. There have always been a number of good effects presets for electric guitar, but the new version of GarageBand has cleared a space in the room for electric guitar players specifically by adding a new track type—Electric Guitar tracks (which, as we discussed, are Real Instrument tracks set up for recording your electric guitar through your line in or audio interface). Instead of the Track Info panel showing you all of the effects and presets available to you through the Browse and Edit tabs, you will have a guitar amp and a row of five stompbox effect slots with which to build your tone (see Figure 5.9).

The top half of the Guitar track Track Info panel is a stage, and on the stage are your guitar amp and your stompbox pedals. You can choose a guitar preset from the pop-up menu, such as Clean Combo, Fat Stack, Punk Rock, Liverpool Bright, and Vibrato Blues. There are 37 presets in all, and you can create and save your own, just like with saving a new instrument with the Real Instrument and Software Instrument effects settings Track Info panel. See Figure 5.10 for a complete list of guitar setting presets that come with GarageBand.

With Electric Guitar tracks, you can click Save Setting at the lower right to capture your customized electric guitar sounds. By clicking on the guitar amp, you will see that

Figure 5.9   The Track Info panel in Electric Guitar track mode.

all of the parameters that can be adjusted for the particular amp will be shown to you in the bottom half of the panel. Just click and drag the knobs to adjust the different aspects of the tone. You can be playing your guitar in real time and make an adjustment and then keep playing to test your changes, but it might be easier to record a short track of you playing your guitar, and then you can just allow GarageBand to play back your guitar part while you tweak your sound settings. Of course, a friend is always good for this task as well. Have someone play your guitar continuously while you adjust the settings on your amp.

If you click the Edit button at the top right of the Electric Guitar Track Info panel or just double-click the amp, you will be able to edit the amp itself and choose different amp models. There are five different base amp models to use as starting points for your guitar effects setting.

Figure 5.10 GarageBand '09's Guitar Track settings presets menu.

The guitar amps included in GarageBand '09 are:

- Small Tweed Combo, based on the '57 Fender Twin-Amp Tweed Combo Amp

- Blackface Combo, based on the '60s Fender Blackface Pro Reverb Combo Amp

- English Combo, based on the Vox AC 30 Combo Amp

- Vintage Stack, based on a vintage '60s Marshall Plexi stack

- Modern Stack, based on the Mesa Boogie Dual Rectifier stack

You'll notice that you can also add Master Echo or Master Reverb (just like the effects sends that you can apply to Real Instrument tracks, Software Instrument tracks, or the Master Track) and choose an alternate input source for your guitar. If you are using the electric guitar adapter and plugged straight into your computer, you'll want to choose line in from the Input Source menu. Otherwise, you'll need to choose your audio interface mono input, or if you don't have either, you can always mike a guitar or your real-world guitar amp, choose your microphone input from the Input Source menu, and still apply amps and stompbox effects to your sound. But overall, that would not be as clean and pure-sounding as when you have the guitar directly connected to your Mac (see Figure 5.11).

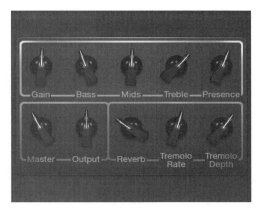

Figure 5.11 The bottom half of the Track Info panel when editing your guitar amp.

Keep in mind that guitar amps and stompbox effects are just as powerful for simply playing your guitar through GarageBand and using your speakers or even headphones. It's like having your own library of amps and stompboxes to play through any time you like. You don't have to be recording to find GarageBand useful.

Electric Guitar Stompbox Effects

A guitar stompbox is a self-contained guitar effect that traditionally was built into a small metal box with a foot switch and some knobs to adjust the parameters of the sound the stompbox was designed to deliver, such as chorus, distortion, or delay. GarageBand offers you 10 software stompboxes that are so nicely designed, you will undoubtedly be as surprised as I was by how fantastic these effects are. You can drag and drop stompboxes into your signal chain on the stage underneath your amp. Click on the stompbox that appears by default for the guitar effect setting preset you chose, and the 10 pedals will all be shown. Click and drag them into place on the stage, and click and drag to reorder your chosen stompboxes. Topnotch pro-sounding stompbox models available in GarageBand '09 are as follows.

Phase Tripper

A phaser divides an audio signal into two paths, one of which is the original sound and the other feeding an all-pass filter and an LFO (low-frequency oscillator). When the two signals are combined, the notches created by the filter and the modulation of the LFO cancel out certain frequencies in the unprocessed signal path, giving a very animated, sweeping sound. The Phase Tripper stompbox effect allows you to adjust rate, depth, and feedback, and clicking the Sync button will set a rate that suits the tempo of the song project you are working on (see Figure 5.12).

Figure 5.12   The Phase Tripper guitar stompbox effect adds a phaser effect to your guitar tone.

Vintage Drive

An overdrive is an effect that mimics the overloading of the input stage of an amplifier. This creates a low level of harmonically rich distortion that adds excitement to the signal. The Vintage Drive stompbox effect allows you to adjust drive, level, and tone, and it has a fat switch you can click to add some real beefiness to your over-driven tone (see Figure 5.13).

Figure 5.13   The Vintage Drive guitar stompbox effect adds an overdrive effect to your guitar tone.

Grinder

Distortion is overdrive taken to the extreme; the input signal is fully clipped, which adds even more harmonics to the sound and changes the fundamental waveform in a more drastic manner. The Grinder stompbox effect allows you to adjust grind, filter, and level, and it includes a switch for full scoop to create a particular EQ sound often associated with particularly teeth-grinding metal guitar sounds (see Figure 5.14).

Figure 5.14 The Grinder guitar stompbox effect adds a distortion effect to your guitar tone.

Fuzz Machine

Fuzz is another flavor of distortion that adds dissonant intermodulation harmonics due to the levels of clipping to the original signal. The Fuzz Machine stompbox effect allows you to adjust fuzz, tone, and level so that you can add in just the right measure of it to sculpt your sound (see Figure 5.15).

Figure 5.15 The Fuzz Machine guitar stompbox effect adds a fuzz effect to your guitar tone.

Retro Chorus

Chorus is produced by delaying a sound by 10 to 30 milliseconds and blending it with the original signal. This delayed sound is also slowly modulated in pitch by an LFO, producing a doubled effect. The Retro Chorus stompbox effect allows you to adjust rate and depth, and clicking the Sync button, just as with the Phase Tripper stompbox effect, will set a rate that suits the tempo of the song project you are working on (see Figure 5.16).

Robo Flanger

Flanger is similar to a chorus, but the delay times are shorter (1 to 20 ms on average), and the LFO modulates the delay time, not pitch. The output of the delayed signal is

Figure 5.16 The Retro Chorus guitar stompbox effect adds a chorus effect to your guitar tone.

then fed back to itself, causing resonances that enhance the depth of the modulation. The Robo Flanger stompbox effect allows you to adjust rate, depth, feedback, and manual, and once again, clicking the Sync button will set a rate that suits the tempo of the song project you are working on (see Figure 5.17).

Figure 5.17 The Robo Flanger guitar stompbox effect adds a flanger effect to your guitar tone.

The Vibe

Vibrato is the modulation of pitch via an LFO. The Vibe stompbox effect allows you to adjust rate and depth and lets you choose between six vibrato types. Clicking the Sync button will set a rate that suits the tempo of the song project you are working on (see Figure 5.18).

Auto-Funk

Filtering is simply the boosting or cutting of a specific frequency or frequencies. The Auto-Funk stompbox effect allows you to adjust sensitivity and cutoff and has three toggle switches allowing you to set different pass filters, such as BP or LP, HI or LO, and UP or DOWN. You will want to experiment with these different filters to see what effect they have on your overall tone (see Figure 5.19).

Figure 5.18 The Vibe guitar stompbox effect adds a vibrato effect to your guitar tone.

Figure 5.19 The Auto-Funk guitar stompbox effect adds a filter effect to your guitar tone.

Blue Echo

Delay is sometimes also referred to as *echo*; it is simply the repeating of a signal. If the delayed signal is fed back to itself, the repeat can happen anywhere from once to an infinite number of times. The Blue Echo stompbox effect allows you to adjust time, repeats, and mix and offers a Tone Cut switch that you can set to Hi cut, Lo cut, or Off (see Figure 5.20).

Figure 5.20 The Blue Echo guitar stompbox effect adds a delay or echo effect to your guitar tone.

Squash Compressor

Compression is an effect that limits the dynamic range of the input signal by a chosen ratio. The Squash Compressor stompbox effect allows you to adjust sustain and level and offers an attack switch, allowing you to set a fast or slow attack on when the compression begins to sustain your tone (see Figure 5.21).

Figure 5.21 The Squash Compressor guitar stompbox effect adds a sustain or compression effect to your guitar tone.

Recording

Let's walk through setting up some effects and recording something step by step. Suppose I want to record an Electric Guitar track, since we've been talking about guitar amps and stompbox effects. First, I create a new Electric Guitar track and check to make sure I have the record light armed on the track itself. If it's not, I click it so it turns red. My guitar patch cord is plugged into Input 1 on my audio interface, and I have the level set to about 70% (which is recommended for my audio interface). Then, I select Mono 1 Lexicon Omega (the Lexicon Omega is my audio interface) as my input source in GarageBand. Choose the input source that is your audio interface or line in if you're using a guitar adapter plugged directly into your Mac. Next, I set Monitor to On. Because my guitar is plugged in and is a direct signal (as opposed to placing a microphone on my real-world guitar amp), I don't have to worry about feedback or accidentally tracking any extraneous noise along with my performance. This way, I can sit back and hear my guitar playing through my speakers along with the mix I'm playing to; I don't have to be wearing headphones, which will free me up to be more at ease. This is a personal preference.

I start browsing through the five major guitar amp models by clicking on the right or left arrows next to the picture of the default guitar amp on the stage in the top half of the Track Info panel, or I select a preset from the drop-down menu. I choose Seattle Sound from the preset menu, and GarageBand sets up the Blackface Combo amp model for me, with the Fuzz Machine and Phase Tripper stompboxes on the stage. I play a little more and see whether I like it. I'm not feeling it, so I choose Super Flange from the presets menu. If I like the sound of that and I want to name my track, I double-click on the track name (which changed to Super Flange when I selected that guitar effect preset) and type Rhythm Guitar in the Name field of the track itself, and then I hit Enter or Return to lock it in. You can feel free to leave the tracks named with the name of the preset you have chosen, but I find that the more tracks you create, the more confusing things become if you leave every track name set to its default name. Finally, I select Metronome from the Control menu, as well as Count In (also from the Control menu). Then I press R on the keyboard for record, and after four clicks (assuming my song is in 4/4), I start playing away, recording my next hot guitar track.

You would use essentially the same process if you wanted to record a Real Instrument track. By way of comparison, let me take you through the process I use for recording an acoustic guitar through a microphone onto a Real Instrument track. First, I create a new Real Instrument track by clicking the plus button in the lower-left corner of GarageBand, and I choose Real Instrument and click Create. Then, I check to make sure I have the record light armed on the track itself. If it's not, I click it so it turns red. My microphone is connected to Input 1 on my audio interface, and once again, I have the level set to about 70% to start with. Then, I select Mono 1 Samson C01U (the Samson is my USB condenser microphone) as my input source in GarageBand. Next, I set Monitor to On, plug my headphones in, and turn off my speakers by powering them down, to avoid feedback in the room while I track my acoustic guitar.

I select Automatic Level Control and strum some loud chords for about 15 to 20 seconds, and I let GarageBand set the level for me. Then I click off Automatic Level Control and play a bit more to see whether I like where the level is set. It looks good to me, so I start browsing the guitar effects by clicking on the Acoustic Guitars group in the left column under Browse in the Track Info panel, and I click on Large Reverb. I might play a little more and try to determine whether I want to use this sound. I'm not in love with it, so I click on Shimmering Chorus instead. I really like the sound of that, so I double-click on the track name (which changed to Shimmering Chorus when I selected that effect preset) and type Acoustic Guitar 1 in the Name field, since I like to name my tracks manually. Then I hit Enter or Return to lock it in. Finally, just as with recording an Electric Guitar track or a Software Instrument track, I select Metronome from the Control menu, as well as Count In (also from the Control menu). Then I press R on the keyboard for record, and after four clicks (assuming my song is in 4/4), I begin recording.

Undo and Re-Record

If I make a mistake that's so bad I want to start all over, my process is as follows. I press the spacebar to stop, press Command+Z to undo, press Home to make the playhead go back to the beginning, and then press R one more time to give it another take. That's my preferred key sequence for, "Aw crap, I want to do it again."

If you're a perfectionist like me, you'll get used to that keyboard sequence very quickly. If you're doing fine, then play the song all the way through, and you can use the powerful editing tools that we will cover later on in this book to clean up any little errors. Most times, a fresher take done early in the session is going to have better energy, and fixing a few clams is easier than trying to recapture a golden moment, so don't be too eager to press Undo. That said, I tend to press spacebar, Command+Z, Home, R pretty frequently.

Experiment with Post-Processing

After you finish recording a track, you can select new amps and add or reorder your stompboxes as much as you'd like to experiment with different sounds. Or if the sound is close to what you're going for but not quite there, just click the guitar amp or any of your stompboxes to edit their individual settings. You might even want to duplicate your track by pressing Command+D or selecting Track > Duplicate and then copying the audio region by clicking on it and pressing Command+C or selecting Edit > Copy. Then paste your performance from the original track down into your new second track by pressing Command+V or selecting Edit > Paste. Keep your playhead exactly at the beginning of the original audio region so that when you paste on the new track by selecting it and pressing Command+V, it will end up exactly in sync with the original, and you can apply a different set of effects, adjust the pan position, raise or lower the volume level of one or the other to find a good balance, or do anything you like to that second guitar track for a really cool effect.

If you want to be very precise about the placement of the duplicate region, double-click it to open it in the Track Editor, and you can zoom in to a degree where there will be no mistaking where you are positioning the region. If you position your mouse on the waveform region in the Editor just under the ruler that runs along the top of it, you will get a double-headed arrow cursor, which will allow you to click and drag the region left to right from within the Editor itself, aiding you in incredibly precise positioning.

You could have Seattle Sound slightly panned left and Super Flange panned slightly right, and both sounds will be triggered by the same performance, making everything sound really tight, and now you've got a huge-sounding guitar part with two different tones playing at the same time. Experiment with these types of ideas; your imagination is the only limit.

For an added effect, try offsetting one of the duplicated guitar parts by just the slightest bit. Select all the guitar audio regions in one of your tracks and then zoom way in. Click and drag it slightly one way or the other and experiment with the widening effect this can have. You'll find there is a limit to moving the guitar parts and having them still sound in sync, but a gentle touch when making this adjustment might give you a nice double-tracking effect. In the example in Figure 5.22, I set my timeline grid

Figure 5.22   A duplicated electric guitar track with a different effect setting, offset by 1/64 note in the timeline. Try this experiment!

resolution setting to 1/64, the smallest amount by which you can move anything in GarageBand, and then slid the Super Flange guitar track ahead in time by 1/64 note.

Another fun post-processing experiment is to actually perform the part a second time on a brand-new track. This technique is called *double-tracking* and is used constantly in professional music recording. If you track the same part over and over, then things start to sound *really* big. Double-tracking is especially effective for guitars and vocals but can be used for any instrument, including MIDI performances. You can position the double-tracked parts in different areas of the stereo spectrum by adjusting their pans individually as well.

Punching In

One function of the traditional recording process that hasn't changed at all in the digital world is the ability to punch in. *Punching in* means inserting a new recording into an existing recording for a certain amount of time. Punching in is commonly used to fix mistakes or to re-record tracks. Another way punching in is often used might be if you record a whole guitar track all the way through, for example, and play your rhythm stuff really tight, but when the guitar solo comes up, you sort of lay out or just noodle around, knowing that later you'll want to go back and punch in a new guitar solo onto that same physical track.

By way of explaining how punching in can be used to fix a mistake, suppose you played a nice, fat, wrong note in the middle of the second verse, but you really liked your performance overall. You could opt to fix only that spot in the second verse by punching in. Conceptually, the process is like setting some in and out points in your timeline and then cueing the playhead and hitting Record so you can sort of play along to the part leading up to the second verse. (Playing along with the pre-existing part while leading up to your punch-in location will require monitoring to be set to On in the Track Info panel!) Then, when GarageBand gets to the beginning of the region that you set for your punch, the input turns on, and you are recording live. You play through the second verse and a little past it to make sure you are not leaving an unwanted gap, and GarageBand stops recording at the right time. What you've done is essentially "inserted" a new second verse. This can be very powerful and can help you get really great performances on your recording. It's very calming for some musicians to know that they don't necessarily have to play the part perfectly all the way through. Make-or-break situations can often introduce a lot of stress. This should be fun. Use the technology to your advantage. You can fix things very easily by punching in. See Figure 5.23.

Figure 5.23 A punched-in section in an audio region that once was one continuous region.

Let's look at how it works and how to set up what's known as a *cycle region* to identify where you want GarageBand to punch you in and out. Incidentally, you don't have to have a punch-out spot set; you can just as easily punch in and then play through to the end of the piece or even stop your punched-in recording at any time by positioning the playhead where you want to punch in, pressing the R key, or clicking the Record button—and then just hit the spacebar when you're finished, which is effectively punching out by stopping.

Suppose you had a handful of mistakes in the repeat choruses at the end of the song. You could opt to punch in after the second guitar solo and play the whole rest of the song from there. It's very flexible. Later on in this chapter, in the section called "Recording Multiple Takes," we'll also talk about doing multiple takes of a given section of the song automatically, without having to press anything in between the takes. This way, you can make your specific choices later about which take you'd like to use for the final mix.

The most straightforward way to punch in simply requires that you place the playhead where you want to punch in and press the R key or click the Record button. Then you begin playing. An example of this might be if you wanted to replace a section of your recorded take with a new pass. So again, let's assume we're doing a guitar track, and the second verse is sloppy and should probably be replaced. Play the song until you get to the point where you'd like to punch in and then find the right spot for the playhead to start. To do this you can also zoom in and look at the visual representation of the audio waveform while you listen to the track. Keep your finger ready to press the spacebar to stop right on the beat at which you want to start the new recording. This is totally up to you, but very often starting on the beat is most desirable—it might even help mask a slight unevenness that might result if you play something on the new track that is quite different from what you were playing just before your selected punch-in location. This will take some practice, but after a while you'll get very good at choosing the right spot for a punch, and when you start using the Track Editor as a playhead-positioning aid (see the next section, called "Additional Tips for Punching In," and the upcoming "Splitting a Recorded Region" section for more examples of using this versatile tool), your punches will become very precise. See Figure 5.24.

Think about it this way: Try to find a spot that is in between discrete sounds. For instance, if your guitar part has moments where it stops for a second and then resumes

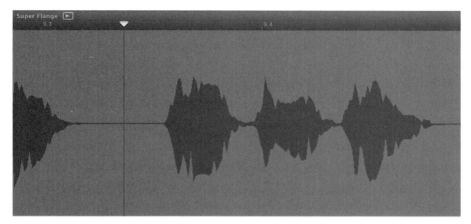

Figure 5.24 An example of choosing a spot between sounds to place your playhead for precise-sounding punches.

(or maybe right at the end of a chord just a few milliseconds before the next chord begins, you've muted the strings for just a brief moment), these can be good places to punch. Look at the waveform and try to find the spot (zoomed in all the way in the Editor) where the waveform is very slight, just before it gets huge again. This is going to be the best spot for a punch in when there are no actual breaks in sound. Sometimes there is even a nice visual valley in the waveform that you can see clearly—this is a good punching choice as well.

Additional Tips for Punching In

Here are a few more things to add to your arsenal when thinking about punching in and choosing your punch location:

- You can further adjust the point at which your track switches from the old take to the new punch in *after* it has been recorded, so don't worry too much about being surgical in your choosing of a punch spot on behalf of the preexisting track. It will still be there "under" your newly recorded, punched-in part.

- You can adjust the "resolution" of the playhead's movement and set it so the playhead drags in finer and finer increments to make exact positioning much easier. Do so by changing the value of the timeline grid in the tiny ruler icon in the upper-right corner of the timeline and choosing a note value of 1/16 or 1/32. This means when you are dragging the playhead manually, it will move in increments of a sixteenth note or a thirty-second note, which are both much smaller than eighth notes and quarter notes.

- You can open up the Editor, sometimes called the *Track Editor*, by clicking on the scissors/waveform icon at the lower left, just next to the New Track plus button. You'll have a very large, zoomed-in view of the audio waveform, allowing you to be extremely precise about the placement of the playhead. After you've clicked the Editor button, you can place your cursor on GarageBand's chrome (the metal-looking area of the interface just off to the right of where you clicked the Editor button), and it will become a "hand" cursor, allowing you to click and drag upward, expanding the waveform view even further. This movement, in combination with zooming in even further, will allow you to see such a fine resolution view of the waveform that you will have complete control over where you position the playhead and/or where you cut (or split) the audio waveform for your editing purposes.

- The playhead in the top part of the window, your Track view, will always match the location of the playhead in the bottom part of the window. Think of them as two views of the same physical thing. If you move the playhead in one view, it moves in the other. This gives you a lot of flexibility in the tasks you can perform on the playhead's location from either your Track view or your Editor view.

- The tiny ruler menu in the upper right of the Editor view allows you to set a new value for the grid of the Editor window. This setting is independent of the grid value in the main Track view window, and setting it to 1/64 gives you the finest level of movement possible. You will even be able to see light-gray vertical lines running throughout the Editor view—these are the 64th notes of your audio waveform. As you move the playhead manually, by clicking on its top triangle indicator and dragging it or even just clicking in the top ruler area of the Editor window, the playhead will "click" along those notches, allowing you to be very precise about its placement.

The Power of the Editor

Using the Track Editor is a great way to get an extreme zoom in on your individual audio waveforms. As shown and described in many of the examples throughout this chapter, it is the perfect tool for analyzing your audio and making decisions about edits because it's a directly linked, alternate view of the exact same instance of the audio region from the Timeline view. Anything you do to the region in either one of the two windows—the Timeline or the Editor—will be visible in real time when you look at the region in the other window.

This behavior allows you to choose the right tool for the job, so to speak, on the fly. If you try to do something such as trim an edit or slide it left or right in the timeline, and you realize that the method you chose is too fine or too coarse an adjustment, you can press Command+Z or select Edit > Undo and try the same task in the other tool. Clicking the scissors icon next to the New Track plus button will open and close the Editor, and whatever you have selected in the timeline will always be visible in the Editor. This goes for audio regions and for MIDI regions. In the next chapter, "Software Instruments," you will learn more about the specifics of using the Editor with MIDI regions. You can also double-click on any region in your timeline to automatically open the Editor window and have it focus on the region you double-clicked.

Splitting a Recorded Region

You can apply many of the principles involved in precise placement of the playhead when thinking about editing one of your recorded regions. The main function that you will use when editing a region is something called *splitting* the region (also loosely called *cutting* or *dividing* the region). It's much like the analog tape editing idea of using a razorblade to physically cut the tape on which your recording is made. Often, you will have a recorded region, and you will want to break it up into two or more pieces and then do something with those pieces. This is the process of splitting the region.

The process of splitting has three distinct steps, as follows:

1. Select the region to be split by clicking on it once in the Track window. Be sure to click on the actual region, and not the track itself.

2. Precisely place the playhead within the region where you want to split it and use the Editor for precise placement.

3. Choose Split from the Edit menu. The GarageBand keyboard shortcut for splitting is Command+T.

For the sake of explanation, suppose you have a recorded region, and in it you are singing five words: "You've got to break free." See Figure 5.25 to see the waveforms of those lyrics in the Timeline view and the Track Editor view. Suppose you want to split your region so you have "You've got" in one region and "to break free" in the second, so you can move them independently in your timeline. Or maybe you even want to delete the "You've got" and keep the "to break free." The reasons for wanting to do this are entirely your own and entirely up to your creativity. Maybe you just want this vocal part to be a backup part, and after you have already made the recording, you decide that you only want this particular part to be singing "to break free" as a backup vocal part. To achieve this, you'd want to delete the "You've got" from that audio region.

First, you need to find the location in the region that is between "got" and "break" and place the playhead there. Refer to Figure 5.25 once more—the playhead is just after the "t" sound in "got" and right before the word "break" begins. The first thing to do is click on the audio region. Then, you might even want to solo this track so you are only listening to the vocal part and none of the other instruments.

Click the Headphones button to solo the track—when it's yellow, it's soloed. Then, press the spacebar to hear the track. After you hear the word "to," quickly press the spacebar to pause playback. You'll see that the playhead has stopped right after one of the large waveforms. Zoom in and look closely at it—you can even see where the "t" of the "got to" happens. It's a really small indentation, but it's there. Make sure the playhead is positioned in between the "to" and "break" words, and with the track selected, press Command+T to split the track. You now have two regions—one with "You've got to" and another with "break free." See Figure 5.26.

Figure 5.25 The audio waveform of the vocal part singing "You've got to break free" in the Timeline view and in the Editor.

Figure 5.26 The vocal line split right between the words "to" and "break."

At this point, both regions are still selected. If your goal is to delete just the "You've got to" part, you need to be sure it's the only region selected. The easiest way to do this is to click in an area of the Track view that has no information in it—one of the empty tracks, for example—which will deselect all regions. Then, simply click once on the region you want to delete. Click in an empty area and then click on the "You've got to" region and choose Delete from the Edit menu (or press Delete). See Figure 5.27.

Figure 5.27 "You've got to" has been deleted. All that remains after the split is now "break free."

Now you're left with "break free," which is an independent audio region with which you can do anything you'd like. You can move it around by clicking and dragging. You can copy and paste it multiple times in the same track or into other tracks by selecting it and choosing Copy from the Edit menu or pressing Command+C, and then selecting Paste from the Edit menu or pressing Command+V. You can loop it by moving your cursor over the upper-right corner of the region and dragging it out to the right with the looping cursor. You can do anything you'd like with it, including splitting it further. Select the region, place the playhead between "break" and "free," and simply press Command+T again to split it once more.

If you need to join two regions that have been split—even two that didn't originally go together—there is a function in GarageBand called Join. Joining requires you to position the two regions where you want them in relation to one another (either together or separated by some space if need be), select them both together (either by clicking on one and Shift-clicking the other or by dragging your selection cursor around both regions), and then choose Join from the Edit menu or press Command+J. This will create one new region consisting of both parts that were originally independent. If there was some space between them, this will just be built into the new region as a silent section.

Recording Multiple Takes

Very often in the recording process, you will want to record multiple takes of the same thing. A common example of this is an improvised solo. It could also be just that you want to take multiple stabs at doing the vocal part in the verse or any other thing that you are recording. Sometimes, the key here is that you are looking to give yourself several shots at nailing the part, and then you can go back later with your editor's hat on and make a decision about which one to use, or even which parts of your various performances to combine (or composite, sometimes called *comping*) into one final version. Since GarageBand '08, the process of recording multiple takes has been made very simple.

This is accomplished by creating a cycle region in the timeline (detailed in the section called "The Step-By-Step Process of Recording Multiple Takes") and then pressing Record. Each time you get to the end of the section, GarageBand will return the playhead to the beginning of the region automatically and allow you to take another pass at the section. This will go on for as long as you want, until you press the spacebar or the Stop Play/Pause button. After recording multiple takes, you will notice that GarageBand has kept track of all of your takes, and this newly recorded section will have a small yellow indicator number in the upper-left corner of the audio region. This is a drop-down menu that gives you direct access to all of your takes. You can then choose the best one for your song and even combine parts of different takes into one new composite take.

What Is a Solo? A musical *solo* is a section of a song where one musician in the ensemble (or band) essentially takes over by playing instrumental melodies (and sometimes rhythmic chords or a combination of both) while the rest of the ensemble continues playing the rhythm and chords of the song behind him, supporting him. A solo is usually considered a spotlight of sorts, where the musician can shine—or even show off his chops—by really going for it and embracing the adventurous spirit of flying alone, with the safety net of the band providing a bedrock while he lets it rip! Often, solos are improvised, meaning that they are made up on the spot. The musician trusts his instincts and relies on his technical and conceptual understanding of the musical piece and his own prowess on the instrument to spontaneously create a melody, harmony, or even completely "whacked out" noises that move him. Ultimately, his band mates and the audience may be moved as well.

Some soloists may prefer to compose an instrumental musical section that acts as a solo, rather than improvising. This approach may still involve pushing the limits of his technical abilities, but at the same time the solo itself is something decided upon ahead of time and then played when it becomes the musician's turn to take a solo. Jazz, rock, and bluegrass musicians are probably the most famous for relying on the improvisational techniques, but indeed, musicians in all genres have been known to embrace the improv approach to one degree or another. Pop and classical musicians might be the more common examples of the "composed soloing" approach, or at the very least—especially in the pop genre—solos tend to become canon once they are heard hundreds of times on the radio and then are repeated by musicians when performing the songs live.

Soloing essentially means playing by oneself or in groups in a more prominent musical role than usual, over the top of what the band is playing. It can mean playing planned, composed notes as well as improvised notes created on the spot, caught up in the whimsy of a moment.

An interesting story about guitarist Alex Lifeson of the band Rush comes to mind. Regardless of whether you are a fan (I happen to be one!) of the Toronto-based power trio, which has been releasing records and touring together since 1974/1975, I would wager that this technique is something you haven't considered and something that GarageBand's Multiple Takes function provides for. Before I share the technique, keep in mind that it seems to me there are two distinct approaches to creating a guitar solo (or any kind of musical solo). One approach is the improvisation route. Many musicians feel that improvisation is the soul of creativity. Others enjoy the power and flexibility of the recording studio, which provides them the space and flexibility to "craft" a solo or essentially "compose" their solo, practice it like crazy, and then perform the composition to tape. Whichever method you are more drawn to is the one you should pursue, but I urge you to try the technique that you are less drawn to as an exploration of the world of soloing. By trying both approaches (or even an approach that avoids soloing altogether!), you will find the method that best suits your style and abilities.

The Alex Lifeson story is about the method he used for coming up with many of his guitar solos in the records the band made during the '80s and '90s. This isn't meant to imply that this is the only way he came up with his solos, but it was said to be the way many of his guitar solos were composed. Alex recorded several takes of the solo until he got four or five takes recorded that he really liked. In fact, many times he would just come in and blow down some 10 takes of a solo, and then Geddy Lee and Neil Peart (the bassist/vocalist and the drummer of Rush, respectively) would edit together a grand composite of his many solos, creating one master version of the solo. They referred to it as a Frankenstein solo because it was stitched together from all the different passes. After Geddy and Neil had "composed" a new solo from Alex's series of disparate performances, the guitarist would be called back into the room and would learn to play this Frankenstein solo, teaching it to himself by listening over and over to the stitched-together version and practicing it. Then, a final process of recording the performance of the newly learned solo would take place.

To recap Lifeson's process for our purposes in using GarageBand to compose a solo using the Multiple Takes function: Record multiple takes of a solo, construct a composite of the solo using track splitting and track joining; teach yourself the new Frankenstein solo by listening and learning from the composited version; create a new track; mute the composite; record multiple takes of the new, learned solo; and then review the takes and choose your best performance. You could opt to stop once you have the composite created and just use that, but if any of the edits are less than perfect or the energy of one to the next was a little different, it might not sound even. Re-recording the learned version is one way to make this whole unnatural process sound very natural. By owning the new composition and playing the hell out of it, you might just have yourself a blazing solo!

The Step-by-Step Process of Recording Multiple Takes

First, you will want to create your track and arm it for recording. Then, click the Cycle Region button in the main Transport controls. It's the button with two circular arrows (see Figure 5.28) just to the right of the Play and Fast Forward buttons. This will reveal the cycle region strip at the very top of the Timeline window under the ruler. Click and drag your mouse within this cycle region strip to draw in a yellow bar, which designates the area of your piece that you'd like to "cycle" through multiple times, recording a new take each time as you go. You can adjust the ends of the yellow cycle region bar just by clicking and dragging them, and you can click in the center of the bar to drag the whole thing to a new location while keeping its length constant. See Figure 5.29.

Figure 5.28 The Cycle Region button.

Figure 5.29 The Cycle Region button on and a cycle region drawn in for the area where the multiple takes will take place.

You may also want to visit the Control menu to activate the metronome. If you want there to be a preceding one-bar count-off each time you do a new take (of four beats), you can also select Count In from the Control menu to have GarageBand give you a four-count of the metronome *before* where the playhead is started. This is a powerful feature that you might want to experiment with to get more used to it. If you need to start playing right on the downbeat of a given bar, starting the playhead at that bar without the Count In function activated means that you will have to press Record and then play your first chord almost immediately to not be late. If the Count In function is activated, you will position the playhead where you want to begin (or, in the case of Multiple Takes, at the place where the cycle region begins), and GarageBand will count off in time, 1 - 2 - 3 - 4 -. And then, bang—you can start playing right in time and not come in late.

After the metronome and count in are activated and your cycle region is created, press R to begin recording, wait for the count in, and then begin playing. When you reach the end of the cycle, GarageBand will automatically snap the playhead back to the beginning of the cycle region (this time with no countdown), and you will continue playing to start automatically recording your second take. When you reach the end, GarageBand will again return to the beginning of the cycle, and you can make as many takes as you want. When you are finished, let GarageBand cycle around once more (to get a clean ending to your last take), and once it has started rolling into the *next* cycle, you can just press R to stop recording or hit the spacebar, since this final cycle will be treated as extraneous for the purpose of preserving your performance and focus and can just be deleted at will.

Give Yourself Some Breathing Room

I like to leave a little breathing room in my cycle region for several reasons—so I don't feel rushed at the beginning, so that I actually *do* have a countdown for each take, and so that I can allow the last notes of each take to ring out into the next section of the song. Suppose I'm recording a guitar solo, and I don't want the cycle to end on the downbeat of the first bar of the next section of the song—I'd like to let it extend a few bars *into* the next section, so that it's not abruptly cut off. That way, I can make my own specific edit, fade, or whatever at the end of the solo and craft it to my liking with options.

To use a more specific example, suppose the guitar solo section of the song goes from Measure 132 to Measure 136. I will not make my cycle region be from Bar 132 to Bar 136; I will actually make it from Bar 131 to Bar 137. See Figure 5.30. This means on the first pass, with the Count In function activated, I will have to wait one bar, or two counts of four (if my song is in 4/4), before playing. Then I will always have a bar at the end of the solo to let my last note ring out over the next section. (I can edit the way in which it rings out later in the mixing stage.) Also, when the cycle repeats, I will always have one full bar of metronome to let me count off before I begin soloing. In fact, if I want to, I can even come in a little early to really "take it" and solo my heart out. See Figure 5.31.

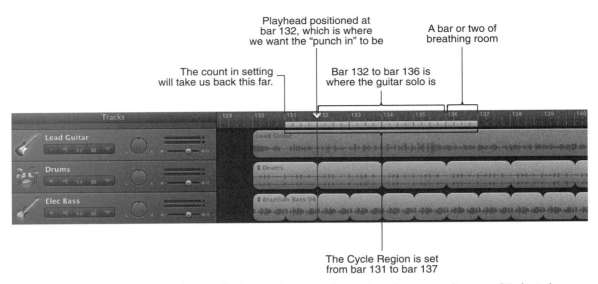

The count in setting
will take us back this far.

Playhead positioned at
bar 132, which is where
we want the "punch in" to be

Bar 132 to bar 136 is
where the guitar solo is

A bar or two of
breathing room

The Cycle Region is set
from bar 131 to bar 137

Figure 5.30 An example of a well-planned-out cycle region for recording multiple takes.

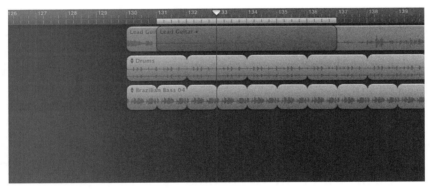

Figure 5.31 Press Record and begin to track your first take of the guitar solo. Notice how the new part punches in over the old part (which will appear red while recording).

Select Your Take

When you are finished cycle recording your multiple takes (let's say you did three or four of them), you will see a little yellow box in the upper left of the recorded audio region with the number 4 in it. The 4 means you will currently hear Take 4 if you press Play. The Multiple Takes feature defaults to showing you the last take you recorded unless you choose a different one to listen to. If you click and hold on this number 4, you will see the Multiple Takes menu. In this menu (again, let's say you did four takes), you will see Take 1, Take 2, Take 3, and Take 4 (which you can select to hear each one individually), followed by Delete Unused Takes (which you can select once you've finalized what you want to use if you'd like to save hard drive and project storage space as well as RAM memory). Finally, since you are still selected on Take 4, the last menu item is Delete Take 4. This menu item will update depending on the take you have selected. You can review one of the takes, and if you decide that you don't like it at all and you want to get rid of it, you can easily just delete that take from the list and be done with it. If you choose to delete a take, GarageBand will confirm that you would like to discard the take; you can opt to suppress this confirmation in the future by clicking the check box that says Do Not Ask Me Again. See Figure 5.32.

Figure 5.32   A Multiple Takes section with three takes to choose from. Click once on the small 3 in the upper left to access the Multiple Takes selection menu.

Combine Different Parts of Different Takes

After reviewing your takes, if you want to use the first half of Take 2 and the second half of Take 3, you can start by deleting Take 1 and Take 4. Click on the yellow number and choose Take 1. Then, click again on what will now be a yellow number 1 and select Delete Take 1 from the menu. Follow the same process for deleting Take 4. Now you have Take 2 and Take 3, but keep in mind this little pitfall: Notice that they are now named Take 1 and Take 2 in the yellow number menu. I honestly hope Apple will fix this in a future update to GarageBand. When you delete a take, GarageBand re-sorts the list to absorb the one you deleted and then renumbers them all. So if you had four takes and you delete Take 3, the take that used to be called Take 4 will now suddenly (and without warning or confirmation) be called Take 3 in the list. If you're planning to do some intricate take mashing, I would keep a notepad nearby and make notes about what each take is called. Otherwise, you'll be sitting there saying something like, "I was *positive* that Take 9 was the one with the cool tremolo lick. Why can't I find it anywhere?!"

When you have eliminated the takes you don't want to use, you can use the Split (Command+T) technique to create a split in the track where you want to switch over from the original Take 2 to the original Take 3 (now called Take 1 and Take 2, respectively). You'll notice after you make the split that there will be a little yellow number on each region, allowing you to choose which one you want. You will now have two separate Multiple Takes audio regions from which to choose. See Figure 5.33.

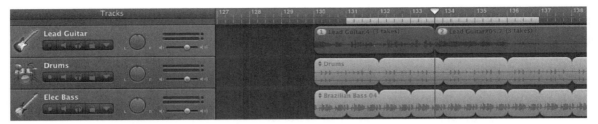

Figure 5.33 A Multiple Takes region that has been split. Take 1 is chosen for the first half, and Take 2 is chosen for the second half. If you leave them like this, the "hidden" takes for each section will remain tucked away for future reference or use.

You can do this as many times as you want throughout any multiple take that you record. When you are finished choosing, you can either leave things the way they are to allow further editing in the future, or you can select all the regions that represent your new composite and press Command+J to join them into one region. GarageBand will do all the cross-fading for you, and you will have a new cohesive-sounding composite of your multiple takes. See Figure 5.34.

Figure 5.34 The new guitar solo region merged with the Join command. The "hidden" takes are now deleted.

Tuning and Timing Enhancers

GarageBand has some very powerful features for enhancing (read: fixing—love the euphemism, Apple!) the timing and the tuning of your performances. *Tuning* refers to the pitch of notes that are played or sung and recorded into GarageBand, while *timing* refers to the beat—or in this case, the tightness, accuracy, or rhythm—of your recorded tracks. GarageBand has a tuning feature, which is meant to get notes that are nearly right on more into tune, as well as a pitch adjustment feature that lets you change the pitch of a note by full steps, up to an octave in either direction.

Let it be said up front that the existence of these features in the application should not in and of itself be a reason to use them. Tuning Enhancers (also called *auto-tuners*) can be overused very easily. Sometimes you might not want anyone to know that you had to apply some tuning to that one vocal part to get the pitch in better shape, but the trained ear can spot tuning enhancements very easily. So, using this function sparingly and in very measured doses may well be the order of the day. Sometimes, the effect of over-enhancing the tuning of something is just what you're looking for, and then by all means use it.

The Pitch feature can provide some really incredible sounds, and this so-called pitch-shifting technology has been used in many professional recordings—to the delight of some pop music fans and the dismay of others. Artists and producers have used some of this pitch shifting to create an almost robotic-style sound with their voices.

It's true that sometimes getting those four-part harmonies just right the old-fashioned way can be really difficult, especially if the singers aren't very experienced with recording harmony vocals. GarageBand's Tuning Enhancer might be just the thing to help get you over that hump and make the track sound a lot better, perhaps with only a modicum of the effect being applied to get it just right.

Timing enhancements, often called *quantizing* your rhythm, can be used to make things sound more even. Percussion parts are the most commonly quantized, but you can use this function in GarageBand on any track. GarageBand takes the selected track or region and attempts to adjust the higher-velocity sound waves and reposition them in closer proximity to the evenly spaced markers of the timeline grid. Said another way, GarageBand attempts to make the part have a more solid beat, or more dependable clocklike accuracy, by making slight adjustments to the positioning of the beats relative to the beats in your song—in other words, where the metronome would be clicking. When you apply a Timing Enhancer setting, GarageBand tries to fix sloppy rhythm.

Enhancing Tuning

To enhance the tuning of a track, you need to select the track and then open the Editor by clicking the scissors/waveform icon in the lower left. When you have the track selected and the Editor pane open, you will see the two sliders in the lower left that will allow you to adjust the tuning of the track. This is accomplished by positioning a slider along a continuum of minimum to maximum use of the Enhance Tuning effect, and you'll have to use your ears to determine where you should set it. If you leave the Limit to Key check box deselected, GarageBand's Tuning Enhancer will attempt to put the note in tune with the closest half step (semi-tone) to the note being sung. If you select the Limit to Key check box, GarageBand will keep the notes specifically within the key of your song; it will ignore notes that are out of the key and "round" up or down to the nearest note in the actual key automatically. See Figure 5.35.

Suppose the note you wanted to sing was an F#, and the song was in the key of D major. F# is in the key of D major; it's the major third of the scale. If you sang off pitch and hit a note that was almost (but not exactly) an F (in other words, closer to an F than an F#), GarageBand would make it an F# if the Limit to Key check box was checked, and it would make it an F if the box was not checked.

If you only want to tune a specific section of the song—for instance the chorus—you will want to split the chorus out into its own region and place it on an individual track

Figure 5.35 The Tuning and Timing Enhancers for audio regions.

using Command+D to duplicate the track to maintain all of your other settings, and then click and drag the chorus region that you just created onto the new track. Be sure to zoom in a bit before you drag it so you can be sure it will end up on the exact same beat that it was on in its original track. You want to avoid moving something out of sync accidentally. Then you can apply the Tuning Enhancer to that track, thereby only affecting the chorus region. See the section called "Splitting a Recorded Region" earlier in this chapter for more information on performing the split.

Enhancing Timing

To enhance the timing of a track, follow the same process as in the previous "Enhancing Tuning" section, and apply the Enhance Timing slider to your taste. Realize, though, that you are asking GarageBand to kind of take apart and put back together the audio into a new, tighter pulse with the beat of the song, so using too much of it will result in little skipping-sounding gaps in the audio. It works really well for drums, which have a lot of empty spaces naturally between the percussive attack of each sound in the beat, but not so well for something like violin or any instrument with continuous, sustained notes (although it can be done).

You can set the resolution of the beat grid that you want GarageBand to try and place notes into by choosing a resolution from the drop-down menu, which you'll notice is the same menu as the timeline grid value selectors. Choosing 1/8, for example, will ask GarageBand to attempt to place every note in the track as close as possible to its nearest eighth note within the grid. This process is usually called *quantizing*, which means putting notes in time with one another. The more you add of the Timing Enhancer, the more "on the beat" all of the notes will be, and possibly the less "human." So, once again, be sparing in your use of this effect. If you can hear that it's being used, then chances are you've used too much. Unless, of course, that effect is what you're going for, in which case you should crank it up to the max.

Next Up: Software Instruments

Now that you know how to record and edit Real Instrument and Electric Guitar performances, it's time to look at recording and editing performances made with Software Instruments on Software Instrument tracks. The huge sound library made available to you in GarageBand, plus those included in the various Jam Packs from Apple, will open up a wide palette of choices that go far beyond any real-world physical instruments you own or have access to for recording. These Software Instrument libraries can add an intricate tapestry of amazing—and original—sounds to your recordings. Additionally, the amazingly flexible editing functions and endless creative possibilities available to you in the world of MIDI and Software Instruments in GarageBand will add tremendously to your final product. Not to mention, they're a lot of fun!

6 Software Instruments

In addition to recording tracks using Real Instruments or Electric Guitars, you can create performances and recordings using a wide variety of sound samples and synthesizers that are included in GarageBand by using a MIDI controller. These are known as *Software Instrument* tracks in GarageBand. No microphones are involved, but you do need a MIDI controller device to transmit into GarageBand what notes you want played and the velocity of those notes, as well as the attack, decay, and other parameters over which you will continue to have complete control, even after they have been recorded.

Customization is very easy in GarageBand, so you can make these sounds your own and build up a musical piece that has an original sound—not something where you are just choosing from a bag of cookie-cutter tricks. All of the effects settings, synthesizer and musical instrument parameters, and, of course, the mix of the song itself are at your fingertips. The creation is up to you, and the steps in this chapter will get you there quickly and confidently.

We will be covering the nuances when tracking a performance using a Software Instrument versus recording a Real Instrument track, the sometimes very different method for editing your performances and takes with the Piano Roll view in the Track Editor, and even using GarageBand's musical notation view, called the Score view, to prepare a printed musical score of your latest masterpiece!

Check Those MIDI Prefs!

If you want to be sure your MIDI connection is working properly, create a new Software Instrument track in GarageBand to test it. Choose New Track from the Track menu, choose Software Instrument from the radio buttons, and click Create. Once you have a Grand Piano (green-colored) default Software Instrument track, you should be able to press the keys of your MIDI keyboard and hear a piano sound. If you cannot, check all your settings by revisiting Chapter 3 to get your connections configured properly.

If things are not working properly, the quickest way to ensure that you're not experiencing a USB, MIDI, or hardware connection glitch of some kind (as opposed to a larger issue) is to quit GarageBand, shut down your computer, and unplug all of the connections to your computer, your audio interface, and your MIDI controller. Some would even suggest unplugging the power cable from the wall, then from your computer itself as well, to get everything freshly reseated. After about 15 seconds, plug your power cable back into the computer and then plug it into the wall socket. Then reconnect your USB devices, your MIDI controller, and your audio interface and make sure every connection is firmly attached.

After you've done that, you can restart your computer. When you get to the desktop, revisit System Preferences and go to the Sound pane. Check to see that your input and output settings are as you want them. Then you can launch GarageBand. Choose Preferences from the GarageBand menu and click the Audio/MIDI button at the top of the window. Then, you can check your audio input and output and make sure they are as you want them. Look about halfway down the window and you'll see MIDI Status. Figure 6.1 shows a successful MIDI connection notice. The text following MIDI Status will tell you how many MIDI connections GarageBand currently recognizes. If you have one MIDI device connected properly, as I have in the example shown in Figure 6.1, it will say, "1 MIDI Input(s) Detected."

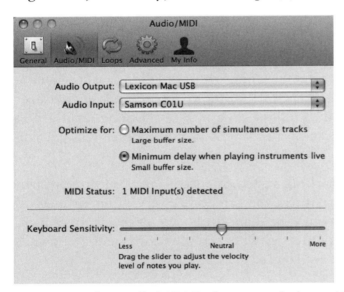

Figure 6.1 The Audio/MIDI Preferences window with the MIDI input(s) detection notice and, below that, the Keyboard Sensitivity slider.

While you're in the Preferences window, notice the Keyboard Sensitivity slider at the bottom. (Refer to Figure 6.1.) If you find later on down the road that your MIDI tracks are consistently tracking with low velocity (meaning the notes that you play are perceived as "quiet" by GarageBand, even though you may be pressing the keys like Keith Emerson on a really good day), you can drag this slider to the right to have your MIDI device send a higher velocity for each key press than it normally sends by default. The opposite case might be true as well: If you find that you are unable to attain nuance and subtlety with your keyboard playing, and all of your notes are getting sent to GarageBand as quite "loud," then you might want to drag this slider to the left a bit and experiment with getting a nice, solid track that is balanced with your keyboard-playing style. This is something that you will probably be able to set once and leave it, unless you have various keyboardists tracking into GarageBand. In that case, you'll want to revisit the Keyboard Sensitivity slider with each new performer. Sometimes, this can be a "set it, do a test, reset it, do a test" process.

One other thing I'd like to point out is that if you connect or disconnect a MIDI controller while GarageBand is running, it will inform you that it has detected a new input and that the total number of inputs has changed. (I like to use the verb "complains," but that paints GarageBand's handy dialog boxes in a negative light!) It is nice that GarageBand has no problem detecting and using a hot-swapped MIDI connection, but it's even nicer that GarageBand tells you when one has been detected! See Figure 6.2.

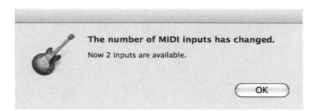

Figure 6.2 New MIDI input detected dialog box.

Create a Software Instrument Track

We covered how to create Real Instrument tracks and Electric Guitar tracks in the previous chapter, and creating a Software Instrument track is no different, save for the one radio button you'll need to click differently. To create a Software Instrument track, click the plus button at the bottom of the GarageBand interface. Alternatively, you can choose New Track from the Track menu or press Option+Command+N. Then, click the Software Instrument radio button in the dialog box and click Create. You now have a Software Instrument track, armed and ready to be recorded into using a MIDI controller. See Figure 6.3.

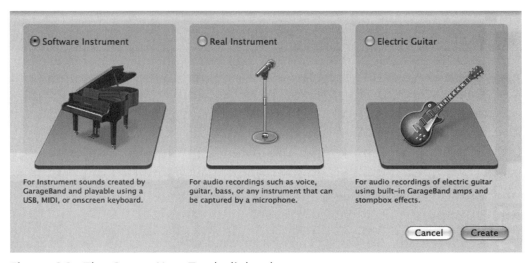

Figure 6.3 The Create New Track dialog box.

Tracking with Your MIDI Controller or Keyboard

The workflow for tracking MIDI in GarageBand is fairly simple. You create a Software Instrument track, choose a Software Instrument from the GarageBand library, adjust any parameters or effects that you are so moved to adjust, press Record, and begin playing on your MIDI controller. When you are finished playing, you can press Stop and then play back your recording.

All of the principles for recording with Software Instruments are the same as for recording Real Instruments, in terms of starting, stopping, using metronome settings, counting in, playing, and pausing. If you skipped Chapter 5 because your intent is to record using only MIDI, I suggest you take a few minutes and review that chapter. A lot of techniques, keyboard shortcuts, and workflow ideas in Chapter 5 will apply to the work you do with Software Instruments, and Chapter 6 assumes that you have read the material in Chapter 5.

There are a few distinct differences in the process of recording Software Instruments. When you are recording Real Instruments, you are recording actual audio files, which get stored inside your GarageBand project file and are only editable in the sense that they can be split, moved, deleted, and rejoined, and they can have effects applied to them to alter the sound of the original track. Short of the Timing and Tuning Enhancer features we discussed at the end of Chapter 5, you can't ever truly edit the performance that was recorded. With Software Instrument performances recorded via your MIDI controller, every note you play, every foot pedal pressed, and every nuance in rhythm, velocity, and sustain is fully editable, movable, deletable, duplicatable, and so on. In essence, you have complete control to monkey with everything you record in order to make your final piece the best it can be.

Later in this chapter, we will cover using the Editor to edit your MIDI data, and you will see that when you are editing a Software Instrument track, a "piano-roll" version of the Editor takes the place of the waveform display that you see when working in the Editor with a Real Instrument track (as the primary difference between a Real Instrument track and a Software Instrument track is that the former is a digitally recorded audio waveform and the latter is MIDI data), giving you complete control over your performance, right down to the finest variation. The Editor is a contextual tool, used for both purposes. There is even an easy method of editing your MIDI data using musical notation that is generated automatically by GarageBand while you play or view the MIDI notes you've played, so technically there are three ways to use the Editor. The term *Track Editor* is used to generically refer to that area of the GarageBand interface that allows you to make fine adjustments and edits to your tracks, be they MIDI data or audio waveforms.

You can also do multiple takes (as opposed to allowing each new take to "merge" with the previous ones) with Software Instrument tracks, but you need to be sure you do not have Cycle Recording set to Automatically Merge Software Instrument

Recordings when Using the Cycle Region when doing so (the check box for this is in the GarageBand Preferences window under General), so that GarageBand knows not to merge your multiple takes into one MIDI recording region. With this function turned off, GarageBand will give you the Multiple Takes yellow number icon on your MIDI region, the same way it did with your audio regions in a Real Instrument track. For more information on the differences and how to activate this feature, see the section called "Using Cycle Recording and Multiple Takes to Build a Drum Beat" later in this chapter.

Let's Record Some MIDI Data

Software Instrument tracks record MIDI data that you play. Let's do that now. Create a Software Instrument track and choose an instrument from the Track Info panel's Browse column. (Press Command+I or click the little "i" button at the lower right to open it if it's closed.) Be sure you're clicked on the Software Instrument tab at the top of the Track Info panel, and you will see the Browse tab and the Edit tab below it (see Figure 6.4).

The list on the left contains groups of instruments, such as Bass, Guitars, Strings, Synth Leads, and so on. You can click on any of these groups to reveal in the right column the instruments that you have available to you within that group. Each instrument you click on will load into the Software Instrument track. If you click on Pianos and Keyboards on the left and then Electric Piano on the right, your Software Instrument track will update its icon on the left and its track name. You can also see a full-color detailed image of the instrument (a nice touch in GarageBand '09) on the stage at the top of the Track Info panel. Also, remember that you can double-click the track name to change the name to something less default. If you play your MIDI keyboard, you will hear an electric piano sound. Then you can create a new track and add another new sound, or you can simply change the electric piano to another sound that suits your mood.

If you click on the Track Icon Selection button (the small keyboard icon below the Software Instruments library list—refer to Figure 6.4), you will see that it is easy to change the track icon for any track. However, Apple does not make it very easy to add your own icons, although after a few minutes of Googling around, I found some steps for doing it. Because it's not a supported feature, I will refrain from including that information here, but you can feel free to pursue that if it's something you'd like to accomplish. For a view of all the icons available for tracks, see Figure 6.5.

Press R to record and then begin playing, and you will be tracking MIDI data into GarageBand. As the red recording bar begins to draw left to right across the timeline, you will see the notes you are playing represented by thin gray bars. These are the actual notes that you are playing, simplified to show you that GarageBand is in fact getting notes recorded as you play. As soon as you press the spacebar, the recording will stop, the recording bar will change from red to green, and you can press Command+S to save your performance.

Figure 6.4 The Software Instrument tab in the Track Info panel in Browse mode.

You might recall discussing one of the settings in GarageBand Preferences: General, which can be checked to automatically merge Software Instrument recordings when using the cycle region function to record multiple passes. This function will *combine* your various passes when recording, useful for creating drum beats and other complex, layered parts. This means that if you have this setting checked in Preferences and you create a cycle region that spans the recording you've just made and press Record again, you will hear the old part, and any new notes you play on this pass will get saved directly to the original part—as though you have four hands instead of two. See Figure 6.6.

Once you have a MIDI region in the timeline, you can perform any of the tasks you were introduced to in Chapter 5. You can place the playhead and split the region, select and delete, click and drag the bottom-right corner of the region to loop it, stretch the head or tail, join two regions—you can do everything with a MIDI region that you can with an audio region in the timeline.

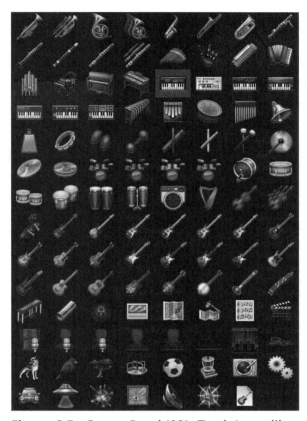

Figure 6.5 GarageBand '09's Track Icons library.

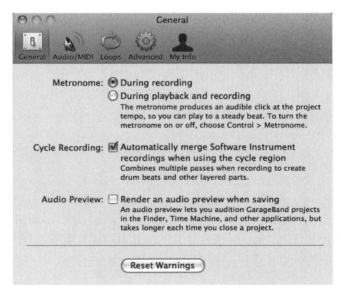

Figure 6.6 The check box in GarageBand Preferences: General pane where you can set a cycle region recording to merge MIDI data instead of doing multiple takes.

Using Cycle Recording and Multiple Takes to Build a Drum Beat

The Cycle Recording Using Multiple Takes functionality works particularly well for building drum beats. To try building an eight-bar drum beat, create a new Software Instrument track, and from the Software Instrument Track Info panel, under Browse, choose a drum kit that you like from the Drum Kits category. Within that drum kit, you will find that each key on your MIDI controller will trigger a different sound in the kit. Much like a piano Software Instrument will play each note as you press each key (A, B flat, B, C, and so on), a drum kit Software Instrument doesn't have notes as much as voices. Almost always, low C will produce the kick drum sound. The low D and E often will be snare drums or some variation of a snare drum, and the D sharp key often will have a hi-hat sound. You'll have to hunt around a bit to find the sound you want. If you are surprised to not be getting kick drums and snares on the bottom C note of your controller, check to see what your transpose setting is set to on the controller and adjust it accordingly.

Set the metronome to On and the count in to On and then press R to record. Remember that you will have a one-bar count in, and then start to play after the metronome counts to four. But if you recall, the idea of giving yourself some breathing room may also apply here. If you are trying to record an eight-bar drum part that you may intend to loop and reuse in many places later throughout your song, why not plan to play from the beginning of Bar 2 to the end of Bar 9 and have your cycle region extend from Bar 1 to Bar 10? This will always give you two full bars of rest to find your next sound and to get ready to come in cleanly on the downbeat.

The process will go like this: When you press Record, the playhead will go back to Bar −1 (off the screen) and give you your initial count in. Let's do the hi-hat part first. You wait for the count in of two bars—the count-in bar plus your one "breathing-room" bar, which is Bar 1 in this example (see Figure 6.7). After an eight count, you come in at the beginning of Bar 2, playing the hi-hat part. Tap that out on the keyboard, and then after eight bars you can stop playing and allow GarageBand to continue recording. You can hunt around and press a key or two to find the kick drum and the snare in the interim, as long as you're listening and/or watching to know when to come in. We will clean out the breathing-room bars later.

When Bar 2 arrives, you can start playing the kick and snare part, and you'll still hear the hi-hat part coming out of the speakers or your headphones. This new kick and snare will simply get added to the part, overlaid onto the MIDI data of the initial part. As you can see illustrated in Figure 6.8, the hi-hat part is a darker color on the second pass, and your new MIDI notes—the kick and snare—are a lighter color in the Editor as you are tracking them.

Notice the shadings are reversed in the timeline—this is because the new notes are actually displayed as red as you record on the timeline track. For a third go around,

Figure 6.7 Start with the hi-hat part in Cycle Record mode, with the Automatically Merge Software Instrument Recordings When Using the Cycle Region option checked in the GarageBand General Preferences.

Figure 6.8 Add the kick and snare part on the second pass. GarageBand merges the MIDI notes into your MIDI region and treats them as a single performance.

how about adding a few choice cymbal crashes or shakers? It's up to you, but if you try this experiment, you'll see what the process is. It's like automatic looping over-dubbing. It's fun! See Figure 6.9.

Figure 6.9 Adding a shaker part on the third pass. The shaker is played on a much higher note on the keyboard, and as such it is displayed far above the notes of your hi-hat, kick, and snare in the Editor.

When you are finished with your tracking, let GarageBand cycle around one more time and then press Stop. You'll see that the MIDI notes have all been layered on top of one another, and if you play the part back (you might want to turn off the metronome now), you'll hear everything you did on each of the cycle recordings playing together. Turn cycle recording off by clicking the Cycle Record button and then double-click on the green bar that is your new MIDI region. Double-clicking any region in the timeline is a shortcut for viewing that region in the Editor.

In the previous chapter you viewed and moved the audio waveforms of your Electric Guitar recording in the Editor, so you saw GarageBand's Editor display audio wave-forms. In this chapter, we are dealing with MIDI regions, so we will be using the Editor in a different way, visualizing notes in what's called "piano-roll" style and for editing musical notation with the Score. It's only a little confusing in the nomen-clature. GarageBand calls the lower third of the interface the *Track Editor*, or just the

Editor, referring to any track or region that is being edited in close-up view down in that lower area, whether it be an audio region's waveform or a MIDI performance's "piano-roll" matrix. Just as a reminder, the Editor is the name of the lower area of GarageBand's interface, where you zoom in and finely edit things that have been tracked. Depending on which type of region you double-click on, the Track Editor updates with the appropriate editing tool—one version for editing audio regions and the "piano-roll"-style version for editing MIDI regions. One final detail is that the MIDI Track Editor has two distinct views with different features depending on your style, abilities, and approach to editing music. There is the Piano Roll view and the Score view, between which you can toggle at will by clicking either of the two main tab selectors at the top left of the Editor, only visible when viewing the MIDI data or a Software Instrument track in the Editor.

Renaming a Region in the Editor

The Editor is also where you can rename individual regions within a track. Open a region in the Editor and double-click its name in the upper-left portion of the blown-up region, edit the name, and press Return or Enter to lock it in. You can play an individual region from the Editor interface as well, by clicking the small Play button located right near the region name in the blown-up representation of the region displayed in the Editor (see Figure 6.10).

Figure 6.10 Edit a region name or play a region directly from the Editor in GarageBand '09.

Using the Editor for Editing MIDI Information

The Editor has some very powerful and nicely designed tools for making adjustments to your MIDI notes after they have been played and recorded into GarageBand. This so-called "piano-roll"-style editor is constructed in a system of columns and rows in a rectangular array. While a piano keyboard is horizontal in orientation, it's important to note that the piano-roll editor is vertically oriented.

The rows in the Editor (which extend up and down) represent the notes on your MIDI keyboard, where the very top of the grid is the highest note you can play, and the bottom is the lowest. You can use the small vertical representation of a piano keyboard on the left edge of the Editor to reference what notes have been played, and you can even click on the tiny piano keys to produce a note to check and decide what note you might want to move things to.

The columns of the Editor (which extend across the Editor panel from left to right) represent the timeline of the song (or the beats and measures) within which your notes occur. You can scroll the Editor up and down to see the far reaches of the notes on the keyboard and from left to right to see ahead and back in time. The zoom sliders are in effect here as well, just as they are when you're editing an audio waveform on a Real Instrument track. See Figure 6.11.

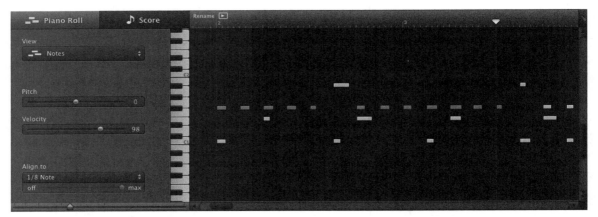

Figure 6.11 The Editor with MIDI data for a drum-beat pattern being viewed.

The left-to-right timeline aspect of the Editor, as well as its content, specifically represents the length of the particular MIDI region you have selected in the timeline. As you click around the timeline onto different MIDI regions, the notes and time span shown below will change. Double-clicking a region in the timeline is a shortcut for opening the region in the Editor window. When the Editor is already open, single-clicking a region in the timeline updates the Editor to highlight the region you've clicked and focuses it on a similar view to what the Timeline view is focusing on. Double-clicking another region while the Editor is already opened will not only show you the close-up of that region, but will refresh the windows if need be so that the playhead in the Editor is locked to the same vertical position as the playhead up in the Timeline window. It's a way of placing the playhead specifically and then loading regions into the Editor for inspection—but with some foreknowledge of exactly what you'll be looking at when it gets there, instead of just loading it and then having to scroll around to find your place.

Piano Roll and Score

There are two diverse ways to view the information in the Editor—the Piano Roll view and the Score view. There is a small button in the lower left of the Editor window, just below the zoom slider, that allows you to toggle between these two views.

It's quite nice for Apple to have included these disparate views of the same information in GarageBand, because there are certainly people with differing abilities and approaches to music. For example, I don't read music. I have been playing music since I was a very small child, but I have always played by ear and instinct. For me, the piano roll's graphical view is much more appealing in that I experience and perceive music spatially and somewhat mathematically (as in math's relationships, not necessarily in its operations). Because I never learned to read musical notation, the Score view is of little or no use to me. For someone else, it may be the only way they'd ever consider working with MIDI note values. GarageBand allows you to use the view with which you're the most comfortable. You can switch easily back and forth, and the edits you make in one view always carry over to the other. If you're skilled enough to use both views, it might just come down to your mood. One additional benefit of the Score view is its ability to automatically print beautifully formatted sheet music directly from the MIDI notes that you played to a PDF file or to your printer.

Piano Roll View

When you open up a MIDI region for editing, the default view of the Editor window is the Piano Roll view, or what was called Graphic view in GarageBand '08 and earlier. It displays the notes of your keyboard represented along a vertical axis on the left and the timeline and length of the Editor left to right, representing the beats and measures of the region you have selected. Your recorded notes are shown as blocks or bars of varying shades of gray, denoting the velocity with which you struck the note. (Charcoal gray represents a note that was struck hard, and light gray represents a note that was struck lightly.) The recorded notes are also shown as varying lengths, denoting the sustain—or duration—of the notes that you played.

Mousing over any note will give you a little tooltip that displays the name and the velocity of the recorded note. The notes are named by their musical names and a number. C2 means the second C note on your keyboard from the left, E4 means the fourth E note, and so on. Essentially, the numbers refer to the octave that the note is in—the higher the number, the higher the note. The velocity is a value from 1 (virtually silent) to 127 (you actually can't play the note any harder). Some sounds even have extra flourishes in their attack when you strike the note very hard, such as an extra pluck, a slide, or some type of accent. This makes it advantageous to be able to edit the velocity of each note, not just because this affects the relative volume of the note, but because it will allow or disallow the nuances and flourishes that some Software Instrument sounds have built in.

To adjust the velocity of a note, select the note in the Editor and adjust the velocity slider on the far left. You can also type in a value and press Return to save the adjustment.

If you look at the top of the Advanced pane in the Editor, you will see a drop-down menu that defaults to Notes. You can access other aspects of the MIDI controller's information, such as sustain pedal, modulation wheel, pitch shift, and more. I'll provide a quick overview of these functions, but some of them will not even come into play if you do not have these features on your MIDI keyboard or you don't own a foot pedal. For instance, if you do not have a sustain pedal for your keyboard, you will not see any information recorded to the Sustain Pedal view in the Editor. If that is the case, you can still create values in the Sustain Controller Edit view, almost as though you have played the part with a pedal, but it's a lot more time-intensive to try to enter these values manually, which is why you might want to consider investing in a sustain pedal.

Most MIDI keyboards have two wheels on the far left, next to the lowest piano keys. These are modulation and pitch bend wheels, and they are both accessible from the Advanced Display drop-down menu in the Editor. These are two very common features to keyboards, and most Software Instruments are programmed to respond to their use in interesting ways. When you use these functions on your keyboard while performing, the movements get tracked by GarageBand and represented there by lines connecting control points. It's very similar to adjusting automation for volume up in the Track Mixer, which we will cover in more detail in Chapter 11, in the sections on automation. Choose the control you want to edit from the menu, and you will notice the green control points that have been recorded. You can move these points up or down to change the intensity of the effect or to the left or right to adjust when each point occurs. If you want to delete a point, click it once and press Delete. To add a new control point to any of the controller parameters, hold the Command key down while you click on the line. You can select multiple points for movement or deletion by clicking and dragging a marquee box around the desired points, and then you can affect them simultaneously.

Focusing back on viewing your MIDI data as notes, you can adjust the duration of any note played by dragging the ends of your notes to the left to shorten them and to the right to lengthen them. Position your cursor at the tail end of the note, and you'll see the standard cursor change into the same region-stretching cursor you saw earlier, when you were changing the length of regions in the timeline. Move your cursor until you see the double-arrow bracket cursor at the tail end of a note and then click and drag. You can click once on any note to hear it play. If you click and release quickly, you will hear the note sound as if you had just played it the same way you clicked your mouse. If you click and hold the mouse down on a note, you will hear its duration as recorded or presently adjusted.

You can click and drag any note—or selected group of notes—up or down in the Editor to change its pitch. If you played a wrong note, but it's in the right position rhythmically, you can simply click and drag it into place to make it play the correct note. If you played a "clam," as it were, you can often see that little straggler there out of place, and you can just select it—by clicking once on it or drawing a box around it—and delete it.

Just as you used the Timing Enhancer while dealing with audio regions, you can align MIDI notes to the grid to further nudge the whole rhythm of the piece back into shape—

Figure 6.12 Choosing a resolution for the timing enhancement, or quantization, of your drum part from the Note drop-down menu.

provided that you are interested in having your notes aligned to a grid. You can choose the resolution of the grid to which you want to align (see Figure 6.12), and the best part is you can adjust a slider from minimum to maximum, which tells GarageBand just how much to change your original performance.

Most often, something in the 40–60 percent slider range will probably be what you're looking for. The more important the exact alignment of your notes is for your composition, the more you will want to slide the slider all the way to the right, which is maximum zoom. The keyboard shortcuts are Control+Left Arrow for zooming our and Control+Right Arrow for zooming in.

Quantizing, timing enhancement, and aligning to the grid will affect the human aspect— or the feel—of your performance, but once again, I will leave that up to your tastes and desires. Sometimes quantizing the drum part or the keyboard part can really tie it all together, and other times it can kill the song. As long as you use your ears, you can't say you didn't listen to the effect your decisions had on your final mix. In Figure 6.13, I have enhanced the timing of my performance to eighth notes and to the maximum, bringing the "alignment" of all my hi-hat, kick, snare, and shaker notes to a completely tight and squared-off grid.

Figure 6.13 Maximum timing enhancement on the new merged drum part.

Adding New Notes to Your Performance

Finally, you can add a new note to the song simply by holding down the Command key and clicking where you want the note to be. Use the keyboard diagram to the left to guide your Pencil tool and click (see Figure 6.14). Then you can adjust the length and velocity of the note. You can select and then copy and paste groups of notes in the Piano Roll view, and you can easily duplicate notes that are already in the Editor by selecting one and then holding the Option key down while you click again and drag the duplicate notes to where you want them.

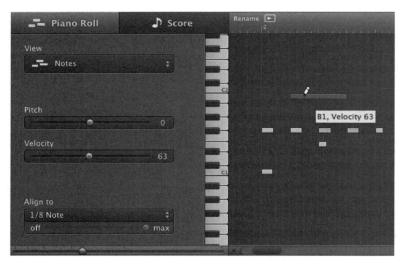

Figure 6.14 The drum track in Piano Roll view, with a new note drawn in by holding the Command key down and clicking in the grid. Notice the velocity slider on the left to adjust the intensity of the note after drawing it in.

Score View

The Score view focuses on musical notation. The MIDI notes you recorded into Garage-Band are displayed in musical notes on a staff and can be edited with as much ease as in the Piano Roll view—if you know how to read and write music. You can click and drag notes up and down to change their pitch, and you can click a note to select it and then adjust the light-green tail of the note to tell GarageBand how long you want that note to hold out. You can add a new note by holding down the Command key and clicking where you want the note to be. You can then adjust its length and copy and paste it. Many of the same editing functions are available to you in Score view as in Piano Roll view, only they are visually represented differently. See Figure 6.15.

You can print your MIDI region as musical notation by going into Score view and then choosing Print from the File menu or by pressing Command+P. The printed sheet-music document will pick up the name of your GarageBand project for the title, your administrator username from your Mac as the author, and the name of the region

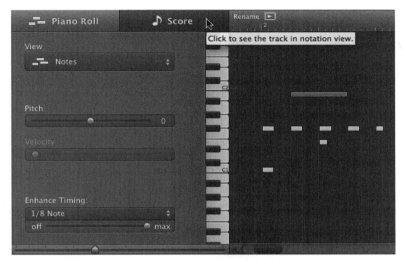

Figure 6.15 Click to see the drum track in Score view.

as the "instrument." GarageBand will print the tempo and then bar after bar of your beautiful creation. If you need to adjust the author information, remember to visit the GarageBand Preferences under the main GarageBand menu and make your edits there, and then go back to GarageBand and choose Print from the File menu or press Command+P to print your score. See Figure 6.16.

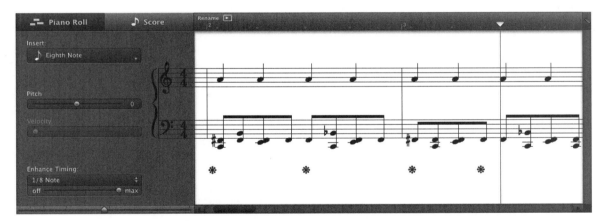

Figure 6.16 The drum track in Score view.

Now on to Apple Loops

Now that you know how to record and edit a Software Instrument MIDI performance, it's time move on to using the vast library of Apple Loops in GarageBand. The extensive loop library made available to you standard in GarageBand, plus the additional Apple Loops libraries included in the various Jam Packs from Apple, will really blow the doors off your song creation process. Loops open up a whole new set of possibilities by allowing you to add to your song's professional recordings of studio pros laying down grooves, riffs, licks, beats, and vocalizations. These so-called loops are short segments of high-quality audio and MIDI that can be seamlessly repeated, and in many cases customized and edited, that will make your projects sound as if you have a full backup band, even if it's just you in your garage. Let's get to it!

7 Working with Apple Loops

We've looked at a number of ways that we can get audio into GarageBand, including by recording Real Instruments into tracks and by using a MIDI controller to input a performance using a sound or a set of sounds from the vast sound library that GarageBand comes stocked with. We have also looked at editing and manipulating those tracks—be they tracks containing audio regions or MIDI regions—using GarageBand's audio editing tools and multiple interface windows, including the Editor with its different views, such as the Piano Roll view and the Score view. There is another major component in the GarageBand digital composition and recording arsenal that we have yet to discuss, and that is Apple Loops.

These wonderfully flexible files are known as *Apple* Loops because Apple, Inc. invented the file format. They are known as Apple *Loops* because they are audio regions and MIDI regions that are designed to loop, or repeat, seamlessly. What does this mean? *Loop* is an audio recording and compositional term referring to a short snippet of audio—again, loops can be comprised of audio information, MIDI information, or both, depending on the loop at hand—that has been recorded and edited specifically to be repeated again and again cleanly.

What do I mean by "cleanly?" Imagine recording yourself playing a guitar for two full minutes. Let's say you are in 4/4 time and just strumming chords, perhaps playing a little lead melody now and then. Then, you open that recorded region in GarageBand's zoomed-view Editor window, and you simply split out a short section of the track willy-nilly, by using the Split function at two points of your choosing, resulting in a shorter, three- or four-second region. Let's also suppose that you cut out this shorter region without a care in the world about what part of the larger two-minute region you use or specifically where you split the region. Then you take that region—let's imagine it's roughly five seconds of guitar-playing audio—and you drop it into a new GarageBand track. Then you use the looping tool to make that region repeat some number of times. Because you did not take great care to both create your starting point exactly on the beat and end the region just before the beginning of a new measure— maybe you even caught it right smack in the middle of a rhythmic strum—you will likely have a choppy-sounding moment every time the loop repeats.

The effect would sound much like a skipping vinyl record. You know how when the record skips, it never really seems to maintain the beat? If you were to count the rhythm of the song on your broken record and attempt to incorporate the skip into your count, you might end up counting like this: 1 - 2 - 3 - 4, 1 - 2 — 1 - 2 - 3 - 4, 1 - 2 — 1 - 2, and so on. It's not even. It's not clean. It sounds wrong. Dancing people would trip over their feet. Furthermore, if you were to take an even four or eight beats of your strumming guitar and surgically split out one or two bars of it and then loop it in a GarageBand track, even if your beat were steady, you might still have a little popping sound at the moment when the loop repeats. Experiment with this and see whether you get some of the results I am describing here. This is why audio editors use the Apple Loops Utility to create their Apple Loops: It takes these things into account and aids in the process of creating a clean, even loop. It also allows them to add metadata, such as genre, style, and other keywords, to the Apple Loop, allowing the user to easily browse for it in GarageBand.

If a file is crafted to be a loop—especially with the degree of care that a company such as Apple takes in the things that it releases—you can bet that there will be no popping sounds between loops and that the loops will all be nice and clean and an even number of beats in length. This is what distinguishes a loop from a run-of-the-mill audio snippet. When you use GarageBand's looping tool to make it repeat, it sounds as if it's just being played again and again, and no one can tell that it's being looped—it just sounds groovy and plays for as long as you'd like it to.

What Is a Region?

We've covered regions to some degree in previous chapters, but a discussion of Apple Loops requires being able to refer to a region and know what its attributes are.

A *region* in GarageBand is any discrete section of audio in use in your audio project. It can be a voice, a guitar, a Real Instrument, a Software Instrument, or anything that appears in the timeline in a track and can be interacted with. A region is a singular audio object that can be selected in the timeline. See Figures 7.1 and 7.2.

Figure 7.1 A GarageBand MIDI region (which appears in green).

Figure 7.2 A GarageBand audio region (which appears in blue).

Regions are sections of audio or MIDI and are of a certain specific length. They can be in a certain key (but not always) and can have a tempo (but not always), a head (beginning), and a tail (end). Regions can be copied and pasted, selected and moved, or deleted. They can also be played, be split, and have effects applied to them, and you can automate the changing of their volume level or panning (among a great number of other attributes) over time.

What Is a Loop?

In the next section, "What is an Apple Loop?" I'll explain specifically what an Apple Loop is, but I'd like to talk about loops in general before we get there. In electronic music, the generic term "music loop" is used to describe a sample that is repeated through some electronic means. What's a sample? It's a recording—usually digital—of some particular bit or snippet of audio. For example, you could sample the sound of your dog barking, you hitting a wooden spoon on the side of your fridge, or a drummer hitting a snare drum.

The process of sampling them might be to use a microphone and record these sounds into a digital recorder of some kind. Essentially, it could be anything like a portable digital recorder, such as the Zoom H2 that I use, your laptop running GarageBand, or even a dedicated sampler device. The purpose of such a sampler device is to capture sounds, edit and customize them, and then re-purpose those sounds in some broader way in terms of building a sound library or simply making it so that when you press some key on your MIDI keyboard (such as the lowest C# key, for example), you hear your dog bark. Right there, onstage, at that exact right spot in the third chorus, you can reach over and press that C# key, and the dog barks in the song, right where she's supposed to. If someone asks you after the show, "Hey, how'd you get that dog bark to happen?" you could reply, "I sampled my dog, Wilma, barking and then mapped it to my keyboard and just triggered the sample by hitting a predetermined note on my MIDI keyboard during the concert."

Sampling   Here is what the Wikipedia entry for sampling had to say on the subject at the time of this writing:

"In music, sampling is the act of taking a portion, or sample, of one sound recording and reusing it as an instrument or element of a new recording. This is typically done with a sampler, which can be a piece of hardware or a computer program on a digital computer. Sampling is also possible with tape loops or with vinyl records on a phonograph."

With regard to loops as a type of sample, Wikipedia says:

"The drums and percussion parts of many modern recordings are really a variety of short samples of beats strung together. Many libraries of such beats exist and are licensed so that the user incorporating the samples can distribute their recording without paying royalties. Such libraries can be loaded into samplers. Though percussion is a typical application of looping, many kinds of samples can be looped. A piece of music may have an ostinato, which is created by sampling a phrase played on any kind of instrument. There is software which specializes in creating loops."

Thus, looping is the act of taking a sample (which can be anything from a single note on a single instrument to a snippet of audio from an entire mix or performance—including things that are not particularly musical, such as a chatting dinner crowd, a bomb exploding, or a noisy traffic jam) and using MIDI or a sequencer or even mapping samples or loops to a MIDI controller, such as a keyboard, electronic drum pad, or foot switch, so that the loop may be triggered either at will or at a predetermined time or beat in the piece.

In the case of GarageBand, GarageBand itself could be called the sequencer that you are using to organize, present, and trigger your samples, or loops. Now let's take a look at what is meant by the term "Apple Loop."

What Is an Apple Loop?

Apple Loop is the standard file format invented by Apple that allows for next-generation audio and MIDI looping in Apple's audio software products. The fact that the Apple Loop format is a universal standard means that third-party developers can release Apple Loops (such as those produced by Big Fish Audio, PowerFX, and others), and they will be compatible with applications such as GarageBand. Developers and musicians alike can use a tool called the *Apple Loops Utility* to create Apple Loop files, and the utility is included with Apple's pro audio software bundles.

The Apple Loop format has a couple of very interesting features—one uncommon and the other completely unique. While many third-party loops are created as WAV or AIF files that will seamlessly repeat when looped, Apple Loops will time-stretch. This means they will automatically adjust to the tempo of your project. Currently, the only other types of loops in the marketplace that offer this tempo adjustment feature are ACID Loops and REX Loops, which in addition to being invented and developed by Sony and Propellerhead, respectively, are regularly produced by many third-party developers. Automatic tempo adjustment is incredibly powerful and means that you will not be required to hunt endlessly for loops that just so happen to have been created at the exact tempo of the song you're working on. Even worse would be having to create your song at a particular tempo just so that you can use that kickin' loop you really love. This advanced feature of Apple Loops makes all of that go away.

With Apple Loops, you can drag them into your project, and they will automatically change to the tempo of your piece. A word of warning, however: If your song's tempo differs more than roughly 30 or 40 beats per minute from the tempo at which the Apple

Loop was created, you may start to hear distortion and possibly some digital artifacts because Loops do begin to break down if you stretch them too far. You will be able to tell if that is happening, and you can always try a different loop if you don't like the results.

The completely unique feature of Software Instrument Apple Loops is that they contain the MIDI data of a performance as well as instructions for GarageBand to set up a Software Instrument track with a specific Software Instrument and some preset effects settings in place. They may also contain specific plug-in information, effects information, and even audio information. If you use a Software Instrument Apple Loop in your project, you can add it to a Software Instrument track to retain full control of its instrument, plug-in, and effects settings. Alternatively, you can drag and drop the Software Instrument Apple Loop onto a Real Instrument track, and GarageBand will instantly change the Software Instrument Apple Loop into an audio Apple Loop. If you do this, it can be far less processor-intensive than letting the loop remain in the MIDI realm, because the Real Instrument Apple Loops are loaded entirely into RAM. However, if your computer is at all RAM starved, you may still run into issues with Real Instrument Apple Loops overloading your system. In addition, remember that if you place Software Instrument Apple Loops into Real Instrument tracks, you will not be able to change any of the MIDI information contained in the Software Instrument Apple Loop unless you go back to the original version.

Indeed, Apple Loops are very well conceived and produced—they are infinitely usable, cleanly prepared for looping, and often quite creatively designed and well suited to the genre categories of loops into which Apple breaks down its library. One more distinction that ought to be made is that the Apple Loops that come with GarageBand, the Garage-Band Jam Packs, and Apple's other audio software packages are all provided as royalty-free music loops, like the licensing example given in the Wikipedia definition earlier in this chapter. This means you can use Apple Loops in any of your musical creations as you desire; you can release the resulting composition commercially and make a profit from it, and Apple will not claim a cent from you. These loops are free to use as you like.

Within GarageBand, there are vast libraries of Apple Loops. In the next section, we will look at some ways of browsing and auditioning the available audio and Software Instrument Apple Loops. You can search and filter them by a variety of criteria, including genre, style, mood, and instrument. GarageBand comes loaded with a healthy library of loops right out of the box, but I will say this: If you spend some time working with GarageBand loops, you might quickly begin to say to yourself, "I've heard this one before," or, "This doesn't have what I'm looking for." This may result in you wanting to expand your Apple Loop library.

To expand your Apple Loop library, one thing you can do is purchase software packages, known as *GarageBand Jam Packs*, from Apple. These CDs or DVDs are expansion libraries or refills of new Apple Loops of a certain genre. In Appendix A, "GarageBand Jam Packs," we will discuss the contents of the Jam Packs specifically, but as of this printing, there are five GarageBand Jam Packs available from Apple. These are called Rhythm Section, Symphony Orchestra, Remix Tools, World Music, and Voices. They each retail for $99. If you own Logic Studio, that package includes all of the available Jam Packs except the newest one, Voices. It does, however, include the original Apple Loop library that ships with GarageBand.

If you are considering buying all of the Jam Packs to outfit your GarageBand studio, allow me to recommend that you instead purchase the Logic Studio bundle, which is the same price as all five Jam Packs ($499). With the bundle, you get not only the complete library of Jam Pack Apple Loops, Software Instruments, and samples, but you get Logic Pro 8, MainStage, Soundtrack Pro 2, and an incredible array of studio effects and sound libraries that can be used in GarageBand as well as Logic Pro 8. Even if Garage-Band is the application you prefer, and you have no intention of using Logic, it seems a waste not to put that same investment into the Logic bundle, even if there's only a five percent chance you'll use it. As a result of your Logic Studio installation, many new things will appear in GarageBand's menus and libraries. You can expect to see new Apple Loops as well as new instrument presets, AU instruments, audio effects, and more.

In addition to purchasing loops from third-party music software companies, you will also find a large number of websites and web resources that offer free loops to download and import into GarageBand. Some of these sites are like free discussion board communities, where you will need to register (for free) to have access to the downloadable loops. iCompositions (www.icompositions.com) is one such example. A quick Google search with a search string such as "free loop download," "free Apple Loops," or "GarageBand loops" will yield page after page of great resources. I'll list a few of them here. Because websites change frequently, let this list be a jumping-off point and then perform your own search online for sites that offer free (and commercial) loop downloads. There are literally hundreds of them.

- **Macloops:** www.macloops.com
- **Silicon Beats:** www.siliconbeats.com/garageband_loops.php
- **Macidol:** www.macidol.com/downloads.php
- **BandmateLoops:** www.bandmateloops.com/storefront.php
- **Smart Loops:** www.smartloops.com
- **Samples4.com:** www.samples4.com
- **The GarageDoor:** www.thegaragedoor.com
- **MacJams:** www.macjams.com
- **iCompositions:** www.icompositions.com
- **Basslines:** www.apple.com/downloads/macosx/audio/basslinesappleloopsdemo.html

Those links should get you started, but I'm always a little wary of link lists that appear in printed books, because websites and companies come and go. For the *GarageBand '09 Power!* edition of this book, I have added a few new ones. Although many of these resources may in fact be around for years to come, I always feel better doing my own searches. I encourage you to dig around the web, download a few .dmg files (Mac OS X–formatted disc images—software ready for installation on your Mac), and then see the section called "Importing Loops" later in this chapter for information about importing loops into GarageBand.

If you are interested in finding out how to create your own Apple Loops, the Apple Loops SDK provides the tools and guidelines for creating audio loops in the Apple Loops format for use within GarageBand or any other audio application that supports Apple Loops. You can search the web for "Apple Loops SDK" or use this link to download the .dmg file directly: ftp://ftp.apple.com/developer/Development_Kits/Apple_Loops_SDK_1.3.1.dmg. Or you can go to developer.apple.com/sdk and scroll down to find the download.

The Loop Browser

GarageBand makes it very easy to browse, audition, and insert loops into your song projects. As you saw in the interface overview earlier, there is an area called the *Loop Browser* located within the right-hand side of your GarageBand interface, where the Track Info panel is displayed. Click the Show/Hide Loop Browser icon to slide the panel open in your GarageBand window, giving you access to all of your loops currently installed. (The Show/Hide Loop Browser icon is the open eye icon in the lower right of the GarageBand window, next to the Track Info "i" button and the Media Browser filmstrip button.) See Figure 7.3.

Figure 7.3 The Show/Hide Loop Browser icon.

Any time you install new Jam Packs or import new loops, you'll need to save your project, quit GarageBand, and relaunch it for your new loops to be visible in the Loop Browser. The truth is, the loop installation process can sometimes be a little glitchy. Occasionally, newly added loops show up without restarting; other times, it's the only way to get them to show up. You can click and drag with your cursor (which will become a two-directional arrow cursor when positioned between your Loop Browser and your track timeline) to adjust the relative sizes of top half and the bottom half of your Loop Browser window. Sometimes, you will want to see more loops in your found set in the bottom half, and you can slide the separator up to make the bottom list longer (see Figure 7.4).

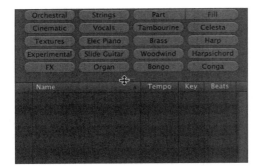

Figure 7.4 The Loop Browser window in GarageBand '09.

The Loop Browser offers a host of methods for achieving a single thing—listening to loops for the purpose of deciding which one(s) to include in your project. The reason why there are so many ways to sort, search, filter, and group your loops is that even in the most basic GarageBand Jam Packs, there are thousands of loops. With the entire collection of GarageBand Jam Packs installed, the total cranks up to around 18,000 loops. To make any sense of a collection that huge, you need good filtering tools for sorting your view so that you can be looking at only a couple hundred at a time. Then it becomes much easier to sift through them all reasonably and eliminate the ones that simply won't work for you right out of the gate. Then, you can hone in on that perfect groove or line to suit your creation. Be warned, though—browsing loops is addictive! I have literally spent hours just listening to them all and marking my favorites—a process we'll cover in just a bit in the section called "Saving and Browsing Favorites"— just so that when I really need a loop of a particular feel, style, length, or tempo down the road, I will be able to locate it quickly.

The Process of Browsing Loops

Browsing loops with your auditioning hat on is a fun process, but it can also be overwhelming. Sometimes you know exactly what you are looking for and you can't find it, and other times you have no idea what you need, and you find dozens of things that you like. Especially for those of you who are new to using loops, many of the Apple Loops provided within GarageBand's default set of loops may sound really cool to you. That's not to suggest that those of you to whom I'm referring have non-discerning taste; it's more to say that they are, in fact, really cool. They are hip, modern, professionally produced loops that sound hot. The only time you might think, "Blech, that one stinks," is in a scenario where you might be putting together a metal tune, and the loop is a country lick or just something totally unmatched to what you're looking for. I've found that it's usually an appropriateness thing, not a quality thing.

This is why the sort functions are really useful. When you first click on the Show/Hide Loop Browser icon and the Loop Browser slides open, you will notice the top half of the Browser is set up in a button grid. This grid contains filter buttons that let you allow—or disallow—loops of a certain type to be shown or hidden from the list view on the right.

At the very top of the Loop Browser, in its title bar, is the word "Loops" or "Garage-Band" (depending on your setup and current installation) and a set of double arrows to the right of the word. These double arrows indicate a menu underneath, and if you have more than the default GarageBand loops installed (in other collections like the Jam Packs I mentioned or custom loops), these collections will be listed in the menu. The menu shown in Figure 7.5 is from my system, where I have Logic Studio installed, and that includes all of the GarageBand Jam Packs and the Apple Loops that come with Soundtrack Pro.

Figure 7.5   The Loops title bar, where you can choose which loops to view.

If you choose Show All, then the Loop Browser will allow you to sort and search through your entire collection of loops. Yours might be different from mine, so the specific examples may not match up with your collection, but all of the principles will be exactly the same, whether you're listening to 12 Bar Blues Bass or Promenade Viola 01.

In the lower-left of the Loop Browser, there are three buttons that toggle the general view of the left side of this window. From left to right, they are Column view, Musical Button view, and Podcast Sounds view. Click each of them and see how they change the loop browsing environment. See Figure 7.6.

Column View

Column view behaves much like the Mac OS X Finder, with its multi-column view—you single-click on a category or loop type in the first column, and the second column reveals what is "underneath" that category or loop type. You click on something in the

Figure 7.6 The Loop Browser in Column view.

second column and dig deeper. The first column breaks down your library into five master categories. You can view by genre, instrument, or mood, or you can view your favorites or all loops. Each category has a whole litany of choices under it, and once you get to the third column and you see things such as Bass, Beats, or Experimental, these will often have parenthetical numbers next to them, telling you how many loops are in that category or grouping given your current filter or sort criteria. Click on that third column, and the right side of the Loop Browser will fill with the actual loops that you can begin to browse by single-clicking the loops to hear them play. Single-click a second time to make a loop stop playing. See Figure 7.7.

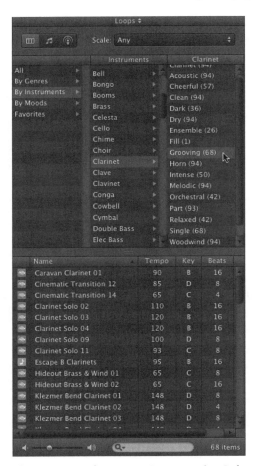

Figure 7.7 The Loop Browser in Column view, showing loops to browse.

Musical Button View

The second button is the Musical Button view. The buttons in the Musical Button view allow you to filter the display to only show loops that correspond to the buttons you click on—which can be either a single button or multiple buttons—to hone in on your loop collection more specifically. See Figure 7.8.

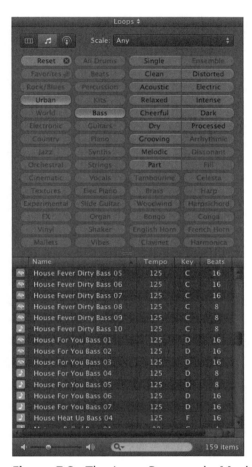

Figure 7.8 The Loop Browser in Musical Button view.

The musical buttons themselves are generally of three types—Genre (for example, Rock/Blues, Jazz, Orchestral), Instrument (for example, Bass, Synths, French Horn), or Descriptor (for example, Relaxed, Distorted, Ensemble, Dark). So by clicking on the Rock/Blues, Guitars, and Distorted buttons, you can become very specific in your searches for loops to use in your projects. In a library of many thousands of loops, clicking three or four buttons may only yield eight or ten loops. This method prevents long scrolls through many hundreds of loops when you already know a little bit about what you are looking for.

Aside from any time you might spend actually investigating or browsing through your Loops library to see what you have access to, most of your searches will likely take place when you already have something in mind. You might say to yourself, "I need a mellow xylophone riff to go in this section," and then begin to hunt for it with that description, instrument, or genre in mind. If you have several buttons clicked (they will appear light blue when activated), you can deselect them one by one to widen your search. If you find that certain musical buttons are more often the kinds of loops that you tend to like, you can easily rearrange or move them around as you like. Simply click and drag the musical buttons to position them where they are of the most use to you. You can always click the Reset button, when it is glowing orange, to deselect all musical buttons with one click.

You also can easily reassign the actual musical keywords (and therefore, the filter behavior) that are on each button by right-clicking (or holding the Control key down as you click) on one of the buttons and using the Genre and Instrument sub-menus to choose a keyword term that is not in use. See Figure 7.9.

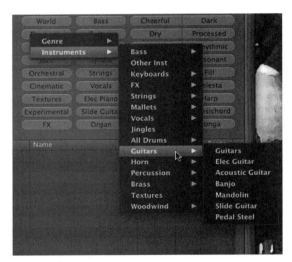

Figure 7.9 The Genre and Instrument right-click menu system, used for changing the label and behavior of musical buttons.

Podcast Sounds View

The third button is Podcast Sounds view. This is handy when you are working on a podcast or movie score because it filters your library down to just those loops and sounds that are designed for creating radio-style projects. There are sound effects (twangs, bonks, birds, booms, atmospheres, sports sounds, guns), jingles (brief, catchy songs; grooves, jams, or melodies to be used under titles; theme songs; and even music beds for scoring—these tend to be more songlike than cinematic scoring), and stingers (like those whiz-bang effects that you commonly hear used as transitions between one hot moment and another on FM radio).

In Appendix A, I'll present a much deeper look at what each of the Jam Packs offers, with a number of specific examples of all of the various sets. This topic is difficult to cover in a book like this because it makes the most sense to just open up the Garage-Band application, open the Loop Browser, and start clicking. You can audition all of the loops in your collection for yourself. See Figure 7.10.

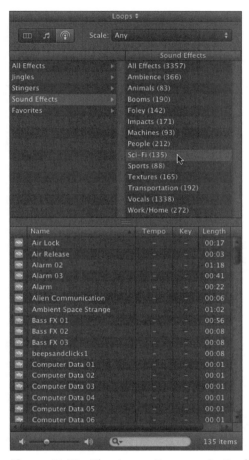

Figure 7.10 The Loop Browser in Podcast Sounds view.

Scales

Additionally, there is a drop-down menu to the right of these three sort buttons labeled Scale. This menu allows you to filter your view in yet another specific way, by the musical scale around which the loops are based. Sometimes it makes sense to use a loop that was created with your key in mind—or, at the very least, the type of scale. By that I mean the two main types of scales used in almost all of so-called Western or American music—what we call the major scale and the minor scale. In this case, when I say "Western," I do not mean the genre Country and Western. I mean the Western world—as opposed to, say, the Far East. Chinese, Indian, and Middle Eastern music (to name *very* few) often use very different types of scales and tunings than those used in American/European music or music taught in Western schools and universities under the banner of "musical basics." See Figure 7.11.

Figure 7.11   The Scale menu in the Apple Loops search area in GarageBand.

The choices in the Scale filter menu are:

- **Any.** This choice is basically the "no filter" state for this menu, showing you all of the Apple Loops available.

- **Minor.** This displays all of the loops that are in one of the 12 minor keys.

- **Major.** This displays all of the loops that are in one of the 12 major keys.

- **Neither.** This displays all of the loops that aren't specifically good for major or minor keys.

- **Good for Both.** This displays loops that may be in major or minor keys, but given their mode, the notes played or general approach could be used for songs that are in either major or minor keys.

The Major Scale

It would be foolhardy at best to attempt to explain and teach the musical theory behind minor and major scales in a sub-subsection of a book on GarageBand, but it will help to offer a basic overview for those of you who have no experience whatsoever with these concepts.

A scale is a series of notes arranged in a specific pattern of whole and half steps. A half step is the smallest distance between two notes. A whole step is twice as far. On the piano, the keys are separated by half steps. The arrangement of these half and whole steps gives a scale its distinctive sound.

The major scale is the familiar do, re, mi scale we all learned in elementary school and is the most common scale sound in Western music. A major scale has seven distinct notes and then repeats the starting note an octave (a doubling of the frequency of the note) higher. The scale can be continued through as many octaves as an instrument can play. The major scale sequence is whole, whole, half, whole, whole, whole, half. The scale can be started on any note (the root), and the notes are named in alphabetical order. If you start on C, the scale would be C - D - E - F - G - A - B - C and so on. This scale has a fairly bright sound.

The Minor Scale

Like the major scale, a minor scale is a succession of tones in alphabetical order. A minor scale has a different quality because the sequence of whole and half steps is different. The scales have a "darker" sound, and there are slight variations in the types of minor scales. The most important characteristic of a minor scale is the flattened third. This means the distance from the first to the third note is a half step smaller than in the major scale.

One common minor scale is the natural minor scale. This scale has a sequence of whole, half, whole, whole, half, whole, whole. It can also be created by playing a major scale starting from the sixth note instead of the first note. In other words, A - B - C - D - E - F - G - A. If we started on C, the notes would be C - D - E♭ - F - G - A♭ - B♭ - C.

Classical composers use variations of this scale to suit melodic invention. One common variation is the harmonic minor scale. In this scale the seventh degree is raised a half step to create a half step between the seventh note and the octave. This is called a *leading tone*, and in C minor the B♭ would be raised to B.

Importing Loops

There are three main ways to get new loops into GarageBand. The first way is to insert a DVD-R or CD-R into your computer and run the installer (as with GarageBand Jam Packs). This will allow the installer program on the disc itself to place all of your new Apple Loops and Software Instruments within the correct directories on your computer. You will want to be sure to quit GarageBand before running this installer. Once you launch GarageBand after installation, the new loops and Software Instruments will appear in your Loop Browser and in your Media Browser windows within GarageBand.

Another variation of this type of installation would be to install downloaded .dmg files, which also contain installer programs. Once the .dmg is mounted (by double-clicking the .dmg image), you can double-click to open the disk icon that appeared on your desktop, and you will see an installer application or package (.pkg) file. When you double-click either of those, your new Apple Loops and Software Instruments will be installed to the correct locations on your hard drive. Launching GarageBand once again will reveal all of these new loops and Software Instruments in your Loop Browser and your Media Browser pane within GarageBand.

You can use the other general method of installing new Apple Loops into GarageBand when you have Apple Loops in a folder, on a CD, or downloaded from a site that are, for lack of a better term, *loose*—just Apple Loop files in a folder of any kind, on your hard drive or on an external drive of a mounted disc (such as a CD-R or DVD-R that contains Apple Loop files but not an installer application of any kind). You can manually install these independent, loose loops into GarageBand, but you need to do so while GarageBand is actually open and launched. All you need to do is to open your

Loop Browser window and then drag and drop these Apple Loops directly into your GarageBand window, into the Loop Browser area itself. When you hover over the Loop Browser with your dragged files, you will see a round, green "plus" cursor attached to your main pointer cursor. This is the indication that it is safe to drop these new Apple Loops into GarageBand. The files will automatically "copy" over to the correct directory for Apple Loops to be stored and will be available immediately in your Loop Browser for use in your project. See Figures 7.12, 7.13, and 7.14.

Figure 7.12 To manually import or install Apple Loops into GarageBand, drag and drop the Apple Loop files into your Loop Browser window while GarageBand is running.

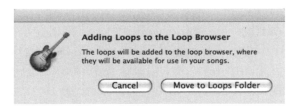

Figure 7.13 Click to authorize GarageBand to move your imported loops to your Loops folder.

Figure 7.14 The progress bar during importing. With a large group of loops to import, this may take several minutes.

Setting Loop Preferences

Within the GarageBand Preferences window (choose Preferences from the GarageBand menu), the Convert to Real Instruments check box will allow you to convert Software Instrument loops into Real Instrument audio files on the fly. Once a loop is converted, it lives within your GarageBand project as an actual audio file—essentially, an external rendering of itself. Real Instrument (or actual audio) regions (loops or regular recordings) require far less processor power on playback, and you can use this technique if your computer is having a difficult time playing back all of your tracks, yet you still want to add more tracks or more Software Instrument loops. Keep in mind, however, that if you want to be able to still edit and modify the Software Instrument Apple Loops you have added to the timeline, you should allow GarageBand to leave them as native MIDI (Software Instrument) loops in your tracks. See Figure 7.15.

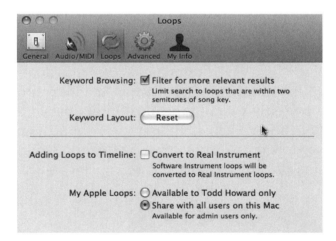

Figure 7.15 The Loops pane in your GarageBand Preferences window.

Adding Loops to the Timeline

The processes of installing and browsing Apple Loops will only take you halfway there. These processes will merely make those Apple Loops available to you in GarageBand but will not yet make them part of your song. This is a manual process that you will do by choosing the desired Apple Loop and dragging it from the right-hand preview window of the Loop Browser and dropping it into your timeline. Just like the round green plus icon attached to your cursor when installing Apple Loops into GarageBand via the drag-and-drop function of the Loop Browser, adding Apple Loops to the timeline will give you the same indication of where it is (and isn't) safe to drop your chosen loop. There are two distinct differences, however.

The first thing to notice is what type of loop you are adding. Is it a Software Instrument Apple Loop, which is colored green in the Loop Browser, or an audio loop (a Real Instrument loop), which is colored blue in the Loop Browser? When you hover over your potential destination track for the loop, blue audio loops need to end up in Real Instrument tracks, and green MIDI Software Instrument loops need to end up in Software Instrument tracks.

If you want to place the loop into its own new track of the appropriate type, you can drag and drop the loop into the empty space *below* your last track (the empty gray area that is labeled Drag Apple Loops Here). GarageBand will create a new track that matches the requirement of the loop being dragged into the timeline. Again, if you have the Convert to Real Instruments check box turned on under Adding Loops to Timeline in GarageBand Preferences: Loops, GarageBand will convert green Software Instrument Apple Loops to actual blue audio loops on the fly, as you drag them in. Remember, if you do this, you will not be able to edit the MIDI notes or any of the other parameters contained the original loop. See the previous section, called "Setting Loop Preferences," or the subsection called "Preferences: Loops" within the "GarageBand's Preferences Window" section in Chapter 3 for an expanded description.

The second thing to notice is the vertical black "hairline" position indicator that floats just to the left of your cursor when you are still in the process of dragging a loop into the timeline. This indicator allows you to precisely position the loop within the context of your piece. See Figure 7.16. Although it is incredibly easy to move a loop around in the timeline after it has been placed there, sometimes you'd rather do things in one step than in two. See the next section on moving, splitting, or copying loops.

Figure 7.16 The position indicator when adding loops to the timeline.

Moving, Looping, Splitting, and Copying Loops

All of the same standard editing functions that you learned about with regions apply to Apple Loops. After all, Apple Loops are nothing more than Real Instrument audio regions and Software Instrument MIDI regions once placed in the timeline, and you can interact with them in the same manner as the regions of those types that you create yourself. For a complete review of these functions, or in case you are most interested in using loops and you have not read the other chapters, refer to Chapters 5 and 6 on Real Instruments and Software Instruments and the subsections on working with regions.

You can select a loop and copy and paste it somewhere else by pressing Command+C and Command+V. You can delete a loop by selecting it and pressing Command+X or the Delete key. You can hold down the Option key and click and drag a loop to make a copy of it and move the new copy somewhere else. You can place the playhead within the region of an audio loop or a Software Instrument Apple Loop after selecting the region and press Command+T to split the region, after which you can select and move, copy, paste, delete, or further split your regions, just like with regions that are the result of recording actual audio into a track or a MIDI performance. See Table 7.1 for a list of useful keyboard shortcuts.

As with other regions, if you hover your cursor over the upper-right corner of the loop region itself, your cursor will change into a circular arrow—the looping

Table 7.1 Keyboard Shortcuts

Action	Command
Copy	Command+C
Paste	Command+V
Delete/cut	Command+X
Split	Command+T
Duplicate and move	Option-click, drag and drop

cursor. Even though you can click and drag the upper-right corner of any region in GarageBand and loop it (repeat it), Apple Loops and other audio files that are designed to be looped have the characteristic that they sound cohesive, clean, neat, in rhythm, and meant to be looped. Apple Loops will always sound like they have not been looped even when they have. This is to say, there are no botchy telltale signs of the loop itself repeating like a skipped beat, a popping sound, or another noncontiguous anomaly. See Figure 7.17.

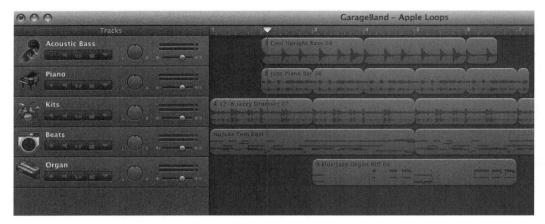

Figure 7.17 Several looped Apple Loops in the timeline.

Swapping Apple Loops

Many of the Apple Loops available in GarageBand or in any of the Jam Packs have one or more counterparts—or siblings—that are often just slight variations on a theme. Although sometimes the various versions are quite different from one another, I think this example might be best illustrated by describing a situation in which the loops in a given series *are* in fact similar, as the swapping function will most often be utilized when what you are looking for is perhaps a slight variation.

In the upper-left corner of any Apple Loop, you will see a double-headed arrow (pointing up and down) anytime a loop that you are using in the timeline has any counterparts in your library. This menu is in the same location as the Multiple Takes menu, which appears in audio regions created using the Multiple Takes function when you are recording Real Instruments or MIDI Software Instruments. (See Chapter 5, in the section called "Recording Multiple Takes.") When I say "counterparts," I'm talking about a case where you have a loop—let's say it's called Brazilian Guitar 04. This menu is accessed by clicking on the double arrows and will display all of the other loops that are in the series. You will see Brazilian Guitar 05, Brazilian Guitar 06, Brazilian Guitar 07, Brazilian Guitar 08, and so on. If you choose one of these from the menu, the entire loop region (including any number of times that you may have looped it) will be swapped out for the new loop.

For the sake of description, let's say you have the Brazilian Guitar 04 loop in the timeline, and you've repeated it four times. See Figure 7.18.

If you swap Brazilian Guitar 04 for Brazilian Guitar 08 by choosing Brazilian Guitar 08 from the Loop Selection menu (the small double-headed arrow at the top left of any loop region), all four repeats of the loop will be replaced by your new choice. If you only wanted to replace the third repeat of the loop with Brazilian Guitar 08, then

Figure 7.18 Brazilian Guitar 04, looped four times.

you'd have to perform a split of your loop between the second and third repeats and again between the third and fourth repeats. By placing the playhead at those two locations, selecting the loop region, and pressing Command+T, you will perform the splits, revealing three separate loop regions (the first lasting from the beginning of the loop to the third measure, and the second lasting from the third measure to the fourth measure, and then the fourth and final measure). Each newly split Apple Loop region will now have its own Loop Selection menu. You can change the menu selection on the third repeat of the loop to read Brazilian Guitar 08, and the musical loop that is played during that measure only will be the new Brazilian Guitar 08 loop. See Figures 7.19 through 7.21.

Figure 7.19 The original loop repeated four times and split into three pieces to isolate the third repeat for swapping to a different loop.

Figure 7.20 Choosing Brazilian Guitar 08 from the Loop Selection menu, under the double-headed arrow at the top left of the loop.

Figure 7.21 The third measure, now replaced with Brazilian Guitar 08.

Editing Software Instrument Apple Loops

Editing Software Instrument Apple Loops involves the same processes and techniques as editing any MIDI performance that you have recorded yourself. You can use all of the same cursor tools. Keyboard shortcuts apply, and you can double-click the MIDI region to open it up in the Editor. There, you can move MIDI notes around by clicking and dragging, alter the sustain of notes by clicking and dragging the tails (right edges) of the notes out to the right to lengthen them and to the left to shorten them, and make any other adjustments that you learned to make to MIDI notes in Chapter 6, in the section called "Using the Editor for Editing MIDI Information." See Figure 7.22.

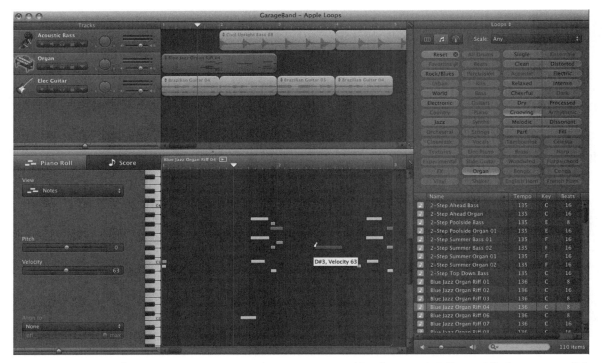

Figure 7.22 A Software Instrument Apple Loop opened in the Track Editor. All the same editing rules, features, and functions apply.

Saving and Browsing Favorites

In the course of your travels through the vast libraries of Apple Loops that you have with GarageBand and any Jam Packs or loop downloads you have installed, you are likely to encounter certain loops, sounds, and sound effects that you really like. Maybe you don't have an ideal project for their use at hand, but you might suspect that someday they may come in handy. GarageBand provides the ability to mark a given Apple Loop as a favorite. In the right-hand column of the Loop Browser, there is a column of check boxes labeled Fav. Any time you wish, you can check that check box, and it will flag that loop as one to show you at a later time, whenever you click the Favorites button in the Loop Browser in Musical Button view or Column view. Anything you have marked as a Fav will show up when you click Favorites in either view. If you would like to remove a loop that you have made a Fav in the past, simply select the Apple Loop and uncheck the box in the Fav column at the far right of the Loop Browser. See Figures 7.23 through 7.25.

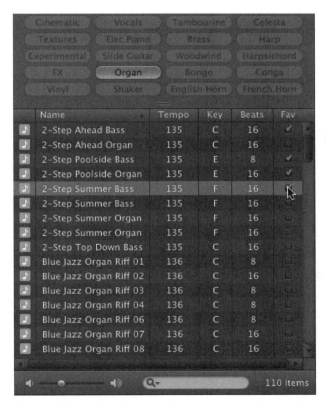

Figure 7.23 The Fav, or Favorites, check box in the Loop Browser's far-right column.

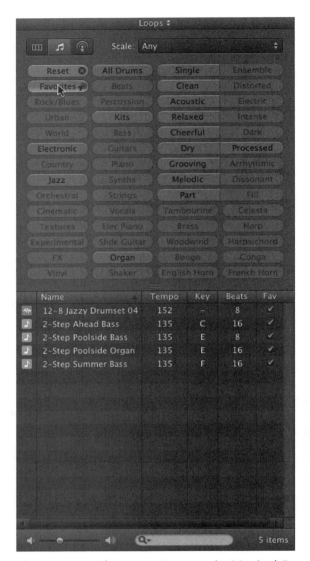

Figure 7.24 The Loop Browser in Musical Button view with Favorites selected.

Becoming a Conductor: Magic GarageBand

Constructing songs out of Apple Loops and editing them to further customize your project is an exciting way for musicians and non-musicians to create music; enhance existing music; add effects, jingles, stingers, and beds to scores or podcasts; and experiment with the endless possibilities of creative combining. GarageBand offers another way to approach assembling loops into songs or starting places for songs. This feature was introduced to GarageBand users in the '08 version and is called *Magic Garage-Band*. I will cover Magic GarageBand extensively in the next chapter. Discover how to

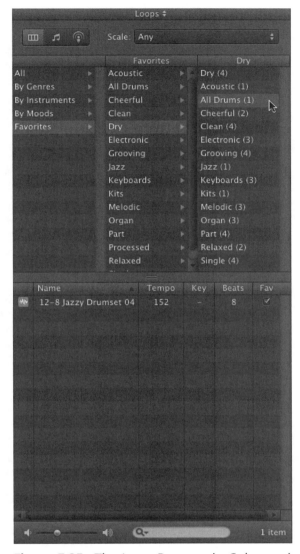

Figure 7.25 The Loop Browser in Column view with Favorites selected.

become your own bandleader and assemble the players and parts of your own backup band using GarageBand's unique and fun interface for creating your Apple Loop–based jumping-off points. You can even jam along with your Magic GarageBand band in full-screen mode for great practice and fun playing along with professionally produced grooves!

8 Magic GarageBand Jam Walkthrough

Magic GarageBand was added to the GarageBand application in iLife '08. It allows you to build up a song from predetermined "song structures" that Apple has created. The songs are each in a certain genre, and within each genre (jazz, funk, country, blues, and so on), you can make specific decisions about which instruments will be playing in the band. Magic GarageBand also allows you to choose an instrument (a Software Instrument via MIDI) to play yourself, so you can jam along with the band that you create. To start a Magic GarageBand project, launch GarageBand, and in the New Project dialog box, click Magic GarageBand in the left column and see all of the genre choices you have. See Figure 8.1.

Apple and Inspiration

One of the things I love most about Apple's software design and development team is that the products they release to the public indicate a never-ending desire to explore, create, and inspire users of their software. They are always trying new, innovative things. They seem to believe in—even directly pursue—paradigm shift. You never see an Apple software application come out in version 1.0 or 2.0 and then just languish along, relegated to a life of something seen as fine the way it is. In my opinion, Garage-Band was a fabulous application in version 2.0, as a relatively free multitrack digital recording tool included with every new Mac that was easy to learn and performed quite well even when stacked up against professional tools at 10 times the cost. Yet version 3, and most recently the versions of GarageBand in iLife '08 (version 4) and iLife '09 (version 5), have continued to push the boundaries even further.

Even though GarageBand '08 had brought more pro-level effects and new Software Instruments, plus 24-bit recording and other features that would be unheard of in most companies' consumer-level audio production products, Apple still had their finger on the pulse of the brand-new-user sector of the market. When I saw that Apple had created a new feature called Magic GarageBand, I knew in an instant that they weren't simply continuing to evolve the application with a trajectory toward becoming a pro-only tool. The addition of GarageBand Learn to Play music lessons in GarageBand '09 has further proven Apple's ability to deliver new features that invite new users and beginners into the fold. While making the application more robust and increasing

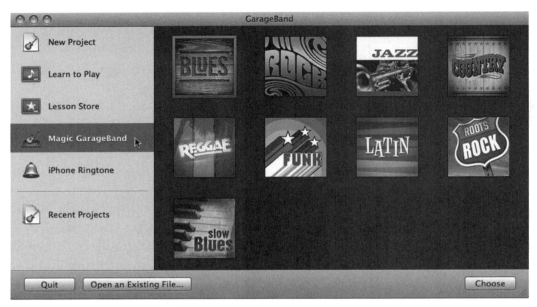

Figure 8.1 Choose Magic GarageBand from the New Project dialog box.

the quality and functionality under the hood to rival pro-level apps, they also continue to keep the new user—maybe even the non-musician—clearly in mind.

Magic GarageBand is a function—an approach, really—to creating digital music that is unprecedented. It gives you a virtual representation of a stage with the curtain closed, and like a true bandleader, a creator of songs, you get to choose the genre of the song you'd like to build, and GarageBand plays a song for you. You can then choose which instruments you want to hear and which ones to turn off. You can decide to have a certain player in the band play a different type of instrument or play his instrument in a different style. You can even play along yourself and record with the band with a Real Instrument, a MIDI Software Instrument, or a microphone. GarageBand '09 has added the ability to go full screen and jam with the band. You might make up your own lyrics and record a vocal part, play solos, or even eliminate one of the players in the band and take over his part.

Magic GarageBand is very flexible in almost every way, except for the specific grooves/chord progressions themselves—those are predetermined, and until there is a refill or Jam Pack for Magic GarageBand, the list is not very long. However, the variety is there, and all you need to do is experiment and listen. It can be really fun to feel as if you're mixing or conducting a live band. The song loops that Apple has created to make Magic GarageBand come together sound truly excellent.

Choosing a Song Genre

The genres, or styles, that GarageBand offers are listed as icons within the New Project dialog box, when you click on Magic GarageBand in the left column. Refer to Figure 8.1.

Genres or styles of music as a starting point are fairly ambiguous. For example, The Beatles, Toad the Wet Sprocket, and Porcupine Tree are all rock bands, yet they're so different it's hardly a plausible categorical statement to say they are all the same. Likewise, in Magic GarageBand, when you select Rock as your genre, for example, you sort of get what you get—a single flavor of rock. It's a good flavor, but there's only one. Magic GarageBand in GarageBand '09 presents its particular brand of jazz, funk, slow blues, and others in the way that it presents them…categorically, take it or leave it.

What the genres deliver is great for what they are, but they're rather specific and exclusive. It's almost like you're deciding what musical *stereotype* you want to play or sing over. Magic GarageBand is not a creative composition engine; it's a platform for you to experiment with hearing different sounds, being a band leader or arranger, and trying different combinations of parts and instruments, making decisions that satisfy your own whims. You can jam or sing—and by all means, record—on top of these predetermined tracks, but it's not compositionally flexible in the way that perhaps a future version of the Magic GarageBand tool might be.

Don't get me wrong; in one sense, it is very limited. But in another sense, I actually think it's marvelous, and for people who don't play a lot of instruments or who might not be proficient at starting a song from scratch, it's an excellent way to learn how to do this stuff—arrange, record, mix, and edit—and also to have a tight band to play along with, seasoned to taste.

Inasmuch as they are, in fact, different musical styles, the genres provided get you in the ballpark of a mood, theme, or feel, but they don't allow you to actually customize the musical composition or performances of the song itself. I don't want to sound too down on Magic GarageBand—I actually think it's fantastic for what it is—but I don't want to give you false hope about what it's like to work with a Magic GarageBand "band."

Choosing a genre is a simple matter of clicking on one of the genre icons. When it's selected, a blue outline will surround the genre square. When you mouse over one of the genre icons, you will see a Preview button. Click it, and the basic Magic GarageBand song will begin to play. Click again to stop the preview from playing. See Figure 8.2.

When you decide what genre you'd like to start with, click the Choose button at the far right of the bottom bar to open Magic GarageBand with the genre you have selected, or simply double-click the genre icon.

The genres available are:

- Blues
- Rock
- Jazz
- Country

Figure 8.2 The Preview button on a Magic GarageBand genre in the New Project dialog box.

- Reggae
- Funk
- Latin
- Roots Rock
- Slow Blues

The main window when you are in a Magic GarageBand project is called the *stage*. All the instruments you are using will be displayed on a virtual stage, with lighting, a brick backdrop, and a wooden stage floor. Within the stage area of the window, there are a few items you can interact with. One is the full screen button. (See Figure 8.3 in the lower-right portion of the stage floor, in the shadows.) Clicking this button will open Magic GarageBand into its new full-screen mode, allowing you to enjoy the lack of any distraction from your computer desktop or any other windows you may have open and get down to jamming.

Additionally, each instrument has an indicator that appears when you mouse over the instrument. The spotlight shines on the instrument, and its name appears above it. Once you click on the instrument, the name indicator persists, allowing you to click its disclosure triangle to access mute, solo, and volume controls for that individual instrument, essentially allowing you to mix your band while still in stage mode. In front of the stage—underneath it, in your GarageBand interface—there are several elements you can interact with. This are all outlined in Figure 8.3 and shown close up in Figure 8.4. These elements include your Transport controls, such as playhead, arrangement indicators, play, stop, and record, master volume, the snippet and entire song toggle (for focusing on a single part of the song over and over), as well as your instrument selectors, allowing you to change the style of part that your selected instrument will be playing in your band. Finally, in the lower right is the Open in GarageBand button, which you can click once you've made all your selections and load the entire band into a standard GarageBand song project window, allowing you to record additional parts, change the arrangement, mix, add effects and other sounds, and so on.

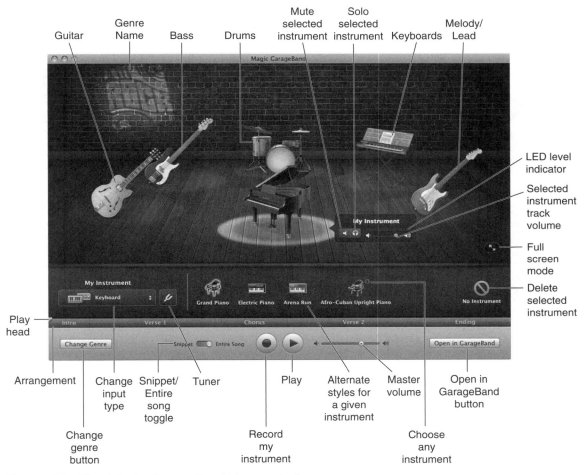

Figure 8.3 The Magic GarageBand stage window.

Figure 8.4 The controls interface at the bottom of the Magic GarageBand stage.

The Genres and Style Options in Magic GarageBand

Let's take a look at each of the genres in Magic GarageBand a little more closely. Each instrument in the band has a series of different styles that can be played. Each genre listed in the following sections will be followed by a list of the instruments and styles available to you.

The best way to experience these variations is to click on them in GarageBand and experiment for yourself, but I'll list them here.

Blues

When you select the Blues genre, your stage will open up with the instruments shown in Figure 8.5.

Figure 8.5   The Blues genre stage in Audition mode with the new Shuffle Instruments button.

Blues Guitar Styles

Figure 8.6   The Blues Guitar styles in Magic GarageBand.

Blues Bass Styles

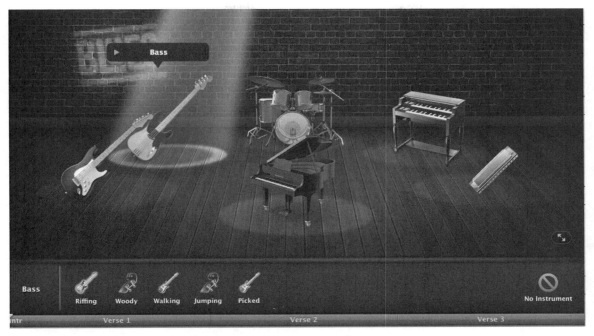

Figure 8.7   The Blues Bass styles in Magic GarageBand.

Blues Drums Styles

Figure 8.8   The Blues Drums styles in Magic GarageBand.

Blues Keyboard Styles

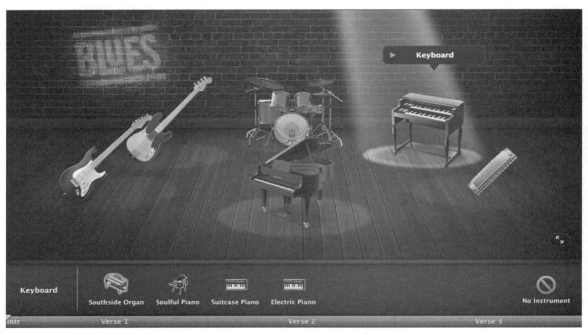

Figure 8.9　The Blues Keyboard styles in Magic GarageBand.

Blues Melody Styles

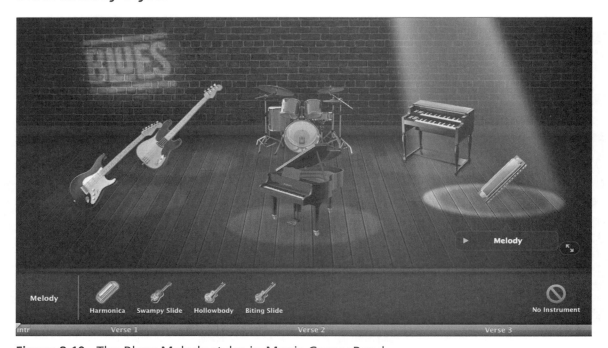

Figure 8.10　The Blues Melody styles in Magic GarageBand.

Blues My Instrument Styles

Each genre provides for a series of styles for My Instrument. These are the instruments that you can select to play along with. There is further discussion later in this chapter, in the section called "Auditioning a Band and Creating Your Project," about the role of the My Instrument styles in each of the genres.

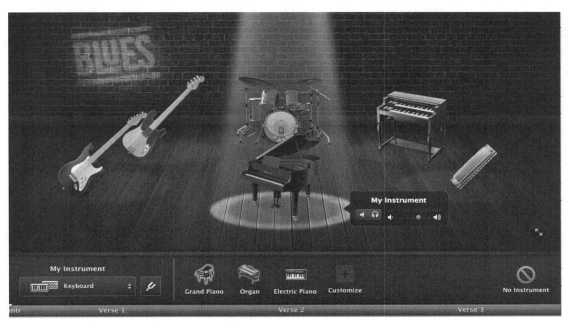

Figure 8.11 The Blues My Instrument styles in Magic GarageBand.

Rock

When you select the Rock genre, your stage will open up with the instruments shown in Figure 8.12.

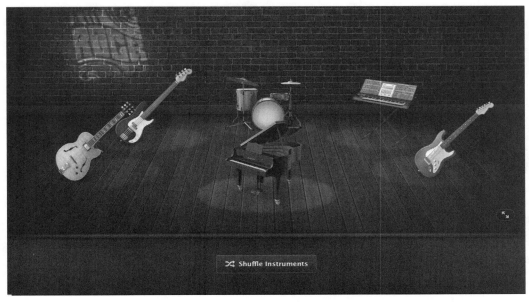

Figure 8.12 The Rock genre stage in Audition mode with the new Shuffle Instruments button.

Rock Guitar Styles

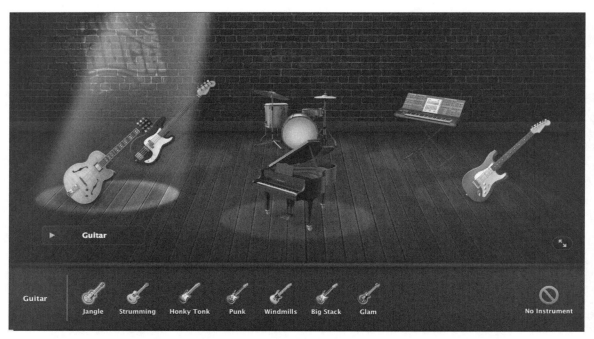

Figure 8.13 The Rock Guitar styles in Magic GarageBand.

Rock Bass Styles

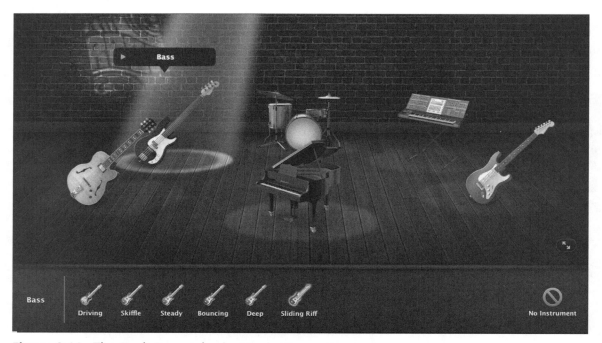

Figure 8.14 The Rock Bass styles in Magic GarageBand.

Rock Drums Styles

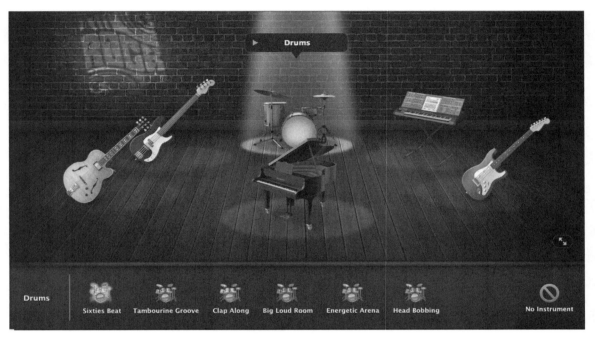

Figure 8.15 The Rock Drums styles in Magic GarageBand.

Rock Keyboard Styles

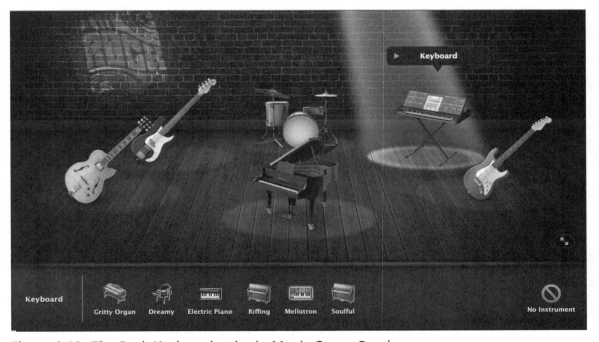

Figure 8.16 The Rock Keyboard styles in Magic GarageBand.

Rock Melody Styles

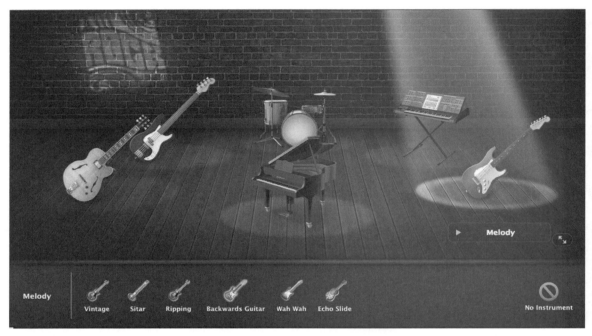

Figure 8.17 The Rock Melody styles in Magic GarageBand.

Rock My Instrument Styles

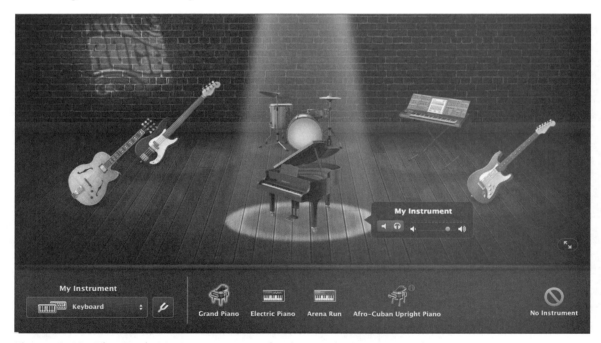

Figure 8.18 The Rock My Instrument styles in Magic GarageBand.

Jazz

When you select the Jazz genre, your stage will open up with the instruments shown in Figure 8.19.

Figure 8.19   The Jazz genre stage in Audition mode with the new Shuffle Instruments button.

Jazz Guitar Styles

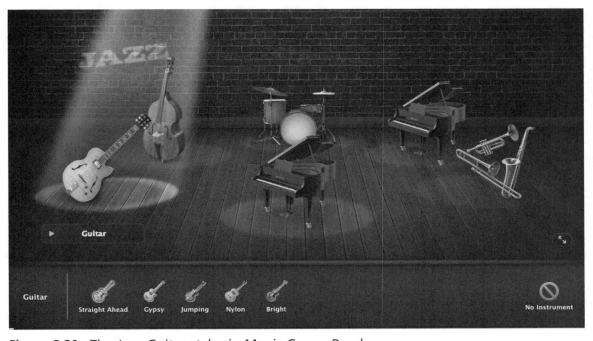

Figure 8.20   The Jazz Guitar styles in Magic GarageBand.

Jazz Bass Styles

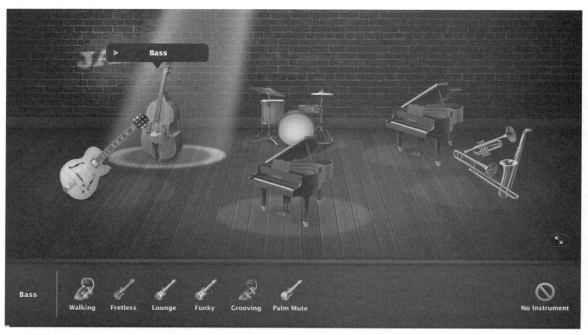

Figure 8.21 The Jazz Bass styles in Magic GarageBand.

Jazz Drums Styles

Figure 8.22 The Jazz Drums styles in Magic GarageBand.

Jazz Keyboard Styles

Figure 8.23   The Jazz Keyboard styles in Magic GarageBand.

Jazz Melody Styles

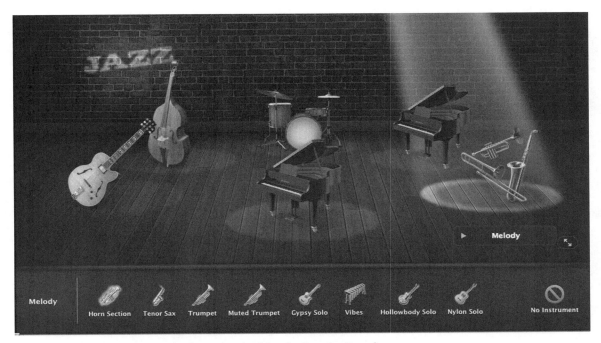

Figure 8.24   The Jazz Melody styles in Magic GarageBand.

Jazz My Instrument Styles

Figure 8.25 The Jazz My Instrument styles in Magic GarageBand.

Country

When you select the Country genre, your stage will open up with the instruments shown in Figure 8.26.

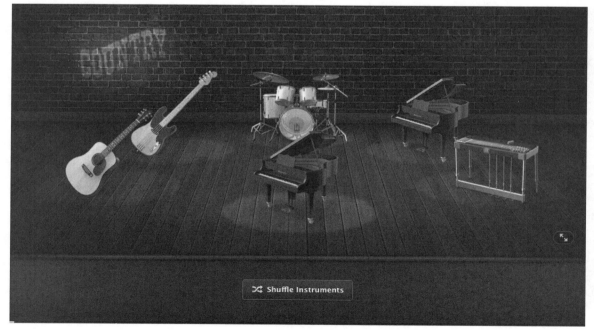

Figure 8.26 The Country genre stage in Audition mode with the new Shuffle Instruments button.

Country Guitar Styles

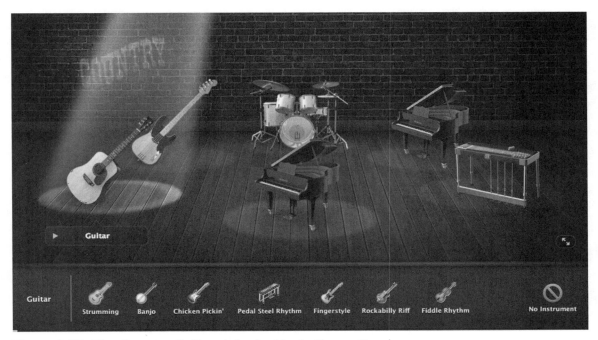

Figure 8.27 The Country Guitar styles in Magic GarageBand.

Country Bass Styles

Figure 8.28 The Country Bass styles in Magic GarageBand.

Country Drums Styles

Figure 8.29   The Country Drums styles in Magic GarageBand.

Country Keyboard Styles

Figure 8.30   The Country Keyboard styles in Magic GarageBand.

Country Melody Styles

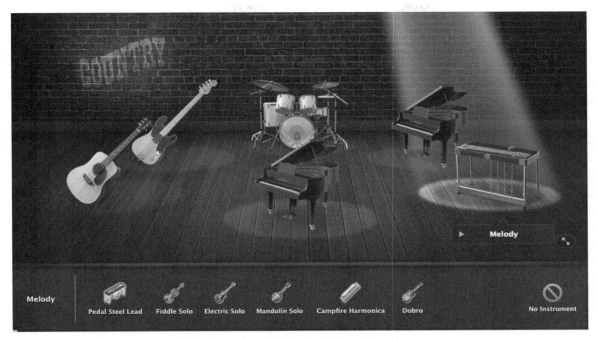

Figure 8.31   The Country Melody styles in Magic GarageBand.

Country My Instrument Styles

Figure 8.32   The Country My Instrument styles in Magic GarageBand.

Reggae

When you select the Reggae genre, your stage will open up with the instruments shown in Figure 8.33.

Figure 8.33 The Reggae genre stage in Audition mode with the new Shuffle Instruments button.

Reggae Guitar Styles

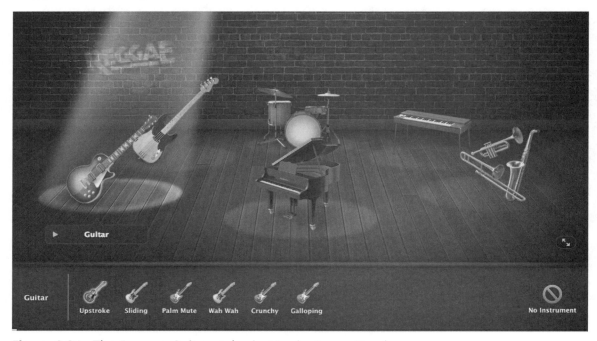

Figure 8.34 The Reggae Guitar styles in Magic GarageBand.

Reggae Bass Styles

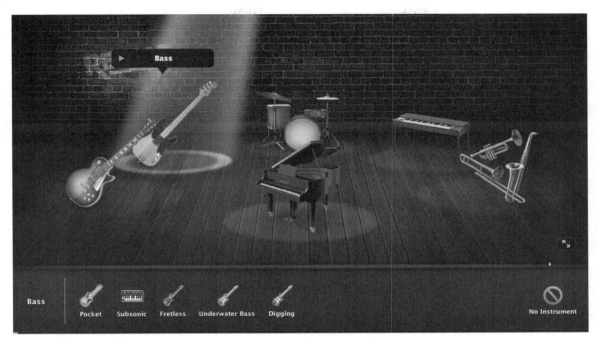

Figure 8.35   The Reggae Bass styles in Magic GarageBand.

Reggae Drums Styles

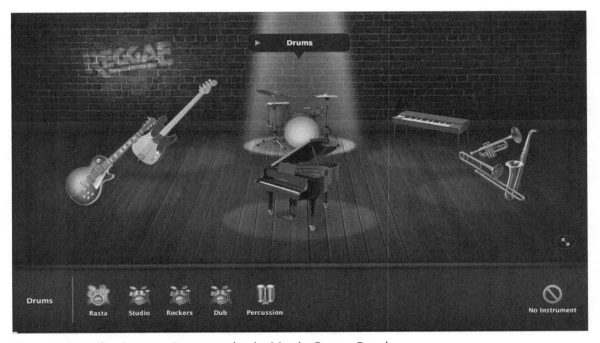

Figure 8.36   The Reggae Drums styles in Magic GarageBand.

Reggae Keyboard Styles

Figure 8.37 The Reggae Keyboard styles in Magic GarageBand.

Reggae Melody Styles

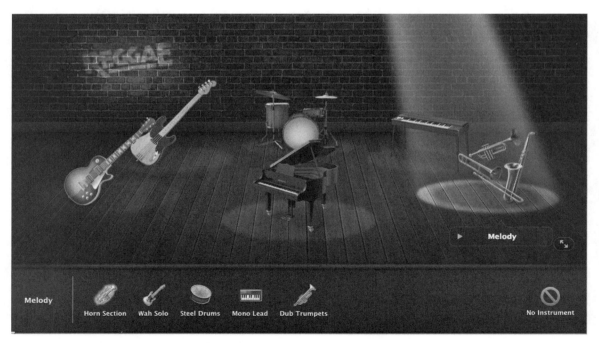

Figure 8.38 The Reggae Melody styles in Magic GarageBand.

Reggae My Instrument Styles

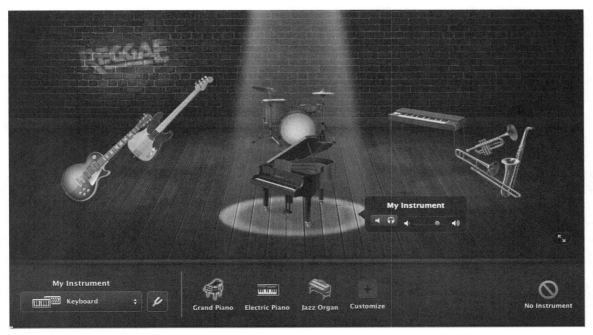

Figure 8.39   The Reggae My Instrument styles in Magic GarageBand.

Funk

When you select the Funk genre, your stage will open up with the instruments shown in Figure 8.40.

Figure 8.40   The Funk genre stage in Audition mode with the new Shuffle Instruments button.

Funk Guitar Styles

Figure 8.41 The Funk Guitar styles in Magic GarageBand.

Funk Bass Styles

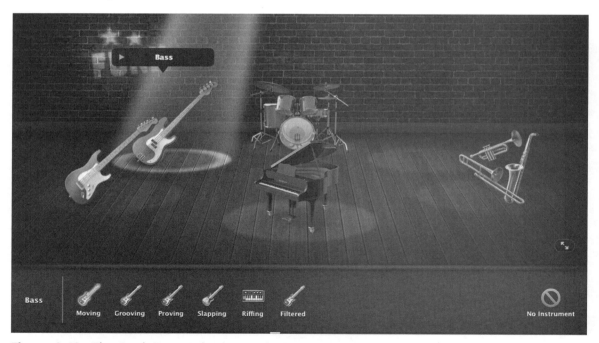

Figure 8.42 The Funk Bass styles in Magic GarageBand.

Funk Drums Styles

Figure 8.43   The Funk Drums styles in Magic GarageBand.

Funk Keyboard Styles

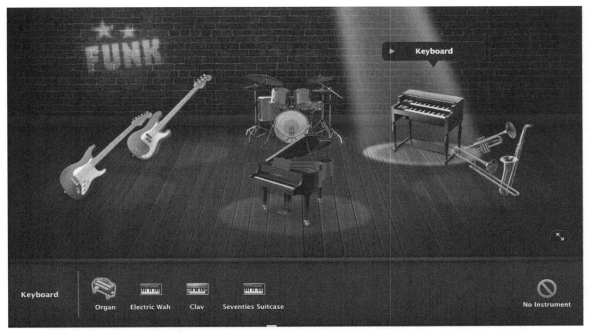

Figure 8.44   The Funk Keyboard styles in Magic GarageBand.

Funk Melody Styles

Figure 8.45 The Funk Melody styles in Magic GarageBand.

Funk My Instrument Styles

Figure 8.46 The Funk My Instrument styles in Magic GarageBand.

Latin

When you select the Latin genre, your stage will open up with the instruments shown in Figure 8.47.

Figure 8.47 The Latin genre stage in Audition mode with the new Shuffle Instruments button.

Latin Guitar Styles

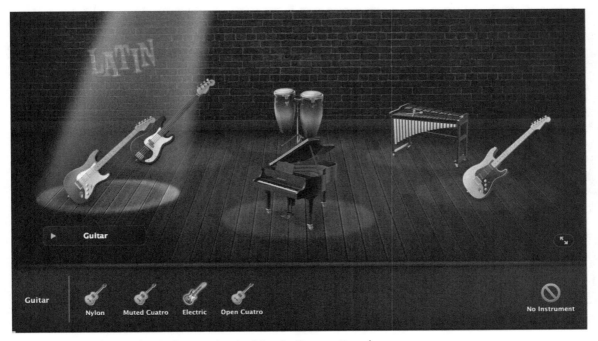

Figure 8.48 The Latin Guitar styles in Magic GarageBand.

Latin Bass Styles

Figure 8.49 The Latin Bass styles in Magic GarageBand.

Latin Drums Styles

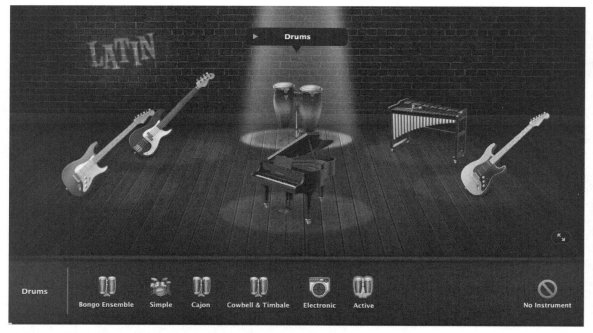

Figure 8.50 The Latin Drums styles in Magic GarageBand.

Latin Keyboard Styles

Figure 8.51   The Latin Keyboard styles in Magic GarageBand.

Latin Melody Styles

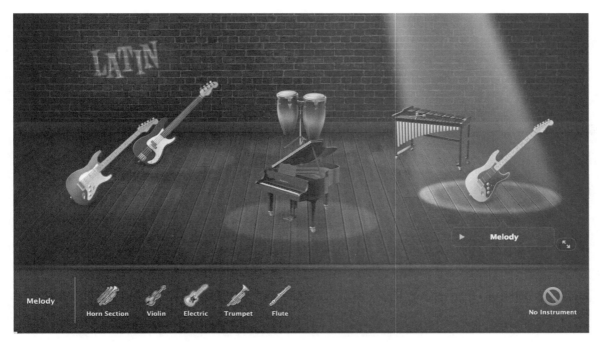

Figure 8.52   The Latin Melody styles in Magic GarageBand.

Latin My Instrument Styles

Figure 8.53 The Latin My Instrument styles in Magic GarageBand.

Roots Rock

When you select the Roots Rock genre, your stage will open up with the instruments shown in Figure 8.54.

Figure 8.54 The Roots Rock genre stage in Audition mode with the new Shuffle Instruments button.

Roots Rock Guitar Styles

Figure 8.55 The Roots Rock Guitar styles in Magic GarageBand.

Roots Rock Bass Styles

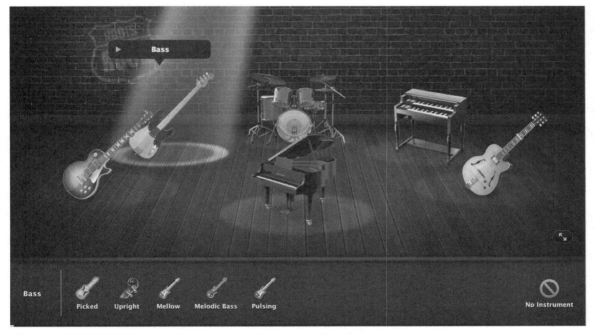

Figure 8.56 The Roots Rock Bass styles in Magic GarageBand.

Roots Rock Drums Styles

Figure 8.57   The Roots Rock Drums styles in Magic GarageBand.

Roots Rock Keyboard Styles

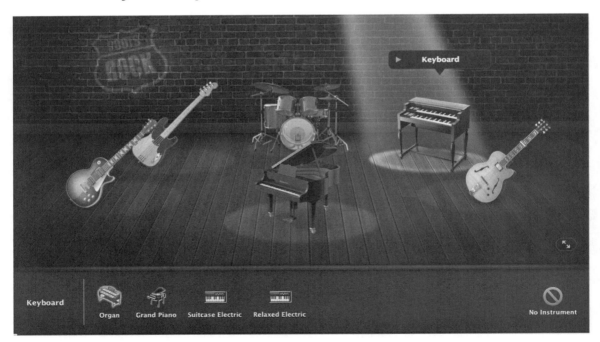

Figure 8.58   The Roots Rock Keyboard styles in Magic GarageBand.

Roots Rock Melody Styles

Figure 8.59 The Roots Rock Melody styles in Magic GarageBand.

Roots Rock My Instrument Styles

Figure 8.60 The Roots Rock My Instrument styles in Magic GarageBand.

Slow Blues

When you select the Slow Blues genre, your stage will open up with the instruments shown in Figure 8.61.

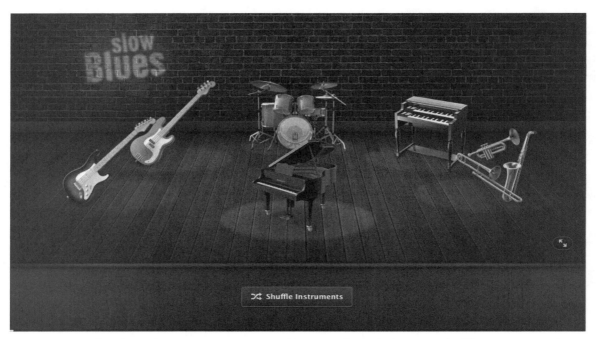

Figure 8.61   The Slow Blues genre stage in Audition mode with the new Shuffle Instruments button.

Slow Blues Guitar Styles

Figure 8.62   The Slow Blues Guitar styles in Magic GarageBand.

Slow Blues Bass Styles

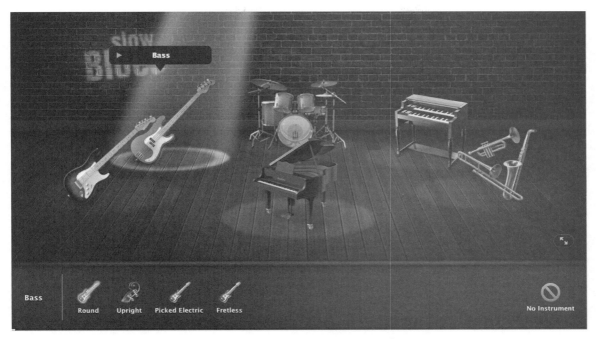

Figure 8.63   The Slow Blues Bass styles in Magic GarageBand.

Slow Blues Drums Styles

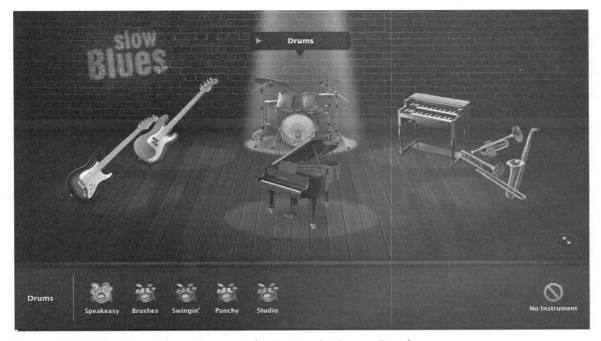

Figure 8.64   The Slow Blues Drums styles in Magic GarageBand.

Slow Blues Keyboard Styles

Figure 8.65 The Slow Blues Keyboard styles in Magic GarageBand.

Slow Blues Melody Styles

Figure 8.66 The Slow Blues Melody styles in Magic GarageBand.

Slow Blues My Instrument Styles

Figure 8.67 The Slow Blues My Instrument styles in Magic GarageBand.

Auditioning a Band and Creating Your Project

When you have chosen your desired genre, click Audition, and the curtain will pull back to reveal your band on stage. Detailed graphics are enhanced by a mouse rollover effect that drops a spotlight on each instrument and prints the name of the instrument underneath. These instrument names are general and ostensibly name the "player" in the band (such as Drums), more so than they name the specific instrument or style of playing (in the case of Drums in the Blues genre, you get the drumming styles of Road-house, Sidestick, Brushes, Swinging, and so on). When you click on one of the instruments (as shown in Figures 8.6 through 8.67), the styles of playing and the types of instruments available will appear in a list underneath the stage, or in the pit, as it were.

Each genre provides you with five instruments, which are Guitar, Bass, Drums, Keyboard, and Melody. There is also a spot at center stage for you to personally occupy, called My Instrument. The instrument/style options for each player are pretty diverse, and it's fun to click on each instrument and make choices from the different options to hear how the whole band sounds together with each new style of instrument you click on. You can click None in the pit to essentially mute an instrument during the audition. If you want to hear just one instrument by itself to see what it's doing and how its musicality and tonality might be affecting the entire band, you will need to click on each instrument that you want to mute and click the None selection in the pit.

If you want to change genre and try something else before committing to creating your project, you can click the Change Genre button at the lower-left of the bottom bar.

This will take you back to the previous screen, where you were able to choose your genre, and you can click a new one—sampling it if you like—and then audition that band and start making your selections with that new genre regarding what instruments you would like to play and what style their parts should be.

If you click on My Instrument, one of the choices is Live Performance, which will allow you to play a Real Instrument performance with the song once you create your project. The Audition mode part of the process of using Magic GarageBand is where you will make all of your decisions about what the constituent elements of your project will be. When you are satisfied that you have the genre, instrumentation, and style nailed down, all you have to do is click Create Project in the lower right, where the Audition button was in the genre selection screen.

The following sections detail the basic song structures provided for each genre in Magic GarageBand, with their arrange regions in place, showing you what structural song elements are included in each genre's song by default.

Basic Blues Song Structure in Magic GarageBand

This is the song structure that Magic GarageBand provides when you go with defaults and create a Blues project. This structure has a brief one-bar intro for you to fill in any way you like, followed by three verses, all with some variation of the loops that are used—these are akin to the loop counterparts or siblings I mentioned in Chapter 7. See Figure 8.68.

Figure 8.68 The Blues song structure in Magic GarageBand.

Basic Rock Song Structure in Magic GarageBand

This is the song structure that Magic GarageBand provides when you go with defaults and create a Rock project. This one has an intro and a verse-chorus-verse pattern followed by a structural section called an *ending*. I referred to this structural element earlier as the *outro*. Outro is not a real word (given that there's no such word as *outroduction*), but it's one of those words that if you ever spend any time playing with other musicians, it will come up. It's essentially an opposing extrapolation of the term *intro*. See Figure 8.69.

Figure 8.69 The Rock song structure in Magic GarageBand.

Basic Jazz Song Structure in Magic GarageBand

This is the song structure that Magic GarageBand provides when you go with defaults and create a Jazz project. As I mentioned earlier, sometimes jazz tunes have a head, or an A section, and then there are three B sections (Magic GarageBand calls them *choruses*, which in instrumental jazz is a fair term for the sections that all the players play over), followed by a repeat of the head, which has an ending incorporated into it. In this case, it's a nice, big hit that everyone can blast on. See Figure 8.70.

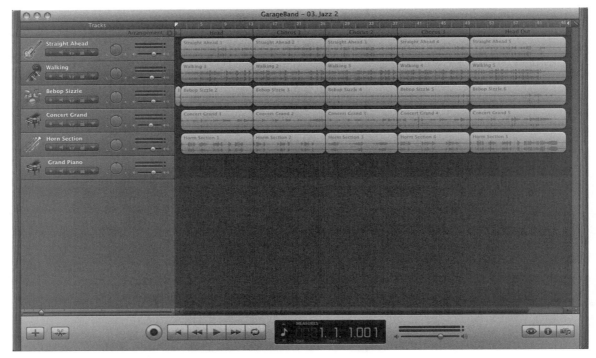

Figure 8.70 The Jazz song structure in Magic GarageBand.

Basic Country Song Structure in Magic GarageBand

This is the song structure that Magic GarageBand provides when you go with defaults and create a Country project. This is essentially three repeats of the verse-and-refrain methodology. Country tunes are often story songs, and this structure reflects the multiple-verse format, which would be filled with lyrics that tell a story of some kind, and then a refrain for everyone to be able to sing as some kind of catchy hook at the end of each pass. See Figure 8.71.

Basic Reggae Song Structure in Magic GarageBand

This is the song structure that Magic GarageBand provides when you go with defaults and create a Reggae project. This structure, like many of those created by Magic Garage-Band, is ready to be Option-click-and-dragged out to whatever length you like, ripe for jammin'. This Reggae tune comes with a verse, a chorus, and a verse, and the second verse has some elements that make a nice ending. You can copy and paste these regions, just like in normal recording and editing mode, and place them wherever they need to be. Think "repurposing" when you are playing with your Magic Garage-Band song files. See Figure 8.72.

Basic Funk Song Structure in Magic GarageBand

This is the song structure that Magic GarageBand provides when you go with defaults and create a Funk project. The Funk song ships with an intro, verse, bridge, short

Figure 8.71 The Country song structure in Magic GarageBand.

Figure 8.72 The Reggae song structure in Magic GarageBand.

verse, and ending. There is lots to play with here and good space for soloing—instrumentally or vocally! See Figure 8.73.

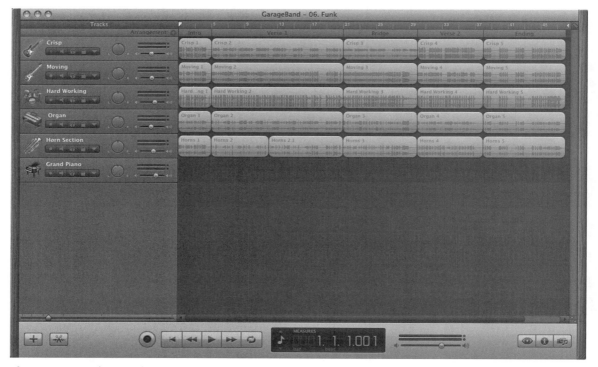

Figure 8.73 The Funk song structure in Magic GarageBand.

Basic Latin Song Structure in Magic GarageBand

This is the song structure that Magic GarageBand provides when you go with defaults and create a Latin project. This song has a verse, verse, bridge, verse structure, and like many of these songs, endless opportunities for taking extended breaks or solos. These Magic GarageBand songs are fantastic for practicing your lead playing. It's like karaoke without the "everybody knows this song" element, so it becomes a good way to practice your chops with no need for a real band or for trying to emulate the way the original band did the song. Throw those headphones on, duplicate out a 15-minute version of one of these grooves, and go to it!

A nifty Magic GarageBand hack is to create one band in a particular genre, create the project, and save it. Then create another project with the same genre but different instruments and styles, and then open the second project and copy all the regions (by pressing Command+A to select all and Command+C to copy). Next, go back into the first project, position your playhead at the end of the whole song, and paste (Command+V) the regions into the tracks. Now you have twice as much music to use as your building blocks to "compose" your song! Move them around, copy and paste, and make different combinations than Apple ever intended. See Figure 8.74.

Figure 8.74 The Latin song structure in Magic GarageBand.

Basic Roots Rock Song Structure in Magic GarageBand

This is the song structure that Magic GarageBand provides when you go with defaults and create a Roots Rock project. This song has an intro, verse, chorus, bridge, second verse, and outro to play with. See Figure 8.75.

Basic Slow Blues Song Structure in Magic GarageBand

This is the song structure that Magic GarageBand provides when you go with defaults and create a Slow Blues project. This Blues song comes with an intro, a verse, a second shorter verse, and an ending. Build it up into a long, slow blues tune and play that slide or mouth harp until your neighbors scream! See Figure 8.76.

Jamming Along and Overdubbing More Parts

New to Magic GarageBand for GarageBand '09 is the ability to jam along with the band in full-screen stage mode and even record your parts. You don't need to play along in this mode or record your part in full-screen mode; it's just been made available to you if that's how you would like to work with Magic GarageBand. You can assign yourself an instrument for your My Instrument part by selecting My Instrument on the stage and selecting a different instrument from the options list at the bottom of the interface. The icons that are shown are just the instruments and styles that have been predetermined to "fit well" within the genre that you have chosen. You are not

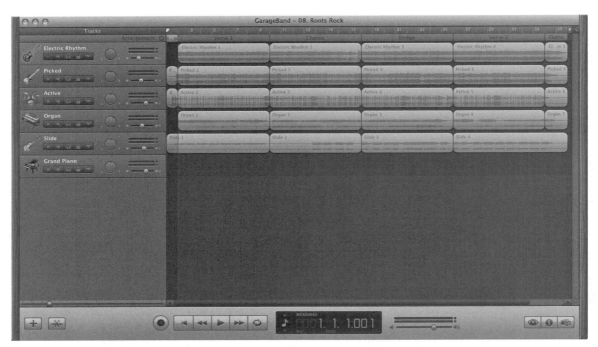

Figure 8.75 The Roots Rock song structure in Magic GarageBand.

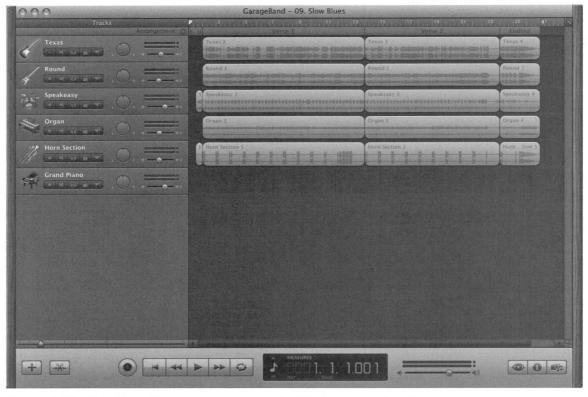

Figure 8.76 The Slow Blues song structure in Magic GarageBand.

limited to those, however; you can click the Customize button and gain access to the full list of all GarageBand instruments. Choose an instrument type from the drop-down menu at the top of the Customize Instrument window and then select your style from the list to load it into Magic GarageBand (see Figure 8.77).

Figure 8.77 The Customize Instrument selection window in Magic GarageBand.

Once you have selected a custom instrument, that instrument's icon appears in the list below, with a small "i" icon to its upper right. To select a new custom instrument or to adjust the settings for the instrument you chose, simply click the "i" to access the Customize Instrument window again (see Figure 8.78.)

Figure 8.78 Click the "i" to further customize your instrument choice.

If you would like to record your part with the band in the stage or full-screen mode, you can make sure that your MIDI controller, guitar, or microphone is connected and choose your input type for My Instrument in the menu on the lower left of the Magic Garage-Band window. By default, it's set to Keyboard. Other choices are Guitar, External Microphone, or External Guitar. To use a tuner to tune your guitar, click the Tuner icon, just to the right of the My Instrument input selection menu (see Figure 8.79).

If you would like to play along with the band, you can press the Play button in the Magic GarageBand controls bar and begin playing via the input type that you have selected in the My Instrument input type selection menu. If you'd like to record while

Figure 8.79 Choose your My Instrument input type or tune your guitar or any instrument being picked up by your external microphone.

you jam along, just press the Record button instead. Once you have recorded a part, when you move on to the next section on loading your band and song into Garage-Band, your part will appear in the project in the track for the instrument you chose.

Open in GarageBand

Once you have made all of your decisions about your band, you can click Open in GarageBand. When you have clicked Open in GarageBand, GarageBand will open a standard song project window and create all of the individual tracks needed for the band, instrument styles, parts, and tracks (including a mixture of Real Instrument and Software Instrument tracks) that you have customized. The song will be arranged in the timeline using arrangement markers (as we will cover in the next chapter). At this point, you have access to all of the normal functionality of GarageBand, including muting, soloing, recording, playing, adjusting volume, applying effects, adding loops, editing MIDI and audio regions—it's all there. Everything you've learned about GarageBand up to this point (and more) is available to you. Magic GarageBand is merely a different way to get tracks of music *into* GarageBand to work with, so now that they're here, it's time to work! It's as though you tracked all these individual performances, and they're ready to be added to or mixed for completion.

As I mentioned, you can add Apple Loops, you can split tracks and delete sections of tracks, and most importantly, perhaps, you can create *new* tracks to play into. You can create Real Instrument tracks and play along with the song for practice or recording. For example, you could create a new Real Instrument track for your electric guitar and create some solos and lead licks to go over the song. You could even grab a microphone, create a new Real Instrument track, and write some lyrics. Or, you could use someone else's and sing a vocal part, and even lay down some backing vocals.

Adding a MIDI part is just as easy. Create a new Software Instrument track with your MIDI keyboard connected, choose a Software Instrument, put the playhead at the beginning of the song by pressing the Home key or by clicking and dragging it there manually, enable recording on that track, and start recording by pressing the R key or by clicking the Record button at the bottom of the interface. Then you can start jamming along with your new song and go back and adjust your MIDI performance with quantizing or by adding and deleting notes. And you have a backup band to practice or play along with.

It's even worth experimenting with just using one of the tracks Magic GarageBand creates for you—such as the drums, for example—and creating your own entire song around that one drum part using the method I've just described. It's incredibly flexible and an awful lot of fun. You can think of the Magic GarageBand band as your idea generator and style guide (something like a wizard or stock template) and then fill in the slots with your own creativity.

One thing that is fun to try is to take the genre and form that are provided and, by selective muting and soloing, learn the part that is provided and then change it to suit your own desire and play along until you are practiced. Then mute the part you're replacing and re-record a new part over it. By the time you are finished, you could replace all of the elements of the entire song with your own parts and mute all the parts that came from Magic GarageBand.

Magic GarageBand has a lot of potential to be used in some very creative ways, and I encourage you to try anything that you are inspired to try, no matter what it might be. It's a jumping-off point, and I expect it will only get more interesting and flexible as newer versions are developed. If you like where Magic GarageBand is going, but you have some suggestions or ideas, one thing you can do is go to Apple's website and submit some user feedback for a particular product. The URL for the GarageBand feedback page is www.apple.com/feedback/garageband.html. The link to the main page where you can choose your software or hardware and then submit specific feedback on any Apple product is www.apple.com/feedback.

Another thing you can do is visit http://discussions.apple.com and follow the navigation folder links on the left side of the website to get to GarageBand '09. (The actual complete URL is http://discussions.apple.com/forum.jspa?forumID=1308.) Then, you can make a posting there. Maybe someone at Apple will read it. Nothing is a guarantee, but you never know…your feature request might already be something that you can do with GarageBand, and someone will post a reply and give you some direction.

Changing Keys and Tempos

Once you have opened your song in GarageBand, you can use the Transport controls' Time view to alter your key and tempo. If the Magic GarageBand song is too slow or too fast for the idea you have in mind or for the type of approach you want to take for singing or playing with the song, you can use the tempo slider to increase or decrease the tempo. One thing to be careful of, however, is that the further away from the original Magic GarageBand tempo you go, the more obvious to your ears it will be that you have changed the tempo. If you change it by 20 or more beats per minute, you will start to hear little breakups in the quality of the audio. It might sound a little like it's skipping or there are some herky-jerky qualities to the sound overall. As I've suggested before and as I'm sure you would assume, if it sounds good to your ears, go for it—and if it sounds bad…well, you might decide to back off your alteration just a bit. See Figure 8.80.

Figure 8.80 Use the tempo slider to adjust the tempo of your Magic GarageBand song.

The same goes for changing keys. If the song is a bit too high or too low for you to sing to, you can change the key to find a more comfortable range in which to sing. This can also be helpful if you are playing a fixed-key instrument along with your song. Some examples of this might be a harmonica, a dulcimer, or an Irish flute. Instruments like these are usually in a specific key. A didgeridoo is the same way. They play well in certain keys and not so well in others. You can use the Key menu in the Transport area of the GarageBand interface to change the key of your Magic GarageBand song. As with the tempo changes, key changes that are several steps away from the original key start to sound a little processed, but if you use your ears and it sounds good to you, who am I to tell you not to go for it? See Figure 8.81.

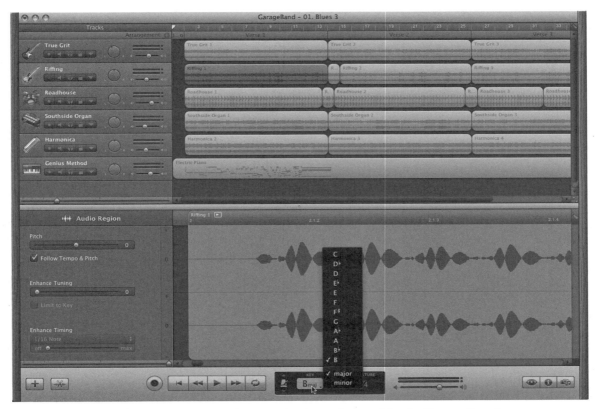

Figure 8.81 Use the Key menu to change the key of your Magic GarageBand song.

Constructing Your Own Arrangements

Magic GarageBand builds your song projects with the sections laid out in arrangements. That row of information at the top of the Track Region window in a project created by Magic GarageBand shows you where the verses, the chorus, and so on are and allows you to deconstruct the arrangement provided and drag sections around, duplicate them, or delete them altogether. In the next chapter, you'll learn how to use the tools that allow you to create those arrangement markers for yourself in your own projects and how to work with them and move them around. You'll see how easy it can be to solve a situation like, "Whoa, I think we really need a fourth verse here!" With a few clicks, drags, and keyboard commands, you can make it happen!

9 Arrangements

A very powerful feature in GarageBand, introduced in '08, enables you to arrange your song into sections and label them. These types of labels are often known as *markers* in the digital recording software realm, and the function's presence in an application usually refers to the user's ability to create a track that has no audio in it but that does contain information about where you are in the song. You could conceivably name these sections anything you desire, but there is a common system of nomenclature that has its inherent flexibilities and limitations, and we will cover that throughout this chapter. Some of these common names for song sections are verse, bridge, and chorus. The use of the word "arrangement" can be misleading—it indeed makes sense to arrange your song's parts or sections into a certain specific order, but the word "arrangement" in music composition has traditionally had another meaning.

Song Form and Song Arrangement

Let's play the semantics game for a moment, and then we'll roll along with the terminology that Apple has decided to use in GarageBand, since that is the focus of this book. It's sort of an argument between the term "form" and the term "arrangement" that I am referring to here. I feel it's important to make these distinctions when they are relevant and say that, for the record, I'm not sure why Apple allows these kinds of anomalies to stand, just for the sake of making something simple. On a personal note, the thing that is truly funny to me is that for years I used the term "arrangement" (incorrectly) to describe this same thing. The aspect of songwriting, composition, and song structure that I'm referring to (by any name you like, apparently) is what is known officially as the *form* of the song. I will submit, however, that it's possible this is what some call *language change*. If you say "arrangement," and everyone interprets the meaning to be "the order of verses, choruses, and so on," then you have new usage.

In common practice, the term "arrangement" usually is used to describe the process of taking existing musical material, making decisions about other instruments that might be used to play on the piece, and specifically deciding what they will be playing musically. Another term that has been traditionally used to describe this process is "orchestration." The American Federation of Musicians defines arranging as "the art of preparing and adapting an already written composition for presentation in other than its original form. (In this definition, the word "form" does not necessarily refer to structure; it means overall original presentation or nature.) An arrangement may include reharmonization, paraphrasing, and/or development of a composition, so that it fully represents the melodic, harmonic and rhythmic structure."

The form, as I am using the term here, is the way in which the sections of the songs are ordered, or physically arranged in relation to one another. And this is where the terminology blunder comes into play. The verb "to arrange" makes sense because you are making decisions about what comes first, what comes next, and so on. For instance, you're deciding what comes after the first chorus. Is it a vamp? Maybe it goes directly into the second verse. Or is there a guitar solo and *then* the second verse? This could be described by using the term "arranging the song." Apple, in fact, calls this process "arranging" in GarageBand and includes something called the Arrange Track for you to use in organizing, naming, keeping track, and even rearranging the sections of your song. In reality, in the musical lexicon, this is not called the arrangement of the song; it's called the form—or even more loosely, the structure. The form is a description of what comes first and what comes next in terms of compositional sections.

Keep in mind that on some level these terms are arbitrary, and the composer of the song has a right to call the sections anything he or she wants to call them. However, you might refer to a section as the pre-chorus, whereas someone else talking about your song might call it the bridge. At the end of the day, it doesn't matter what the sections are called, because it's all about you knowing what they are. Naming them in the Arrange Track in GarageBand (to bring this discussion back around) is a functional and organizational act only and is really for your use. Within GarageBand, this process allows you to very easily rearrange the form at the drop of a hat by clicking and dragging the chorus, for example, from one location and moving it to another location within the Arrange Track.

The only other bona fide purpose for naming the sections of your song form is communication. If you are playing with other musicians, it's convenient and coherent to say, "Hey guys, let's take it from the beginning of the third verse all the way through the piano solo one more time." If you were to say this, and a structure had been agreed upon prior to the statement being made, the whole band would know exactly what to do. In jazz music, the sections are often just labeled with a letter—the A section or the B section, for example. Often there is even something called the *head*, which in jazz form usually refers to the main melodic section at the beginning of the song—the motif around which the whole piece is constructed. In an instrumental jazz tune, the head is the section of the form at the beginning that everyone recognizes. It's the tune.

Some examples of words commonly used to denote sections of a song's form (and some rather loose definitions) might be:

- **Intro.** This, of course, refers to the introduction. The term *intro* is usually used to describe the first thing that happens in the song. It could be a fade-in, or it could be a solo instrument (a piano, for example) that comes in by itself at the beginning.

- **Vamp.** This is a musical figure, usually a fairly short sequence of chords or rhythms that are repeated an indeterminate number of times. This is another example of the kind of thing that musicians can say to each other and everyone present knows what to do. For example, "After the intro, everyone just vamp on the E minor riff." It means to just hang out there for a few moments, perhaps even visually check in with the rest of the players, the vocalist, or the band leader, and wait to be signaled to start playing the next section. This is used more in the live performance of a song than in a recorded song, but only because once a song is recorded, the number of times becomes determined. However, a band can still vamp on a certain section live that was played a specific number of times in a recording. You can think of the vamp like a loop. It doesn't have to be looped, however; it can just be a section that hangs out on some subsection of the form to which you wouldn't be inclined to give a name, such as verse or bridge. A vamp can be an all-purpose filler moment.

- **Verse.** Usually, a verse is one section of unique lyrics—a stanza of the poetry of the song, if you will. It's not always limited to that, but it's the part of the form that is the primary building block. Although some songs in fact begin with a chorus, most pop or rock songs start with some kind of intro and then go into the first verse. Often, the place where you first hear lyrics being sung is the verse. If there are sections of your song that have the same musical backdrop but different lyrics each time, it's a safe bet that that's your verse.

- **Pre-chorus.** Many songs have a short tag, or added part, at the end of a verse, before you get to a chorus, but the music is a little different than what was going on in the verse. I often call this the *pre-chorus*. It's a distinct section of the form that leads up to the chorus.

- **Chorus.** This is the repeated section of the lyrics that you keep coming back to. It's the part that everyone in the room usually knows to sing along with. It's the section that usually contains the hook, which is a musical or lyrical phrase that is the essential catchy idea of the song. It's the section that sits in contrast to the verse. In one of the simplest song forms, you have verse, chorus, verse, chorus, verse, chorus. If the verse is "I think I'm gonna be sad, I think it's today, yeah…. The girl that's drivin' me mad is going away, yeah," then "She's got a ticket to ride, she's got a ticket to ride, she's got a ticket to ride, but she don't care" is the chorus.

- **Bridge.** This term refers to a new musical construct, a section that takes you from one musical section to another and is unique in and of itself. The analogy is the building of a bridge between the last verse—or maybe even a solo section—and the final chorus. There are no hard-and-fast rules about any of these terms, but there are commonalities from song to song about how these terms are used. The bridge is often a musical and lyrical section of the song that comes somewhere in the middle or after the middle and takes you out to that final chorus section. In the example of the classic Beatles song mentioned a moment ago, the bridge of "Ticket to Ride" is the part that goes, "I don't know why she's ridin' so high, she ought to think right, she ought to do right by me…before she gets to sayin' good-bye, she ought to think right, she ought to do right by me."

- **Solo.** This is usually used to describe a section in which the band continues to play the chords of the song, and one or more instrumentalists improvises melodically over the song. The guitar solo, for example, is the section where the guitarist starts playing out front, and there is usually no singing over a solo section. This term is most often used in rock, pop, and many forms of jazz.

- **Break.** Another word for a solo section, this term is more often used in bluegrass and country music. One musician is featured. It's his turn to take the foreground and play his heart out.

- **Breakdown.** This is often a section where only percussion and rhythm are played. It's a time when all melodic and harmonic musical elements and vocals stop and the drummers keep things going. Often used by DJs mixing in clubs, it's a time when the drums can keep going while another section is cued up or set up for the next major musical element. The breakdown just breaks the song form down to its foundation—the rhythmic groove.

- **Middle eight.** This is a term that The Beatles often used—in the book *Beatlesongs* by William J. Dowlding (Fireside, 1989)—when discussing the form of their songs. It refers to eight bars (or measures) in the middle of the song that are unique and up until that point have not been heard. This could be called a bridge, but the way it was used sometimes was more standalone, rather than serving to connect two sections together, and there sometimes could be a bridge that existed separate from the middle eight.

- **Middle section.** This a slightly more generic way of describing what The Beatles called the middle eight. While the middle eight might actually be eight bars, a middle section could go on for longer than that. In fact, when I think of a middle section, I usually think of a part of the song that has even more than one subsection, sort of a mini-song within the song. It might have its own A, B, and C sections and then return to the main song. Longer-form rock tunes (especially in the progressive rock or art rock genre) often have many different sections and tend to stretch the concept of a concise form. Middle section is a nice, generic term for "that other part of the song in the middle that's different from the rest of the song."

- **Build.** This could be used to describe a section that has the purpose of building up from a quiet section or a lower-energy middle section to the full energy of the chorus—maybe even a sort of vamp or repeating figure that gains in energy or volume. Think "A little bit louder now, a little bit louder now, a little bit louder now..." in "Shout!" by the Isley Brothers.

- **Refrain.** This is sometimes used as another term for the chorus. This is the section that gets repeated. You always come back to the refrain. It contains the musical and lyrical hook of the song. Others feel that the refrain is often a one- or two-line phrase that resolves the verse but perhaps is not elevated to what might be termed a chorus proper. Simon and Garfunkel's "Like a bridge over troubled water, I will lay me down...like a bridge over troubled water, I will lay me down..." is more of a refrain than a chorus.

- **Jam.** This refers to a section of the song that has a rhythmic and chordal structure (sometimes just implied) that repeats, but the number of repeats is not decided ahead of time. It's the kind of section in which all of the musicians may improvise rhythmically, chordally, and melodically. The structure is intact, but the musical interpretation is approached improvisationally by the whole band. Bands such as Phish, Dave Matthews Band, and The Grateful Dead have jams in almost every song, especially live. Often, a section like this is where musicians might go out on a limb and deconstruct and reconstruct the song on the fly. Whereas a solo is a section in which one instrumentalist may improvise a melody over the song, a jam is where the entire band might improvise together, taking the train anywhere they like, so to speak.

- **Outro.** This is a section of the song that only comes at the end. It's the ride out. Outro does not usually mean a repeating chorus that fades out. It refers to a composed structural segment of the song that operates as the ending. This might be a thematic recurrence of the intro, depending on the song, but it is almost always a certain specific structural element. As I said, the term is not usually used if the music is just repeating from the last chorus, but it could be. Again, most of these terms are used quite loosely.

Although this chapter is not meant to be a dissertation on song structure, I thought it might be useful to have some examples of how these terms might be used to help you make some decisions about how to structure your own songs from a songwriting perspective and to give you some ideas about terms you can use when incorporating GarageBand's Arrange Track functionality into your projects. To recap, this will help you communicate with others about the sections of your song, it will help you stay organized, and it will make it easy to know where you are in your song and move around from one section to another.

Another powerful thing you can do with the Arrange Track is easily alter the form, or "arrangement," of your song with a click and drag of the mouse. It's great for experimenting with the order of your sections easily, and it allows you to move something around or duplicate a section and quickly hear what that change would do to your song, all without having to play anything again or re-record something. It's extremely handy to be able to do this while writing.

I'll use Apple's term from here on out—what might normally be called the form will be called the arrangement, and I will acknowledge GarageBand's use of the term Arrange Track to refer to the track in the Timeline window that displays the sectional divisions of your song, named whatever you decide to name them.

Creating Arrangements with the Arrange Track

The first thing you'll need to do is make sure the Arrange Track is visible. You can do that by choosing Show Arrange Track from the Track menu or by pressing Command+Shift+A. See Figure 9.1.

Track	Control	Share	Windo
Show Track Info			⌘I
Show Arrange Track			⇧⌘A
Show Master Track			⌘B
Show Podcast Track			⇧⌘B
Show Movie Track			⌥⌘B
New Track...			⌥⌘N
Delete Track			⌘⌫
Duplicate Track			⌘D
New Basic Track			⇧⌘N
Fade Out			

Figure 9.1 Choose Show Arrange Track from the Track menu to make the Arrange Track visible in your timeline.

The Arrange Track will always appear at the very top of your Timeline window in a thin lane about the same size as your timeline ruler. Over on the left side, above your Track Mixer column, is an area that is labeled Arrangement, with a little plus icon in it. This plus icon is a button that, when clicked, creates a new arrange region. New arrange regions will always appear at the end of your current arrangement, so you don't have to be concerned with where the playhead is at any time when creating new arrange regions. See Figure 9.2.

Figure 9.2 The Create New Arrange Region button.

Creating an Arrange Region

To create a new arrange region, click the Create New Arrange Region button (the plus button) that sits at the right edge of the Track Mixer side of the Arrange Track. To start this example, I'm going to create four arrange regions in an empty project and work with them. You can create new arrange regions regardless of whether you have an empty song project or one that has tracks in it already. The process is usually to create a new arrange region, name it, and then resize or reposition it. You can always rename, move, resize, delete, or copy any of your arrange regions later on, so they remain infinitely flexible. If you click the Create New Arrange Region button four times, you will have four arrange regions. By default, they will be named untitled, untitled 1, untitled 2, and untitled 3. See Figure 9.3.

Figure 9.3 Four new untitled arrange regions.

Naming an Arrange Region

To name an arrange region, you use the same technique that you use to name an existing file or folder in the Finder or on the desktop in Mac OS X. You select the arrange region, and it will be highlighted, just like a selected file. Then you click on the name (click where it says "untitled"), and a moment after clicking, the text will be selected in an editable text field so you can type the name and press Return or Enter to lock in the name. See Figure 9.4.

Figure 9.4 Naming the untitled arrange region verse.

For this example, I'm going to name the remaining three arrange regions we just created chorus, bridge, and outro, so that I can refer to them in later examples. This is one good argument for naming your regions: They become very easy to refer to. I can say, "Look at the chorus," "Delete the bridge," or "Play verse 3," and you will know exactly what I mean. See Figure 9.5.

Figure 9.5 Naming the remaining three arrange regions chorus, bridge, and outro.

Resizing an Arrange Region

To resize an arrange region, click and drag on the right edge of the arrange region in the Arrange Track. You can resize any region at any time. If the arrange region you are resizing is the last one (in other words, there are no other arrange regions to the right of it), you will simply be extending or trimming the region's size. If you are attempting to resize an arrange region that is in between other arrange regions, the arrange region after the one you're attempting to resize will absorb—called *rippling*—the change you make, whether it is forward or back in time. See Figure 9.6.

Figure 9.6 Resizing the length of the chorus. Notice how it affects the length of the bridge.

Deleting an Arrange Region

To delete an arrange region, select it and press the Backspace key. If you delete one by mistake, you can press Command+Z to undo your change or select Undo from the Edit menu. Keep in mind that if you *do* have tracks with MIDI or audio regions in them, deleting an arrange region will delete everything in that vertical column first, and then if you press Backspace one more time, it will delete the whole arrange region. Selecting an arrange region is one way to select everything (on every track) that falls vertically under that arrange region. See Figures 9.7 and 9.8.

Moving an Arrange Region

You can easily move all arrange regions. To make the bridge in this example come before the chorus, just select the bridge and then click and drag it back before the chorus. GarageBand will automatically shuffle things around to accommodate the change. It's just like moving one of your icons in the Dock in Mac OS X or even moving webpage tabs around in Safari or Firefox. Click and drag, and everything falls into place around whatever move decision you make. See Figures 9.9 and 9.10.

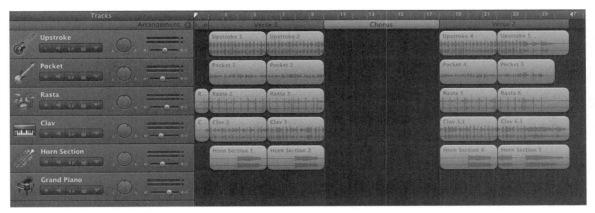

Figure 9.7 Deleting an arrange region's contents. (Select the arrange region and press Backspace.)

Figure 9.8 The timeline after deleting the arrange region itself. (Press Backspace a second time.)

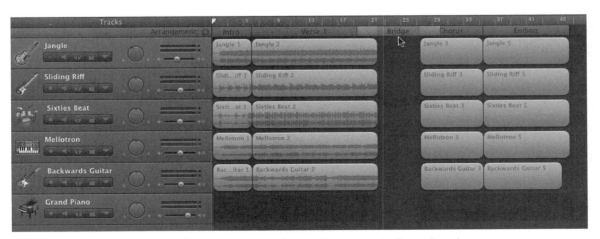

Figure 9.9 Moving the bridge arrange region so it comes before the chorus.

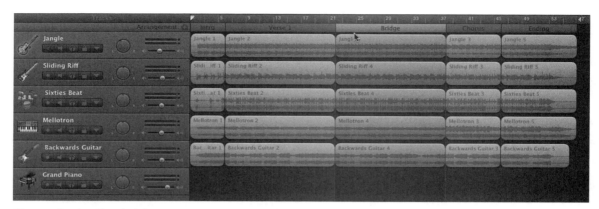

Figure 9.10 The bridge arrange region in its new location before the chorus.

Copying an Arrange Region

You can't actually copy and paste arrange regions in the conventional select/copy/ paste workflow. It happens a little differently in GarageBand. It's a keyboard and mouse technique that can also be used in the Mac OS X Finder for duplicating files. This is the Option-click-and-drag method. Hold down the Option key on the keyboard and keep it held down *while* you click and drag an arrange region. You will end up making a copy of the arrange region and then positioning it where you want it to go. Again, GarageBand will accommodate your move and shift everything else around accordingly, so you don't have to be absolutely precise about where you drop an arrange region. They just collapse and fall into place around one another. If there are tracks of audio or MIDI in your song, and you Option-click-and-drag an arrange region, you will also bring with you trimmed-out snippets of all the tracks in that vertical column. Entire arrange regions move together. There is no way to move or copy an arrange region without also taking its contents with you. That's fine, because if you are trying to extrapolate out your song by duplicating and positioning its constituent building blocks down the timeline, this is what you would want to have happen anyway. See Figure 9.11.

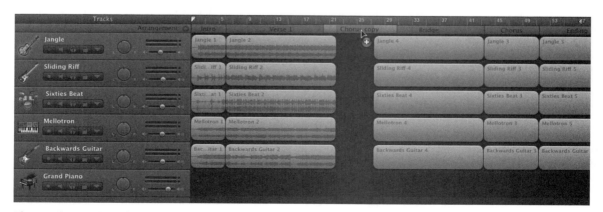

Figure 9.11 Copying an arrange region by using Option-click-and-drag.

Suppose you are creating a song, and you make a verse and a chorus, but you decide you want there to be an arrangement that goes like this: verse, verse, chorus, verse, verse, chorus, verse, chorus, chorus. You can write and record the verse once and the chorus once, and then Option-click-and-drag a copy of the verse and drop it between the first verse and the chorus. Now you have verse, verse, chorus instead of just verse, chorus, which you started with. Now you can select the first verse and hold down the Shift key while you click on the second verse and the chorus, and you have all three selected. Then you can Option-click-and-drag in the Arrange Track of any of the three selected arrange regions, and you will duplicate all three. Now you have verse, verse, chorus, verse, verse, chorus! To do your final duplication, Option-click-and-drag another verse to the end, another chorus after that, and then duplicate the chorus one final time, and you have a full arrangement (or form) made out of two short parts that you recorded and performed. Now you can sing your lyrics over the parts, and you have a whole song! See Figure 9.12.

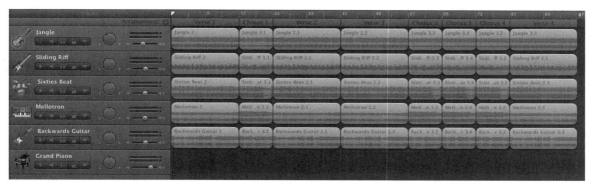

Figure 9.12 A more complex and fleshed-out arrangement made from only one verse and one chorus, all renamed after the copying process was completed.

Opening GarageBand Projects with Arrangements in Logic Pro

One final thing I'd like to mention—and I will cover this more in detail in Chapter 12, "Sharing and Archiving Your GarageBand Projects"—is that your GarageBand arrange regions will translate perfectly into Logic Pro if you open your GarageBand projects in Logic. If you make the move to the higher-end Apple digital audio recording application, you will be able to convert all of your GarageBand projects into Logic projects, and everything will transfer—your MIDI tracks, your audio tracks, all of your automation, all of your effects and mixing decisions, as well as all of your arrangements. Your arrange regions will become elements in the Marker Track in Logic and will serve exactly the same purpose in Logic as they did in GarageBand. My personal opinion is that it's a good idea to add arrange regions to your projects, because it will remind you of what your sections are if you open a project months or years later. It also will help you know where you are anytime you are zoomed way in.

You just look to the top of the window, and without even pressing the Play button, you will know that you are in the third verse, for example.

Ready to Create Your First Podcast?

Now that you have a good understanding of organizing and building your projects with the use of the Arrange Track and you know how to manipulate arrange regions, it's time to move on to another new topic. GarageBand has a specialized working environment for you to use when creating podcasts. I'll cover what podcasting is, how to create a podcast, and the nuances and differences between creating a podcast and a regular song in GarageBand. I'll also show you how to publish your podcasts on your blog or website and how to get them up on the iTunes Store!

10 Podcasting

Nowadays, the term "podcast" is as much a buzzword as ever there was, and it is a whole lot more than just a fad. I once viewed it as neat that Apple's iPod device had found its way, portmanteau-style, into a pop culture phrase and content-distribution revolution, but I now think of podcast as a term that is somewhat hobbling and stunting to the growth of the actual revolution in content distribution. It is damaging to the movement itself insofar as some people hear the word "podcast" (as in, "Have you heard that podcast from so and so?") for the first time and assume they must have an iPod to participate.

Nothing could be further from the truth! Many people who do not use iPods or know much about Apple computers in general have found themselves still in the dark about this incredibly powerful technology for distributing—nay, syndicating—digital audio, slideshow, and video content. The truth is that all you need is a computer and an Internet connection, and all the podcasts of the world can be yours, the lion's share of them for free. You can participate in the revolution not only by listening to the burgeoning library of syndicated podcasts, but by creating and publishing one of your own if you happen to also have Apple's GarageBand.

Before we move on, let's check in with Wikipedia.org on the word "podcast." This definition was printed in Chapter 2, on choosing project types, but because this chapter is on podcasting, I figured I should mention it again.

Podcast   A podcast is a series of digital-media files which are distributed over the Internet using syndication feeds for playback on portable media players and computers. The term *podcast*, like *broadcast*, can refer either to the series of content itself or to the method by which it is syndicated; the latter is also called *podcasting*. The host or author of a podcast is often called a *podcaster*. The term is a portmanteau of the words "iPod" and "broadcast," the Apple iPod being the brand of portable media player for which the first podcasting scripts were developed. Such scripts allow podcasts to be automatically transferred to a mobile device after they are downloaded. Though podcasters' websites may also offer direct download or streaming of their content, a podcast is distinguished from other digital media formats by its ability to be syndicated, subscribed to, and downloaded automatically when new content is added, using an aggregator or feed reader capable of reading feed formats such as RSS or Atom.

—Wikipedia (en.wikipedia.org/wiki/Podcast)

Creating a Podcast

In the New Project dialog box that comes up when you first launch GarageBand, in the New Project section, select Podcast. Doing so will prompt you to save your new project, and then will automatically open a new GarageBand project with the podcast-related panels, tracks, and Media Browser visible. As mentioned earlier, you can certainly create a standard music project and *make* it look and behave the same as what you get when you click Podcast by showing the Podcast Track in the Track menu and turning on the Ducking function in the Control menu. Turning a podcast project into a regular music project would likewise be a simple matter of hiding these elements. Choosing Podcast from the New Project dialog box makes it one convenient step to create a podcast. Additionally, GarageBand creates three tracks for you by default: a Mail Voiceover track, Female Voiceover track, and a Jingles track. These can be customized at will. See Figure 10.1.

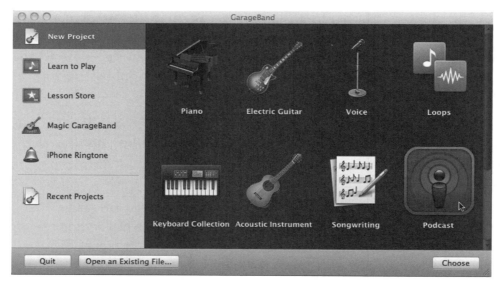

Figure 10.1 Click Podcast in the New Project dialog box to begin working on your podcast episode.

Creating an Episode

I'm going to sidestep redundancy here and get into the heart of creating podcasts with GarageBand. I am going to assume at this point that you have read Chapters 5 and 6 and you know how to create tracks, name them, insert Software Instruments, and edit their settings. There is an understanding throughout this chapter that you know how to browse Apple Loops, and in the case of podcasts, how to look to the Podcast Sounds view of the Loop Browser. I'm not going to pause between the steps to reiterate this. Also, I'm going to lean on your knowledge and understanding of the names of the areas of the interface, such as the Track Mixer, the Track Info panel, the Editor, and the Add Automation menu. I'm also going to rely on your understanding of how to do all the basic functions of working with regions—be they audio or MIDI—and how to split them; trim them; copy, delete, or move them; and create nodes for automation. If you don't know what each and every thing I just mentioned is and how to use these functions, I recommend you take a few minutes and review Chapters 3 through 7, where all of these functions are covered in detail.

The unique aspects of a podcast project are specifically:

- The Podcast Track (or the Movie Track if you are creating a video podcast).

- The ability to add markers, which may represent named chapters and/or display clickable URLs (web links) to listeners, if they are listening in iTunes.

- The Ducking feature can be enabled, forcing audio tracks of lesser priority to drop in volume as tracks of higher priority come in.

- You can embed metadata into the podcast file, allowing the file to be indexed by feed mechanisms as well as by feed readers and podcast aggregators (pod-catcher software applications such as iTunes).

- You can export a podcast directly from GarageBand to iWeb (the webpage design application included in the iLife suite) and build a page automatically, and all of your metadata will be supplied to your RSS feed for one-click syndication. Colloquially, RSS stands for *really simple syndication.*

- GarageBand can generate any of the accepted podcast formats for distribution, such as MP3, M4A (AAC), and M4V (QuickTime MP4 Video). To have support for chapters, still images, or URLs in the player window, you cannot use the MP3 format. The MP3 format is fine as an option for audio export, but in that format you *will not* have your designated chapters, markers, URLs, or images that change throughout your program. You *will* have normal MP3 metadata (such as artist, album, and so on) and album art, but the so-called *enhanced podcast* is only available when you export your project as an M4A (AAC) or M4V (video podcast) format.

See Figure 10.2 for a full view of the GarageBand project window in Podcast mode.

Creating a Video Podcast

The unique aspect of a video podcast project in GarageBand is that it has a Movie Track instead of a Podcast Track. The Podcast Track is the place where you can

Figure 10.2 A GarageBand podcast project.

specify still images that change at marker points within your timeline, whereas the Movie Track simply plays a movie file in real time, and you can still create chapters and markers within your video podcast.

A movie score is a normal GarageBand song with a Movie Track, and a video podcast is a normal podcast episode with a Movie Track. If you drag a video into the Podcast Track of a regular podcast episode, GarageBand will ask you whether you want to convert to a video podcast, so you can start with a podcast and go to a video podcast just by introducing a video into the timeline. See Figure 10.3.

With video podcasts, you import a video file into GarageBand by simply dragging and dropping it onto the Movie Track, which is at the very top of the timeline and Track Mixer. You will need to use a video that is either an iMovie project or any of the QuickTime-compatible formats. When the video has been converted and imported, you can create any additional tracks of narration, music, sound effects, jingles, and so on that you require. When you have completed that, you can mark the timeline with chapter markers, which we will cover in depth later in this chapter, in the section called "Markers: Chapters and URLs." Markers can contain a chapter stop, a URL link, or both. I'll be going through the steps for creating those in just a bit.

Figure 10.3   A GarageBand video podcast project.

The Media Browser's Role

As you build your podcast, you have your normal timeline, which is your program from start to end, and all of your audio tracks in the standard GarageBand timeline are used for anything from creating music, to creating narration, to creating a combination of the two. You can also add sound cues, sound effects, stingers, or jingles—of which there is a huge library included with GarageBand—or anything that you want heard in your show.

The Loop Browser gives you access to many things that are part of the commercial release of GarageBand and are provided royalty free for your use, but you likely have your own media that you'll want to use in your podcasts. This might include songs, your own jingles and sound effects, still images for the Podcast Track, or videos for your video podcasts. These are all accessible through the Media Browser in the far-right pane, where the Track Info panel normally appears. Click on the Media Browser button in the lower-right of the GarageBand interface to open the Media Browser window. See Figure 10.4.

Figure 10.4   Click the Media Browser button to open the Media Browser.

All of the media in your iLife applications and in your Movies and Music directories on your computer's hard drive will be made available to you through the Media Browser. This includes iPhoto photos, iTunes music, iMovie projects, and QuickTime movies from any source that you have on your hard drive. The Media Browser is broken up by Audio, Photos, and Movies and is your one-stop shop for elements that you can easily drag and drop into your project.

The Podcast Track

The Podcast Track is for your visuals. In a regular MP3 podcast, you can have one image—so-called *album art*—that displays on a listener's MP3 player video screen or in a window on his or her computer. It's a still image that usually is the logo of the show, a picture of the hosts or stars, or some other representative image. With an enhanced podcast—a podcast created in GarageBand and exported as an AAC file—you can have still images that change whenever you decide to make them do so. You can also set markers within the timeline of the Podcast Track that can act as chapters, which allow a listener to advance to predetermined starting points throughout the program. This is much like chapters on a DVD or tracks on a CD, but these are chapters within the podcast program. You can also name each chapter and choose whether to make a marker point display a clickable URL. The Podcast Track starts out empty, with no markers, artwork, or URLs. See Figure 10.5.

Figure 10.5 The Podcast Track is empty when you first create a podcast project.

If you are going to use markers in your podcast, you should create your first one at the very beginning so that if someone is in the middle of the show and wants to get back to the beginning, he can choose that chapter and get there easily. But more importantly, a marker at the beginning gives you an image of your choice right from the start. Having no image specified in the Podcast Track will result in the podcast displaying whatever you have chosen for the episode artwork/album art of the podcast episode itself. There are several ways to go about this.

Episode Artwork

The podcasting mode in GarageBand refers to album art as *episode artwork*. The Episode Artwork square is where you can drag a photo from your desktop or your Media Browser and create one exemplary image that will display for people who are listening to your MP3 version of the show. Those using a Mac will see this image in their Coverflow view in the Finder in Mac OS X or in Coverflow in iTunes as the image that acts as the front cover to your whole piece. You can use a logo, name, or image of the program to identify the podcast. Whenever there are blank sections among your still images in the Podcast Track in GarageBand, the episode artwork is what will be displayed. See Figure 10.6.

Figure 10.6 Drag an image into the Episode Artwork square to give your podcast a "cover."

Markers: Chapters and URLs

Place your playhead at specific points throughout your program and use any of these three methods to create markers at those points in time.

■   Click the Add Marker button at the bottom of the Podcast Track edit window. (This displays artwork and marks a chapter by default.) See Figure 10.7.

Figure 10.7   Clicking the Add Marker button.

■   Drag and drop a photo from the Media Browser or from your desktop into the timeline of the Podcast Track at the top of your Timeline window. Wherever you position and drop the image, a marker will be created. (This displays artwork only by default. URL and chapter markers will not be automatically activated. You can manually activate them by clicking their respective check boxes.) See Figure 10.8.

■   Position the playhead and drag and drop a photo on the marker position of your choice in the middle of the Podcast Track edit window. (This displays artwork only by default.) See Figure 10.9.

You have some flexibility with your photos, even after you have dragged them into the Podcast Track. Sometimes you may want to reposition the photo or crop it. Double-click the photo icon in the podcast marker list, and you are golden. Click and drag the image to reposition it, and use the slider to zoom in or out. See Figure 10.10.

Even though these actions have their default behaviors in terms of being a marker only, a marker with artwork that is displayed, a marker that is also a chapter point, or a marker that has a URL attached, these can all be mixed, matched, and combined by using the check boxes in the Podcast Track Editor with a marker selected from the list and editing the text fields in the marker list itself. When you enter a URL, you must use a fully qualified address—for example, http://www.toddhoward.com. See Figure 10.11.

Figure 10.8 Drag and drop a photo into the Podcast Track timeline.

As mentioned earlier, for any span of time that does not have a marker or artwork in the Podcast Track, the enhanced podcast file will just revert to showing your default episode artwork.

Ducking Audio in Podcasts

If you don't have the time or inclination to create a lot of complex volume level automation in the mixing process of your podcast, you have a convenient option in GarageBand called *ducking*. Ducking is a function that allows you to set what's known as a *ducking priority* to each track in your show, and when there are sounds or audio of any kind playing at the same time as one another in your mix, those tracks that have ducking seniority will automatically stay loud, and those that are subordinate will get quieter. Those tracks that have no ducking designation will just stay as they are. The idea with the term "ducking" is that a piece of audio ducks down, or gets out of the way of some other piece of audio.

A good example of this is a situation in which a show begins with theme music that plays for 15 seconds or so, and then the host comes on and starts talking, welcoming people to the show. At that moment, the accepted convention is to lower the music a

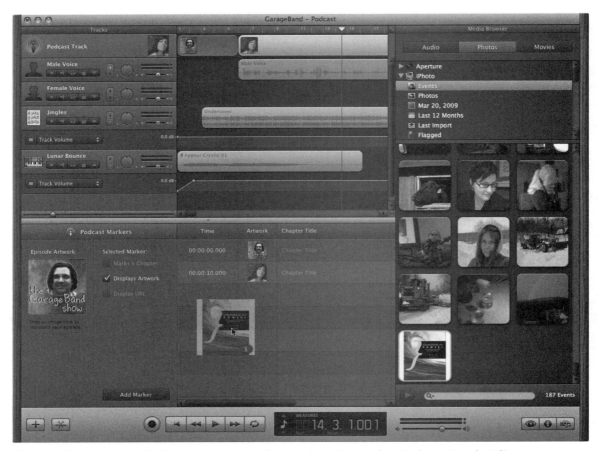

Figure 10.9   Drag and drop a photo in the marker list in the Podcast Track Editor.

bit so you can hear the announcer. That's referred to as *ducking the music*. So you set the host voice track to cause other tracks to be ducked, and the music track to be ducked by other tracks. Clicking the top arrow on the Ducking buttons will cause other tracks to duck, leaving them both off means the track will have no effect on other tracks and also will not be affected by other tracks, and clicking the bottom arrow means the track will be ducked by other tracks that are set to cause ducking. See Figure 10.12.

Working with Episode Information

When syndicating a podcast, the feed on which you host your file requires certain metadata, or information about the file (or "data about the data," as the feller says), to be embedded within the file itself. GarageBand takes care of this process for you with an easy-to-understand, simple-to-edit interface. Click on the Podcast Track in the Track Mixer and then click the little "i" icon next to the LCD readout (or press Command+I) to open the Track Info panel for the Podcast Track. In the bottom third, you will see the Episode Info area, complete with editable fields for information to be entered. You will need to fill out Title, Artist, Composer, Parental

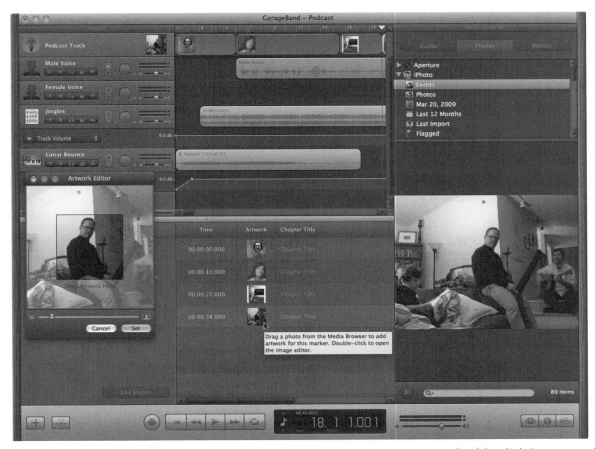

Figure 10.10   After a photo appears in the podcast marker list, you can double-click it to open it in the Artwork Editor and then recrop and reposition your photo.

Figure 10.11   Click the text fields in the marker list to edit them. Editing marker list text fields for Chapter Title, URL Title, and URL makes the marker a chapter and a URL, respectively.

Figure 10.12   Click the arrows to set whether the track is ducked or causes other tracks to duck.

Advisory, and Description fields to complete your file's metadata. This allows your file to be searched for and indexed properly or to be made available for subscription on the iTunes Store Podcast Directory. This is the premier source for podcast fans to find out about new podcasts. See Figure 10.13.

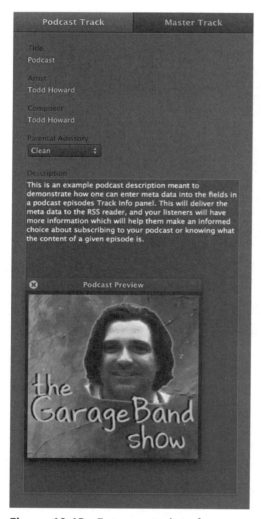

Figure 10.13　Enter metadata for your podcast into the Episode Information fields. Don't forget to do this part!

Exporting Your Project as a Podcast Episode

I will go into great detail about exporting files from GarageBand to iTunes, your hard drive, and even iWeb in Chapter 12, "Sharing and Archiving your GarageBand Projects." In the spirit of not leaving you hanging at the end of the podcast creation process, however, allow me to draw your attention to the Share menu in the main menu bar. These selections, such as Send Podcast to iTunes, Send Podcast to iWeb, and Export Song to Disk, are all methods for creating a final version (or mixdown) of your podcast project in the form of a digital file that can be used for something specific. Sending the podcast to iTunes means you will have an enhanced AAC podcast or a regular MP3 podcast in your iTunes library, ready to be played, shared, FTP'd to a server somewhere, or perhaps just saved in iTunes as a version of your program in the case of a preliminary mix.

Refer to Chapter 12 for an in-depth discussion of all of your saving and exporting options. If you have created an enhanced podcast with a podcast image track, chapters, and URLs, you'll want to click the Compress option in the Send Podcast to iTunes, Send Podcast to iWeb, or Export Song to Disk dialog box. Then, when a listener plays your podcast in an AAC-compatible player (such as iTunes or an iPod or iPhone), he will enjoy your podcast artwork and be able to click on URLs and use chapters to navigate around your show with the click of a mouse or the tap of a finger. See Figure 10.14.

Figure 10.14 Choose Send Podcast to iTunes from the Share menu.

Submit Your Podcast to the iTunes Podcast Directory

If you are interested in getting your podcast submitted to the iTunes Store Podcast Directory, Google "submit a podcast to iTunes" or visit the following URL, which will take you to the podcast submission process in the iTunes Store: https://phobos. apple.com/WebObjects/MZFinance.woa/wa/publishPodcast. For detailed specs on what Apple expects from you in your podcasts that you would like listed on the iTunes Store Podcast Directory, refer to this page: http://www.apple.com/itunes/whatson/podcasts/ specs.html.

The Nitty Gritty: Mixing and Automation

The next chapter will take you into the world of mixing. Mixing is the part of the process in which all of the elements come together, and you will define the relationships they have to one another and to your whole piece. We will work with GarageBand's extensive effects library; make final decisions about which Software Instruments you want to use in your song; learn about using the flexible Visual EQ plug-in; and automate volume levels, panning, and even specific parameters within your audio effects. Get ready for the fun part. Mixing and automation are next!

11 Mixing and Automation

One of the greatest challenges in creating professional-sounding songs and podcasts in any digital recording application—GarageBand included—is the mixing phase. Like the word that was chosen to describe it, this part of the process is quite like mixing all of your ingredients together in a recipe—when you've got hundreds coming to dinner, and everyone's a food critic. Deciding what the exact amount should be of any given ingredient can make or break the final product. I think mixing audio, especially for a beginner, can be even more difficult than that. You've got a number of considerations going in. For example, who are you mixing the song for? Yourself? The artist? The artist's management? Where will people be listening to the final product? Through their headphones? In the car? Through a PA system? On the radio? Streaming from the Internet compressed down to 64 kbps?

There are two answers to what I've posed here, and you're probably not going to like either of them. You are mixing the song for each of those people and none of them, and you are mixing the song for all of those situations and none of them. It's really important to have all of those answers and then to forget about them. The absolute bottom line is that, as the mixing engineer, you have to be happy with the sound of things. If you aren't, you won't want it representing your work, you won't be satisfied, and your heart won't be in it. I've found that for me, in more than almost any other part of the process, if I'm not jazzed during mixing, I'm in big trouble.

A Perspective on Learning to Mix

Before you even read any part of this chapter, the best piece of advice I have for you about mixing is that the only way to become good at mixing is to mix. A lot. Mix and remix. Return to old projects months later on a rainy Sunday and do a new mix. When you get some new speakers, go back and revisit a couple of your old mixes and redo them. Practice every chance you get. Let others (music people and non–music people) hear your mix and ask them questions about it. Do your own informal focus groups. Ask some friends to listen to the song and give you their first impressions about how it sounds. Ask them specific questions about how it makes them feel. If they're musically savvy, ask them about the guitar sounds or the drum levels or anything that may be concerning you, but try to ask open-ended questions, rather than leading ones. Even with a lot of data coming back to you from friends, colleagues, musicians, and interested third parties, you still will have to know what to do to address problems. And sometimes this involves knowing what your limitations are and how to use your gear. Some of this comes through education and resources like this book, but mostly it comes with experience.

One thing that plays a major role in creating limitations is gear—software and hardware gear included. Lots of expensive gear does not make a good mix, but the better the tools available, the more options a mixing engineer has and the more an experienced audio producer has to work with. For example, suppose you had a top-of-the-line outboard tube compressor. Just having the thing would not make vocals sound mint; you'd have to know how to use it. Having it and knowing how to use it puts you in the position of being able to utilize its power, sound, and flexibility when needed to achieve a certain end. This knowledge could come through trial and error, learning from others, and listening. Experience is the greatest teacher. Trial and error is never more valid an approach than when it comes to mixing a song.

One thing that almost never works is thinking about it. You almost always have to hear it to know for sure. For example, if you let an experienced audio engineer listen to your mix, and he gives you some feedback such as, "The bass guitar is too muddy; you should cut some of those low mids," asking him, "Which frequency should I cut and by how much?" would be futile. He might even have a good guess: "Oh, I don't know, bring it down about 2 dB [decibels] at around 125 Hz." You could do exactly what he suggested and show him the result, and he would likely say something like, "Hmmm, maybe a little more," or "Hmmm, that's still pretty muddy down there. What is the electric guitar doing?" My point is that it's all a conversation you need to be having with yourself and with your mixing environment. Listen, ask the question, try one possible answer, listen again, repeat. You might even get a lot out of mixing other people's projects. If you have a friend who is also working with GarageBand, swap files. Mix each other's tracks, if only for practice.

I don't want to overwhelm you with these elaborate warnings about mixing, nor do I want to rant and rave about how to train yourself to be good at it. I have been mixing audio with GarageBand and Logic for about six years now, and I know for a fact that I still have an awful lot left to learn. Let me say this: I know 10 times more about explaining to you how to use GarageBand to mix your song than I could ever know about explaining to you how to become a skilled mixing engineer. However, I can attempt to boil it down to some essential morsels.

Some Food for Thought about Mixing Audio

Here are a few things to think about when mixing audio.

- Know (discover and then keep in mind) the limitations of your software.

- Know the limitations of your hardware.

- Know the limitations and virtues of your source audio tracks. What microphones were used? Cheapies or industry standards? A bad original source track will cause you big problems in the mixing phase. Recording nice, hot (but not peaked) levels is always going to give you a better signal to work with, and a low, mediocre original source recording will introduce problems—including noise—into your mix as you try to raise those elements up to be heard.

- If you have lousy original source tracks for whatever reason, accept that truth and then do the best you can. You still need to mix the track. Unless you can go back and retrack some things with better mics or in a better room or with better instruments, levels, or performances, you might as well face facts about what you have and realize that you may have some issues. There are still a lot of things that can be done, but it's good to be realistic about what you have to work with from the get-go.

- Know the effect that the room or space in which you are mixing has on how you hear things. Trial and error! Bring your speakers into some different spaces and play the same piece of music through them. Get to know your gear and your space. Maybe invest in some bass traps or other acoustic treatments to create a more manageable sound in your room.

- Make sure your speakers, or monitors, are at ear level, equidistant from one another, forming a triangle with your head at the tip and the two speakers at the far points, aimed slightly in at your ears.

- It's generally a bad idea to do a whole mix in headphones. I did this once, on an EP I made with my band Mobile Home in the early '90s in Seattle. Trust me—you want to hear your mix in actual speakers. Be sure to test your mix in headphones, certainly, but don't make that your starting point, unless the only thing that will ever be done with your mix is playing it in headphones. (For example, you might be doing background music for a walking museum tour where the listeners will always be using headphones.)

- Cultivate an understanding of just how important the mix is to the final product of any song or audio creation: It's make or break.

- Listen and trust your ears to tell you what is going on. Mix with your ears, not with your brain. You should also be mixing with your gut. There is an emotional aspect to music to which you should be tuning in and reacting. Mixing is the process that brings all of the aspects of listening and feeling together. If you're not feeling it, it might not be right yet. Trust the goosebumps.

- Experiment. Trial and error (which means tweak, listen, and revise in this context) is a great way to see whether something is working. Try it. You can always press Undo!

- Make a list and have CDs on hand of some of your all-time favorite-sounding recordings in the genres that you are working with in your mixes. Every time you hear something that blows you away, you should add that CD to the list. Even investigate who the producer, recording engineer, and mixing engineer were on the record, and use the Internet to find out what else they've done. These can be your personalized reference guides to making things sound good.

- After a certain number of hours (which is different for everyone, but in my experience it's in the four- to six-hour range), ears develop fatigue. Over time, you fail to be able to hear certain frequencies with the same accuracy that you may have had just a couple of hours before. If you do mix through fatigue, the work you turn out will not actually sound like you think it sounds. Sensitivity to certain frequencies will diminish as your ears become fatigued, and you may start boosting those frequencies in your mix to compensate. When you hear the mix a day or two later, you may realize that those frequencies have been made far too loud for a balanced sound.

- Use the stereo space of your mix to position things, and create sonic space between instruments and voices.

- Learn to use EQ to remove offending frequencies from your tracks. Sometimes the EQ required to make an instrument sound good by itself when soloed is *not* the EQ you want on that sound once the whole mix is up. Too much low end in your individual instrument tracks will compound and make a real problem for you later. Remove the low end from instruments that don't need it, and if your mix is thin at the end of your process, you can always EQ the entire mix and add in some lows. It's often better to cut frequencies than it is to boost frequencies.

- Take frequent breaks. Mixing can be a physically and mentally taxing endeavor (not to mention emotionally taxing when you are mixing by committee!) when you work at it over many hours. Breaks not only keep you rejuvenated and give you time to remember to eat a meal, but they give your ears a rest period as well. You will hear things more distinctly and more clearly if you don't let ear fatigue set in.

- Turn it down! Mixing at loud volumes is almost never advisable. Keep your system at a comfortable, listenable level.

- Get feedback (notes) from others. Find an online forum for your genre of music or type of production, share mixes with the community, and ask for feedback. This is an incredible way of learning how to mix better.

- Be prepared to go back to the drawing board a couple of times. This should be considered normal. Sometimes starting over is the best solution. Know if and when you've hit that point.

- Sleeping on it is a great technique for being able to hear your work clearly. Make a mix and then listen to it again the next day. If it still sounds good, you've got a mix.

- With audio mixing, you are looking for balance and blend. The elements in your mix need to work together, not against each other. Things should be individually discernible but should also sound like they are all in the same space.

- A good tip is to start your mix by reducing the individual levels for every track in your project down to −6 dB and work up from there. If you don't do this, you will run out of headroom very quickly when you start boosting things.

- There is only so much you can actually do in a mix. Very often, it comes down to the quality of the sound of the original recorded elements.

- Listen to your mixes on many different systems: on your mixing station, in the living room, on your surround sound media center, on your cassette clock radio, on your boom box, on good headphones, on bad headphones. ... One of the most telling environments in which to hear your mixes is in the car!

- Keep pen and paper handy and make notes for yourself while listening, but don't forget to keep listening!

- Mixing is a craft and an art, and many people spend their whole lives learning to be master mixing engineers. It is an incredibly technical and creative endeavor.

- Know when to say enough is enough and either start over or call it finished. Contemplate the old artists' adage: "Art is never completed, only abandoned."

- The Best Advice I Ever Got About Mixing™: Mixing is about taking away, not about adding more.

- In my humble opinion, mixing can be one of the most enjoyable aspects of audio production. The more practice you have with it, the more likelihood there is of making truly classic mixes, and the more you will enjoy doing it. Mixing isn't for everyone, but those who end up being really good at it most certainly love doing it. You kind of have to—it can be tedious, repetitive, and very detail oriented. Allow your enjoyment to flow out through the speakers.

Mixing with GarageBand

GarageBand makes the mixing process very easy to understand and learn. A lot of the conventions and tools that we'll cover here are simplified versions of their professional cousins in the pro apps, but the simplification only comes in the area of options or parameters, not overall sound quality. With GarageBand's effects plug-ins, EQs, stompboxes, and Software Instruments, you are getting top-of-the-line professional-level sound quality. Although it is possible to overuse effects and processing to the detriment of your mix, GarageBand makes it very easy to apply just the right amount of a given effect to a track or to your whole mix and gives you a variety of ways to adjust volume levels and the relative positions of your tracks within the stereo-sphere.

Knowing your hardware and software limitations is a key ingredient to success in mixing, especially with GarageBand. As powerful as GarageBand is—and I am not trying to smooth anything over here; GarageBand is capable of producing world-class recordings—it does have its particularities and limitations. However, it is certainly not limited in sound quality of recordings or effects. GarageBand is able to record up to 24-bit audio, and all of its processing, effects, and post-processing is done automatically at 24-bit resolution, so everything you get out of the application is topnotch in terms of sound quality. The GarageBand application ships with a set of professional-grade effects and processing plug-ins, but these are not necessarily *as* high end as some of the commercially available plug-ins you can purchase and install. This additional software will install easily and is usable in GarageBand (and must be offered in the Audio Unit AU format to work with GarageBand), but it is only available from third-party vendors and often can run you hundreds of dollars per effect plug-in or effect library. In this chapter, we are going to focus on what GarageBand can do out of the box and not what it can't, but I do want to drive home the point that while GarageBand is capable of creating excellent-sounding recordings, you can take digital audio processing much further if you desire—but understand that it may also be an additional investment. For starters, you can check out Waves (www.waves.com) and IK Multimedia (www.ikmultimedia .com). IK is the maker of AmpliTube and other fantastic bass and guitar plug-ins—in fact, one of my favorite guitar amp plug-ins. That said, in GarageBand '09, with the addition of amp modeling and stompbox effects, GarageBand does even better with guitar sounds on its own, out of the box, than ever before.

Getting Started with Your Mix

There are some general tips for what to do first when getting ready to dig into your mix. All of your tracks are recorded, and you've done some trimming and editing of your performances and tweaked or quantized your MIDI performances. All your loops are in place, and you're ready to start making it sound great as a finished piece of music or podcast; it's time to get set up for mixing. Please keep in mind that I can show you around GarageBand's mixing interface and tell you how to make it work, but only you can mix your song or audio production. There are so many variables—and even vastly more possible types of projects—that a specific step-by-step walk-through would be unsuitable for far more individual readers than it would be suitable for. What I am going to attempt to do throughout the rest of this chapter is arm you with some ideas and techniques and the facts about what GarageBand does and where to find things in the interface. This will free you and prepare you for your own experimentation. Go to it, and you always have Undo, right? Well...read on.

No Undo with Mixing—What Gives?!

Something that you may find disconcerting is that certain mixing functions, such as raising a volume level in the Track Mixer, repositioning a panorama knob (commonly known as the *pan knob*), muting or soloing a track, and turning on or off automation, are all examples of tasks that are *unaffected* by choosing Undo from the Edit menu or using the Command+Z key command. I would be hard pressed to give you a complete official answer about why this is, but my sense is that the types of mixing adjustments referenced above are considered quite "fluid" adjustments, and not discrete user actions. Splitting a region or moving a MIDI note is an example of a cut-and-dried user action. The volume fader is a fluid setting, meant to be changed at will across a fluid spectrum, in real time, as much—or as little—as you like. If properly "remembered" by GarageBand, changes such as this would generate potentially infinite levels of undo. This would not be practical for the application to try to manage. Try not to be too worried about this fact, but it means that you'll want to be mindful of where you move these settings *from* while you're experimenting. The other thing you can do when trying to "put it back where it was before" is to use your ears. Following are a few more tips for dealing with this fact while mixing.

If you are certain you love where a specific fader is positioned, but you really want to see what it might be like somewhere else, I urge you to write down the setting or press Shift+Command+3 to take a screenshot, which will be saved by default as a PNG graphic file on your desktop. Keep a pad of paper for taking mix notes and a trusty writing implement nearby so that you can write down "Vocal 3, volume +3 dB." That way, if you want to mess with it for some other reason, you can set it back again. To find out what a volume fader or pan knob is set to currently, gently click and hold on the fader or knob without dragging, and a little yellow tool tip will appear with a value such as −3 (pan is expressed in numbers of steps from −1 to −64 on the left side and numbers of steps from 1 to 64 on the right side) or −6.7 dB (volume is expressed in decibels minus or decibels plus from 0.0). That is the number to write down.

Another technique for circumventing this Undo issue is that if you want to mess with a track's settings, duplicate the track, then select all the regions in that track, and Option-click-and-drag them down to the new, blank, duplicate track. Better yet, select all of the regions and then go to where the first region begins in your timeline and zoom way in before you Option-click-and-drag to copy. That way, when you drag down to the empty track, you can see what specific timeline ruler line it's aligned with, and things won't get out of sync. Name the track Trackname Copy and mute the original (which will have the settings you want to preserve), and then you can mess with the copy to your heart's content.

Zeroing/Flattening Out Your Levels

Take a look at Figure 11.1 and refamiliarize yourself with the buttons and functions that make up the Track Mixer, because I will be referring to them fairly often

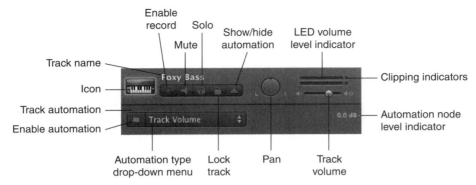

Figure 11.1 The Track Mixer.

throughout the rest of this chapter. The first thing I recommend doing when you are ready to mix is flattening all your levels. *Flattening* is a term that can mean setting everything to 0 or setting everything to the same level. When it comes to volume levels while preparing for a mix, as you'll see in a moment, I recommend starting at −6 dB, giving yourself some headroom or somewhere to go. For the purpose of cleaning your slate, the idea of flattening everything means making sure the following items are true:

- The volume faders on all tracks are set to −6 dB.

- The pan knobs on all tracks are set to the center. (Option-click the pan knob to set it exactly to 0 in one quick step.)

- All the Solo buttons are turned off.

- The only Mute buttons that are turned on are those on tracks you will *not* be using in your mix.

- No tracks are armed for recording.

- The master volume is set to 0.0 dB. (Option-click the master volume to set it exactly to 0.)

- Any locked or frozen tracks are unlocked, since you will conceivably need to alter them to mix.

- Any automation that you have added while tracking that isn't meant necessarily for the final mix should be cleared out. (Select and delete all your nodes in that automation track—see the "Deleting Nodes" section later in this chapter for more info.)

Your First Pass

Every time I mix a song, I lock all my levels to −6 dB and then I do a pass. A *pass* is just a play-through. Start the song at the beginning, make sure the speakers (monitors) are at a good, solid, comfortable level for critical listening, and press Play. While you're listening through your first pass, start clicking, dragging, and tweaking the individual volume levels of each of your tracks. Try to find a good general balance between your main tracks. If your song has several unrelated sections, you can take your passes in sections to focus on one at a time. An example might be a song in which the first third is spoken poetry with one gently plucked mandolin and an Irish drum; the middle third adds two more mandolins and two harmony singers and thrashes away a few dynamic verses; and the last third is a full Celtic rock band, including the voices, mandolins, and other instruments. In this case, it probably makes sense to treat what I've called your first pass as your first three discrete passes.

I am going to cover the use of specific GarageBand effects a little later in this chapter, so look to the section called "Using Effects and Post-Processing" for the ins and outs, but this point in the process is where you'd most likely be introducing those effects you know you will be using. Some effects can be "candy" and just add certain types of spices or flavors to your project, while others are core nutrients. For example, reverb, compression, and EQ get used so often that I'd call them staples.

Subsequent Passes and the Cycle Region

You can keep at it like this until you feel you have a nice balance between your main instruments and voices during the main sections of your song. You might even have made some preliminary decisions, such as starting an instrument out at a level of about –3.5 dB, but when the chorus comes in, you want to raise it to –0.5 dB. You can make note of that or, if you get the idea of creating nodes and doing some basic automation as covered in the next section, you could mark off those areas with nodes and make some basic adjustments, knowing that you can tweak them anytime you like.

When you start getting down to the nitty gritty, the truth is that there are probably sections of your piece that will require more attention than others. Chances are good that those spots will be sections where there is the most going on at once. If all the instruments and voices are playing, it's a lot more challenging (and interesting!) to mix than a solo piano intro is. Not that there's anything wrong with solo piano intros; I happen to love them. This is where the power of using the cycle region can come in. Suppose you're focusing on the first chorus. Why not click the Cycle Region button down in the Transport controls area and mark off the chorus with the yellow bar up in your ruler, and then just let GarageBand play the chorus over and over for you. You can even leave yourself a bar at the beginning or the end (or both!) to give yourself a breather to count in on your next pass or just to be able to play a lead-in phrase or let the last note ring out longer at the end. This can be very helpful because it allows you to focus on things without stopping repeatedly between each listen. You can even section off a very small area and loop that, just to focus on a trouble spot. This is the point at which your spouse, roommates, or house pets will want to go very far away from you. It's also the aspect of mixing that beginners don't tend to realize is a valuable part of the process, and they think it just sounds funny. Or worse—and more likely still—they find it annoying to the *n*th degree!

Muting and Soloing

It can also be incredibly telling to listen to soloed tracks by clicking the little head-phone icon in the Track Mixer. What I like to do when I'm dealing with a complicated section is to listen to my cycle region of the chorus and focus on, say, the bass. I'll click the Solo button on the bass for just a second or two and then turn it back off. Some-times I'll do this repeatedly. It allows my ear to get to know the sound of the bass specifically, focus on it for a second or two, and then just a moment later have it back in the mix with everything. I like to do this because it gives my ears and my brain information about what the bass has to offer sonically and how it's fitting into the mix, while the next second listening to it in context and asking myself, "Are those sonic qualities of the bass coming through when everything is playing? How do they fit?" Then I can make an informed mixing choice.

The Mute button—the little speaker icon in the Track Mixer—can help you out, but in an opposite fashion. Suppose you are working on the chorus, but you want to concen-trate on the rhythm section, which in this imaginary example is a bass, a Hammond organ, and the drums. If you press Mute on all the vocals, as well as the guitars (or was it mandolins?), you can focus on that one group of instruments with the others out of the way for a moment. Once you get them working well together, you can start un-muting the other tracks and adding them back in.

I consider all of these techniques to be looking at (or rather, listening to) the material in as many different lights as possible to learn as much as I can about the sound I'm trying to shape. I think you'll find your own methods for doing this, but if you haven't listened to each and every track in your mix for at least a few moments by itself with solo on, you aren't doing your job.

Final Decisions about Software Instruments

At this point in the mixing process, it's time to start locking down all of those sounds that you may be using for your Software Instrument tracks. You may have been using a Classic Rock Organ sound on your rhythm keyboard track during recording and preliminary mixing, but now is the time to decide whether that's what you actually want to use in your final mix. There are so many options to choose from that it may take you a little time and a little experimenting to settle on something you really love. Fortunately, GarageBand makes it incredibly easy to switch sounds on any given Software Instrument track in the process of seeing what all of your possible organ sounds—and the ways in which you can customize those presets—might be.

All of the Software Instruments in GarageBand are built from the parameters of 24 GarageBand Sound Generator Modules. These so-called modules are sampler instruments. With these 24 basic modules (I mean "basic" as in essential, not as in simplistic—they are quite sophisticated little pieces of technology) that GarageBand currently offers when you have all of the GarageBand Jam Packs installed, you can create almost any sound you can imagine. The Software Instrument patches that come with GarageBand, such as Indian Sitar, Heavy Metal Organ, or Bluesy Acoustic Guitar, are built by the designers at Apple from, respectively, the Strings, Tonewheel Organ, and Guitars Sound Generator Modules, with the parameters tweaked just so. Investigate this absolutely enormous library of sounds, and with each one you select, notice at the top of the Track Info panel's Edit tab for a given Software Instrument track is a Sound Generator icon. If you mouse over it, you can see the overlay of parameter sliders, indicating that these parameters are editable by clicking. Click on the Sound Generator's Edit Parameters icon button to investigate the settings Apple has used to create that instrument's particular sound. Experimenting with these sound modules will get you acquainted very quickly with the building blocks that are available for custom sound creation using these high-quality samples and the instrument modules that utilize them. Take your time and decide what sounds you would like to use in your mix.

If you are starting to hit the limits of your CPU now that you have gotten to the mixing phase and have started to add a lot of effects and customizations to your sounds, it will help you preserve CPU power to lock any tracks that you have finished working with. Even if you think you might need to make further revisions to a particular sound in the future, just click the little padlock icon in the Track Mixer, next to the Mute and Solo buttons, and GarageBand will "freeze" the track, thereby cutting way down on its usage of CPU power. It's a matter of a simple click to unlock a track that has been locked, so go ahead and lock tracks that have a lot of processing and effects in use— this goes for Software Instrument tracks and Real Instrument tracks alike. Remember to notice the color of the triangular top of the playhead. The closer to red it gets, the more of your CPU you are using.

For a complete look at the Sound Generator menu, see Figure 11.2.

Within each Sound Generator, there are a host of individual tones, or stock sounds. The generator module might be Church Organ, but inside of Church Organ there are individual sound presets, such as Bass 1, Bass 2, Flutes + 2 Octaves, Flutes + Fifth, Full Organ, and six others! These lists can be browsed for each instrument by looking through the drop-down menu at the top of the individual module interface, which you can access by clicking the Edit Parameters icon button on the left side of the Sound Generator in the Track Info panel's Edit tab. Alternatively, just to the right of the Sound Generator is the same drop-down menu for even more convenient browsing without having to open the individual Sound Generator's parameters interface. Another example might be under Tuned Percussion, where you'll see the likes of Caribbean Steel Drums, Timpani, and Marimba. These sounds all have different

Figure 11.2 The Sound Generator menu.

waveforms from one another, but they are in the same tonal family of Tuned Percussion, which means the Software Instrument module itself is to play all of those sounds, but with minor modifications given which voice is chosen and how the parameters are adjusted. See Figure 11.3.

Figure 11.3 The Voices menu for Tuned Percussion.

To try looking at one of these Instrument Generators and all of its voices, go to one of your Software Instrument tracks and open up the Track Info panel. Click the Edit tab and look at the top of the list for the Sound Generator drop-down menu. Choose Tuned Percussion from the top drop-down menu. The secondary drop-down menu underneath the Sound Generator menu is the Voices menu. Look inside to review all of the available voices for that instrument. With each one you choose from the menu, play a few notes on your MIDI controller to see what the sound differences are. If you click the Edit Parameters icon button to the left of the Sound Generator listing in the Track Info panel's Edit tab, a small interface for that instrument will open, floating above your GarageBand window, and the Voices menu can be accessed from the top of this interface as well. Watch as the parameter sliders change (in the case of Tuned Percussion, you have Volume, Cutoff, and Release) in response to each new choice from the Voices menu. You can further alter any of these parameters within a certain voice and make your own sound. From the top of the Voices menu, choose Make Preset to save your new voice with a unique name. This way you can expand your GarageBand sound library and save all of your creations. See Figure 11.4.

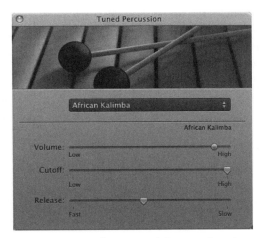

Figure 11.4 The Tuned Percussion instrument module.

Using Effects and Post-Processing

GarageBand has a lot to offer in the way of digital post-processing. This is another way of describing all of the digital effects that you can apply to your tracks after you have recorded them to enhance—and often vastly alter—the sound of them. There are two ways to approach this fun, creative aspect of building up your mix. One is by adding effects one by one; the other is by using GarageBand presets.

Presets versus Effects

When you record a track in GarageBand and you open up the Track Info panel with the left tab (the one labeled Real Instrument) selected, you will notice a list on the left of groups of presets. The idea is you're supposed to choose the group that represents what you have on your track, but the truth is you can choose anything you like—it's just that making your acoustic guitar track sound like Vocoder drums might be a little funky. If funky is what you're going for, then by all means knock yourself out. That's creativity. For the most part, using presets involves choose a preset that matches what is on your track and customizing the parameters from that jumping-off point.

The list consists of Acoustic Guitars, Band Instruments, Basic Track, Bass, Drums, Effects, Guitars (Previous Version), Podcasting, and Vocals. When you click on one of the groups, such as Guitars, you get a list on the right of guitar effects presets. The Guitars (Previous Version) preset group gives you access to all the Guitars presets that came with GarageBand in version '08 (version 4) and earlier. Since GarageBand '09 employs the use of Electric Guitar tracks, all of the amp models and stompbox effects that are available in a Guitar track are considered the "new" way of handling electric guitar sounds and effects in GarageBand. If you want to use anything that you had in an older project or any previous version of GarageBand, you can still access them by choosing presets from the Guitars (Previous Version) group.

Presets in GarageBand are preconfigured groupings of individual effects all added together to make a particular sound. They are effects patches that are created by combining various effects from GarageBand's effects library. The best way to explain this is to say that the next section will cover all of the individual effects in GarageBand, and to see how GarageBand brings the power and uniqueness of these individual effects together into full-blown effects presets, you can click on the selections in the right column of the effects selection list to apply them to your tracks. Once they are applied, you can see which digital effects have been put together to create that sound by looking in the Edit tab. If you need a reminder about how to use the effects editors, the section called "Effects" in Chapter 5 covers how to use them. Let's look now at all of the effects available in GarageBand.

GarageBand Effects

Just as the Instrument Generators have a list of voices or presets built into them, most of the GarageBand effects also have a series of individual presets built in. You can likewise dial in your own custom settings based on those presets or by starting from scratch and save those by choosing Make Preset from the Preset menu to build up a series of possibilities to draw upon in the future. The presets that the GarageBand effects come with are meant to be a jumping-off point. A very close friend of mine, who is an audio guru I look to for sound advice about these things, hates nothing more than using presets. He feels that if you're using a preset, you're either not trying or not listening. Even if you start with a preset, you should listen to it as applied to your track, as integrated into your mix, then move the sliders around and learn specifically what each parameter does to the sound, and then tweak it until the sound sits properly in your mix. With that said, GarageBand comes with an excellent library of effects, and since those are the jumping-off points we have to work with, let's look at each of them individually.

Amp Simulation

The Amp Simulation plug-in offers a variety of different guitar amplifier models to choose from, and you can further customize all of them once you've applied the effect to your track. You have some American and British clean and gain choices for your amp model, which comprises the core of your sound, and in the top drop-down menu there are a host of presets, including American Lead, Big Wheels, and Classic Rock. Remember, these are jumping-off points—a guide to designing your own sounds. Adjust the low, mid, and high of the amp, presence, and master gain and the overall output level. With this amp modeler, you can even adjust your pre-gain. See Figure 11.5.

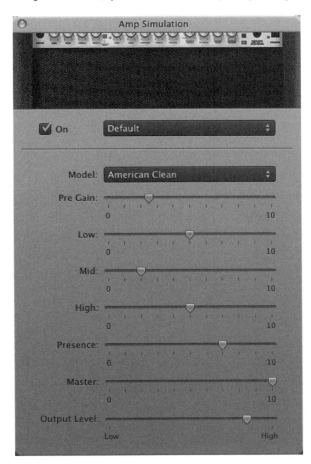

Figure 11.5 The Amp Simulation GarageBand effect.

Auto Wah

GarageBand's Auto Wah effect is a re-creation of an envelope follower, which is a filter effect that responds to the velocity of your tone. You have a lot of control over the effect's sensitivity and the color of the sound. Many variations are available. You have six modes from which to choose. You can set the mode to Thick, Thin, Peak, or Classic 1, 2, or 3. The presets in this case are good to check out to see what the capabilities of the effect are, and once again, I encourage you to go from there to sculpt

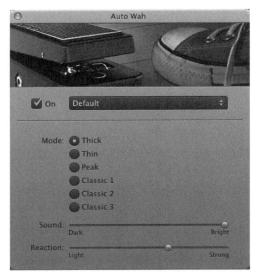

Figure 11.6 The Auto Wah GarageBand effect.

your custom tone. Don't forget to save your new preset by selecting Make Preset from the Presets menu. See Figure 11.6.

Automatic Filter

This effect plug-in lets you apply a variety of filters to your track. Think of filters like audio shapes through which you pass sound. They're like sound lenses. Some are hard to see through, others refract the sound in odd ways, and some even have motion to them, meaning they oscillate or even change over time. You can adjust the frequency, resonance, and intensity, as well as the direction and the speed of the filter. See Figure 11.7.

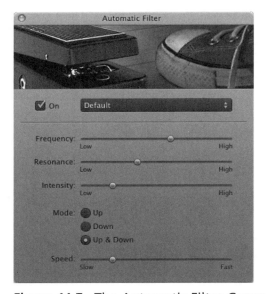

Figure 11.7 The Automatic Filter GarageBand effect.

Bass Amp

Bass Amp is similar to the Amp Simulator plug-in, but it has a set of presets that are optimized for the bass guitar. There are nine amp models to choose from, including Top Class DI Warm and American Scoop. Adjust your lows, mids (with a frequency sweep, which means you set the particular frequency that you will be boosting or cutting, which is ideal for tweaking bass tones), and highs, pre-gain, and master output. See Figure 11.8.

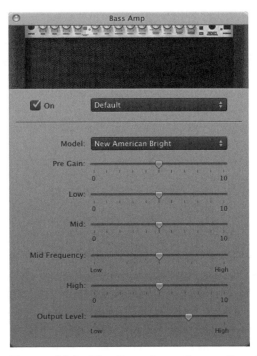

Figure 11.8 The Bass Amp GarageBand effect.

Bass Reduction

With this effect, you can dial in a specific frequency threshold, and all of the frequencies below that threshold will be attenuated (reduced in volume). The bass frequencies below the threshold that you set with the Frequency slider in the effect's interface will still be audible, but significantly reduced in presence and volume. The presets available in GarageBand's Bass Reduction effect are Hi Pass, Remove Bass, and Remove Deep Bass, and these settings simply position the Frequency slider up and down to create a reduction shelf beginning at three different positions in the frequency spectrum.

A good approach to successfully using the Bass Reduction effect is to solo your track, listen to the track with the effect enabled, select the Edit tab in the Track Info panel, and click on the parameter adjustment icon on the left side of the Bass Reduction effect itself. You can then move the slider in the interface manually until you find the sweet spot where the bassy tones you want to reduce are audibly reduced. The Bass

Reduction filter is *very* powerful in removing unwanted low-end rumble and mud from a mix. If you are mixing acoustic guitar and bass guitar together, one thing to consider is creating discrete sonic spaces via EQ (using the Hi Pass preset available in this effect is a great place to start) for each instrument. So taking the recording of the guitar and reducing its low end might be just fine because you have the bass guitar picking up the slack and filling out that portion of the spectrum. In fact, experiment with this, and you'll see that it makes both instruments clearer and more distinct. See Figure 11.9.

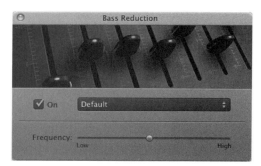

Figure 11.9 The Bass Reduction GarageBand effect.

Bitcrusher

Bitcrusher is an effect that destroys your sound by crushing the bits of data that are there. It takes your original audio source and wrecks it. The effect reduces the available bits of processing, leading to a very coarse, electronic sound. In addition, the presets apply all sorts of digital processing to achieve some really "out there" sounds. Some of the presets might remind you of classic low-tech electronic games of the early '80s. There is even one setting called Meet Atari. Crush some bits and see what your voice might sound like coming out of a 1983 plastic Dick Tracy wristwatch! See Figure 11.10.

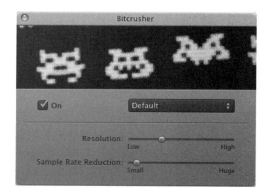

Figure 11.10 The Bitcrusher GarageBand effect.

Chorus

Chorus is an effect that makes a sound appear to be wider than it started. By wider, I mean filling up more space—thicker. It does this by doubling the original signal and slightly detuning the duplicate. Sometimes it gives the sound a little movement and some warble, which is a factor of the amount of detuning. The more detuning applied, the more the warble becomes apparent. Some of the preset names offer insight into what the Chorus plug-in is meant to achieve, such as Atmospheric, Glimmer, and Spread Stereo. See Figure 11.11.

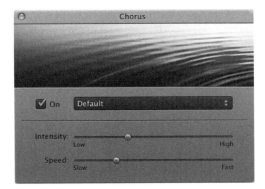

Figure 11.11 The Chorus GarageBand effect.

Distortion

Big, crunchy rock and heavy-metal guitars are all about the distortion. It makes things overdriven, scratchy, abrasive, and dark. Dial it up big with parameters such as Drive and Tone, which go from low to high and dark to bright, respectively, and adjust your overall output level. The more output level, the more heads will bang. Using this effect in combination with the Amp Simulator will create monster sounds. Commercial plug-ins, such as AmpliTube 2 from IK Multimedia, that will run you a few hundred bucks can deliver bigger, better, and louder distortion sounds than the GarageBand defaults, but if you don't have the budget to spring for that, the settings available in GarageBand give you an enormous amount of flexibility if you also pay attention to how you're going to be recording the original guitar track. If you are playing your guitar through an amp and miking the amp, then the distance and position of the mic will affect the sound you're getting to a very large degree, and this in turn will affect how effects such as distortion sound when applied. Mike the amp, plug in your guitar, create a track, and mess with effects and sounds in conjunction with your mic position to dial in your perfect sound before even recording. See Figure 11.12.

Flanger

A flanger produces a sweeping effect that changes over time, and then "comes back," if you will, like a pendulum. The effect is produced by doubling the signal (making two identical sounds out of your one source sound), and both are played simultaneously but slightly out of sync with one another—usually only small fractions of a second. Intergalactic Police, Stadium Flange, and Dolphin Flange are a few presets you can use to start with. You have parametric control over intensity, speed, and feedback with GarageBand's Flanger effect. See Figure 11.13.

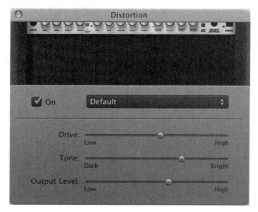

Figure 11.12 The Distortion GarageBand effect.

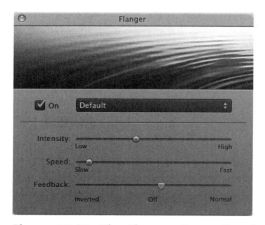

Figure 11.13 The Flanger GarageBand effect.

Overdrive

This effect allows you to crank the gain, which doesn't necessarily mean that your sound gets louder. A good analogy for something that sounds overdriven is when you turn your TV up too loud and the speaker distorts. More power is coming to the speaker than it's equipped to handle, and it sounds raunchy. With parameters of Drive, Tone, and Output Level, this can be just the thing you need to put that sound right out there in front with some guts behind it and a little snot. It will often produce distortion and can be used in conjunction with other effects to boost the grit and texture. See Figure 11.14.

Phaser

Phaser is a type of sweeping comb filter. It has a low-frequency oscillator (LFO) that makes the lower frequency parts of the spectrum start to swim around. Your original sound gets doubled, and the two are played out of phase with one another, the result of which is spacey, chorusy, and trippy. You can adjust the intensity to dial in a

Figure 11.14 The Overdrive GarageBand effect.

mixture of the LFO with the phased signals, and also the speed of the swish of the LFO and the amount of feedback generated to add some additional sweeping tonal noise to the sound of the LFO. Some presets are Circle Phases, Wide Phase, and Rock Phaser. See Figure 11.15.

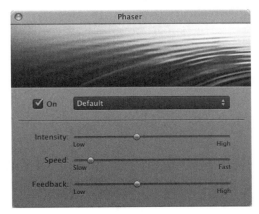

Figure 11.15 The Phaser GarageBand effect.

Speech Enhancer

The Speech Enhancer effect is designed to help you make voices, narration, voiceover, spoken parts, and even sung vocals sound better when not recorded well. You can even dial in the type of mic used, such as iBook or iSight Camera, and then choose the type of voice it is, between male and female and voiceover and solo vocal. There is also an adjustable noise filter to help cut down on the type of noise normally generated in the types of mics available in the list. If you don't want to choose a specific mic and just work with the noise filter, you can uncheck the Microphone Type box to disable that consideration. See Figure 11.16.

Figure 11.16 The Speech Enhancer GarageBand effect.

Track Echo

Sometimes called *delay*, the echo effect can add a repeat to your sound, just like an echo coming back at you when you shout in a canyon. Track echo is meant to be applied to a single track and has an awful lot of presets, including Straight Eight and Straight Quarter, which will produce echoes at eighth notes or quarter notes (respectively) in time with your song, based on the tempo setting of the song. The Echo Time slider gives you more direct control over the speed and even lets you know if you have set it to a quarter-note triplet or a sixteenth note, and so on. Echo Repeat is the number of times the echo repeats, Repeat Color is like a tone control that only affects the sound that is coming back, and Echo Volume and Original Volume allow you to set the relationship in loudness between your source audio and the echo itself. See Figure 11.17.

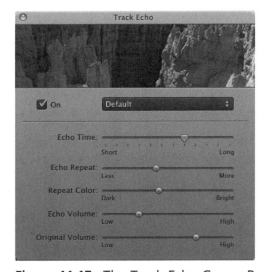

Figure 11.17 The Track Echo GarageBand effect.

Track Reverb

Apply reverb to an individual track with this effect. Reverb is a computer simulation of the reverberation of a sound in a space. It is a sound effect that re-creates how long it takes for a source sound to reflect off of the edges or walls of a space and conveys the size of that space to the listener in the length and depth of the reverb sound returned. Imagine standing in an empty warehouse and clapping your hands loudly. There's the sound of your clap itself, but then that long tail of sound—the sound that makes you know you are inside a big space—is reverb. (As opposed to clapping your hands loudly in, say, a bedroom at home with carpet on the floor, where you would hear the sound of your clap and not much else.)

You can mix how much of the reverb sound you want to come through in relation to the sound of the original track by using the two sliders at the bottom, called Reverb Volume and Original Volume, as well as adjust the length of the reverb effect with the Reverb Length slider. The Reverb Color slider will brighten or darken the overall character of the reverb. The more reverb volume you add, the "wetter" the sound is said to be. The wetter your reverb, the farther away in the mix your sound will appear—or the bigger the re-created space will seem. Reverb is one way to adjust how close or far sounds appear in a mix and can be used to address the problem of one element in your mix not sitting well or not blending with other sounds. Try a sprinkle of reverb. Too much reverb is sometimes a bad thing, though, so be conservative with it unless you're expressly going for that effect. See Figure 11.18.

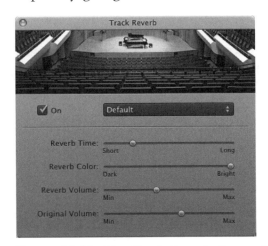

Figure 11.18 The Track Reverb GarageBand effect.

Treble Reduction

Much like the Bass Reduction effect acts like a high-pass filter, the Treble Reduction effect is very similar to a low-pass filter. Set your frequency, and everything above that frequency in the EQ spectrum of the sound will be reduced and shelved. You will still hear some of the highs—this filter will not eliminate the frequencies completely—but it can significantly reduce sharp, harsh tones in the top end of any track to which you apply it. Experiment with moving the Frequency slider manually in the effect's interface (click the parameter adjustment icon on the left side of the Treble Reduction effect in the Edit tab in the Track Info panel) while you have the offending track soloed, and take a moment to listen carefully and find the sweet spot. The idea is to only reduce the frequencies that are creating a problem, and not any of the frequencies that are desirable parts of your sound. Try to position the Frequency slider as high (to the right) as you can while still making sure not to allow any of the problem frequencies through. The presets are Hard, Soft, Medium, and Ultra and are four variations of the positioning of the frequency threshold. See Figure 11.19.

Figure 11.19   The Treble Reduction GarageBand effect.

Tremolo

Tremolo is a rhythmic pulsing of the volume going up and down at a variable intensity and speed. You may think of the classic tremolo sound as that '50s Dick Dale surf guitar sound. It's the result of the amplitude (volume) of sustained notes actually modulating up and down in volume at a certain variable of time that you can set with the Speed slider. You can set the depth to which it modulates with the Intensity slider. See Figure 11.20.

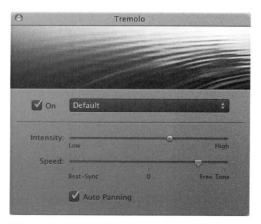

Figure 11.20   The Tremolo GarageBand effect.

Vocal Transformer

The Vocal Transformer effect is what's known as a *formant shifter*. This effect processes the quality of the phonetic sound that vowels make in speech and shifts them wildly and specifically depending on the preset. Make your vocal track sound like a monster, a chipmunk, a robot, or cartoon falsetto. You can also pitch parts up and down a major or minor third or a fourth, or even make a female voice sound male and vice versa. See Figure 11.21.

Figure 11.21   The Vocal Transformer GarageBand effect.

Adjusting Guitar Stompbox Effects and Guitar Amps

Remember that in the mixing phase, you may want to revisit the specific settings that you have dialed in on any of your guitar amps or guitar stompbox effects. Once you have all of your pieces to work with and all the parts have been tracked, the mixing process can very often involve a period of revisiting. As you hone in on your final overall sound, an element or effect that may have sounded perfect earlier on in the recording process may need to be adjusted now that you have the whole picture to work with. Sound is energy, and everything contributes to the noise soup. You need to make sure you are using spices in the soup and not muddy boots.

Select your individual guitar tracks, open up the Track Info panel, and make sure all of the parameters of the individual stompboxes and amps are just how you would like them to be. If they are not, make adjustments. Also remember that you can always rearrange the order of your stompboxes just by clicking and dragging them left to right on the floor of the stage in front of your amp in the Track Info panel. For a complete run-through of all the stompboxes and amps available in GarageBand '09, refer back to Chapter 5, in the sections called "Electric Guitar Amps" and "Electric Guitar Stompbox Effects."

Audio Unit (AU) Effects

Mac OS X uses the Audio Unit (AU) format for audio plug-ins, and you can purchase and install a wide variety of third-party AU plug-ins for use with GarageBand. If you have any installed, they will appear in the second half of the Effects drop-down menu in the Details area of the Track Info panel. If you have other software, such as Logic or other audio applications, they may install libraries of Audio Unit plug-ins by default, and if you have some things listed in that menu under Audio Unit Effects, this is why. They can be used in the same fashion as any of the GarageBand effects, including having their parameters automated with nodes in the Add Automation menu, beneath each Track Mixer on the left. See the following section for a complete explanation of the Add Automation menu and how to automate the changing of individual parameters of GarageBand effects and AU plug-ins over time.

Creating Nodes and Basic Automation

The notion of automation is simple. In the old days of analog music recording and mixing, the process of doing a mixdown of the final song often involved a performance of sorts all its own. To boil it down to one single example, suppose a particular song has all of its levels set perfectly, through hours of tweaking and honing. EQs are all set, reverbs and other effects are dialed in, and everything is ready. Let's also say that there is a place in the song where something has to change. Again, to keep it simple, suppose there is a Reverb setting on the vocals that is really mild. But in the outro of the song, when the band is going into the big finale, you need the reverb to become much wetter, and the volume of the lead vocal has to come up 4 dB.

In the old days, when it was time to do the mixdown, everything was done in real time. The multitrack recorder was connected to a two-track mixdown deck, and the engineer would have to press Record on the two-track deck and then Play on the multitrack deck and "record" the mixdown from the multitrack deck to the two-track, thus creating a two-track master tape. While the song was recording from the multitrack deck to the two-track deck, at the moment where that outro began, the engineer would have had to lean over the board, turn up the wetness of the reverb, and raise the volume fader 4 dB on the lead vocal. For talented engineers this process would be a no-brainer. In fact, if you can imagine complex mixes in songs by bands such as Rush and Yes back in the '70s and '80s, sometimes the band members themselves would have to pitch in just to have enough hands and brains to accomplish the many changes—the guitarist might be in charge of doing these three things, and the singer might be in charge of muting four specific tracks at just the right time, and so on. If one person screwed up and said, "I only raised the vocal 2 dB; I forgot it was supposed to be 4 dB," chances were very good that the engineer would press Stop, and the whole process would have to begin again. Everyone was trying to nail perfectly the technical performance of the mixdown itself. They would go back until everyone did what they were supposed to do, on time and to the perfect point. This was difficult, needless to say. But it's how it was always done.

I can remember crowding around a tiny Ross 4×4 four-track cassette recorder with my band, Mobile Home, in Seattle's Greenwood neighborhood in the mid '90s, when we were working on our first homemade demo. Everyone had responsibility for a track (four tracks, four musicians), and we didn't do our own tracks—we swapped around so we knew that no one was making his part a little louder than he was supposed to! Our "fifth member" and live sound engineer, Aaron Murray, took care to monitor levels on the two-track cassette deck we were mixing down to. There was me, Jesse Howard (my brother), Courtney Hudak, and Jesse Moore, all with our hands reaching into this tiny workspace, with our fingers on knobs and faders, waiting for those prescribed moments to make the minute changes we had painstakingly decided to make. If we screwed it up during the final mixdown, we'd just rewind and do it again. No one even complained—that was just how it was done. I would do anything to be able to go back to that time and have something like GarageBand available to me! I often feel truly envious of kids today. I know that sounds cheap and clichéd, but the truth is that the amount of technology available today to musicians and filmmakers (film is my other passion) makes me tremble.

Mixing automation first arrived on the scene in the form of a motorized mixing console that was programmable, and you could make decisions ahead of time about what fader should change to what degree and at what time in the song. You could decide later that you wanted some fader to be set to something different, and you could just alter the program. It was very convenient, and it revolutionized audio post-production. Some resisted, of course, and I'm certain there are still mixing engineers today who refuse to use automation in favor of keeping up their chops and doing it the old-fashioned way. Just like those filmmakers who continue to edit on film (Steven Spielberg, Francis Ford Coppola, Woody Allen, and Martin Scorsese all come to mind), it is a craft unto itself, and if you're good at it (as those filmmakers and their respective editing teams clearly are), why not continue to do it that way? It's a good question.

This brings us back to the nonlinear world of digital audio recording and GarageBand. Automation in this context is nothing different than the programmable motorized mixing consoles I mentioned before, except that your console in GarageBand is a software mixing console (the Track Mixer), and the automation is done by creating specific points—or *nodes*—in the timeline where you want a particular change to be made with a certain parameter and dragging the node into a new position at that particular time—or gradually over time. Voila—when you do your mixdown, those modifications are made seamlessly and precisely every time, for as long as the digital file of that particular GarageBand project exists and is not modified further. By creating these automation nodes, you are essentially recording those moves of the faders, knobs, and parameters so that they automatically play out every time you play the song, including when you bounce or export your final mix.

In GarageBand, there are two parameters that are considered basic track automation. These are volume and pan.

Track Volume

Volume is the loudness of a track. This is the parameter that you will automate if you want a track to get softer or louder—either instantaneously or gradually over time—at a certain point in your song. When automation is going to be involved with a certain parameter (such as volume) on a certain track, I always like to try to set my main volume setting for that track to the level that is the most appropriate for the whole song. In other words, first set your volume to the level that makes that track work best for most of the song—the highest percentage of the running time will be spent at this level—and then plan to use automation to automatically deviate from your "default" level setting when necessary, perhaps often returning to the proposed default.

After setting your volume level for the track to something that works really well for most of the song, click the View/Hide Automation for Track icon in the Track Mixer on the track for which you want to create some automation. (It's the small, gray, downward-pointing triangle at the right end of the button strip that contains Mute and Solo.) This process has four steps.

First, choose Track Volume from the Track Automation menu. Then click the rectangular indicator button on the left edge of this menu, which enables automation for that parameter on this track. Now, you will see a colored continuum (timeline) in the track timeline area, underneath this track. That colored area shows where the parameter is currently set; think of it as a line graph. As the playhead moves across this automation timeline, if it encounters a change in the parameter, it makes the change in GarageBand. To make your volume decrease a little bit at the two-minute mark in the song, scroll along your timeline until you get two minutes in (or to the chorus or the bridge, and so on) and click once on the line at that point. This is a node. You will need to add at least two nodes every time you want to make a change (the setting you're starting at and the setting you're changing to), and you'll want to add a total of at least four nodes if you need something to change for a bit and then go back to default. So suppose you want the volume to go up 4 dB for a few seconds and then come back down to where it was. You would click four times on the automation timeline. You don't have to be exact when you first place the nodes because you will fine-tune them in a minute. I usually just click four times, spaced out, and then position them exactly where they need to be after all four of my nodes are created. See Figure 11.22.

Figure 11.22 Four automation nodes in the Track Volume Automation track.

After you have placed your four nodes, you can raise Node 2 up your requisite 4 dB. (The reason I drew four nodes is that you always need a place to come from and to go to—any change in automation is always comprised of a starting place/time and an ending place/time.) Then, raise your third node up to match the second. You will know that the third one is exactly matching the second when the line connecting them gets thin, sharp, and perfectly straight. You can also hover your mouse over the nodes to see what their current setting is, which will be reported in the small yellow tooltips. See Figures 11.23 through 11.26 for a step-by-step representation of the rest of the process.

Figure 11.23   Raise Node 2 up 4 dB as desired.

Figure 11.24   Raise Node 3 up to match Node 2.

Figure 11.25   Zoom in, and by clicking and dragging left to right, you can position the start points and end points of your automated move more accurately. Zoom in more for even greater control.

Figure 11.26   Adjust the positioning of the start and end nodes of the fade at the end of your section of audio where the volume returns to its original level.

Gradual Automation Changes over Time

To have something such as volume change gradually over a span of time, all you need to do is space out your nodes. If it takes five seconds to get from Node 3 to Node 4, then it will take five seconds for the volume to change from –7 dB to –12 dB. See Figure 11.27.

Figure 11.27   A volume decrease over time, achieved by spacing out the nodes.

GarageBand figures out all the movement in between and performs it for you more smoothly than a human could. If you want to make it more human, add a few more nodes across the five seconds and make the appropriate adjustments. After the nodes are created, you can click and drag every node into position and fine-tune any of them. See Figure 11.28.

Figure 11.28 Adding more nodes along your continuum to create that less-than-perfect feel.

Deleting Nodes

You can select a node by clicking once on it. When you do, you'll notice that the small dot of the node itself will get a little bigger—I even like to say it gets bold. You can delete any selected nodes by using the Delete or Backspace key. You can select a node and then Shift-click a second node (or more) to group-select them, and then delete all of them at once. You'll notice that every automation timeline starts out with one node at the very beginning. If you delete *all* nodes, including this first one, your level will drop to 0. You can add a node back in at the beginning and raise it up if you'd like, but an easier way is to disable automation (the little blue light on the Track Automation menu to the left in the Track Mixer, under your track), then use the normal volume fader to position the level where you want it to be (which will become your new default), and then enable automation again. There will be an initial node again, and the automation timeline will return to its level throughout.

You can group-select a range of nodes by clicking and dragging a node selection across a series of nodes. You have to click in an area where there is no node and be sure not to click on the line itself, or you'll just create a new node. Once you click and drag across several nodes, they will all be bold and can be deleted or moved together. See Figure 11.29.

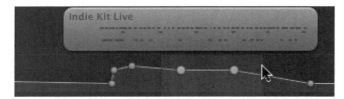

Figure 11.29 Click and drag across nodes to group-select them.

More appropriately, perhaps, to a task you might want to actually perform time and again, once group-selected, you can now click and drag one node to the left or right, and the entire selected range of nodes will move left or right and be positioned in a new place, with their same relative relationships intact. The same goes for raising and lowering a group of selected nodes. If you like the way the intricate little move you made occurs, but the whole thing needs to be a little quieter, just select them all and drag them down. See Figures 11.30 and 11.31.

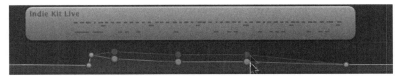

Figure 11.30 Click and drag to the left or right, and a selected group of nodes will move with their relationships intact.

Figure 11.31 Click and drag up or down, and a selected group of nodes will move with their relationships intact.

Track Pan

Panning is the movement of a track throughout the stereo field, or panorama. Making something appear to be coming out of the left speaker a little more than the right is known as *panning left* or *panned left*. Although Track Pan automation (as well as every other type of automation) has its particularity in terms of which parameter it's affecting, it operates exactly the same as Track Volume automation. Set the start point and end point of your nodes and drag them to their new positions. With Track Pan, the center line of the timeline automation continuum (the line graph analogy) represents 0, or centered. Moving your nodes above the line effects a shift to the left side of the stereo field, and moving your nodes below the line moves the sound of the track into the right side. A gradual shift of panning over time can be a neat effect in mixing to make an instrument "wander" from one ear to the other in headphones or one speaker to the other when played through speakers. See Figure 11.32.

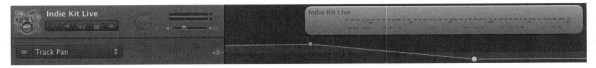

Figure 11.32 Automation nodes in the Track Pan automation track. Up is pan left, and down is pan right.

The Add Automation Menu

Apple beefed up the automation aspect of GarageBand starting in version '08 of the application by adding the ability to automate more than just volume and panning of a track. You can now automate any parameter of any of the GarageBand effects, amps, or stompboxes. Anything that is available to be adjusted by the user in the edit mode for the effect in the Track Info panel Edit area can be added as a new automation track and automated, even things that are simply an on/off toggle—such as when you might want your Retro Chorus stompbox to kick in or out. The following technique will carry over to any effects or instruments you use and would like to automate.

Automating Effect and Instrument Parameters

I've added the Atmospheric Chorus to my Indie Kit Live drum MIDI track, so I can automate one aspect of the Chorus by way of example. See Figure 11.33.

Figure 11.33 The Atmospheric Chorus effect inserted onto the track.

If you click the Edit Parameters icon button for adjusting the parameters of the Chorus effect in the Track Info panel's Edit tab, you can see that there are Intensity and Speed parameters. These are the two standard parameters of almost every chorus (hardware or software) available on the market. Every effect that you try to automate will have its own particular set of parameters that can be automated. See Figure 11.34.

Set your defaults for these parameters to what you might consider the normal position of this effect in your song, again so that if you need to create a deviation, you have a baseline from which to start. If the effect is simply going to appear on one instrument for a few bars and start one way and end another, then set your defaults to roughly

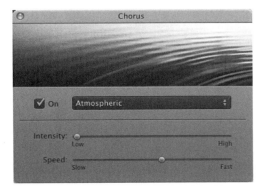

Figure 11.34 The Chorus effect has Intensity and Speed parameters.

where you think you might want to begin or end, and you can work backward from that.

Choose Add Automation from the Automation drop-down menu in the Track Mixer on the left. See Figure 11.35.

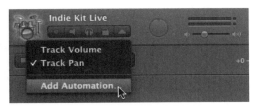

Figure 11.35 Choose Add Automation from the Track Mixer's Automation drop-down menu.

The Add Automation window will come up, allowing you to place check marks next to the parameters that are available for any of the instruments or effects that are inserted on that track. Notice that here you can access not only two parameters from the Chorus effect, but also drums kits (since my Software Instrument is a drum kit), visual EQ (covered in the next section), and echo and reverb. These can all be automated over time independently. Activate them here with the check box. See Figure 11.36.

Click OK and then look to the Automation drop-down menu over in the Track Mixer once again, and see that it reads Intensity instead of Volume or Pan. You can click the little LED button to the left of the drop-down menu to enable or disable automation for the track. See Figure 11.37.

Now your automation timeline for Chorus Intensity is displayed, and you can add nodes and create your automation, just as in the earlier section on automating volume. Add nodes, position and space them, and play your track back to see how you did. See Figure 11.38.

If you click the Edit tab in the Track Info panel and click on the Chorus effect Parameters icon, you'll see that because we have automation enabled for Intensity, the

Figure 11.36 Choose to automate the Intensity parameter of Chorus by selecting the check box.

Figure 11.37 Enable automation for the track by clicking the button at the left of the drop-down menu.

Figure 11.38 Two nodes positioned to change the intensity of Atmospheric Chorus gradually over a period of time.

Intensity parameter slider is now grayed out in the effect interface itself. This is because you can't alter the intensity by moving the slider in the effect interface while there is automation for that parameter. The two approaches are mutually exclusive. The automation nodes are taking care of the moves, and that renders the slider in the parameter's interface moot. If you disable automation for Intensity, this slider will no longer be grayed out, and you will be able to move it around again. See Figure 11.39.

Visual EQ

Adjusting the EQ of a track is the process of identifying certain frequencies within the audio spectrum and with a specific degree of angle and then boosting or cutting the

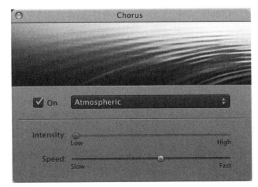

Figure 11.39 The Chorus effect edit pane with Intensity grayed out because it's being automated in the timeline.

gain of those frequencies. GarageBand has a fantastic tool for accomplishing this task, and it's called the *Visual EQ* effect. It's a great-sounding EQ with four bands, and you can determine where the bands are and how much you want to boost or cut the band. Open up Track Info for any track and click on the Edit tab. Visual EQ has been added to every track you create, but with none of the frequencies cut or boosted, as this is left to your discretion. If you click the parameters adjustment icon for Visual EQ, you will see the default frequency ranges of Bass, Low Mid, High Mid, and Treble. They are all set flat to start with, and you can cut and boost frequencies within the Visual EQ interface. There is a small interactive grid that represents the frequencies in hertz (Hz, which is cycles per second). You can click and drag up and down on the Hz boxes and change the point in the EQ spectrum that each of the four nodes will be affecting. Then you can click and drag to set the boost or cut to the desired gain level. See Figure 11.40.

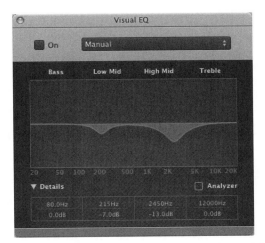

Figure 11.40 Click and drag in the grid to set the frequencies (in Hz) and boost/cut those frequencies (in dB) in the Visual EQ edit pane.

You can also interact directly with the EQ curve in the top half of the Visual EQ pane, and click and drag the peaks to position them any way you like. With Visual EQ, you can really sculpt your sound quite precisely and artistically. See Figure 11.41.

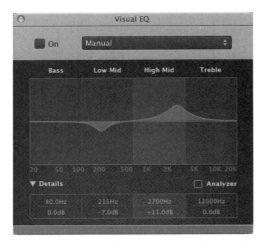

Figure 11.41 Click and drag the peaks and valleys to move them in the frequency spectrum and in the boost/cut amount.

The Visual EQ effect can have its parameters automated just like any effect, as described a moment ago. Try radically changing the EQ on a lead vocal at a certain moment in the song for a dynamic effect.

In the Visual EQ edit pane, you can click the check box next to Analyzer and see a spectrum analysis of the sound that's coming through the Visual EQ effect in real time. This is valuable when you are trying to track down offending frequencies in a sound or even when you're trying to see what frequencies are actually there, which is helpful in deciding at what frequency to position the shelf of a high-pass filter, for example. See Figure 11.42.

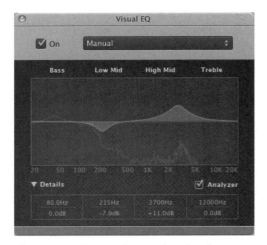

Figure 11.42 Activate the Analyzer to see what ranges of frequencies are most prominent in your track. The higher (vertically) the graph lines reach, the more sonic energy the sound has in that frequency range.

You can always add additional Visual EQ effects if necessary, just by clicking on any empty effects slot in the Edit tab for a given track and choosing Visual EQ from the menu. Just keep in mind that whatever order you place your EQ effects in will affect the track cumulatively. In other words, if you remove the low end with the first EQ in your effects chain and then boost the low end in a second Visual EQ, there will be very little low end left to boost since you had reduced it with the first Visual EQ.

Master Effects

The Track Info panel has another tab next to Real Instruments, Software Instruments, or Guitars, at the top of the Track Info panel, called Master Track. These are the global effects and post-processing that you can apply to your whole mix. The process of using master effects is usually something like putting the icing on the cake. It's that final layer of polish, level adjustment, and maybe even compression or limiting that brings your song the rest of the way up to snuff. Click on the Master Track tab at the top of the Track Info panel and explore some of the presets, which will add combinations of effects to your Master Track. You can then tweak and massage them to get the song sounding exactly as you want. Remember, you can also save your Mastering settings for future use (like on other songs on the same album?) by clicking Save Master at the bottom of the Master Track panel. See Figure 11.43.

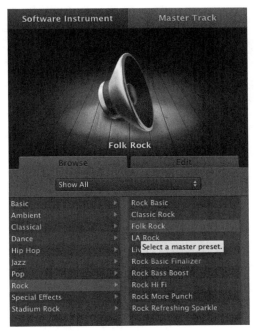

Figure 11.43   The Master Track tab with the Browse tab selected.

Automation in the Master Track

This is where you would create a master fade-out of the whole song. To do this, you have to choose Show Master Track from the Track menu (or press Command+B), which will reveal a track at the bottom of the Track Mixer and Timeline window called Master. This is a track where you can create automation nodes, just like in any individual track, as discussed earlier, but the things that you change in this track affect the entire mix. In the Automation menu for the Master Track, located in the drop-down menu at the far left of the Track Mixer, create nodes along the automation timeline and drag them up and down to change the chosen parameter. Volume is the main option here. To fade the song out, create one node a number of seconds before the end of the song and then another at the very end, and drag the latter down to 0. Then, over time as the song plays, GarageBand will gradually lower the playback volume to 0, automatically performing the fade-out for you. See Figure 11.44.

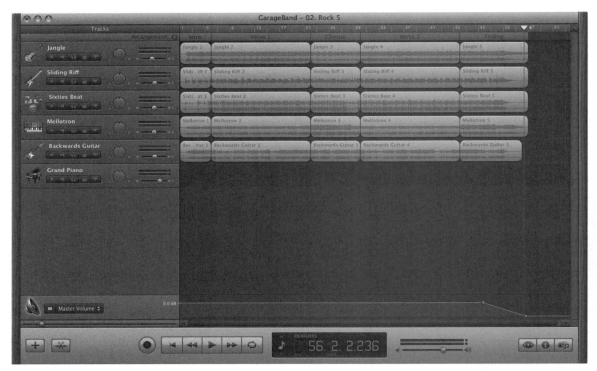

Figure 11.44 A master fade-out automated in the Master Track.

Automating Changes in Tempo and Pitch

In GarageBand '08, Apple added a feature that was sorely missing from all of the previous versions of GarageBand. It's not perfect yet, in my opinion, and it hasn't been improved in GarageBand '09, but it's a real start. I even remember asking my friends about this when GarageBand first came out. You can now have the tempo of your song change at any point in the song. You can also change the pitch of the song, which will transpose (meaning change to a new key) all of your MIDI tracks at a certain point. Just choose Master Tempo or Master Pitch, create your nodes, and drag them up and down at the precise point in time that you'd like to see the change happen. Tempos can even be *ramped*, meaning they can change gradually over time, or you can just have a change instantaneously happen at a specific beat in the song. Just zoom in on your timeline to be as precise as you want to be. Your ramp can be nearly vertical if you like. See Figures 11.45 and 11.46.

Figure 11.45 Automating a change in tempo in the Master Track.

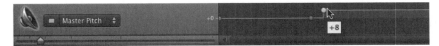

Figure 11.46 Automating a change in pitch in the Master Track.

Mixing Your Own Mash-Ups

Just a final note here for the mash-up artists among you. If you want to create your own mash-ups, it's very easy with GarageBand. Use a track for each song you want to mash—you can use any song file (MP3, AIF, WAV, or AAC) that you have on your computer—and drag the files into their own tracks. Slide the audio regions left and right to sync them up in whatever way you like, and you can even automate fade-ins and fade-outs using the volume automation we just covered in the second half of this

Figure 11.47 A mash-up of two Last Fair Deal songs with automated volume changes and panning set slightly out from center.

chapter. You can adjust the level of each relative track and even the panning of each element. You might get some weird results if you pan things out that were designed to be stereo tracks, but as usual, experimentation and listening are all you need to know. When you are finished, use the Share menu to get your files out of GarageBand and share them with your friends. See the next chapter for an in-depth look at sharing your songs from GarageBand with other applications and with people! That's the real reason we do any of this anyway, right? So people can hear it? I created a mash-up of two songs by Last Fair Deal (my four-piece acoustic roots outfit), "New England" and "Arizona." It seemed like a good juxtaposition. See Figure 11.47.

What's Next: Sharing and Archiving

Now that your masterpiece is recorded and mixed, it's time to get it out of GarageBand and into people's ears! The next chapter will focus on what to do when you're finished making and ready to start sharing. Then we'll look at the all-important practice of backing up, archiving, and the steps for importing GarageBand projects into Logic Pro.

12 Sharing and Archiving Your GarageBand Projects

Digital music and audio production are very broad forms of creativity, art, production, and engineering. Many different kinds of people are involved—often at different levels of participation—with the process. If we're talking about it from the perspective of the producer, recording engineer, or performer on a given project, that person will often have other musicians working with him, as well as other producers or engineers. With collaboration comes a degree of unpredictability with regard to the software and/or hardware your comrades will be using. Sometimes it's a different recording software package, such as Logic Pro, Pro Tools, Digital Performer, or Cubase, and it's even probable that if you are working with someone else who uses GarageBand, that person might be using a different version than you are. This can make life difficult if you are unprepared.

This preparation usually involves understanding a good bit about file types and formats, as well as software versions and the inherent pitfalls and/or benefits associated with them. It also includes knowledge of where and how to acquire and install software patches and updates and how to purchase licenses for plug-ins, Software Instruments, or samples that perhaps you do not own yourself, but that your collaborator has used in the project he is planning to share with you. There are so many possible iterations of these various scenarios that it's very important to consider—almost from a strategic perspective—ways to align yourself technologically before you begin working on a project.

It would be impossible to cover every possible permutation that you might encounter moving forward. To be fair, if you're just starting out with GarageBand and digital audio recording, you might not run into these types of issues right away, but since you are likely to encounter a roadblock at some point in your audio production career, I feel it's worthwhile to talk a little bit about working together, keeping apprised of software updates and related concerns, and sharing not only GarageBand projects with others, but also the exported files that GarageBand generates. These days, in the computer world and in the culture of the Internet, the word *sharing* usually means the methods we employ for allowing others to listen to, download, burn, or share yet again our music or audio programs. In this discussion I am referring to that part of the equation indeed, but also to the idea of taking a project that you have created in GarageBand and actually running it on someone else's computer.

An example might be a rock band whose members all live and record in different places. The drummer might start the GarageBand project and track live drums or program them using MIDI and then send the file (via the Internet or burned to a CD-R and mailed) to the bass player. The bassist, in turn, tracks the bass part and then saves and ships the GarageBand file off to the guitarist. After that, the keyboardist gets a stab at adding parts, and then the file finally makes its way to the vocalist's computer. Vocals get tracked and then it comes back to the drummer, who, for the sake of argument, is the person who started the project and is planning to mix and master the song. He will make the final mastered bounce (mixdown or export) of the song and will upload it to the band's website. This process is also what I would call "sharing your GarageBand project." So, we'll talk about sharing as in file sharing, as well as sharing as in collaboration. This chapter will discuss both scenarios.

The other part of the discussion relates to what to do when you are finished working on a project for the time being, and you need to save, archive, move, or back it up, and what to do when you want to work on the project again a month or a year (or more!) down the road. One thing that happens when you try to work on an older project again is that often your versions have changed on your application, and sometimes you have even changed applications! One example of this might be if you were to use GarageBand for a couple of years and then decide it's time to upgrade, so you start working with Logic Pro. In such a case, you will need to know how to import one of your old GarageBand projects into Logic. This is but one example of how this might play out for you.

Sharing GarageBand Projects

When we talk about sharing GarageBand projects, there are really two types of sharing that require some attention. Sharing as in *file sharing*, which is the exporting and transmitting of any of a variety of file types and modes of transmission, is our first order of business. The second type is sharing in terms of *project collaboration*, which we will cover later in this chapter, in the "Saving and Archiving GarageBand Projects" section.

The Share Menu

When we talk about exporting a song (I'm going to call a project a song for now), we're talking about taking the project file and all of its tracks, decisions, instruments, MIDI data, effects, and automation—*as is*—and writing a new file out to the computer. In the analog world, this part of the process is called the *mixdown*. In some other audio applications, it's called *bouncing*. This basically means the current state of the GarageBand project will be frozen (also sometimes called *baked*) to a new file, which can be any one of a variety of formats, somewhere outside of GarageBand. This can be your hard drive, a server, or a CD, but the idea is that you are making a version of the song and putting it somewhere. It's almost like GarageBand is playing your song all the way through and recording it part and parcel to a new file, the parameters and settings of which you can control to some degree. GarageBand calls this process *sharing* your song. All of the functions in GarageBand that pertain to this process are, as you might imagine, relegated to the Share menu in the main menu bar at the top of your screen. When you want to give your song to someone or make it available somewhere, you are considered to be sharing it. See Figure 12.1.

Figure 12.1 GarageBand's Share menu for songs.

If you are scoring a movie or you have a video file open in GarageBand, the Share menu will update to show options for sending your movie to iTunes, iDVD, or iWeb. See Figure 12.2.

Figure 12.2 GarageBand's Share menu for movies.

When you consider your song to be finished or at a good stopping point where you're ready to share it, you have a number of options. The first and most obvious method of sharing your song is, of course, to play it for someone or listen to it yourself. As you've been doing since the beginning, you can put the playhead at beginning of the timeline, hit Play, and listen to your song out of your speakers or on headphones. Beyond that scenario, there are a number of things you can do from the Share menu.

Send Song to iTunes

This first menu choice initiates the most common practice for getting songs out of GarageBand and into other arenas—in other words, exporting them. It's the basic mixdown idea. Because iTunes is Apple's default Mac OS X audio player, having this function built right into a menu makes a lot of sense. If you like to use another application for managing and listening to audio, it's a simple one-step process to move the song file into your preferred player, and we'll cover that toward the end of this section. By the way, when GarageBand uses the word *send* in a menu, that usually means *export* with a side order of "please put the resulting file somewhere specific for me."

When you choose Send Song to iTunes from the Share menu, you get a dialog box with a couple of pertinent questions that need answering. The dialog box presents you with a series of fields to fill out. You can specify which iTunes playlist you would like your newly exported song to be placed in. If you enter a name that does not yet exist in the iTunes playlists, GarageBand will create a new playlist of that name in iTunes on the fly, and the song you are exporting will be the only song in the list. Naturally, GarageBand will add the exported song to your iTunes Library *and* the playlist. The next three fields are all set to add metadata to your audio file. Artist Name, Composer Name, and Album Name are all available to be filled out. Artist Name is the only one that is optional. If you leave the Composer Name, Album Name, or Playlist field empty, GarageBand will generate an error dialog box warning you to fill out those fields. See Figure 12.3.

Figure 12.3 Remember to fill out the iTunes Playlist, Composer Name, and Album Name fields. Artist Name is optional.

Below the four fields is a Compress check box. If you leave this unchecked, GarageBand will export an AIFF file (CD quality, similar to a WAV file) to iTunes. If you want to create an MP3 or an AAC of your file as you send it to iTunes, you can select the Compress check box, and that will reveal a few more options. Personally, I usually send uncompressed exports to iTunes, and then if I need an MP3, AAC, or something else, I can always go back to my master (the AIFF uncompressed export from GarageBand to iTunes) and generate an MP3 or another file type with the settings that I choose at that particular time. Because creating MP3s is usually situationally specific for me, I like to take control of that process in iTunes manually. See Figure 12.4.

You can choose to compress the file into an MP3 or an AAC file in the Compress Using drop-down menu, and the Audio Settings drop-down is where you set your quality

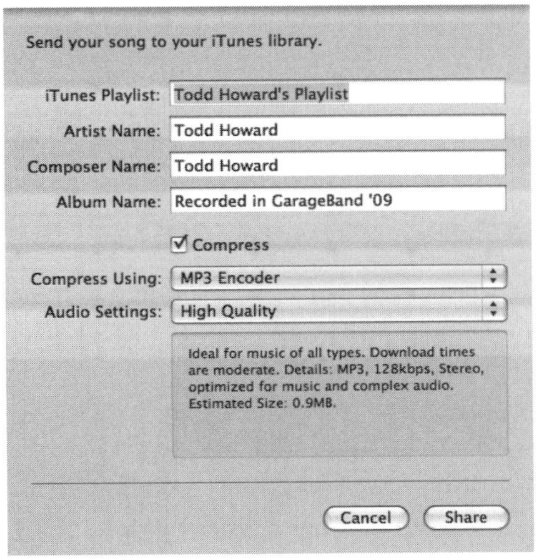

Figure 12.4   Options for compressing your export on the way to iTunes.

settings once you choose a format. GarageBand offers Good Quality, High Quality, and Higher Quality as three preset quality choices, and they deliver as follows:

- **Good Quality:** 64 kbps

- **High Quality:** 128 kbps

- **Higher Quality:** 192 kbps

As a nice convenience, the compression settings summary box at the bottom (which only appears when you have the Compress check box selected) will tell you how big your particular file will be if you choose that particular compression setting. You can always choose Custom from the Audio Settings drop-down menu and make these settings anything you like for your MP3 or AAC files. See Figures 12.5 and 12.6.

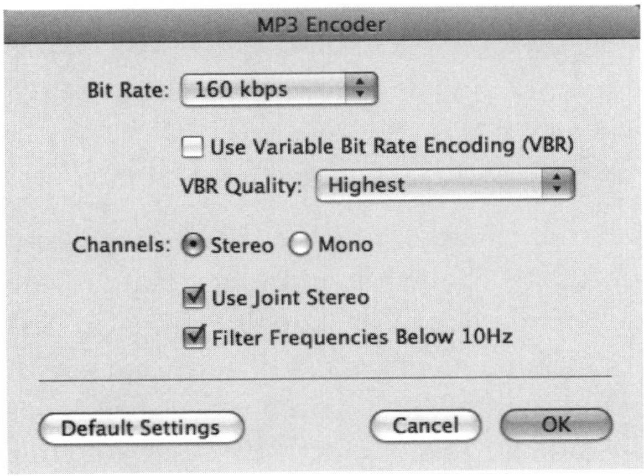

Figure 12.5   Custom compression settings for MP3 files.

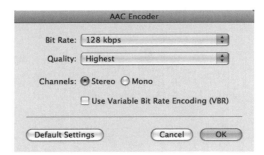

Figure 12.6 Custom compression settings for AAC files.

Auto Normalize   Sometimes, for any number of reasons, your song will be too quiet. This can be the result of recording things at a very low level, or maybe they are very quiet things that you've recorded, such as crickets in a field at night. Another reason might be that you have levels that are loud enough, but you've mixed everything relatively low. There is a feature that can save you from having to go back and remix everything. It's called Auto Normalize, and it is a global preference that you can turn on or off in the GarageBand Preferences window. Under the Advanced tab in GarageBand Preferences, there is a check box for Auto Normalize. This essentially raises the gain, or volume, of your mix to the point where the loudest moment in your song will be right around 98-percent maximum volume. Like the old saying goes, "A rising tide raises all boats," so the rest of the song gets louder to boot.

To have GarageBand Auto Normalize your songs at the moment that you export them, keep this box checked. The only issue with using Auto Normalize is that GarageBand does it for you, and you don't have any control over the degree to which it normalizes the signal. For most GarageBand users this will be sufficient, but if you're really picky about your final product, you should only use this as a temporary measure so you can get something tossed up on MySpace or e-mail a demo to a friend and avoid having a file that's just too darn quiet.

Normalization will never add distortion to a track, and it is likewise unable to remove distortion from source files. See Figure 12.7.

Where Is the File I Just Sent to iTunes? If you need to locate the song file that GarageBand exports to iTunes, the easiest way to go about it is to open iTunes and navigate to the song in your Library. Then, right-click (Control-click) the song's name in the Library list and choose Show in Finder. A new Finder window will pop open with the folder that contains the song file. The file itself will be highlighted when the Finder window opens. Alternatively, you can click and drag any song name out of your library in iTunes, and iTunes will make a copy of the song file and put it anywhere

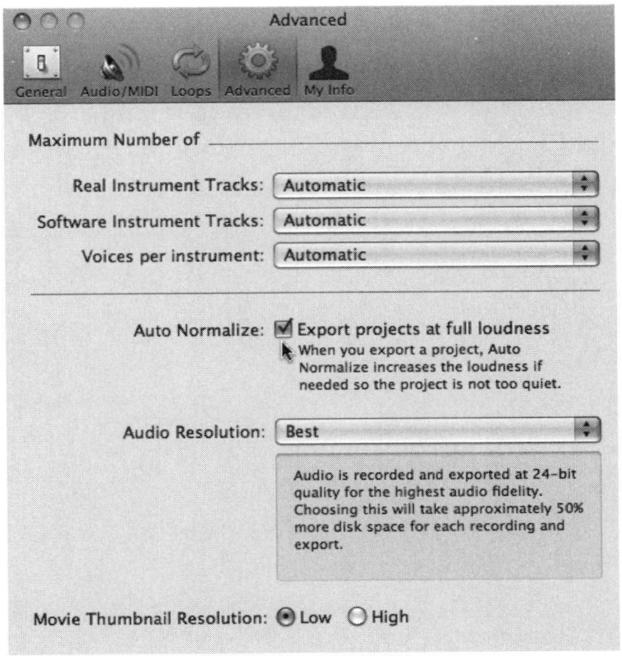

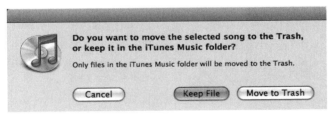

Figure 12.7   The GarageBand Preferences Advanced pane with Auto Normalize turned on.

you drag it to if what you need is to have a copy of it, rather than needing to go to its location.

If you need to move the file from its location in the Finder to another location, I recommend using the Option-click-and-drag method so that you make a copy of it and move it to another location. If you simply move the file, then iTunes will no longer be able to locate it, and you'll start to have a lot of bad links in your iTunes Library. If you *do* move it, be sure to go directly back to iTunes and click and delete that listing in the Library to make sure you've cleaned up after yourself. If you Option-click-and-drag the file, copying it, and then you return to iTunes, select the song in the Library, and press Delete, iTunes will remove that reference from the Library, and while it's doing that, it will ask you whether you want the song to be removed from the Library only or also moved to the trash. If you pay attention to the dialog while you are doing this, your chances of accidentally deleting a file for good are slim, but if you move too quickly, you could end up deleting the only copy you have of a particular file. Be warned! See Figure 12.8.

Figure 12.8   The Remove from Library/Move File to Trash dialog box in iTunes.

Send Movie to iTunes

If you are exporting a movie that you have imported into GarageBand and scored with your own music, when you are finished, you may want to send that movie file to iTunes for viewing on your iPod or Apple TV, or even straight to your hard drive. If you are scoring a movie, and you choose Send Movie to iTunes from the Share menu, your options for compressing will be different than those you saw when sending a song to iTunes. See Figure 12.9.

Figure 12.9 Choosing your target video compression settings when sending a movie to iTunes.

Send Ringtone to iTunes

With the release of the iPhone, Apple has entered the ringtone game. Certain songs on the iTunes store, when purchased, can be (for an additional 99 cents) converted into a ringtone ready for use on an Apple iPhone. In iTunes there is a mini-interface that pops up when you are getting ready to purchase a ringtone that allows you to specify which portion of the song to use as the ringtone (up to 40 seconds) and whether to fade in or out. Once you've decided, you can't change these settings—your ringtone is already baked, and you can't change the amount of fade-out in the recipe, if you get my meaning. See Figure 12.10.

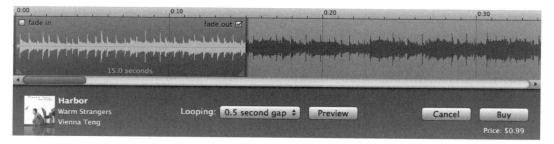

Figure 12.10 Creating a ringtone with an iTunes Store purchase in iTunes.

With the release of GarageBand '08, ringtone-creation functionality (for use in iTunes for syncing with an Apple iPhone) was added to allow you to create ringtones out of any audio you have in your GarageBand timeline. We discussed using the Cycle Record function in the chapters on recording audio and MIDI performances, and this process is no different. To create a ringtone with GarageBand, mark off a section of your timeline of less than 40 seconds with the yellow cycle region bar and select Send Ringtone to iTunes from the Share menu. If you try to make your ringtone longer than 40 seconds, you will get the error/instruction dialog box shown in Figure 12.11.

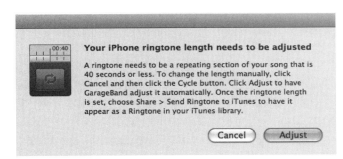

Figure 12.11   Your ringtone length needs to be adjusted!

Activate the Cycle Region button, which is the double-facing curved arrows button in the main Transport controls area at the bottom of the GarageBand interface. See Figure 12.12.

Figure 12.12   Activate the cycle region function.

Adjust the yellow cycle region bar at the top of your ruler to designate the portion of your song out of which you'd like to make a ringtone. Be sure to keep it under 40 seconds. That's a limitation of the Ringtone function in iTunes and on the iPhone. See Figure 12.13.

Figure 12.13   Adjust the cycle region bar to play only that which you would like "ringtoned."

Finally, choose Send Ringtone to iTunes from the Share menu, and the file will be prepped and packaged for use as a ringtone and added to your Ringtones list in iTunes. Your new ringtone is now ready to be synced with your iPhone.

Keep in mind that if you want to make a special version of your project file to do some funky editing with—maybe mute certain tracks or create a loop specifically for your ringtone collection that isn't merely a captured snippet of the song—simply go to the Finder, open your GarageBand folder, and click to select the project file in question. If you press Command+D, you will create a duplicate of the project. Be sure to add the word "Ringtone" or something obvious to the filename so you'll know which file this is two years from now, open the duplicate and begin making as many destructive changes as you need to make your ringtone, and remain worry-free. You can use automation as well to create a fade-out at the end of your ringtone, if you'd like!

What If I Don't Have an iPhone, and I Still Want to Make a Ringtone with GarageBand? Many cell phone companies allow you to make your own ringtones, but you won't be able to use the file GarageBand creates for iTunes. Simply follow all of these steps, but this time just make a 40-second-or-less project file. (You can edit your tracks down by selecting them all, positioning the playhead, pressing Command+T to make a split, selecting everything after and before your desired split, and hitting Delete to clear them out.) Then position your regions as you like, create your automation or fades, and select Send File to iTunes from the Share menu. Check the Compress button to make an MP3 (make sure it's an MP3, not an AAC!), and then you can upload that MP3 file to your phone or to your cell phone company's website for conversion into a ringtone for your particular phone.

Send Podcast to iWeb

As we talked about in the chapter on creating podcasts, Apple makes working with all of the iLife applications awfully easy by uniting them in this way. If you have created a podcast in GarageBand and you have a website that you use iWeb to maintain, choosing this simple menu item will save you loads of time by adding your podcast to your site, giving it its own page, and even adding it to your RSS feed. All this is accomplished with one step. Since the logical next step in Apple's iLife workflow model is to take a podcast and get it on the web, they've made it a one-step process. Choose your compressions settings, and GarageBand will send the file over to iWeb, copy the needed media, and open the iWeb application and bring you directly to the page created for the new episode. Then you can start adding your text and photo content. It's that simple.

Send Movie to iDVD

If you are using GarageBand to score a movie, you can export the movie with all of your new audio work built in and deliver it right over to iDVD for authoring. This might be a movie that you were editing in iMovie and then opened in GarageBand for scoring or sound effects. You can always generate separate audio files if you are delivering them back to an editor or post-production supervisor. To do that you'd use the next menu choice, Export Song to Disk. It's another "reduce it to one step if possible" bit of perfection on Apple's part.

Export Song to Disk

Choosing Export Song to Disk from the Share menu is almost exactly the same as choosing Send Song to iTunes, only this time you won't have to enter a playlist name and the other metadata info. You will save a file to your hard drive in its full, original quality (whatever quality setting you recorded the song at), or you can click Compress (just like when you send to iTunes), choose between MP3 and AAC, and make your compressions settings. This is useful if you need to send the file to someone, burn a data CD of your files, or even if you use another utility for doing your burning, such as Toast, Jam, or WaveBurner. If you only need to export files but you don't need them in iTunes (for example, if you were making some MP3 exports to upload to your MySpace music page), you might use this function. See Figure 12.14.

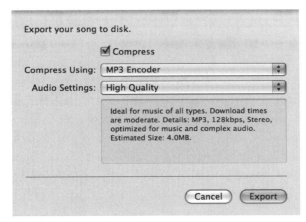

Figure 12.14 The Export Song to Disk compression dialog box.

Burn Song to CD

If you are ready to make a CD of your song, it's a one-step process. Choose Burn Song to CD from the Share menu, and you'll be prompted to insert a blank CD in your CD burner. Click Burn, and within a few minutes you'll have an audio CD of your song! If you have more than one burner, you'll be asked to choose one from the drop-down menu. See Figure 12.15.

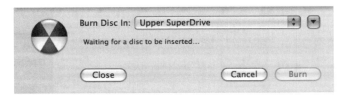

Figure 12.15 Burning a CD directly from GarageBand.

Saving and Archiving GarageBand Projects

There are two different ways to save and archive GarageBand projects. One is a complete, professional, top-to-bottom solution, which we will cover in this section, and the other is a built-in way of reducing file size at the cost of some quality, which we will look at in the next section, called "Compacting GarageBand Projects."

If you choose Save As from the File menu, you are given a couple of options for saving your GarageBand project beyond the name and the location where you wish to save it. In this case, saving is different from exporting or sharing the project, which is considered a mixdown. The process we're discussing now is actually the process of preserving a copy of the native, editable project file itself for the future. These options are selected via two check boxes at the bottom of the Save As dialog box, and they are to archive the project or compact the project.

Archiving the project makes your GarageBand project able to be opened on anyone's computer that has GarageBand installed, including future versions of GarageBand. Suppose you have purchased the World Music GarageBand Jam Pack, and you have used a bunch of Tabla Apple Loops in your song and a MIDI sitar sound, both included in your Jam Pack. If you want to let a friend open the project on his computer, and he doesn't own the World Music Jam Pack, then if you tried to open your project file on his computer, you'd get an error that GarageBand could not find some of the sounds or loops that were used in the file. If you check the Archive Project check box in the Save As dialog box and save the file, GarageBand will embed everything that was used in the song into the project file, allowing your friend to open and work with the file on his computer, even though the World Music Jam Pack is not present on his system. It doesn't mean that GarageBand will give him the World Music Jam Pack, but it will make those sounds and loops that were used in your project available to his computer while your project file is open. These elements will behave as though he owned them, allowing you to further edit, customize settings, and generally work with all of those instruments, loops, and voices—but only for the project into which they were embedded via the Save As archive process.

This is the way I always save my GarageBand projects. Then, I zip the project file and burn it to a CD-ROM or DVD for storage on my shelf or offsite. All you need to do to zip the file is right-click (Control-click) the project file itself and make a choice from the context menu. Suppose the name of your GarageBand project is The Backup Jig.band. If you are using Tiger (Mac OS X 10.4.x), the wording of the menu choice is Create Archive of "The Backup Jig.band," and in Leopard (Mac OS X 10.5.x), the wording of the menu choice you're looking for is Compress "The Backup Jig.band." This will zip your file, protecting it by encoding it and also making it slightly smaller. Later, when you double-click the zip file, it will convert back into the original GarageBand project file you zipped. This function is also available from the Tiger and Leopard File menus if you have selected a file in the Finder. See Figure 12.16.

Figure 12.16 Right-click a file to archive it (also called zipping the file).

Choose either of these options, and you will see a file in the same location as your original GarageBand file called The Backup Jig.band.zip. If you click the file once (and do the same to your GarageBand file) and press Command+I, which is the command for Get Info, you can see what size the file was before and after Zip compression was applied. This Zip file is the file I recommend burning to a CD-ROM or DVD-ROM or uploading to an offsite storage server, such as an FTP server, a web server, or your .Mac account. You can also use a website such as YouSendIt.com to send the file to another person via his e-mail account. However, YouSendIt's file size limit for their free account is 100 MB per file. Remember that CD-ROMs hold 700 MB, so you might want to batch some of your burning to save CDs. You will likely be able to fit 10 to 20 GarageBand projects, zipped, on one CD-ROM. Once you've moved the Zip file off of your computer, you can delete both the original GarageBand file and its zipped counterpart. See Figure 12.17.

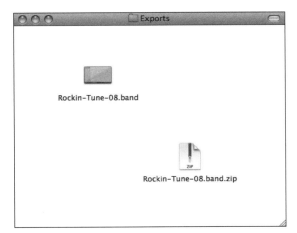

Figure 12.17 A GarageBand project and a zipped archive copy of the file.

Compacting GarageBand Projects

The other method of archiving is pretty clever, but ultimately the file quality loss makes it not worth doing, in my opinion, unless you are really short on storage space or you don't care at all about the quality of your archived projects. This method does, however, have a neat aspect that I will explain. These days, hard-drive storage is so cheap that I have started doing all of my projects at the highest quality possible and building it into my budget to buy a new 500-GB hard drive every year or so. They only cost about $100, which I feel is a small price to pay to guard against some future day when I might say to myself, "Man, I sure wish I'd recorded these vocals at a higher bit rate. They sound terrible in high-def audio [or 10.1 surround sound, or whatever new technological resolutions and fidelities end up becoming available some three or four months down the road]." Of course, I'll have to figure out what to do with stacks upon stacks of hard drives in 10 years, but that's a discussion for another day!

The bottom check box in the Save As dialog box is Compact Project (see Figure 12.18), which converts and encodes all of your audio tracks into a new, smaller format, reducing the overall audio quality of the project. It's essentially a process whereby GarageBand takes all of your audio tracks, everything you've recorded (Real Instrument tracks only), and compresses the original source audio destructively. It's going to make a permanent alteration of the source files themselves, over to another format. This process uses AAC as its method of audio compression, and you can choose between Micro (64 kbps), Small (128 kbps), and Medium (192 kbps). Your audio files will be irrevocably transcoded into AAC files, and the 16-bit or 24-bit AIFF files that GarageBand recorded natively will be destroyed forever. The file size of your GarageBand project will decrease significantly, and if you zip that smaller file, it will be smaller still, but please only use this process if audio quality is not of any concern. It won't sound horrible, mind you, but it will not be the full resolution of the original performances you

Figure 12.18 The File > Save As dialog box in GarageBand '09.

tracked. This option was considered more essential when the hard drives that shipped with new Macs were 20 GB to 40 GB, but now that argument is moot. I can't see a good case to ever use this, but if you want it or need it, it's there for you. Perhaps it would be useful if you were doing a large-scale, long-term audio series, and you were in the Outback with no way to offload any data from your laptop, and your hard drive was fairly small, and your final deliverable was an audio file of fairly low resolution—for example, a streaming audio podcast.

Sharing GarageBand Projects with Logic Pro

With GarageBand '09 and version 8 of Logic Pro, it is now incredibly easy to share GarageBand projects with Logic. Once you open them in Logic, they become Logic projects for good. You can't edit them and go back, but it's nice to be able to "graduate" to Apple's pro audio application and bring all of the work you've done in GarageBand with you. There is nothing special that you need to do to your GarageBand projects to make them able to be used in Logic; however, it's always a good idea to make sure your tracks are named properly, and your Arrange Tracks should all be labeled well if you want to have your song's sections appear in the Marker Track in Logic. All good housekeeping rules apply, but you don't have to do anything in particular. Create any project in GarageBand and import it into Logic. The two apps share all the same recording engines, plug-in libraries, Apple Loops, and so on. See Figure 12.19.

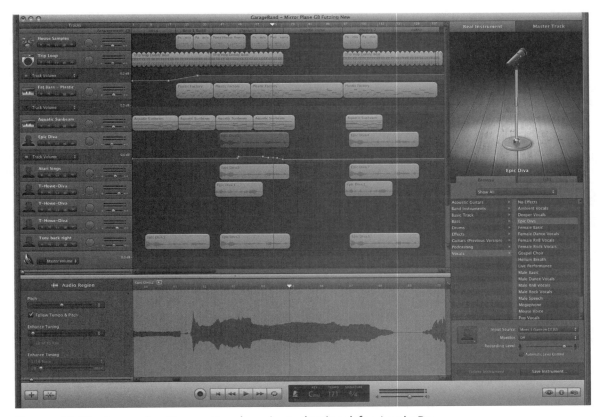

Figure 12.19 A regular GarageBand project, destined for Logic Pro.

Drag and drop the GarageBand project on your Logic Pro icon, name the new Logic project and choose a location to save it, and watch the magic. GarageBand will take all of your audio out of the GarageBand package and create an /Audio subdirectory for you. It will create all of your tracks, maintain your arrangement in the Marker Track in Logic, and plug in all of your effects and MIDI sound choices. Everything will be maintained from GarageBand to Logic. See Figure 12.20.

Figure 12.20   The GarageBand project depicted in Figure 12.19, after being imported into Logic Pro.

Allow Yourself to Write Bad Ones

Before we move on to the final chapter, on GarageBand's Learn to Play music lessons, I'd like to share a little story with you.

In 1999, I wrote and published my first book, called *Who's Afraid of HTML?* (Morgan Kaufmann). In the opening paragraphs of that book, I shared a little anecdote that I'd like to share again here because it is timeless and fits in perfectly well with a second—related, I promise—story that I'll include after it, winding up this part of *GarageBand '09 Power!*

This is to all of you out there who are working on creating music with your computer and who are working with the tools as well as your own creativity and motivation. If there is any part of you that is apprehensive about digging in and starting to work on a project in GarageBand, let me leave you with these two anecdotes. Interestingly enough, they both include little wisdoms that were shared with me by my brother, collaborator, creative giant, and dear close friend, Jesse P. Howard.

Jesse had just completed his first 16mm short film back in 1997, and I thought to ask him what the message of his film was. He said, "It's about just doing it. You know, the only way to start is to begin." Just doing it. Like Nike's advertising slogan, "Just do it." Jesse added, "I'm tired of 'Just do it,' though. I am changing it to 'Just do it NOW!'" He's a wise young man, my brother.

If there's a part of you, like there was a part of me in the past—something inside your head maybe—that can sometimes make it difficult to go be creative, to take the plunge and actually start working on a song, I have some words of advice for you. If "Just do it NOW" makes sense mentally but still doesn't get you in there tracking music, let me offer these closing words. Back to my brother Jesse, once again. I have always considered him to be an excellent songwriter and lyricist. I was having some trouble with songwriting about 15 years ago, and he told me something that got me writing. I was about 23 years old at the time, and I was allowing myself to be held up from writing any new material—frozen even—because I kept thinking that I couldn't write good lyrics. So, as I'm prone to doing, I asked my younger brother's advice.

"How do I write good lyrics, dude?" I asked him.

"Allow yourself to write bad ones," he replied.

Links for the Author

- **My home page:** www.toddhoward.com

- **Last Fair Deal (the four-piece acoustic/folk/bluegrass/swing band I play 5-string bass in with my father, Paul Howard, Tom Hagymasi, and Phil Zimmerman):** www.lastfairdeal.com

- **Chalk/Third Person (my duo with drummer, lyricist, producer/engineer/programmer Don Gunn):** www.thirdpersonmusic.com

- **High Adventure (my duo with Glen Nelson):** www.highadventuremusic.com

- **Spaghetti Cake** (a rock band for the whole family; I play bass and sing, also with Glen Nelson, Sue Birk Nelson, Christopher Eddy, Dennis Fancher, Steve Battistoni, and Mike Tierney): www.spaghetticake.com

- **Karmen Buttler** (my dear friend, also a songwriter/guitarist I play bass, guitar, and sing with): www.karmenmusic.com

- *The Trouble with Boys and Girls* (the independent feature film I produced and co-edited with my brother, Jesse, and our production company, Home Movies, in 2003; Jesse also wrote and directed the film): www.thetroublewithboysandgirls.com

- **Gaillion** (the commemorative site for my high school band with Don Gunn and Jim Vasquenza): www.gaillion.com

What's Next: GarageBand Learn to Play Music Lessons

One of the exciting new features in GarageBand '09 is Learn to Play. It's an innovative new learning system that works right inside of GarageBand, and it will help you learn to play guitar or piano. The lessons start right at the very beginning of the learning curve, so even if you've never played music before, you can follow along and learn the basics. There are also more advanced lessons available, and the GarageBand Artist Lessons are a fun way to learn a particular song from some of today's top popular musicians. Plug in your guitar, connect your MIDI keyboard, and learn to play!

13 GarageBand Learn to Play Music Lessons

New in GarageBand '09 is a revolutionary way to learn to play piano and guitar, Apple-style. This new system is perfect for the beginner, in that the Basic Lessons start right at the very beginning with the instruments themselves, showing you all the different physical parts of the instrument, such as the fretboard, headstock, and sound hole on the guitar, and the black and white keys and the sustain pedal for the piano, and they describe the purpose of each. The lessons utilize an innovative "double-widescreen" viewing area, plus their accessibility and clarity are augmented by an ingenious method of displaying both the instructor's keyboard or fretboard and the student's, as well as the availability of several methods of altering your view on the fly.

GarageBand '09 comes with nine free Basic Lessons in piano and nine more in guitar. It provides a secondary premium service that offers Artist Lessons, where chart-topping musicians teach you how to play their most popular songs. Apple plans to continue to add more Artist Lessons in the future, and one can only hope that they expand into woodwinds and other instruments, especially for instruments where a MIDI controller is available so that the student can truly play along.

Getting Started with Learn to Play

The lessons in GarageBand are video based, interactive music lessons, where you are guided by visual cues and fingerboard and keyboard layouts with clear indicators showing you where to place your fingers on the keyboard or fingerboard. There's even a friendly instructor named Tim to take you through the process.

Launch GarageBand and in the New Project window, click on the Learn to Play icon in the left column. You will see Piano Lesson 1: Intro to Piano and Guitar Lesson 1: Intro to Guitar. To take one of the intro lessons, double-click on it to begin. See Figure 13.1.

One potential that really excites me in terms of this new feature is that with the lessons engine in place and GarageBand's one-step connection to the Lesson Store for immediate downloading of new lessons online, if Learn to Play is successful and users enjoy this method of learning, it could really become a whole new way for people to learn to play an instrument—something that I personally think everyone should try to do at some point in their life.

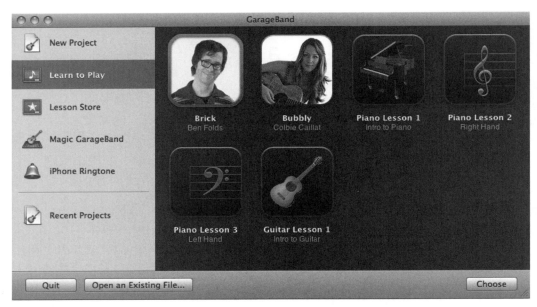

Figure 13.1 The Learn to Play category of the New Project window selected, with the two free intro lessons, some additional free Basic Lessons, and two Artist Lessons available for use.

As mentioned, as of this printing, there are nine lessons in the Intro to Piano series and nine lessons in the Intro to Guitar series. These are designed for people who are brand new to these instruments or intermediate players who would like a refresher. If you played an instrument back in your school days and you want to reacquaint yourself with either the piano or the guitar, this is a great place to start.

The GarageBand Learn to Play lessons will only play in full-screen mode, and when you start a lesson, GarageBand automatically takes over your whole screen. To exit, you can click the small X in the upper-left corner of the Learn to Play interface or just press your Escape key.

Piano Lesson 1: Intro to Piano

The first nine lessons in the Basic Piano Lessons series are free to download, but only Lesson 1 comes preinstalled in GarageBand '09. You will need to click on Lesson Store in the New Project window and download Lessons 2 through 9, all of which are free. Once you have lessons downloaded, they will always be located in the Learn to Play section of your New Project window. Double-click any lesson to watch it.

The Intro to Piano Lesson covers the basics of using a piano and an introduction to the basic techniques involved in playing the instrument. Lessons are divided up into segments, and each covers a different aspect of the piano. Piano Lesson 1: Intro to Piano covers black and white keys, playing position, sustain pedal, chords, chord progressions, and rhythm. These basic skills and understandings will provide a good foundation for moving into the rest of the series of Basic Piano Lessons. See Figure 13.2.

Figure 13.2 Piano Lesson 1: Intro to Piano, with Tim, your instructor, playing a C Major chord in the section on chords.

Guitar Lesson 1: Intro to Guitar

As with the Basic Piano Lessons, the nine lessons in the Basic Guitar Lessons series are free to download, and only Lesson 1 comes preinstalled. You can click Lesson Store in the New Project window to download Lessons 2 through 9 for free.

Guitar Lesson 1: Intro to Guitar covers the basics of using the guitar and some basic techniques for holding the instrument properly and producing a sound. The aspects covered in the first lesson are acoustic guitar, electric guitar, holding the guitar, tuning, picking and strumming, and strumming an E chord. This lesson will prepare you with a good foundation for each of the additional lessons in the Basic Guitar series. See Figure 13.3.

Lesson Store: Basic Lessons

The GarageBand Lesson Store connects to Apple's servers and allows you to download Learn to Play lessons to your computer and use them in GarageBand. You will need to be connected to the Internet to download lessons, but once they are downloaded, you can use them any number of times, regardless of whether you are online. Once you click on Lesson Store in the New Project window, the right side of the New Project window will populate with two tabs labeled Basic Lessons and Artist Lessons. Clicking

Figure 13.3   Guitar Lesson 1: Intro to Guitar, with Tim, your instructor, strumming an E Major chord.

Basic Lessons will display all of the Basic Lessons available. You can download them all and use them at your leisure, or you can download a new one each time you are ready for the next lesson (see Figure 13.4).

Figure 13.4   All of the piano and guitar lessons available for download in the Basic Lessons tab under the Lesson Store.

Piano Lessons

All of the Basic Piano Lessons available for download are listed here. Click the Download button to begin downloading the lesson. Each lesson is roughly 200 MB in size and may take a few minutes to download and install, depending on your connection speed and network traffic. Once Learn to Play lessons are downloaded, they will be available in the Learn to Play category of the New Project window. The following list covers the nine Basic Lessons for piano and the focus of each lesson.

- Basic Piano Lesson 1: Intro to Piano

- Basic Piano Lesson 2: Right Hand

- Basic Piano Lesson 3: Left Hand

- Basic Piano Lesson 4: Rhythm

- Basic Piano Lesson 5: Sharps and Flats

- Basic Piano Lesson 6: Rhythmic Accents

- Basic Piano Lesson 7: Major and Minor Chords

- Basic Piano Lesson 8: Scales

- Basic Piano Lesson 9: Playing the Blues

Guitar Lessons

As with the piano lessons, the Basic Guitar Lessons available for download are listed here. Click the Download button next to each lesson to begin the downloading process. Each lesson is roughly 200 MB in size, as mentioned earlier, and may take a few minutes to download and install. The following list covers the nine Basic Lessons for guitar and the focus of each lesson.

- Basic Guitar Lesson 1: Intro to Guitar

- Basic Guitar Lesson 2: Chords - G, C

- Basic Guitar Lesson 3: Chords - A, D

- Basic Guitar Lesson 4: Minor Chords

- Basic Guitar Lesson 5: Single Note Melodies

- Basic Guitar Lesson 6: Power Chords

- Basic Guitar Lesson 7: Major Barre Chords

- Basic Guitar Lesson 8: Minor Barre Chords

- Basic Guitar Lesson 9: Blues Lead

Learn

The Basic Lessons in GarageBand contain two parts: Learn and Play. Learn is the section where you are taken step-by-step through a process of learning different aspects, parts, or ideas of one lesson. Most of these lessons are working toward playing a piece of some kind or an exercise. The Learn section is where you learn how to actually play it, and the Play section is geared toward letting you play what you have learned. See Figure 13.5.

Figure 13.5 Learn mode in a Basic Piano Lesson.

Play

Once you have gone through the Learn section of a given lesson, you can click the Play button on the upper left of the video overlay and then play along with your own MIDI controller or your own guitar. One nice feature is that if you are connected with a MIDI keyboard, both the instructor's notes *and* your notes will be displayed as well as heard, and you can follow along to make sure you're playing the right notes at the right time. You will also see the musical notation (by default) with a small pointer arrow following along, indicating where you are. If you've ever experienced losing your place while trying to read music notation, you'll quickly see that this can be very helpful. See Figure 13.6.

You can always see what lesson number and title you are working on by looking to the upper-left corner of the screen, next to the Exit button. See Figure 13.7.

Figure 13.6   Play mode in a Basic Piano Lesson.

Figure 13.7   The Exit button, the lesson number, and the title.

In the upper-right corner of the screen are some setup options. In Piano Lesson mode there are buttons for Setup and Mixer, and in Guitar mode there is a button to call up your Tuner as well. See Figures 13.8 and 13.9.

Figure 13.8   Setup and Mixer buttons in Piano mode.

Figure 13.9   Tuner, Setup, and Mixer buttons in Guitar mode.

Piano Lesson Setup

When you click on Setup, a screen comes up that allows you to configure exactly how GarageBand displays information to you in the different quadrants of the screen. You can check at the top to see that your MIDI controller keyboard is connected, and if you do not see your keyboard here, you can click the GarageBand Preferences button at the lower left to adjust your settings.

In Piano mode, the screen has options for automatic layout configurations (these are considered good places to start for most users), notation display modes for chords, left hand staff, right hand staff, and both hands. The appearance and arrangement can be further customized as well, so you can see notation and the instrument, instrument only, or notation only. These can all be selected by clicking on each picture or using the number on your keyboard shown to the right of the selection. You can check the box next to Easy View to show the names of the notes in the score (the musical notation) and on the keyboard and even see text subtitles for the instructor in the video. Below the main area is a button to invoke GarageBand's main Preferences window, and you can click Done in the lower right when you are ready to get back to it. See Figure 13.10.

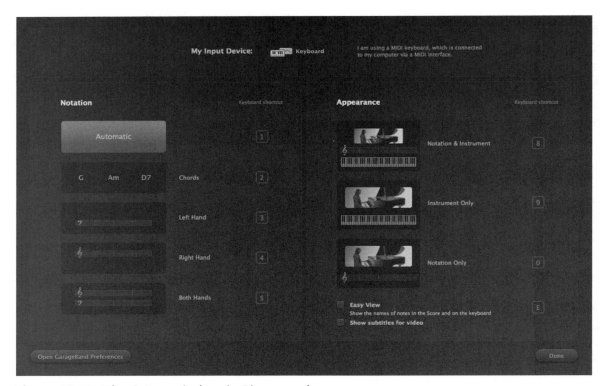

Figure 13.10   The Setup window in Piano mode.

Piano Lesson Mixer

If you click Mixer in the upper right of the Lesson interface, you'll see a small mixing console representing all of the audio elements that you can hear; it will allow you to balance the different parts according to your wishes. The Mixer is dynamic and will show you only the pieces of audio that are present in the lesson—in this example, Teacher's Voice, Teacher's Piano, The Band, and My Instrument. You can solo, mute, or adjust the volume of all of these elements. See Figure 13.11.

Figure 13.11   The Mixer window in a Basic Piano Lesson.

Guitar Lesson Setup

When you click on Setup in Guitar Lesson mode, a screen comes up that allows you to configure how GarageBand displays information to you in the different quadrants of the screen. In Guitar mode, you also have an automatic default option, as well as the option to display chord names, chord grids, TAB (or tablature), or TAB and standard notation together. The appearance of the Lesson window can be changed to show notation and the instrument fretboard, the instrument only, or notation only. The three check boxes at the bottom allow you to see a top-down fretboard view, reorientation for left-handed guitarists, and the video subtitles. See Figure 13.12.

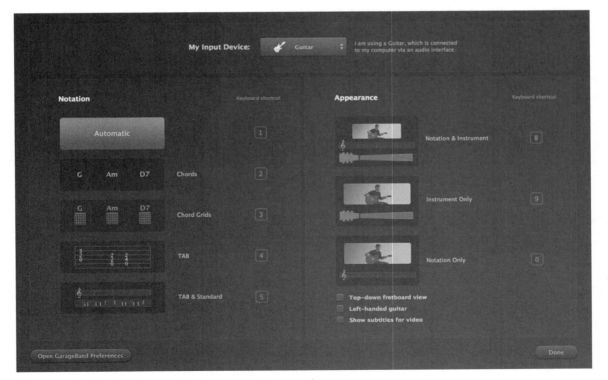

Figure 13.12   The Setup window in Guitar mode.

To choose between Guitar, External Mic, or External Guitar, use the drop-down menu at the top of the Guitar mode Setup screen. You can check to see that your Guitar is plugged in, and if you do not see your guitar input here or hear it playing through your speakers or headphones, you may want to click the GarageBand Preferences button at the lower left to adjust your settings. See Figure 13.13.

Figure 13.13   The Input Device drop-down menu in Guitar mode.

Guitar Lesson Mixer

To adjust the independent levels of all the elements in the mix while in your guitar lesson, click Mixer in the upper right and mute, solo, or adjust the volume level for each of the parts. Click the down arrow next to Band to display the individual parts in the backup band to have independent control over their levels. If you wanted to just play along to the drums and the singer's voice, click the headphones or solo the drums and voice tracks, for example. See Figure 13.14.

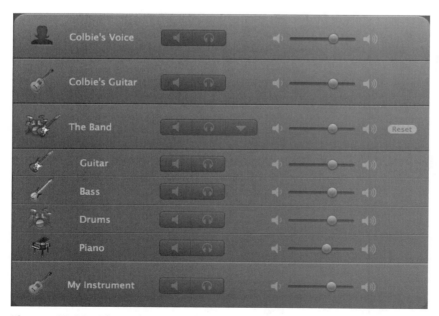

Figure 13.14   The Mixer window in a Guitar lesson with the Band tab expanded to show individual mixer controls for each instrument in the backup band.

Guitar Tuner

If you would like to tune up, click Tuner in the upper right, and you can tune from within your music lesson. This avoids having to create a GarageBand project and tune using the Tuner in the Transport controls display area at the bottom of your main GarageBand window. See Figure 13.15.

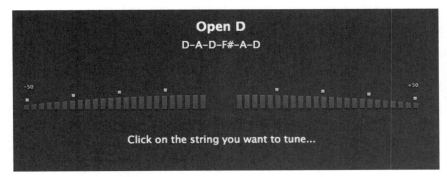

Figure 13.15 The Tuner in Guitar mode.

Lesson Store: Artist Lessons

Clicking this option in the main New Project window connects you to the Lesson Store, where you can preview and purchase GarageBand Artist Lessons. You will need to be connected to the Internet to purchase and download Artist Lessons. For $4.99 each, you can download an interactive video-based lesson in which the artist will teach you how to play one of his or her songs on the guitar or piano. Click the Add to Cart button to add lessons to your cart from the Artist Lessons menu and then click Checkout to be taken to the Apple Store online to sign in with your existing Apple account. (This is the same account you use when you make purchases from the iTunes Store.) You can also opt to create a new account.

Then you will be able to download the lessons to your computer. You can remove Artist Lessons from your cart before checking out by clicking the Remove button on the lesson. Once the lessons are downloaded, you will not need to be connected to the Internet to watch the Artist Lessons. If you would like to preview an Artist Lesson before buying, click once on the portrait of the artist. See Figure 13.16.

Although it can be presumed that Apple will continue to produce and release new Artist Lessons regularly, the complete list of Artist Lessons available in GarageBand '09 as of this printing is as follows:

- Ben Folds: "Brick" (Piano, Advanced)

- Fall Out Boy: "I Don't Care" (Guitar, Medium)

- Fall Out Boy: "Sugar, We're Goin' Down" (Guitar, Advanced)

- Norah Jones: "Thinking About You" (Piano, Advanced)

Figure 13.16 The Artist Lessons tab under the Lesson Store category in the New Project window. Notice the Preview button.

- Sara Bareilles: "Love Song" (Piano, Medium)

- Colbie Caillat: "Bubbly" (Guitar, Easy)

- John Fogerty: "Proud Mary" (Guitar, Easy)

- John Fogerty: "Fortunate Son" (Guitar, Medium)

- OneRepublic: "Apologize" (Piano, Advanced)

- Sting: "Roxanne" (Guitar, Easy)

Artist Lessons are often between 350 and 800 MB in file size and will take several minutes to download, even on a broadband Internet connection. These are pretty large files, so if you purchase many of the Artist Lessons, be sure to keep an eye on your hard drive capacity. You're looking at somewhere around 4 to 5 GB if you buy all 10 of them. While downloading each lesson, there is a progress bar indicating what percentage of the file has transferred to your computer, and any Artist Lessons that are in the queue to download are listed as "pending" in the New Project dialog.

Learn Song

Many of the Artist Lessons include instructions for playing a simple version of the chords or strums of the song, while also including an advanced version about the way the artist actually performed the song. In the list above, as in the New Project Artist Lessons window, there is an indication of easy, medium, and advanced. These should be taken as general guidelines about the level of proficiency you might want to have before tackling the lesson, and they don't have to do with the simple and advanced versions that may or may not be offered within each lesson. This is at

Apple's (or the artist's) discretion. The listing of easy, medium, or advanced on the lesson itself is just a guide; however, if you are ready to work at it and crack each nut, then by all means give it a try. None of the songs taught in these lessons is extremely challenging. Even intermediate musicians who have been playing only a little while might find them fairly easy to learn. See Figure 13.17.

Figure 13.17   Click on Simple in the video overlay to choose the simpler version of the song to learn.

Simple versions are typically in different keys to make the fingerings and chords easier for beginning players, and they often incorporate a more straightforward rhythmic approach, while the advanced versions are exactly what the artist plays on that original track. If you have trouble with the advanced version in a given lesson, try the simple one first and work your way up. Once you have learned the simple version, try the advanced version again. See Figure 13.18.

Figure 13.18   Click on Advanced in the video overlay to choose the advanced version of the song to learn.

The lessons themselves are done in a live video and instructional combination that really works for learning the songs quickly for those who already have some background on the instrument in question, while remaining completely understandable and accessible for people who are approaching guitar and/or piano for the first time. I've been playing for years, and quite honestly, I found the lessons to be really fun simply because the approach and the interface are so innovative. They work really well!

Play Song

Once you've learned the song in the Artist Lesson, it's time to play along with the whole song from beginning to end. Of course, you can stop and start over using the simple controls at the bottom of the window, or move the playhead around to different sections to focus on one area or another, but the goal will be to play the entire piece all the way through. You will have the same choices between the simple and advanced versions if they are provided, and you can click Mixer to adjust the levels of the individual musical elements in the band you are playing along with. See Figure 13.19.

Figure 13.19 Click on Simple or Advanced in the video overlay to choose the version of the song you'd like to play along with.

To switch between different display views on the fly, hover your mouse over the button of the video panel itself and click on the fret view or picking view at will. See Figure 13.20.

Figure 13.20 Alternate between a focused view on the picking hand or the fretboard fingering hand with the video overlay toggle buttons.

Story

In addition to the song lessons, the artists that are featured in GarageBand's Artist Lessons also tell the story of the song itself or the writing of the song. When you mouse over the top area of the lesson, where the teacher is, you will see an overlay panel giving you access to Play, Learn, and Story. Think of these as the extras. Some of the stories are short and sweet, such as Colbie Caillat's story for "Bubbly," and some are quite involved, such as Ben Folds telling the story of his song "Brick." All are quite enjoyable. See Figure 13.21.

Figure 13.21 Click Story on the video overlay buttons to hear the tale of the creation of the song you are learning to play.

The Appendixes

I hope you have enjoyed *GarageBand '09 Power!* Take a good look through both appendixes. I will provide you with a comprehensive list of all of the voices, sounds, Software Instruments, and loops that come with all of the currently available Garage-Band Jam Packs in Appendix A, and Appendix B is an exhaustive list of all of Garage-Band's keyboard shortcuts. Have fun pushing GarageBand to its limits, and by all means send me an MP3 of anything you record with it if you'd like to share! You can email me a link to your finished projects at todd@toddhoward.com or visit my personal website and send me a message from there. It's at www.toddhoward.com.

GarageBand Jam Packs

Jam Packs are Apple-created royalty-free libraries of Apple Loops, Software Instruments, and GarageBand effects that currently come in six flavors. The Jam Packs that are available as of this printing are Jam Pack 1, Rhythm Section, Symphony Orchestra, Remix Tools, World Music, and Voices. Each retails for $99. See Figure A.1.

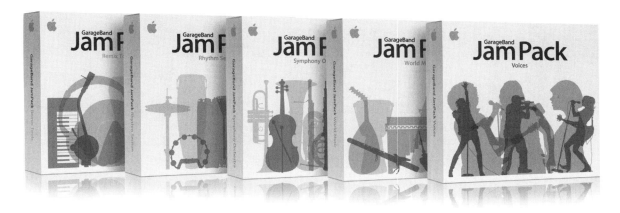

Figure A.1 The GarageBand Jam Pack family. Courtesy of Apple.

Jam Packs are DVDs that you install, and they add hundreds of new loops to your Loop Browser automatically, making it a very painless process to add new sounds, samples, Apple Loops, and Software Instruments to your GarageBand arsenal. They are professionally created—recorded and performed by professional studio musicians. These things sound fantastic and are a no-brainer for adding a huge amount of breadth and variety to GarageBand. Even if you never use Apple Loops for anything at all (some musicians find no need or use for loops, while others cherish them), you will find a wealth of new MIDI Software Instrument sounds to play with. And although the library that ships with GarageBand is adequate to get started, if you have any desire to do some serious work in GarageBand, I suggest you take a look at some of these offerings. This appendix is designed as a Jam Pack reference, and after this brief introduction on installing Jam Packs, I will provide you with a comprehensive list of all of the Apple Loops and Software Instruments that are included in each of the Jam Packs, including GarageBand's default set and the first Jam Pack (now referred to as *Jam Pack 1*).

Installing Jam Packs

Insert the GarageBand Jam Pack DVD into your computer and double-click the disc icon on your desktop. Read the Read Me file before you begin and then double-click the Jam Pack installer. For a look at the steps and how to go about installing your Jam Pack libraries on an external hard drive (or any drive other than your main boot drive), follow the series of screenshots in Figures A.2 through A.9. You may want to install the Jam Packs elsewhere if you don't have enough free space on your boot

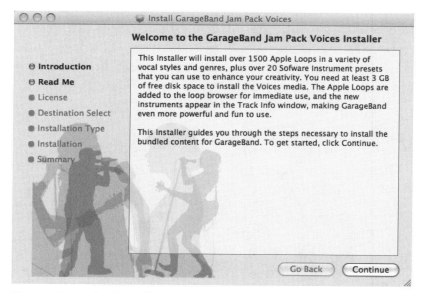

Figure A.2   The installer introduction for the Voices Jam Pack. Read and click Continue.

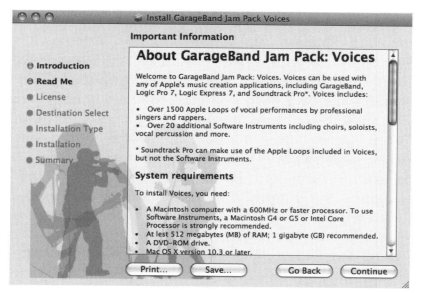

Figure A.3   Read Me file text repeated for convenience and assurance of system requirements, etc.

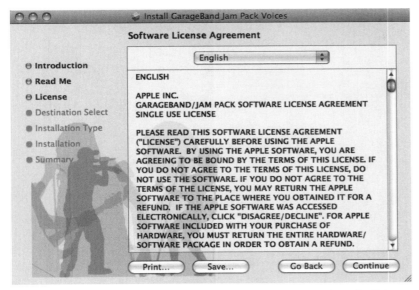

Figure A.4 The Software License Agreement. Read and click Continue. You can print this text out or save it to your hard drive. Most people don't read SLAs, it seems to me, but this is one you might want to read because it has pertinent language regarding your use of Apple Loops in your commercial music. (It's basically okay to do so because they are all royalty free.)

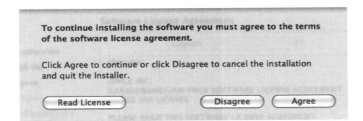

Figure A.5 Agree to the SLA.

drive, because Jam Pack libraries—especially if you install several of them—take up many gigabytes of space each. See each Jam Pack's Read Me file for a listing of the system requirements, including the hard drive space requirements.

Using Jam Packs

Using a Jam Pack is as simple as installing it, launching GarageBand, and then beginning to browse your sound library and your Apple Loops library in GarageBand to discover that your lists have vastly expanded. Just choose the new Apple Loops or Software Instruments and use them in your projects. It's that simple. To learn how to filter and sort your Loop Browser view to show only those loops within a certain Jam Pack, refer to the section in Chapter 7 called "The Loop Browser." You can also refer to the section in that chapter called "Importing Apple Loops" to find out how to install Loops that are from third-party vendors and do not necessarily follow the same series of steps that Jam Packs follow.

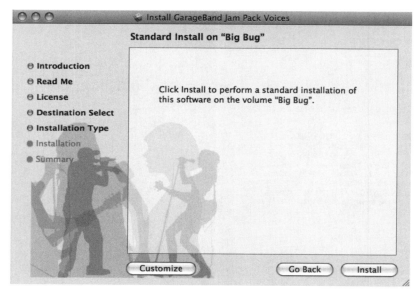

Figure A.6   If you're ready to install, click Install. Or, click Customize to choose alternate locations for your Jam Pack libraries to be installed. Because Jam Packs take up a huge amount of space (often several gigabytes for each Jam Pack), many users prefer to install them on an external drive. If you do that, you'll need to always have that external drive connected to be able to use your Jam Pack libraries. Laptop users have a tough choice to make.

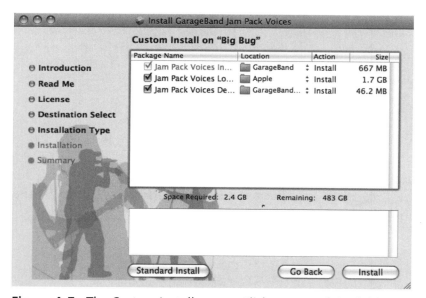

Figure A.7   The Custom Install screen. Click on one of the folders to present options for installation.

Troubleshooting Missing Loops

I have encountered an interesting bug in GarageBand from time to time. It's not entirely explicable, but I can offer you two tips if you encounter the same issue. The issue is a case where some (or all) of your GarageBand Apple Loops are no longer showing up or no longer being recognized by GarageBand. Two things you can do if you run into this

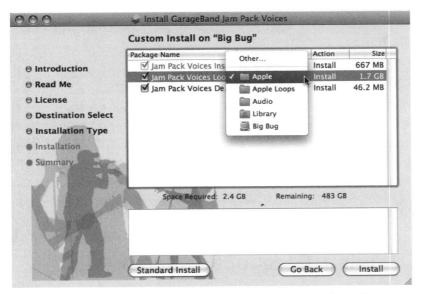

Figure A.8 This menu displays where the Jam Pack installer is currently intending to install your Jam Pack libraries. To change the location, choose Other and select a folder on another hard drive.

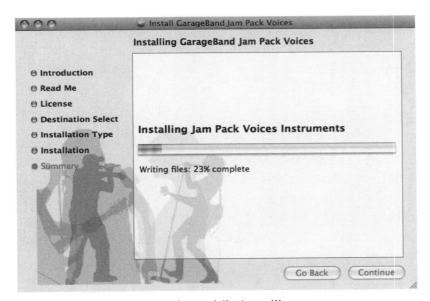

Figure A.9 The progress bar while installing.

issue are detailed in the following sections. First, it's important to know two specific locations on your hard drive.

GarageBand Preferences File

One thing you can do is quit GarageBand, trash your GarageBand Preferences file, and relaunch GarageBand, allowing the application to rebuild its Preferences file and re-index your Apple Loops. The file is located on your hard drive at ~ /Library/Preferences.

The file that you want to drag to the trash and delete is com.apple.garageband.plist.

Default Location of Apple Loops

Another thing you can do is reload your loops into GarageBand manually. You need to locate the Apple Loops folders and drag and drop the folders full of loops into the Loop Browser in GarageBand. If you installed your Apple Loops in a specific location of your choosing during Jam Pack installation, then this location will be different than the defaults listed below, of course, and you will presumably know that location, given that you were required to specify it at the time of installation. The default locations of your Apple Loops files themselves are /Hard Drive/Library/Audio/Apple Loops/Apple and/or /Hard Drive/Library/Audio/Apple Loops/User.

A Walkthrough of Apple's GarageBand Jam Packs

Allow me to present you with a complete list of all of the Apple Loops and Software Instruments that come with GarageBand out of the box and each of the six Jam Packs that have been released to date. This is meant to be a reference, and hopefully it will be of help to readers who are considering investing in the Jam Packs. It's nice to know what you'll be getting before you plunk down money for it, and because Apple does not specifically publish a list like this, I thought it might be helpful to include them all here. The number in parentheses following the name of each Apple Loop below indicates the number of individual loop variations that are included within the particular Jam Pack library.

GarageBand's Default Library

The default GarageBand library of Software Instruments, studio effects, and Apple Loops gets you started with a wide array of commonly used sounds—from guitars and keyboards to drums and basses, a few orchestral voices thrown in for good measure, and a whole host of Apple Loops in all genres. GarageBand '09 now ships with the original GarageBand library, plus the complete contents of Jam Pack 1. This first section will cover the original GarageBand library, and I will break out what is now known as Jam Pack 1 in the next section.

70s Ballad Drums (1)	80s Rock Guitar (1)	Ambient Beat (1)
70s Ballad Piano (5)	Acoustic Noodling (8)	Ambient Guitar (1)
70s Ballad Strings (1)	Acoustic Picking (21)	Ambient Synth (1)
80s Dance Bass Synth (10)	Acoustic Slide (6)	Asian Gamelan (6)
80s Dance Pad (3)	Acoustic Vamp (4)	Backwards Effect (1)
80s Pop Beat (4)	Agogo Groove (1)	Bass Pad (1)
80s Pop Synthesizer (1)	Alternative Rock Bass (4)	Beach Sound Effect (1)

Blip Synth (1)

Blue Jazz Organ Riff (6)

Blue Jazz Piano (2)

Blues Guitar (3)

Blues Harmonica (11)

Bongo Groove (5)

Ceramic Drum (6)

Chordal Synth Pattern (23)

Chunky Metal Guitar (1)

Classic Rock Beat (5)

Classic Rock Fretless (4)

Classic Rock Guitar (2)

Classic Rock Organ (2)

Classic Rock Piano (6)

Classic Rock Steel (5)

Clave (3)

Claypot Percussion (1)

Clean Electric Guitar (1)

Club Dance Beat (63)

Conga Groove (11)

Contemplative Synth (6)

Cool Upright Bass (17)

Cop Show Clav (7)

Country Guitar (1)

Cowbell Groove (1)

Crowd Applause (2)

Crowd Sound Effect (2)

Dance Floor Pattern (45)

Deep Electric Piano (5)

Deep House Bells (2)

Deep House Dance Beat (6)

Deep Pad (3)

Delicate Piano (18)

Disco Pickbass (6)

Distorted Finger Bass (4)

Djembe (3)

Dreamy Guitar Pattern (2)

Dumbek Beat (2)

Eastern Santoor (4)

Echoing String (4)

Edgy Rock Bass (7)

Edgy Rock Guitar (14)

Edgy Synth (2)

Effected Beat (4)

Effected Drum Kit (14)

Electric Guitar Swell (1)

Electric Slap (17)

Electro Beat (1)

Electronic Drum Beat (4)

Emotional Piano (7)

Ethnic Shake Loop (1)

Evolving Atmosphere (10)

Exotic Beat (9)

Exotic Sarod (2)

Far East Drums (2)

Folk Mandolin (8)

Funky Electric Guitar (7)

Funky Latin Drums (15)

Funky Muted Bass (2)

Funky Pop Bass (6)

Funky Pop Conga (2)

Funky Pop Drum (9)

Funky Pop Drums (3)

Funky Pop Synth (3)

Fusion Electric Piano (12)

Groovy Electric Bass (19)

Hip Hop Beat (5)

Holiday Bells (1)

Hooves (3)

Indian Tabla (5)

Island Reggae Bass (8)

Island Reggae Drums (3)

Island Reggae Organ (8)

Jazzy Rock Drums (7)

Latin Horn Stabs (8)

Latin Lounge Beat (1)

Latin Lounge Piano (14)

Latin Triangle (2)

Live Edgy Drums (15)

Long Crash Cymbal (6)

Lounge Jazz Drums (7)

Lounge Vibes (12)

Mediaval Flute (6)

Middle Eastern Oud (6)

Mini Mono Synth (5)

Modern Rock Drums (12)

Modern Rock Guitar (26)

Moody Electric Piano (5)

Motown Drummer (20)

Muted Rock Bass (5)

Natural Drum Kit (14)

Nordic Keyed Fiddle (2)

Office Sound Effect (1)

Old School Funk Line (4)

Orchestra Brass (3)

Orchestra Strings (13)

Percussion Combo (9)

Phone Sound Effect (3)

Picked Steel String (20)

Pluck Synth (3)

Plucky Guitar Loop (2)

Pop Piano (7)

Pop Rock Guitar (2)

Reggae Toy Piano (6)

Relaxed Drum Groove (4)

RnB Bass (2)

RnB Beat (9)

RnB Horn Section (13)

Rock Bass (19)

Rock Guitar Riff (3)

Round Funk Bass (4)

Round Latin Bass (5)

Rural Banjo (6)

Sci Fi Texture (8)

Secret Agent Guitar (9)

Shaker (19)

Short Crash Cymbal (2)

Simple Cabasa (1)

Simple Funk Drums (2)

Single Closing Hat (1)

Single Kick (2)

Single Open High Hat (1)

Single Ride Cymbal (2)

Siren Sound Effect (2)

Slap Bass (5)

Southern Bass (5)

Southern Beat (3)

Southern Rock Bass (6)

Southern Rock Drums (6)

Southern Rock Guitar (5)

Southern Rock Organ (7)

Southern Rock Piano (5)

Spacey Electric Piano (4)

Spacious Guitar (3)

Steel String Slide (7)

Straight Up Beat (4)

Strummed Acoustic (4)

Synth Array (21)

Synth Sweep (2)

Synth Swirl (3)

Synth Tone Bass (5)

Synthbass Sequence (8)

Synthesizer Bass (12)

Synthetic Chime (1)

Tambourine (10)

Techno Bass (5)

Techno Beat (1)

Techno Synth (6)

Texas Blues Guitar (1)

Thick Guitar Delay (1)

Thumpy Hip Hop Bass (5)

UFO Sound Effect (1)

Upbeat Electric Piano (4)

Upbeat Funk Drums (4)

Upright Funk Bass (28)

Upright Hip Hop Bass (6)

Vibraslap (2)

Video Game Synth (1)

Vintage Funk Kit (5)

Vinyl Scratch (9)

Walking Clav (1)

Walking Upright Bass (8)

Woody Latin Bass (8)

World Agogo (2)

World Bongo (3)

World Clave (1)

World Conga (3)

World Drums (3)

World Fretless (2)

World Maraca (2)

World Triangle (1)

Wow Bass (2)

Jam Pack 1

The first GarageBand Jam Pack was released shortly after the release of GarageBand itself and provided an expansion of the original GarageBand library. It added more guitars, synths, pianos, keyboards, drums, horns, and others, and it added many hundreds of new Apple Loops to the library.

12 String Dream (9)	Classic Rock Guitar (3)	Effected Drum Kit (24)
70s Ballad Piano (1)	Classic Rock Organ (1)	Electric Slap (15)
70s Electric Piano (84)	Classic Rock Piano (7)	Emotional Piano (3)
70s Rock Piano (61)	Classic Rock Steel (7)	Ethnic Shake Loop (1)
80s Dance Bass Synth (18)	Claypot Percussion (1)	Exotic Beat (11)
80s Pop Beat (7)	Club Dance Beat (156)	Folk Mandolin (21)
Abstract Atmosphere (157)	Contemplative Synth (21)	Fretless Groove (3)
Acoustic Noodling (7)	Cop Show Clav (11)	Funk Tambourine (1)
Acoustic Picking (12)	Cricket Sound Effects (2)	Funky Electric Piano (31)
Acoustic Slide (3)	Crowd Applause (2)	Funky Latin Drums (17)
Acoustic Vamp (27)	Deep Electric Piano (2)	Funky Muted Bass (1)
Analog Drum Machine (95)	Deep House Bass (10)	Funky Pop Bass (6)
Ancient Didjeridoo (12)	Deep House Bells (1)	Funky Pop Drum (16)
Asian Gamelan (15)	Deep House Dance Beat (2)	Funky Pop Drums (3)
Authentic Dudka (2)	Deep Pad (1)	Funky Pop Synth (3)
Blue Jazz Organ Riff (7)	Delicate Piano (7)	Fusion Electric Piano (7)
Blues Harmonica (17)	Distorted Finger Bass (4)	Glass Breaking Loop (1)
Burning Rock Organ (16)	Dreamy Electric Piano (1)	Groovy Electric Bass (15)
Car Start Loop (1)	Dreamy Guitar Pattern (9)	Hip Hop Beat (25)
Cash Register Sounds (2)	Drive By Sound Effect (1)	Hip Hop Low Bass (1)
Chilled Beats (4)	Eastern Santoor (2)	Hip Hop Piano (4)
Classic Funk Synth (13)	Echo Electric Piano (16)	Hip Hop Shaker (1)
Classic Rock Bass (9)	Echo Guitar (11)	Hip Hop Strings (4)
Classic Rock Beat (5)	Echo Vibes (1)	House Chords (2)
Classic Rock Fretless (4)	Edgy Rock Bass (21)	House Conga (1)

House Organ Riff (1)

House Shaker (1)

Instrumental Shorts (47)

Island Reggae Bass (4)

Island Reggae Organ (1)

Jazz Piano Bar (55)

Jazz Vibraphone (4)

Jazzy Rock Bass (3)

Jazzy Rock Drums (13)

Latin Lounge Piano (7)

Latin Nylon Guitar (8)

Latin Percussion (1)

Light House Bass (1)

Live Edgy Drums (17)

Lounge Jazz Drums (9)

Lounge Vibes (35)

Mellow Latin Conga (1)

Middle Eastern Lute (5)

Middle Eastern Oud (7)

Moody Electric Piano (8)

Motown Bass (8)

Motown Beat (7)

Motown Drummer (4)

Muted Rock Bass (5)

Natural Drum Kit (7)

Nordic Keyed Fiddle (4)

Old School Funk Line (5)

Orchestra Brass (4)

Orchestra Strings (78)

Orchestral Woodwinds (5)

Percussion Combo (44)

Phase Synth (1)

Phone Sound Effect (1)

Pluck Synth (1)

Plucked Balalaika (24)

Pop Bass (3)

Pop Piano (1)

Pop Triangle (1)

Ride Cymbal Solo (1)

RnB Bass (2)

RnB Beat (9)

RnB Electric Piano (2)

RnB Horn Section (34)

RnB Muted Guitar (9)

Rock Bass (25)

Rock Beat (2)

Rock Clav (3)

Rock Steady Bass (17)

Rock Steady Beat (4)

Rock Steady Organ (6)

Rock Steady Sax (5)

Rock Steady Synth (2)

Round Funk Bass (3)

Round Latin Bass (15)

Rural Banjo (28)

Sabahar Riff (4)

Sci Fi Texture (12)

Shaker (1)

Simple Electric Piano (1)

Simple Funk Drums (3)

Slap Bass (6)

Slow Rock Beats (2)

Slow Sub Bass (1)

Smooth Fretless Bass (5)

Smooth Jazz Piano (10)

Smooth Synth Lead (2)

Soda Can Sound Effect (1)

SongBird Sound Effect (1)

Southern Bass (5)

Southern Beat (3)

Southern Rock Bass (7)

Southern Rock Guitar (1)

Southern Rock Piano (10)

Spacey Electric Piano (4)

Steel String Slide (3)

Straight Up Beat (4)

Strummed Acoustic (15)

Swirling Pad (1)

Swirly Filter (15)

Synth Array (42)

Synth Bass Pulse (2)

Synth Swirl (2)

Synth Tone Bass (4)

Synthesizer Bass (17)

Tech House Beat (1)

Techno Beat (5)

Techno Synth (1)

Thick House Bass (1)

Thumpy Hip Hop Bass (9)

Tonewheel Organ (11)

Triangle Combo (1)

Triangle Loop (1)

Turkish Saz Riff (10)

Upbeat Electric Piano (4)

Upbeat Funk Drums (6)

Upright Funk Bass (33)

Upright Hip Hop Bass (7)

Vintage Funk Kit (7)

Vinyl Scratch (19)

Walking Upright Bass (7)

Woody Latin Bass (9)

World Bongo (4)

World Conga (8)

World Electric Piano (1)

World Maraca (1)

World Muted Guitar (9)

World Tribal Dance (2)

Wow Bass (2)

Rhythm Section

The Rhythm Section Jam Pack provides an enormous library of Apple Loops that offer chord progressions, grooves, licks, riffs, and fills in all genres, performed by top studio musicians. You can build an entire song out of the loops provided here, and then some!

12 Bar Blues Bass (1)

12-8 Acoustic Strum (3)

12-8 Afro Cuban Conga (6)

12-8 Electric Arpeggio (11)

12-8 Jazzy Drumset (11)

12-8 Jazzy Fill (2)

12-8 Muted Acoustic Strum (1)

6-8 Acoustic Strum (6)

6-8 Jazzy Drumset (3)

6-8 Jazzy Fill (1)

6-8 Muted Acoustic (4)

60s Shuffle Drumset (12)

60s Shuffle Fill (7)

70s Street Drumset (16)

70s Street Fill (7)

80s Pop Rock Bass (1)

80s Pop Rock Guitar (4)

80s Pop Rock Solo (4)

Acoustic Salsa Guitar (1)

Airy Rhythm Guitar (1)

Alt Metal Drumset (14)

Alt Metal Fill (8)

Alt Pop Acoustic (7)

Alternative Acoustic (10)

Alternative Arpeggio (14)

Backroads Banjo (66)

Backroads Electric (60)

Ballad Acoustic Guitar (1)

Bar Band Basic Drumset (20)

Basic Electric Strum (6)

Basic Rock Drumset (20)

Basic Rock Fill (7)

Bass Strobe (1)

Beachside Clave (1)

Beachside Conga (2)

Beachside Drumset (16)

Beachside Electric (17)

Beachside Fill (8)

Beachside Shaker (1)

Beachside Steel Drums (21)

Bebop Drumset (16)

Bebop Fill (7)

Bedrock Drumset (13)

Bedrock Fill (1)

Big City Drumset (11)

Big City Fill (5)

Big City Harmonics (2)

Big City Rocker Bass (14)

Big City Tambourine (1)

Big Hair Bass (13)

Big Hair Drumset (14)

Big Hair Fill (9)

Big Hair Guitar Chunk (9)

Big Maracas (8)

Big Room Rock Drumset (4)

Big Room Rock Fill (3)

Black Boots Guitar (3)

Blues Bar Bass (2)

Blues Bar Piano (8)

Blues Harp (4)

Bluesy Guitar Chords (4)

Bluesy Guitar Stabs (4)

Boogie Woogie Acoustic (1)

Boogie Woogie Bass (1)

Brazilian Caxia (2)

Brazilian Repique (4)

Brazilian Surdo (4)

Brazilian Timbau (10)

Bread and Butter Bass (67)

Bright Acoustic Lines (5)

Bright Hammer Bass (5)

Bright Tone Bass (10)

British Invasion Bass (21)

Brush Train Drumset (24)

Brush Train Fill (7)

Busy Roundtrip Drumset (2)

Busy Roundtrip Fill (9)

Chaos Guitar (1)

Cheerful Mandolin (28)

Chicago Blues Drumset (2)

Chicago Blues Fill (4)

Chunk Delay Chords (5)

Classic Attitude Rock (19)

Classic Rock Arpeggio (5)

Classic Rock Riffing (26)

Coffee Shop Guitar (12)

Cool Down Slide Guitar (8)

Cool Jazz Drumset (9)

Cool Jazz Fill (3)

Cool Jazz Walking Bass (12)

Country Perfect Bass (1)

Crowd Groove Drumset (7)

Crowd Groove Fill (3)

Dark Bells (1)

Dark and Heavy Riff (20)

Daydream Guitar (1)

Delayed Rock Electric (10)

Delicate Guitar Echoes (6)

Delta Blues Guitar (4)

Delta Blues Solo (21)

Double Punk Drumset (14)

Double Punk Fill (6)

Down Home Dobro (48)

Driving Pick Bass Riff (10)

Droning Guitar (1)

Dusty Road Dobro (10)

Endless Metal Chunk (2)

Essential Drumset (3)

Falling Star Guitar (4)

Farewell Guitar (3)

Fat Maracas (1)

Fingerpicking Melodies (3)

Flannel Guitar (2)

Folk Pop Acoustic (11)

Forever Harmonics (1)

Foundation Drumset (9)

Foundation Fill (3)

Four on Floor Drumset (13)

Four on Floor Fill (3)

Front Porch Dobro (10)

Funked Out Drumset (16)

Funked Out Fill (4)

Funky Brushes Drumset (7)

Funky Brushes Fill (2)

Funky Shuffle Drumset (19)

Funky Shuffle Fill (5)

Funky Strut Drumset (13)

Funky Strut Fill (6)

Funky Strut Shaker (3)

Funky Strut Tambourine (5)

Glam Riffing (4)

Grit Metal (2)

Groove Along Drumset (29)

Groove Along Fill (4)

Groove Along Rock Bass (13)

Half Time Funk Drumset (14)

Half Time Funk Fill (2)

Hardest Working Bass (10)

Harmonic Echoes (6)

Harmonic Strumming (3)

Haunting Octaves (2)

Haunting Pad (1)

Headbop Drumset (11)

Headbop Fill (3)

Heavy Attitude Guitar (1)

Heavy Growling Riff (9)

Heavy Wah Guitar (1)

Hi Hat Foot Count-off (1)

Indian Tambourine (3)

Indie Groove Bass (1)

Indie Rock Riffing (11)

Jam Band Basic Drumset (25)

Jam Band Basic Fill (6)

Jam Funk Drumset (14)

Jam Funk Fill (3)

Jam Funk Hat Intro (1)

Jam Rock Drumset (7)

Jam Rock Fill (3)

Jaws Harp Jingo Jango (9)

Jazz Brush Drumset (4)

Laid Back Classic (4)

Laid Back Dream (5)

Laid Back Jazz Bass (17)

Lava Lamp Wah Guitar (1)

Lazy Conga Shuffle (2)

Lazy Tambourine (1)

Liquid Fretless Bass (4)

Liverpool Skiffle Bass (19)

Lo Fi Country Drums (17)

Long Snare Roll (1)

Lush Guitar Chords (1)

Metal Chunk Bass (2)

Metal Chunk Guitar (2)

Metal Head Guitar (2)

Metal Shaker (8)

Millennium Surf Bass (17)

Monster Speed Metal (7)

Monster Truck Guitar (21)

Monster Truck Solo (40)

Mood Ring Guitar (2)

Moody Fingerpicking (6)

Motown Ballad Bass (20)

Motown Ballad Drumset (11)

Motown Ballad Fill (6)

Motown Guitar Picking (2)

Motown Mixed Drumset (5)

Motown Mixed Fill (2)

Motown Pocket Bass (8)

Motown Pocket Drumset (5)

Motown Pocket Fill (1)

Motown Tambourine (1)

Motown Upbeat Bass (16)

Motown Upbeat Drumset (10)

Motown Upbeat Fill (5)

Mountain Dobro (10)

Music Video Drumset (46)

Music Video Fill (16)

Nashville Pedal Steel (56)

New Attitude Electric (6)

Odd Feel Rock Drumset (3)

Odd Time Pop Drumset (1)

Odd Time Pound Drumset (1)

Odd Time Rock Bass (15)

Odd Time Rock Drumset (15)

Odd Time Rock Fill (4)

Odd Time Shaker (1)

Old Timer Bass Pattern (3)

Overcast Guitar (2)

Picked Rock Bass (27)

Pitch Bender Electric (5)

Pop Groove Drumset (16)

Pop Groove Fill (5)

Pounding Drumset (5)

Pounding Fill (3)

Power Rock Riff (2)

Preaching Slide Guitar (5)

Prog Metal Drumset (4)

Prog Metal Fill (2)

Progressive Acoustic (21)

Progressive Solo (38)

Pure Rock Drumset (14)

Pure Rock Fill (6)

Reflective Arpeggio (19)

Reflective Bass (29)

Reflective Congas (4)

Reflective Cowbell (1)

Reflective Cymbal (3)

Reflective Delay Leads (13)

Reflective Drumset (15)

Reflective E Piano (11)

Reflective Fill (11)

Reflective Percussion (1)

Reflective Rattler (1)

Reflective Rhythm (13)

Reflective Shaker (1)

Reflective Tambourine (4)

Reflective Toms (1)

Reflective Triangle (1)

Reverse Guitar FX (1)

Rhythm & Blues Drumset (8)

Rhythm & Blues Fill (3)

Ringing Power Chords (5)

Rock Riff Bass (4)

Rockabilly Guitar (12)

Rockabilly Upright (23)

Rolling Timbale (1)

Round Tone Bass (11)

Rural Acoustic Strum (19)

Salsa Conga (2)

Serious Strumming (8)

Seventies Conga (2)

Seventies Guiro (1)

Seventies Rock Anthem (1)

Seventies Rock Riffing (7)

Seventies Wah Guitar (1)

Sidestick Drumset (12)

Simple Clean Delay (8)

Skiffle Drumset (10)

Skiffle Fill (4)

Slap Back Drumset (2)

Slapback Echo Drumset (7)

Slapback Echo Fill (7)

Slinky Alt Drumset (6)

Slinky Alt Fill (1)

Slow Chunk Guitar (2)

Solid 70s Drumset (30)

Solid 70s Fill (15)

Sonic Distortion Guitar (1)

Southern Banjo (18)

Southern Basic Drumset (14)

Southern Dobro (15)

Southern Drumset (10)

Southern Fiddle (35)

Southern Fill (3)

Southern Guitar (21)

Southern Smooth Bass (13)

Space Rock Guitar Riff (2)

Stadium Guitar Solo (4)

Stage Effects Guitar (2)

Story Acoustic Guitar (2)

Straight Timbale (3)

Sub Dubby Synth Bass (5)

Sunday Morning Organ (8)

Surf Bingo Guitar (3)

Sweet Lament Guitar (3)

Sweet Strummer (2)

Swinging Conga Groove (1)

Swinging Shaker Groove (1)

Syncopated Drumset (15)

Syncopated Fill (4)

Syncopated Pop Drumset (30)

Syncopated Pop Fill (9)

Tell It Strumming Guitar (1)

Texas Blues Rhythm (3)

Texas Blues Solo (5)

Thrash Drumset (9)

Thrash Fill (3)

Timbale Snare Enhancer (1)

Titanic Fill (1)

Tomboy Drumset (8)

Tomboy Fill (1)

Two Hand Finger Tap (11)

Unplugged Attitude (13)

Upbeat Strummer (1)

Wild Slide Distortion (1)

Wooden Tambourine (6)

World Rock Drumset (11)

World Rock Fill (1)

Software Instruments

Aggressive Fretless

Attitude Bass

Bluegrass Banjo

Bluesy Acoustic

Caribbean Steel Drums

Cavern Kit

Dobro

Eighties Electric

Eighties Power Chords

Headbanger Kit

Indie Kit

Indie Kit Live

Liverpool Bass

Motown Bass

Prog Rock Bass

Roadhouse Kit

Session Bass

Seventies Kit

Shared Percussion

Stinger Bass

Studio Brush kit

Studio Heavy Kit

Studio Tight Kit

Studio Toolkit

Subby Bass

Sunburst Electric

Sunburst Power Chords

Thumbstroke Bass

Twangy Electric

Twangy Strumming

Unplugged Bass

Warehouse Kit

Symphony Orchestra

Everything you might hear in an orchestra is here, added to GarageBand for you in this Jam Pack. There are violins, violas, cellos, basses, woodwinds, horns, percussion, brass, bells, and whole sections of performers. The sound library is topnotch, and the loops are extensive.

Academy All (1)

Academy Cello (1)

Academy Viola (1)

Academy Violin (2)

Adversary All (1)

Adversary Low Strings (2)

Adversary Mid Strings (1)

Adversary Strings (5)

Alliance All (1)

Alliance Brass (1)

Alliance Clarinet (1)

Alliance Hi Strings (1)

Alliance Low Strings (1)

Alliance Mid Strings (2)

Alliance Strings (1)

Antidote All (1)

Antidote Brass (2)

Antidote Clarinet (1)

Antidote Flute (1)

Antidote Hi Strings (1)

Antidote Low Strings (1)

Antidote Mid Strings (1)

Antidote Oboe (1)

Antidote Strings (1)

Antidote Timpani (1)

Antidote Woodwinds (1)

Aperitif All (1)

Aperitif Cello (1)

Aperitif Viola (1)

Aperitif Violin (2)

Autumn All (1)

Autumn Cello (1)

Autumn Viola (1)

Autumn Violin (2)

Avenger All (1)

Avenger Cello (1)

Avenger Viola (1)

Avenger Violin (2)

Banquet All (1)

Banquet Cello (1)

Banquet Viola (1)

Banquet Violin (2)

Baroque Harpsichord (7)

Beacon All (1)

Beacon Cello (1)

Beacon Contra Bass (1)

Beacon Flute (1)

Beacon No Timpani (1)

Beacon Strings (1)

Beacon Timpani (1)

Beacon Viola (1)

Beacon Violin (1)

Behold All (1)

Behold Brass & Wind (12)

Bounty All (1)

Bounty Clarinet (1)

Bounty Flute (1)

Bounty Harp (1)

Bounty Hi Strings (1)

Bounty Low Strings (1)

Bounty No Timpani & Harp (1)

Bounty Strings (1)

Bounty Timpani (1)

Cabernet All (1)

Cabernet Cello (1)

Cabernet Viola (1)

Cabernet Violin (2)

Canopy All (1)

Canopy Cello (1)

Canopy Viola (1)

Canopy Violin (2)

Capitol A Basses (1)

Capitol A Bassoon (1)

Capitol A Cellos (1)

Capitol A Clarinets (1)

Capitol A Deep Bass (1)

Capitol A Flutes (1)

Capitol A French Horns (1)

Capitol A Harp (1)

Capitol A Oboe (1)

Capitol A Orchestral Kit (1)

Capitol A Timpani (1)

Capitol A Trombones (1)

Capitol A Violas (1)

Capitol A Violins (2)

Capitol B Basses (1)

Capitol B Cellos (1)

Capitol B Clarinets (1)

Capitol B Deep Bass (1)

Capitol B Flutes (1)

Capitol B French Horns (1)

Capitol B Harp (1)

Capitol B Orchestral Kit (1)

Capitol B Timpani (1)

Capitol B Trombones (1)

Capitol B Trumpets (1)

Capitol B Violas (1)

Capitol B Violins (2)

Capitol C Basses (1)

Capitol C Bassoon (1)

Capitol C Cellos (1)

Capitol C Clarinets (1)

Capitol C Deep Bass (1)

Capitol C English Horn (1)

Capitol C French Horns (1)

Capitol C Harp (1)

Capitol C Oboe (1)

Capitol C Orchestral Kit (1)

Capitol C Timpani (1)

Capitol C Trombones (1)

Capitol C Trumpets (1)

Capitol C Tuba (1)

Capitol C Violas (1)

Capitol C Violins (2)

Capitol D Basses (1)

Capitol D Cellos (1)

Capitol D Clarinet (1)

Capitol D Deep Bass (1)

Capitol D Flute (1)

Capitol D Flutes (1)

Capitol D French Horn (1)

Capitol D Harp (1)

Capitol D Trombones (1)

Capitol D Violas (1)

Capitol D Violins (2)

Capitol E Basses (1)

Capitol E Cellos (1)

Capitol E Clarinet (1)

Capitol E Deep Bass (1)

Capitol E Harp (1)

Capitol E Orchestral Kit (1)

Capitol E Timpani (1)

Capitol E Trombones (1)

Capitol E Tuba (1)

Capitol E Violas (1)

Capitol E Violins (2)

Capitol F Basses (1)

Capitol F Cellos (1)

Capitol F Deep Bass (1)

Capitol F Harp (1)

Capitol F Orchestral Kit (1)

Capitol F Violas (1)

Capitol F Violins (2)

Caravan All (1)

Caravan Clarinet (1)

Caravan Flute (1)

Caravan French Horn (1)

Caravan Hi Strings (1)

Caravan Low Strings (1)

Caravan Mid Strings (1)

Caravan Strings (1)

Caravan Timpani (1)

Caravan Woodwinds (1)

Church Organ Bass (3)

Church Organ Comp (14)

Church Organ Melody (25)

Cinematic Transition (80)

Clarinet Solo (13)

Classic Harpsichord (11)

Classical Piano Left (5)

Classical Piano Right (128)

Classical Waltz Piano (25)

Clearing All (1)

Clearing Brass (1)

Clearing Flute (1)

Clearing Harp (1)

Clearing Hi Strings (1)

Clearing Low String (1)

Clearing Marcato (1)

Clearing No Percussion (1)

Clearing Percussion (1)

Clearing Strings (1)

Clearing Tremolo (1)

Concert Hall Piano (20)

Costly All (1)

Costly Cello (1)

Costly Viola (1)

Costly Violin (2)

Countdown All (1)

Countdown Cello (1)

Countdown Viola (1)

Countdown Violin (2)

Courier All (1)

Courier Brass (1)

Courier Flute (1)

Courier Hi Strings (2)

Courier Low String (2)

Courier Mid Strings (2)

Courier Strings (1)

Courier Timpani (1)

Court Harpsichord (11)

Culprit All (1)

Culprit Cello (1)

Culprit Viola (1)

Culprit Violin (2)

Cunning All (1)

Cunning Cello (1)

Cunning Viola (1)

Cunning Violin (2)

Daffodil All (1)

Daffodil Cello (1)

Daffodil Viola (1)

Daffodil Violin (2)

Decorum All (1)

Decorum Cello (1)

Decorum Viola (1)

Decorum Violin (2)

Demur All (1)

Demur Cello (1)

Demur Viola (1)

Demur Violin (2)

Desire A Basses (1)

Desire A Cellos (1)

Desire A Deep Bass (1)

Desire A Flutes (1)

Desire A French Horns (1)

Desire A Harp (1)

Desire A Orchestral Kit (1)

Desire A Timpani (1)

Desire A Trombones (1)

Desire A Tuba (1)

Desire A Violas (1)

Desire A Violins (2)

Desire B Basses (1)

Desire B Cellos (1)

Desire B Deep Bass (1)

Desire B French Horns (1)

Desire B Orchestral Kit (1)

Desire B Timpani (1)

Desire B Trombones (1)

Desire B Tuba (1)

Desire B Violas (1)

Desire B Violins (2)

Desire C Basses (1)

Desire C Cellos (1)

Desire C Deep Bass (1)

Desire C Orchestral Kit (1)

Desire C Violas (1)

Desire C Violins (2)

Desire D Basses (1)

Desire D Cellos (1)

Desire D Deep Bass (1)

Desire D French Horns (1)

Desire D Orchestral Kit (1)

Desire D Timpani (1)

Desire D Trombones (1)

Desire D Tuba (1)

Desire D Violas (1)

Desire D Violins (2)

Desire E Basses (1)

Desire E Cellos (1)

Desire E Deep Bass (1)

Desire E French Horn (1)

Desire E French Horns (1)

Desire E Orchestral Kit (1)

Desire E Timpani (1)

Desire E Trombones (1)

Desire E Tuba (1)

Desire E Violas (1)

Desire E Violins (2)

Desire F Basses (1)

Desire F Cellos (1)

Desire F Deep Bass (1)

Desire F French Horns (1)

Desire F Orchestral Kit (1)

Desire F Trombones (1)

Desire F Tuba (1)

Desire F Violas (1)

Desire F Violins (2)

Dogma All (1)

Dogma Brass (1)

Dogma Hi Strings (1)

Dogma Low Strings (1)

Dogma Strings (1)

Dogma Timpani (1)

Dogma Woodwinds (1)

Escape A Basses (1)

Escape A Celesta (1)

Escape A Cellos (1)

Escape A Clarinets (1)

Escape A Deep Bass (1)

Escape A Flutes (1)

Escape A French Horns (1)

Escape A Orchestral Kit (1)

Escape A Timpani (1)

Escape A Trombones (1)

Escape A Tuba (1)

Escape A Tubular Bells (1)

Escape A Violas (1)

Escape A Violins (2)

Escape B Basses (1)

Escape B Bassoon (1)

Escape B Cellos (1)

Escape B Clarinets (1)

Escape B Deep Bass (1)

Escape B Flute (1)

Escape B Flutes (1)

Escape B French Horns (1)

Escape B Harp (1)

Escape B Oboe (1)

Escape B Orchestral Kit (1)

Escape B Piccolo (1)

Escape B Timpani (1)

Escape B Trombones (1)

Escape B Trumpets (1)

Escape B Tuba (1)

Escape B Violas (1)

Escape B Violins (2)

Escape B Xylophone (1)

Escape C Basses (1)

Escape C Bassoon (1)

Escape C Cellos (1)

Escape C Clarinets (1)

Escape C Deep Bass (1)

Escape C Flutes (1)

Escape C French Horns (1)

Escape C Oboe (1)

Escape C Orchestral Kit (1)

Escape C Timpani (1)

Escape C Trombones (1)

Escape C Trumpets (1)

Escape C Tuba (1)

Escape C Violas (1)

Escape C Violins (2)

Escape D Basses (1)

Escape D Celesta (1)

Escape D Cellos (1)

Escape D Deep Bass (1)

Escape D Harp (1)

Escape D Orchestral Kit (1)

Escape D Timpani (1)

Escape D Tubular Bells (1)

Escape D Violins (2)

Escape E Basses (1)

Escape E Cellos (1)

Escape E Deep Bass (1)

Escape E Flutes (1)

Escape E French Horns (1)

Escape E Orchestral Kit (1)

Escape E Piccolo (1)

Escape E Timpani (1)

Escape E Trombones (1)

Escape E Trumpets (1)

Escape E Tuba (1)

Escape E Violas (1)

Escape E Violins (2)

Escape F Basses (1)

Escape F Cellos (1)

Escape F Clarinets (1)

Escape F Deep Bass (1)

Escape F Flutes (1)

Escape F French Horns (1)

Escape F Glockenspiel (1)

Escape F Harp (1)

Escape F Orchestral Kit (1)

Escape F Timpani (1)

Escape F Trombones (1)

Escape F Trumpets (1)

Escape F Tuba (1)

Escape F Violas (1)

Escape F Violins (2)

Escape G Basses (1)

Escape G Cellos (1)

Escape G Clarinets (1)

Escape G Deep Bass (1)

Escape G Flutes (1)

Escape G French Horns (1)

Escape G Harp (1)

Escape G Orchestral Kit (1)

Escape G Timpani (1)

Escape G Trombones (1)

Escape G Trumpets (1)

Escape G Tuba (1)

Escape G Violas (1)

Escape G Violins (2)

Espionage All (1)

Espionage Cello (1)

Espionage Viola (1)

Espionage Violin (2)

Farewell All (1)

Farewell Basses (1)

Farewell Cello (1)

Farewell Flute (1)

Farewell Staccato (1)

Farewell Violin (1)

Fireplace All (1)

Fireplace Cello (1)

Fireplace Viola (1)

Fireplace Violin (2)

Float A Basses (1)

Float A Cellos (1)

Float A Flutes (1)

Float A French Horns (1)

Float A Orchestral Kit (1)

Float B Basses (1)

Float B Bassoon (1)

Float B Cellos (1)

Float B Clarinets (1)

Float B Flutes (1)

Float B French Horns (1)

Float B Oboe (1)

Float B Orchestral Kit (1)

Float B Piccolo (1)

Float B Trombones (1)

Float B Tuba (1)

Float B Violas (1)

Float C Bassoon (1)

Float C Celesta (1)

Float C Clarinets (1)

Float C English Horn (1)

Float C Flute (1)

Float C Flutes (1)

Float C Timpani (1)

Float D Basses (1)

Float D Bassoon (1)

Float D Cellos (1)

Float D Clarinets (1)

Float D Crotales (1)

Float D Flutes (1)

Float D French Horns (1)

Float D Glockenspiel (1)

Float D Harp (1)

Float D Oboe (1)

Float D Orchestral Kit (1)

Float D Timpani (1)

Float D Tubular Bells (1)

Float D Violas (1)

Float D Violins (2)

Float E Basses (1)

Float E Bassoon (1)

Float E Celesta (1)

Float E Cellos (1)

Float E Clarinets (1)

Float E English Horn (1)

Float E Flute (1)

Float E Flutes (1)

Float E French Horns (1)

Float E Glockenspiel (1)

Float E Harp (1)

Float E Oboe (1)

Float E Orchestral Kit (1)

Float E Piccolo (1)

Float E Timpani (1)

Float E Trombones (1)

Float E Trumpets (1)

Float E Tuba (1)

Float E Violas (1)

Float E Violins (2)

Float F Basses (1)

Float F Celesta (1)

Float F Cellos (1)

Float F Clarinets (1)

Float F Flute (1)

Float F Flutes (1)

Float F French Horns (1)

Float F Orchestral Kit (1)

Float F Timpani (1)

Float F Trombones (1)

Float F Trumpets (1)

Float F Violas (1)

Float F Violins (1)

Float G Basses (1)

Float G Bassoon (1)

Float G Cellos (1)

Float G Clarinets (1)

Float G English Horn (1)

Float G Flutes (1)

Float G French Horn (1)

Float G French Horns (1)

Float G Harp (1)

Float G Orchestral Kit (1)

Float G Timpani (1)

Float G Trombones (1)

Float G Violas (1)

Float G Violins (2)

Float H Basses (1)

Float H Bassoon (1)

Float H Cellos (1)

Float H Clarinets (1)

Float H English Horn (1)

Float H Flutes (1)

Float H French Horn (1)

Float H French Horns (1)

Float H Harp (1)

Float H Oboe (1)

Float H Orchestral Kit (1)

Float H Piccolo (1)

Float H Timpani (1)

Float H Trombones (1)

Float H Trumpets (1)

Float H Tuba (1)

Float H Violas (1)

Float H Violins (2)

Flurry All (1)

Flurry Brass (1)

Flurry Clarinets (1)

Flurry Hi Strings (1)

Flurry Low Strings (1)

Flurry Strings (1)

Flurry Timpani (1)

Flurry Violas (1)

Flurry Woodwinds (1)

Fondness All (1)

Fondness Cello (1)

Fondness Viola (1)

Fondness Violin (2)

Fortify All (1)

Fortify Brass (1)

Fortify Hi Strings (1)

Fortify Low Strings (1)

Fortify Mid Strings (1)

Fortify Strings (1)

Fortify Timpani (1)

Fortify Woodwinds (1)

French Horn Solo (26)

Graduate All (1)

Graduate Cello (1)

Graduate Viola (1)

Graduate Violin (2)

Gravity All (1)

Gravity Basses (1)

Gravity Cellos (1)

Gravity Clarinet (1)

Gravity Flute (1)

Gravity Pizzicato (1)

Gravity Strings (1)

Gravity Timpani (1)

Gravity Violas (1)

Gravity Violin (1)

Harbor All (1)

Harbor Brass (2)

Harbor Brass & Woodwinds (1)

Harbor Flutes (1)

Harbor Low Strings (1)

Harbor Mid Strings (2)

Harbor Oboe (1)

Harbor Strings (1)

Harbor Violins (1)

Harpsichord Left Hand (13)

Harpsichord Right Hand (59)

Heavenly Pipes (8)

Henchman All (1)

Henchman Cello (1)

Henchman Viola (1)

Henchman Violin (2)

Hideout All (1)

Hideout Brass & Wind (8)

Hoist All (1)

Hoist Brass (2)

Hoist Flute (1)

Hoist Hi Strings (1)

Hoist Low Strings (2)

Hoist Mid Strings (1)

Hoist Strings (1)

Indulge All (1)

Indulge Brass (1)

Indulge Cymbals (1)

Indulge Flute (1)

Indulge Harp (1)

Indulge Hi Strings (1)

Indulge Low Strings (2)

Indulge Melody (2)

Indulge No Percussion (1)

Indulge Pizzicato (1)

Indulge Run (1)

Indulge Strings (1)

Indulge Timpani (1)

Kingdom Church Organ (18)

Laureate All (1)

Laureate Brass & Wind (18)

Longing A Basses (1)

Longing A Celesta (1)

Longing A Cellos (1)

Longing A Clarinet (1)

Longing A Deep Bass (1)

Longing A Flute (1)

Longing A Harp (1)

Longing A Violas (1)

Longing A Violins (1)

Longing B Basses (1)

Longing B Bassoon (1)

Longing B Cellos (1)

Longing B Clarinet (1)

Longing B Deep Bass (1)

Longing B English Horn (1)

Longing B Flute (1)

Longing B French Horns (1)

Longing B Harp (1)

Longing B Oboe (1)

Longing B Piccolo (1)

Longing B Violas (1)

Longing B Violins (2)

Longing C Basses (1)

Longing C Bassoon (1)

Longing C Cellos (1)

Longing C Clarinets (1)

Longing C Deep Bass (1)

Longing C English Horn (1)

Longing C Flutes (1)

Longing C French Horns (1)

Longing C Harp (1)

Longing C Oboe (1)

Longing C Orchestral Kit (1)

Longing C Piccolo (1)

Longing C Trombones (1)

Longing C Violas (1)

Longing C Violins (2)

Longing D Basses (1)

Longing D Bassoon (1)

Longing D Cellos (1)

Longing D Clarinets (1)

Longing D Deep Bass (1)

Longing D English Horn (1)

Longing D Flutes (1)

Longing D French Horns (1)

Longing D Oboe (1)

Longing D Orchestral Kit (1)

Longing D Timpani (1)

Longing D Trombones (1)

Longing D Trumpets (1)

Longing D Tuba (1)

Longing D Violas (1)

Longing D Violins (2)

Longing E Basses (1)

Longing E Bassoon (1)

Longing E Cellos (1)

Longing E Clarinets (1)

Longing E Deep Bass (1)

Longing E English Horn (1)

Longing E Flutes (1)

Longing E French Horn (1)

Longing E French Horns (1)

Longing E Harp (1)

Longing E Oboe (1)

Longing E Orchestral Kit (1)

Longing E Piccolo (1)

Longing E Timpani (1)

Longing E Trombones (1)

Longing E Tuba (1)

Longing E Violas (1)

Longing E Violins (2)

Longing F Basses (1)

Longing F Bassoon (1)

Longing F Cellos (1)

Longing F Clarinets (1)

Longing F Deep Bass (1)

Longing F English Horn (1)

Longing F Flutes (1)

Longing F French Horns (1)

Longing F Harp (1)

Longing F Oboe (1)

Longing F Orchestral Kit (1)

Longing F Timpani (1)

Longing F Trombones (1)

Longing F Trumpets (1)

Longing F Tuba (1)

Longing F Violas (1)

Longing F Violins (2)

Longitude All (1)

Longitude Brass & Wind (9)

Magna All (1)

Magna Brass & Wood-winds (1)

Magna Clarinet (1)

Magna Cymbals (1)

Magna Flute (1)

Magna French Horn (1)

Magna Hi Strings (1)

Magna Low Strings (1)

Magna Mid Strings (1)

Magna Strings (1)

Magna Timpani (1)

Majestic Church Organ (52)

Mastermind All (1)

Mastermind Brass (2)

Mastermind Clarinet (1)

Mastermind Flute (1)

Mastermind Hi Strings (1)

Mastermind Low Strings (2)

Mastermind Mid Strings (1)

Mastermind Strings (1)

Mastermind Timpani (1)

Maternal All (1)

Maternal Cello (1)

Maternal Viola (1)

Maternal Violin (2)

Memoir All (1)

Memoir Cello (1)

Memoir Viola (1)

Memoir Violin (2)

Memorial All (1)

Memorial Brass & Wind (9)

Metro All (1)

Metro Brass (1)

Metro Flute (1)

Metro Low Strings (2)

Metro Mid Strings (1)

Metro No Timpani (1)

Metro Strings (1)

Metro Timpani (1)

Misty All (1)

Misty Cello (1)

Misty Viola (1)

Misty Violin (2)

Modern Waltz Piano (2)

Momentum All (1)

Momentum Cello (1)

Momentum Viola (1)

Momentum Violin (2)

Monastery Organ (21)

Moody Harpsichord (8)

Musing Harpsichord (8)

Mystery All (1)

Mystery Cello (1)

Mystery Viola (1)

Mystery Violin (2)

Mystic A Basses (1)

Mystic A Bassoon (1)

Mystic A Celesta (1)

Mystic A Cellos (1)

Mystic A Clarinets (1)

Mystic A Crotales (1)

Mystic A Flutes (1)

Mystic A French Horns (1)

Mystic A Glockenspiel (1)

Mystic A Harp (1)

Mystic A Orchestral Kit (1)

Mystic A Piccolo (1)

Mystic A Timpani (1)

Mystic A Violas (1)

Mystic A Violins (2)

Mystic A Xylophone (1)

Mystic B Bassoon (1)

Mystic B Clarinets (1)

Mystic B Flutes (1)

Mystic B French Horns (1)

Mystic B Orchestral Kit (1)

Mystic B Timpani (1)

Mystic C Basses (1)

Mystic C Celesta (1)

Mystic C Clarinets (1)

Mystic C Clarinets2 (1)

Mystic C Flutes (1)

Mystic C Harp (1)

Mystic C Orchestral Kit (1)

Mystic C Piccolo (1)

Mystic D Basses (1)

Mystic D Celesta (1)

Mystic D Cellos (1)

Mystic D Clarinets (1)

Mystic D Deep Bass (1)

Mystic D Flutes (1)

Mystic D French Horn Solo (1)

Mystic D French Horns (1)

Mystic D Glockenspiel (1)

Mystic D Harp (1)

Mystic D Piccolo (1)

Mystic D Tubular Bells (1)

Mystic D Violas (1)

Mystic D Violins (2)

Mystic E Basses (1)

Mystic E Cellos (1)

Mystic E Deep Bass (1)

Mystic E French Horns (1)

Mystic E Harp (1)

Mystic E Timpani (1)

Mystic E Trombones (1)

Mystic E Violas (1)

Mystic E Violins (2)

Mystic F Bassoon (1)

Mystic F Celesta (1)

Mystic F Clarinets (1)

Mystic F Crotales (1)

Mystic F Flute Solo (1)

Mystic F Flutes (1)

Mystic F French Horns (1)

Mystic F Oboe (1)

Mystic G Basses (1)

Mystic G Bassoon (1)

Mystic G Cellos (1)

Mystic G Clarinets (1)

Mystic G Deep Bass (1)

Mystic G Flutes (1)

Mystic G French Horns (1)

Mystic G Oboe (1)

Mystic G Orchestral Kit (1)

Mystic G Timpani (1)

Mystic G Trombones (1)

Mystic G Trumpets (1)

Mystic G Tuba (1)

Mystic G Violas (1)

Mystic G Violins (2)

Nuptial All (1)

Nuptial Cello (1)

Nuptial Viola (1)

Nuptial Violin (2)

Oath All (1)

Oath Brass (1)

Oath Flute (1)

Oath Hi Mid Strings (1)

Oath Hi Strings (1)

Oath Low Strings (1)

Oath Mid Strings (1)

Oath Oboe (1)

Oath Strings (1)

Oath Timpani (1)

Officer All (2)

Officer Brass (1)

Officer Clarinet (1)

Officer Flute (1)

Officer Low Strings (1)

Officer Mid Strings (1)

Officer Strings (1)

Officer Timpani (1)

Old World Harpsichord (22)

Orchard All (1)

Orchard Cello (1)

Orchard Viola (1)

Orchard Violin (2)

Orchestra Flute Solo (23)

Orchestra Harp Pattern (34)

Orchestra Harp Strum (47)

Orchestra Oboe Solo (13)

Orchestra Trumpet Solo (13)

Paranoid All (1)

Paranoid Cello (1)

Paranoid Viola (1)

Paranoid Violin (2)

Pastoral All (1)

Pastoral Cello (1)

Pastoral Viola (1)

Pastoral Violin (2)

Patrol All (1)

Patrol Basses (2)

Patrol Brass (1)

Patrol Hi Strings (1)

Patrol Mid Strings (1)

Patrol Strings (1)

Patrol Timpani (1)

Patrol Woodwind (1)

Phoenix All (1)

Phoenix Brass (2)

Phoenix Clarinet (1)

Phoenix Cymbal (1)

Phoenix Flutes (1)

Phoenix Hi Strings (1)

Phoenix Low Strings (2)

Phoenix Mid Strings (1)

Phoenix No Percussion (1)

Phoenix Strings (1)

Phoenix Timpani (1)

Phoenix Woodwinds (1)

Power Low Strings (20)

Prance All (1)

Prance Cello (1)

Prance Viola (1)

Prance Violin (2)

Promenade All (1)

Promenade Cello (1)

Promenade Viola (1)

Promenade Violin (2)

Protege All (1)

Protege Cello (1)

Protege Viola (1)

Protege Violin (2)

Pugilist All (1)

Pugilist Cello (1)

Pugilist Viola (1)

Pugilist Violin (2)

Pursuit All (1)

Pursuit Brass (2)

Pursuit Hi Strings (1)

Pursuit Low Strings (2)

Pursuit Mid Strings (1)

Pursuit Strings (1)

Pursuit Timpani (1)

Rampart All (1)

Rampart Brass (1)

Rampart Hi Strings (1)

Rampart Low Strings (1)

Rampart March (1)

Rampart Strings (1)

Rampart Timpani (1)

Rampart Woodwinds (1)

Reception All (1)

Reception Cello (1)

Reception Viola (1)

Reception Violin (2)

Reminisce All (1)

Reminisce Cello (1)

Reminisce Viola (1)

Reminisce Violin (2)

Retro Cinema Brass (5)

Retro Cinema Strings (31)

Retro Cinema Winds (7)

Reunion All (1)

Reunion Cello (1)

Reunion Viola (1)

Reunion Violin (2)

Ricochet All (1)

Ricochet Cello (1)

Ricochet Viola (1)

Ricochet Violin (2)

Romantic Piano (39)

Saber All (1)

Saber Brass (1)

Saber Clarinet (1)

Saber Flute (1)

Saber French Horn (1)

Saber Hi Strings (1)

Saber Low Strings (1)

Saber Mid Strings (1)

Saber Strings (1)

Saber Timpani (1)

Saber Trombone (1)

Salute All (1)

Salute Brass & Wind (7)

Sanctum All (1)

Sanctum Cello (1)

Sanctum Viola (1)

Sanctum Violin (2)

Saunter All (1)

Saunter Cello (1)

Saunter Viola (1)

Saunter Violin (2)

Scheme All (1)

Scheme Brass (2)

Scheme Hi Strings (1)

Scheme Low Strings (1)

Scheme Mid Strings (1)

Scheme Strings (1)

Scheme Timpani (1)

Scholar All (1)

Scholar Cello (1)

Scholar Viola (1)

Scholar Violin (2)

Scrutiny All (1)

Scrutiny Brass (2)

Scrutiny Clarinet (1)

Scrutiny Flute (1)

Scrutiny Hi Strings (1)

Scrutiny Low Strings (2)

Scrutiny Mid Strings (1)

Scrutiny Strings (1)

Scrutiny Timpani (1)

Showdown All (1)

Showdown Cello (1)

Showdown Viola (1)

Showdown Violin (2)

Skyline All (1)

Skyline Flute (1)

Skyline Low Strings (1)

Skyline Strings (2)

Skyline Trumpet (1)

Soaring All (1)

Soaring Brass (1)

Soaring Hi Strings (1)

Soaring Low Strings (1)

Soaring Mid Strings (1)

Soaring Strings (1)

Solace All (1)

Solace Cello (1)

Solace Viola (1)

Solace Violin (2)

Sprightly All (1)

Sprightly Cello (1)

Sprightly Viola (1)

Sprightly Violin (2)

Steadfast All (1)

Steadfast Cello (1)

Steadfast Viola (1)

Steadfast Violin (2)

Stormy A Basses (1)

Stormy A Bassoon (1)

Stormy A Cellos (1)

Stormy A Clarinet (1)

Stormy A Deep Bass (1)

Stormy A Flutes (1)

Stormy A French horns (1)

Stormy A Harp (1)

Stormy A Orchestral Kit (1)

Stormy A Timpani (1)

Stormy A Trombones (1)

Stormy A Trumpets (1)

Stormy A Tuba (1)

Stormy A Violas (1)

Stormy A Violins (2)

Stormy B Basses (1)

Stormy B Cellos (1)

Stormy B Deep Bass (1)

Stormy B Orchestral Kit (1)

Stormy B Violas (1)

Stormy B Violins (2)

Stormy C Basses (1)

Stormy C Bassoon (1)

Stormy C Cellos (1)

Stormy C Clarinets (1)

Stormy C Deep Bass (1)

Stormy C Flutes (1)

Stormy C French horns (1)

Stormy C Oboe (1)

Stormy C Orchestral Kit (1)

Stormy C Piccolo (1)

Stormy C Timpani (1)

Stormy C Trombones (1)

Stormy C Trumpets (1)

Stormy C Violas (1)

Stormy C Violins (2)

Stormy D Basses (1)

Stormy D Cellos (1)

Stormy D Deep Bass (1)

Stormy D French horns (1)

Stormy D Orchestral Kit (1)

Stormy D Timpani (1)

Stormy D Trombones (1)

Stormy D Trumpets (1)

Stormy D Tuba (1)

Stormy D Violas (1)

Stormy D Violins (2)

Stormy E Basses (1)

Stormy E Bassoon (1)

Stormy E Cellos (1)

Stormy E Clarinets (1)

Stormy E Deep Bass (1)

Stormy E Flutes (1)

Stormy E French horns (1)

Stormy E Harp (1)

Stormy E Oboe (1)

Stormy E Orchestral Kit (1)

Stormy E Timpani (1)

Stormy E Trombones (1)

Stormy E Trumpets (1)

Stormy E Tuba (1)

Stormy E Tubular Bells (1)

Stormy E Violas (1)

Stormy E Violins (2)

Stormy F Basses (1)

Stormy F Bassoon (1)

Stormy F Cellos (1)

Stormy F Clarinets (1)

Stormy F Deep Bass (1)

Stormy F Flutes (1)

Stormy F French horns (1)

Stormy F Harp (1)

Stormy F Oboe (1)

Stormy F Orchestral Kit (1)

Stormy F Timpani (1)

Stormy F Trombones (1)

Stormy F Trumpets (1)

Stormy F Tuba (1)

Stormy F Tubular Bells (1)

Stormy F Violas (1)

Stormy F Violins (2)

Strategy All (1)

Strategy Brass (2)

Strategy Flute (1)	Vendetta Brass (2)	Victory B Flutes (1)
Strategy Hi Strings (1)	Vendetta Clarinet (1)	Victory B French Horns (1)
Strategy Low Strings (1)	Vendetta Hi Strings (1)	Victory B Harp (1)
Strategy March Mix (1)	Vendetta Low Strings (1)	Victory B Oboe (1)
Strategy Mid Strings (1)	Vendetta Mid Strings (1)	Victory B Orchestral Kit (1)
Strategy Oboe (1)	Vendetta Strings (1)	Victory B Piccolo (1)
Strategy Strings (2)	Vendetta Timpani (1)	Victory B Timpani (1)
Strategy Timpani (1)	Victory A Basses (1)	Victory B Trombones (1)
Sunflower All (1)	Victory A Cellos (1)	Victory B Trumpets (1)
Sunflower Cello (1)	Victory A Clarinet (1)	Victory B Tuba (1)
Sunflower Viola (1)	Victory A Clarinets (1)	Victory B Violas (1)
Sunflower Violin (2)	Victory A Deep Bass (1)	Victory B Violins (2)
Suspense All (1)	Victory A English Horn (1)	Victory C Basses (1)
Suspense Cello (1)	Victory A Flutes (1)	Victory C Bassoon (1)
Suspense Viola (1)	Victory A French Horns (1)	Victory C Cellos (1)
Suspense Violin (2)	Victory A Harp (1)	Victory C Clarinets (1)
Terrace All (1)	Victory A Oboe (1)	Victory C Deep Bass (1)
Terrace Cello (1)	Victory A Orchestral Kit (1)	Victory C French Horns (1)
Terrace Viola (1)	Victory A Timpani (1)	Victory C Glockenspiel (1)
Terrace Violin (2)	Victory A Trombones (1)	Victory C Harp (1)
Tribute All (1)	Victory A Trumpets (1)	Victory C Oboe (1)
Tribute Cello (1)	Victory A Tuba (1)	Victory C Orchestral Kit (1)
Tribute Viola (1)	Victory A Violas (1)	Victory C Timpani (1)
Tribute Violin (2)	Victory A Violins (2)	Victory C Trombones (1)
Tryst All (1)	Victory B Basses (1)	Victory C Trumpets (1)
Tryst Cello (1)	Victory B Bassoon (1)	Victory C Tuba (1)
Tryst Viola (1)	Victory B Cellos (1)	Victory C Violas (1)
Tryst Violin (2)	Victory B Clarinets (1)	Victory C Violins (2)
Vendetta All (1)	Victory B Deep Bass (1)	Victory D Basses (1)

Victory D Bassoon (1)

Victory D Cellos (1)

Victory D Clarinets (1)

Victory D Deep Bass (1)

Victory D Flute (1)

Victory D Flutes (1)

Victory D French Horns (1)

Victory D Harp (1)

Victory D Oboe (1)

Victory D Orchestral Kit (1)

Victory D Timpani (1)

Victory D Trombones (1)

Victory D Trumpets (1)

Victory D Tuba (1)

Victory D Violas (1)

Victory D Violins (2)

Victory E Basses (1)

Victory E Bassoon (1)

Victory E Cellos (1)

Victory E Clarinets (1)

Victory E Deep Bass (1)

Victory E Flutes (1)

Victory E French Horns (1)

Victory E Oboe (1)

Victory E Orchestral Kit (1)

Victory E Timpani (1)

Victory E Trombones (1)

Victory E Trumpets (1)

Victory E Tuba (1)

Victory E Tubular Bells (1)

Victory E Violas (1)

Victory E Violins (2)

Victory F Basses (1)

Victory F Bassoon (1)

Victory F Celesta (1)

Victory F Cellos (1)

Victory F Clarinets (1)

Victory F Deep Bass (1)

Victory F Flutes (1)

Victory F French Horns (1)

Victory F Oboe (1)

Victory F Orchestral Kit (1)

Victory F Timpani (1)

Victory F Trombones (1)

Victory F Trumpets (1)

Victory F Tuba (1)

Victory F Tubular Bells (1)

Victory F Violas (1)

Victory F Violins (2)

Victory G Basses (1)

Victory G Cellos (1)

Victory G Deep Bass (1)

Victory G Flute (1)

Victory G Flutes (1)

Victory G French Horns (1)

Victory G Harp (1)

Victory G Marimba (1)

Victory G Orchestral Kit (1)

Victory G Timpani (1)

Victory G Trombones (1)

Victory G Trumpets (1)

Victory G Tuba (1)

Victory G Violas (1)

Victory G Violins (2)

Victory H Basses (1)

Victory H Cellos (1)

Victory H Clarinets (1)

Victory H Deep Bass (1)

Victory H French Horns (1)

Victory H Harp (1)

Victory H Orchestral Kit (1)

Victory H Timpani (1)

Victory H Trombones (1)

Victory H Trumpets (1)

Victory H Tuba (1)

Victory H Violas (1)

Victory H Violins (2)

Vigilante All (1)

Vigilante Brass (2)

Vigilante Hi Strings (1)

Vigilante Low Strings (1)

Vigilante No Timpani (1)

Vigilante Strings (2)

Vigilante Timpani (1)

Vigilante Woodwinds (1)

Whole Tone Piano (14)

Software Instruments

Orchestra Deep Bass

Orchestra Percussion Kit

Orchestra Brass Ensemble

Orchestra French Horn Sect

Orchestra French Horn

Orchestra Trombone Section

Orchestra Trumpet Section

Orchestra Tuba

Xtra Brass Ens Legato

Xtra Brass Ens Staccato

Xtra French Horn Legato

Xtra French Horn Sect Cresc

Xtra French Horn Sect Leg

Xtra French Horn Sect Stacc

Xtra French Horn Staccato

Xtra Trombone Sect Legato

Xtra Trombone Sect Staccato

Xtra Trumpet Sect Legato

Xtra Trumpet Sect Stacatto

Xtra Tuba Legato

Xtra Tuba Staccato

Orchestra Glockenspiel

Orchestra Marimba

Orchestra Xylophone

Orchestra Baroque Organ

Orchestra Bass Organ

Orchestra Cathedral Organ

Orchestra Deep Organ

Orchestra Flute Organ

Orchestra Fugue Organ

Orchestra Mellow Organ

Orchestra Noble Organ

Orchestra Romantic Organ

Orchestra Toccata Organ

Orchestra Wedding Organ

Orchestra Celesta

Orchestra Harpsichord

Orchestra Steinway Piano

Orchestra Bass Section

Orchestra Cello Section

Orchestra Harp

Orchestra String Ensemble

Orchestra Viola Section

Orchestra Violin Section 1

Orchestra Violin Section 2

Xtra Base Section Legato

Xtra Base Section Pizzicato

Xtra Base Section Staccato

Xtra Base Section Tremolo

Xtra Base Section Trill 1

Xtra Base Section Trill 2

Xtra Cello Sect Legato

Xtra Cello Sect Pizzicato

Xtra Cello Sect Staccato

Xtra Cello Sect Tremolo

Xtra Cello Sect Trill 1

Xtra Cello Sect Trill 2

Xtra String Ens Legato

Xtra String Ens Pizzicato

Xtra String Ens Staccato

Xtra String Ens Tremolo

Xtra String Ens Trill 1

Xtra String Ens Trill 2

Xtra Viola Sect Legato

Xtra Viola Sect Pizzicato

Xtra Viola Sect Staccato

Xtra Viola Sect Tremolo

Xtra Viola Sect Trill 1

Xtra Viola Sect Trill 2

Xtra Violin Sect 1 Legato

Xtra Violin Sect 1 Pizzicato

Xtra Violin Sect 1 Staccato

Xtra Violin Sect 1 Tremolo

Xtra Violin Sect 1 Trill 1

Xtra Violin Sect 1 Trill 2

Xtra Violin Sect 2 Legato

Xtra Violin Sect 2 Pizzicato

Xtra Violin Sect 2 Staccato

Xtra Violin Sect 2 Tremolo

Xtra Violin Sect 2 Trill 1

Xtra Violin Sect 2 Trill 2

Orchestra Crotales

Orchestra Timpani

Orchestra Tubular Bells

Xtra Timpani Hit

Xtra Timpani Tremolo Cresc

Xtra Timpani Tremolo

Orchestra Bassoon

Orchestra Clarinet Section

Orchestra Clarinet

Orchestra English Horn

Orchestra Flute Section

Orchestra Flute

Orchestra Oboe

Orchestra Piccolo Flute

Xtra Bassoon Legato

Xtra Bassoon Staccato

Xtra Clarinet Legato

Xtra Clarinet Sect Legato

Xtra Clarinet Sect Staccato

Xtra Clarinet Staccato

Xtra English Horn Legato

Xtra English Horn Staccato

Xtra Flute Legato

Xtra Flute Sect Legato

Xtra Flute Sect Staccato

Xtra Flute Staccato

Xtra Oboe Legato

Xtra Oboe Staccato

Xtra Piccolo Flute Legato

Xtra Piccolo Flute Staccato

Remix Tools

Get your club on. Mix your DJ-style tracks in GarageBand with this groove-filled pack for creating jammin' remixes and club-inspired beats.

2-Step Ahead Bass (1)

2-Step Ahead Guitar (1)

2-Step Ahead Organ (1)

2-Step Ahead Piano (2)

2-Step Ahead Strings (1)

2-Step Back Flip Beat (2)

2-Step Balancing Beat (2)

2-Step Behind Beat (2)

2-Step Boxer Beat (1)

2-Step Calling Beat (2)

2-Step Electric Bass (2)

2-Step Flatland Beat (3)

2-Step Flux Beat (2)

2-Step Freak Beat (2)

2-Step Jump Beat (2)

2-Step Knuckle Beat (2)

2-Step Lockstep Beat (1)

2-Step Machine Beat (2)

2-Step Missed Beat (2)

2-Step Percussion (2)

2-Step Poolside Bass (1)

2-Step Poolside Guitar (1)

2-Step Poolside Organ (1)

2-Step Poolside Piano (2)

2-Step Push Beat (2)

2-Step Shifter Beat (2)

2-Step Snapper Beat (4)

2-Step Sparse Beat (1)

2-Step Spin Beat (2)

2-Step Summer Bass (2)

2-Step Summer Guitar (2)

2-Step Summer Organ (2)

2-Step Summer Piano (1)

2-Step Summer Strings (1)

2-Step Thump Bass (18)

2-Step Thump Beat (29)

2-Step Thump Beat FX (21)

2-Step Top Down Bass (1)

2-Step Top Down Piano (3)

2-Step Top Down Strings (1)

2-Step Tricky Beat (2)

Autumn Electric Bass (3)

Autumn Synth Bass (1)

Awaiting Arrival Pad (1)

Breaks Biggie Beat (5)

Breaks Blastoff Beat (1)

Breaks Bombastic Bass (1)

Breaks Brick Wall Beat (3)

Breaks Bump Beat (2)

Breaks Chopper Beat (2)

Breaks Crusher Beat (2)

Breaks DJ Dream Beat (8)

Breaks Dig It Beat (1)

Breaks Driver Beat (12)

Breaks Driver FX (2)

Breaks Driver Fill (2)

Breaks Driver Guitar (2)

Breaks Drop Top Beat (2)

Breaks Dub Plate Beat (2)

Breaks Electro Beat (2)

Breaks Energy Beat (2)

Breaks Fat Hammer Beat (4)

Breaks Fat Hammer Fill (1)

Breaks Hieroglyph Beat (2)

Breaks In Two Beat (1)

Breaks Knocking Beat (1)

Breaks Kung Fu Beat (1)

Breaks Lava Beats (5)

Breaks Low Funk Beat (2)

Breaks Low Hand Beat (2)

Breaks Pigpen Beat (1)

Breaks Prowler Beat (2)

Breaks Pushed Beat (5)

Breaks Rim Rocker Beat (1)

Breaks Slow Funk Beat (1)

Breaks Snare Master Beat (1)

Breaks Soul Patch Beat (1)

Breaks Stealth Beat (4)

Breaks Stick Cow Beat (1)

Breaks Stride Step Beat (1)

Breaks Tai Chi Beat (2)

Breaks Tight Beat (2)

Breaks Tiny Funk Beat (2)

Breaks Trashy Beat (3)

Breaks Tricky Rim Beat (1)

Breaks Viscous Beat (1)

Broken Beat Flip Bass (26)

Broken Beat Flip Beat (18)

Broken Beat Flip Synth (2)

Broken Beat Shadow Beat (1)

DnB Acoustic Beat (1)

DnB Angular Beat (1)

DnB Armor Beat (1)

DnB Aurora FX (5)

DnB Aurora Pad (6)

DnB Bang Beat (5)

DnB Bell Beat (2)

DnB Chase Bass (2)

DnB Chase Pad (1)

DnB Chase Piano (1)

DnB Chase Strings (1)

DnB Climber Beat (1)

DnB Climbing Bass (1)

DnB Cracker Beat (1)

DnB Dark Bass (1)

DnB Double Beat (1)

DnB Eerie Bass (1)

DnB Eerie Organ (1)

DnB Eerie Piano (2)

DnB Escape Beat (1)

DnB Flame Beat (2)

DnB Flash In The Pad (1)

DnB Floating Beat (1)

DnB Fog Bass (2)

DnB Gentle Bell (1)

DnB Ghost Beat (2)

DnB Go Beat (2)

DnB Guitar (3)

DnB Haunted Beat (1)

DnB Knock Beat (2)

DnB Lockout Synth (1)

DnB Mayhem Beat (1)

DnB Minimal Bass (1)

DnB Mystery Bass (1)

DnB Mystery Piano (1)

DnB Mystery Strings (1)

DnB Mystic Bass (1)

DnB Percussion (7)

DnB Phase Beat (1)

DnB Pincher Bass (1)

DnB Pit-bull Bass (1)

DnB Quake Beat (1)

DnB Quick Beat (1)

DnB Rivet Beat (1)

DnB Roller Beat (1)

DnB Rubber Bass (1)

DnB Running Beat (1)

DnB Rush Beat (3)

DnB Shifter Beat (1)

DnB Shimmering Piano (1)

DnB Shy Beat (1)

DnB Simple Beat (1)

DnB Sledge Beat (1)

DnB Slide Beat (1)

DnB Stab Bass (1)

DnB Steam Beat (1)

DnB Stiff Bass (1)

DnB Sub Low Bass (1)

DnB Swerve Beat (1)

DnB Tense Beat (2)

DnB Thin Beat (1)

DnB Tight Beat (1)

DnB Tiny Beat (1)

DnB Traffic Beat (1)

DnB Trick Beat (2)

DnB Twister Beat (1)

Downtempo Bounce Beat (2)

Downtempo Cut Up Beat (4)

Downtempo Dream Beat (1)

Downtempo Flex Beat (2)

Downtempo Flight Beat (2)

Downtempo Flip Beat (1)

Downtempo Friendly Beat (1)

Downtempo Funk Bass (19)

Downtempo Funk Beat (14)

Downtempo Funk Clav (16)

Downtempo Funk FX (2)

Downtempo Funk Out Beat (1)

Downtempo Funky Guitar (1)

Downtempo Love Snare Beat (1)

Downtempo Making Beat (1)

Downtempo Mellow Piano (4)

Downtempo Mellow Synth (3)

Downtempo Move Beat (1)

Downtempo Piano FX (5)

Downtempo Ragga Beat (1)

Downtempo Rider Beat (5)

Downtempo Sexy Bass (3)

Downtempo Sexy Guitar (2)

Downtempo Smokey Bass (1)

Downtempo Solid Beat (1)

Downtempo Space Kitten (1)

Downtempo Tribal Beat (3)

Downtempo Vertical Beat (1)

Eastern Mystery String (2)

Eastern Wind Dulcimer (2)

Electric Bass Slide FX (1)

Electro Ascension Beat (1)

Electro Automation Beat (1)

Electro Bass Bin Drum (4)

Electro Battle Bots Beat (1)

Electro Breather Beat (2)

Electro Car Beat (2)

Electro Cycling Beat (1)

Electro Deep End Beat (1)

Electro Destruct Beat (3)

Electro District Beat (1)

Electro Double Click Beat (1)

Electro Drift Bass (2)

Electro Drift Pad (1)

Electro Drift Synth (2)

Electro Elevate Bass (2)

Electro Elevate Pad (1)

Electro Elevate Synth (4)

Electro Emotion Bass (3)

Electro Emotion Pad (1)

Electro Emotion Synth (5)

Electro Fascination Beat (1)

Electro Flight Bass (2)

Electro Flight Synth (3)

Electro Foundation Beat (1)

Electro Frenzy (1)

Electro Future Beat (1)

Electro Generator Beat (2)

Electro House Beat (1)

Electro Infinity Beat (1)

Electro Intellect Beat (2)

Electro Intelligent Beat (1)

Electro Kicker Beat (2)

Electro Love Circuit Beat (1)

Electro Mainframe Beat (2)

Electro Moment Beat (1)

Electro Moon Base Beat (4)

Electro Pop and Lock Beat (1)

Electro Puzzle Beat (1)

Electro Resonance Beat (1)

Electro Robot Rocker Beat (1)

Electro Sector Beat (4)

Electro Shake It Beat (1)

Electro Sharp Shape Beat (1)

Electro Sneak Beat (1)

Electro Soft Pop Beat (5)

Electro Stealth Beat (4)

Electro Structure Beat (4)

Electro Talking Beat (2)

Electro Transistor Beat (1)

Electro Transit Beat (1)

Electro Wired Beat (1)

Electro Wormhole Beat (1)

Electroclash (1)

Electroclash Dirty Beat (1)

Electroclash Glam Beat (2)

Electroclash Low Beat (3)

Electroclash Mini Beat (1)

Electroclash Pop Beat (4)

Euro Accelerator Beat (1)

Euro Anthem Chords Synth (1)

Euro Anthem Synth (2)

Euro At The Party Beat (1)

Euro Backstage Beat (2)

Euro Basic Beat (4)

Euro Big Tent Drama (1)

Euro Chimes Synth (1)

Euro Chord Slicer (2)

Euro Chordal Slicer (1)

Euro Clav Slicer FX (1)

Euro Climbing Synth (1)

Euro Comfort Pad (3)

Euro Didgeridoo Synth (1)

Euro Doppler Beat (1)

Euro Elastic Bass (1)

Euro Energy Stab FX (2)

Euro Foundation Beat (2)

Euro Funk Synth (1)

Euro Hero Bass (1)

Euro Hero Piano (1)

Euro Hero Synth (3)

Euro Honeycomb Bass (1)

Euro Honeycomb Piano (1)

Euro Honeycomb Synth (3)

Euro Kaleidoscope Synth (1)

Euro Lift Off Beat (1)

Euro Lost Robot Synth (1)

Euro Mechanics Beat (1)

Euro Melody Machine Synth (1)

Euro Move Bass (1)

Euro Move Beat (1)

Euro Move Synth (4)

Euro Nosy Freestyle Synth (1)

Euro Odd Mechanical Synth (1)

Euro Oscillation Synth (1)

Euro Pad Slicer FX (1)

Euro Paradise Beat (1)

Euro Party Slicer FX (1)

Euro Pitstop Beat (1)

Euro Pot Boiler Beat (11)

Euro Power Bass (1)

Euro Pulse Pad Slicer (3)

Euro Pushing Red Beat (2)

Euro Quirky Melodic Synth (1)

Euro Raceway Beat (1)

Euro Reach High Organ (1)

Euro Reach High Piano (1)

Euro Reach High Synth (3)

Euro Reach the Top Bass (1)

Euro Reach the Top Pad (1)

Euro Reach the Top Synth (1)

Euro Revelation Bass (2)

Euro Revelation Pad (1)

Euro Revelation Synth (3)

Euro Shimmer Slicer (1)

Euro Slicer Synth (52)

Euro Slipping Away Beat (1)

Euro Snare Roll (4)

Euro Stomp Beat (1)

Euro Sunrise Bass (2)

Euro Sunrise Piano (1)

Euro Sunrise Synth (3)

Euro Super Bass (1)

Euro Supreme Bass (1)

Euro Supreme Synth (3)

Euro Talking Synth (1)

Euro Tapper Beat (1)

Euro Tranquility Pad (3)

Euro Traveler Beat (1)

Euro Tribal Beat (2)

Euro Tribal Boom FX (1)

Euro Urgency Synth (1)

Euro Urgent Cut Pad (1)

Euro VIP Beat (1)

Euro Vox Slicer (3)

Euro Warehouse Beat (4)

Euro Warm Slicer Synth (1)

Floating To Shore Pad (1)

Force Double Bass (1)

Force Electric Piano (1)

Force Flute (1)

Force Pad (1)

Force Strings (1)

Force Synth Bass (1)

Garage Artisan Beat (1)

Garage Break Off Beat (1)

Garage Chopper Beat (1)

Garage Chunk Bass (1)

Garage Chunk Organ (2)

Garage Circus Bass (1)

Garage Circus Organ (2)

Garage Circus Piano (1)

Garage Clack Attack Beat (1)

Garage Empty Space Beat (1)

Garage Fever Beat (1)

Garage Fluid Bass (2)

Garage Fluid Organ (3)

Garage Freestyle Beat (1)

Garage Friday Beat (1)

Garage Friday Fill (1)

Garage Friday Organ (4)

Garage Friday Piano (1)

Garage Friday Strings (2)

Garage Friday Synth (1)

Garage Loose Change Beat (1)

Garage Mathematics Beat (1)

Garage Mover Bass (1)

Garage Mover Organ (3)

Garage Mover Piano (1)

Garage Nasty Beat (1)

Garage Plastic Beat (1)

Garage Pull Back Beat (1)

Garage Push Forward Beat (1)

Garage Sharp Lift Beat (3)

Garage Simple Style Beat (1)

Garage Slush Funk Beat (1)

Garage Smooth Flux Beat (1)

Garage Strut Beat (3)

Garage Stumpy Beat (1)

Garage Superior Beat (1)

Garage Tip Your Hat Beat (1)

Garage Tom Club Beat (1)

Genius Thinker Pad (8)

Goa Aliens Beat (2)

Goa Head Space Beat (2)

Goa Mind Bender Beat (2)

Goa Mind the Gap Beat (2)

Goa Nepal Beat (2)

Goa Psychic Beat (8)

Goa Pulse Beat (2)

Goa Swirling Up Beat (4)

Goa Towards Beat (2)

Hip Hop (1)

Hip Hop 70s Clav (1)

Hip Hop Air Hands Beat (1)

Hip Hop Bad Boy Bass (1)

Hip Hop Bandit Beat (5)

Hip Hop Beginning Beat (1)

Hip Hop Berlin Beat (2)

Hip Hop Blip Beat (2)

Hip Hop Bounce Organ (2)

Hip Hop Breakaway Beat (1)

Hip Hop Breath Out Beat (1)

Hip Hop Broke Beat (1)

Hip Hop Bumper Beat (1)

Hip Hop Caramel Beat (1)

Hip Hop Chunky Beat (1)

Hip Hop Clap Beat (1)

Hip Hop Clap It Beat (2)

Hip Hop Clean Guitar (1)

Hip Hop Cow Beat (1)

Hip Hop Crate Digger Beat (1)

Hip Hop Cruiser Bass (1)

Hip Hop Deep Beat (2)

Hip Hop Deep Jam Beat (1)

Hip Hop Distant Hit FX (1)

Hip Hop Dominoes Beat (1)

Hip Hop Doom Beat (1)

Hip Hop Double Up Bass (1)

Hip Hop Drama Funk Guitar (1)

Hip Hop Drop The Beat (1)

Hip Hop Egyptian Bass (1)

Hip Hop Elevate Bass (1)

Hip Hop Everybody Beat (1)

Hip Hop Fat Frog Beat (2)

Hip Hop Fearless Bass (12)

Hip Hop French Beat (1)

Hip Hop Funky Walk Bass (1)

Hip Hop Gems Beat (1)

Hip Hop Gentle Piano (1)

Hip Hop Hard Driving Beat (1)

Hip Hop Hard Hat Beat (1)

Hip Hop Hard Hitting Beat (1)

Hip Hop Hard Times Beat (1)

Hip Hop Hectic Beat (1)

Hip Hop Here We Come Bass (1)

Hip Hop Hollow Beat (1)

Hip Hop Hot Bass (1)

Hip Hop Hot Hot Beat (1)

Hip Hop Human Beat Box (7)

Hip Hop Lake of Bass Beat (1)

Hip Hop Little Beat (3)

Hip Hop Little Man Beat (1)

Hip Hop Little Story Bass (1)

Hip Hop Loose Clav (1)

Hip Hop Low Boy Bass (1)

Hip Hop Made Easy Beat (1)

Hip Hop Mature Bass (5)

Hip Hop Mature Drums (2)

Hip Hop Mature Piano (1)

Hip Hop Mature Synth (1)

Hip Hop Mic It Bass (4)

Hip Hop Minimal Bass (1)

Hip Hop Money Beat (2)

Hip Hop Muscle Beat (6)

Hip Hop Mystery Guitar (1)

Hip Hop Natural Beat (1)

Hip Hop Naughty Beat (1)

Hip Hop No Pain Beat (1)

Hip Hop Old Kit Beat (10)

Hip Hop On Edge Beat (1)

Hip Hop Once Again Bass (1)

Hip Hop Phantom Beat (6)

Hip Hop Pounding Beat (1)

Hip Hop Punching Bag Beat (1)

Hip Hop Puny Beat (1)

Hip Hop Putty Beat (1)

Hip Hop Rapid Beat (1)

Hip Hop Reggae Beat (1)

Hip Hop Remember Beat (3)

Hip Hop Resistance Beat (1)

Hip Hop Riding Beat (1)

Hip Hop Roll Back Beat (2)

Hip Hop Round Corner Beat (1)

Hip Hop Shifter Beat (1)

Hip Hop Shop Beat (2)

Hip Hop Similar Sub Bass (1)

Hip Hop Simple Sub Bass (1)

Hip Hop Slam Bass (4)

Hip Hop Slinky Beat (3)

Hip Hop Slip Beat (1)

Hip Hop Slow Low Beat (1)

Hip Hop Small Box Beat (5)

Hip Hop Solid Ground Beat (1)

Hip Hop Song Form Beat (1)

Hip Hop Soul Piano (1)

Hip Hop Sprinkler Beat (1)

Hip Hop Steady Beat (16)

Hip Hop Stick It Beat (1)

Hip Hop Stick To It Beat (1)

Hip Hop Story Hook Synth (1)

Hip Hop Strong Arm Bass (1)

Hip Hop Sub Heaven Bass (1)

Hip Hop Subtle Hat Beat (1)

Hip Hop Swirl Beat (1)

Hip Hop Swish Beat (2)

Hip Hop Tease Beat (2)

Hip Hop Technique Beat (1)

Hip Hop Tick Tock Beat (1)

Hip Hop Titanium Beat (5)

Hip Hop Together Beat (1)

Hip Hop Turn About Beat (1)

Hip Hop Twist Stick Beat (1)

Hip Hop Two Punch Beat (2)

Hip Hop Two Ton Beat (1)

Hip Hop Waiting Beat (1)

Hip Hop Wakka Guitar (2)

Hip Hop Working Beat (1)

Hip Hop Zap Beat (1)

Hip Hope Low Tone Beat (1)

Hip Reverse Hat Beat (2)

House Always Open Beat (1)

House Baby Pad (3)

House Baby Piano (11)

House Backstage Beat (2)

House Basement Beat (1)

House Bender Bass (1)

House Big Cat Beat (1)

House Big DJ Beat (2)

House Big Up Beat (1)

House Boxed Beat (1)

House Broken Beat (8)

House Busy Bee Beat (1)

House Clap Attack Beat (2)

House Classic Drive Beat (1)

House Component Beat (7)

House Crazy Conga Beat (2)

House Curious Tiny Synth (1)

House Dance Floor Beat (1)

House Deep Bass (3)

House Deep Beat (1)

House Deep Hot Beat (3)

House Deep Pickup Beat (1)

House Deep Rocker Beat (1)

House Deep Tribal Beat (11)

House Detroit Synth (1)

House Dirty Organ (2)

House Disguised Beat (1)

House Dreamlike Pad (1)

House Drum FX (2)

House Earthy Beat (1)

House Exciter Synth (5)

House Fabulous Beat (2)

House Fever Beat (5)

House Fever Burning Sax (1)

House Fever Dirty Bass (10)

House Fever Disco Strings (1)

House Fever Hot Guitar (4)

House Fever Hot Piano (3)

House Fever Soft Piano (4)

House Filter Organ (5)

House Filthy Beat (2)

House Flanging Sweep Beat (1)

House Fly Flute (2)

House Fly Organ (2)

House Fly Piano (2)

House Foil Pad (1)

House For You Bass (7)

House For You Brass (1)

House For You Flute (1)

House For You Guitar (3)

House For You Piano (4)

House For You Strings (1)

House Fresh Beat (1)

House Genius Chords (2)

House Girl Beat (2)

House Grounded Beat (2)

House Hands Together Beat (1)

House Hats On Beat (1)

House Heat Up Bass (4)

House Heat Up Clav (1)

House Heat Up Guitar (3)

House Heat Up Piano (1)

House Heat Up Sax (1)

House Heavenly Chords (4)

House Hot Hot Beat (2)

House Juicy Beat (2)

House Jump Beat (1)

House Keep It Steady Beat (1)

House Kink Beat (2)

House Knock Down Beat (1)

House Latin Love Beat (2)

House Launch Pad (2)

House Layering Synth (1)

House Lazy Beat (2)

House Light Touch Beat (1)

House Little Alien Beat (1)

House Little Synth (1)

House Lock Steady Beat (1)

House London Club Beat (1)

House Lucid Chords (2)

House Magic Hats Beat (2)

House Music Female Vox (2)

House Nerd Synth (2)

House Over The Edge Beat (1)

House Paris Beat (2)

House Paris Club Beat (2)

House Parisian Beat (1)

House Perfection Beat (1)

House Piano FX (2)

House Potent Beat (2)

House Return Bass (6)

House Return Piano (13)

House Searing Bass (2)

House Searing Organ (5)

House Shape Shifter Beat (1)

House Shark Pad (2)

House Shiver Beat (2)

House Silky Piano (1)

House Slippery Bass (1)

House Slow Burn Beat (1)

House Smooth Organ (3)

House Snappy Beat (2)

House Solitary Pad (1)

House Spicy Beat (2)

House Starter Beat (1)

House Stomper Beat (1)

House Stride Bass (1)

House Strong Beat (2)

House Strut Beat (1)

House Sweet Beat (2)

House Sweet Turn Beat (1)

House Swim Pad (2)

House Swimming Beat (1)

House Tambourine Beat (1)

House Tension Organ (1)

House Ticky Tack Beat (1)

House Tip Hats Beat (1)

House Trickling Synth (2)

House Tricky Bass Beat (2)

House VIPs Lounge Beat (1)

House Ware Beat (2)

House Warm Chord Synth (1)

House Warm Flowing Pad (1)

House Warm Fuzzy Pad (5)

House Warp Bass (5)

Jazz Hustle Bass (2)

Jazz Hustle Flute (4)

Jazz Hustle Guitar (5)

Jazz Hustle Sax (3)

Jazz Muted Trumpet (2)

NuJazz Air Beat (2)

NuJazz Chop Beat (1)

NuJazz Compact Beat (1)

NuJazz Folded Beat (1)

NuJazz Fractured Beat (1)

NuJazz Frozen Beat (1)

NuJazz Gig Beat (1)

NuJazz Jam Bass (5)

NuJazz Jam Flute (1)

NuJazz Jam Guitar (7)

NuJazz Jam Organ (2)

NuJazz Jam Piano (4)

NuJazz Jam Sax (3)

NuJazz Jam Strings (1)

NuJazz Ladybug Bass (4)

NuJazz Ladybug Flute (3)

NuJazz Ladybug Guitar (5)

NuJazz Ladybug Horn (4)

NuJazz Ladybug Piano (5)

NuJazz Nucleus Beat (1)

NuJazz Rain Beat (1)

NuJazz Ride Beat (2)

NuJazz Ringer Beat (1)

NuJazz Rolled Beat (1)

NuJazz Roller Beat (1)

NuJazz Safari Beat (1)

NuJazz Side Stick Beat (2)

NuJazz Smart Snare Beat (1)

NuJazz Stick Digger Beat (1)

NuJazz Sticky Beat (1)

NuJazz Tom Beat (1)

NuSchool Breaks Beat (2)

Percolating Cavern FX (1)

Pop (2)

Pop Beauty Piano (1)

Pop Beauty Synth (1)

Pop Beloved Beat (4)

Pop Block Beat (2)

Pop Body Beat (2)

Pop Bubblegum Beat (2)

Pop Chart Topper Beat (2)

Pop Clay Pot Funk Beat (1)

Pop Complex Beat (1)

Pop Contemplate Bass (1)

Pop Contemplate Drums (1)

Pop Contemplate Piano (2)

Pop Curious Piano (3)

Pop Digging Hard Beat (2)

Pop Dirty Secret Beat (1)

Pop Disco Force Beat (1)

Pop Disco Returns Beat (1)

Pop Easy Beat (1)

Pop Egyptian Sky Beat (10)

Pop Emotive Beat (5)

Pop Euro Beat (1)

Pop Feel It Return Beat (1)

Pop Freeze Beat (1)

Pop Frenzy Step Beat (2)

Pop Funky Stick Beat (1)

Pop Get Up Beat (5)

Pop Get-Ready-Set Beat (5)

Pop Go Beat (2)

Pop Hands Up Beat (1)

Pop Humble Beat (1)

Pop Jump Jumble Beat (1)

Pop Let It Ride Beat (1)

Pop Lift and Push Beat (1)

Pop Listen To Me Piano (2)

Pop Lock Step Beat (1)

Pop Looker Beat (1)

Pop Low Flow Bass (1)

Pop Low Swinging Beat (2)

Pop Low and Slow Beat (1)

Pop Mini Song Beat (1)

Pop Movement Beat (1)

Pop New Disco Beat (1)

Pop Pink Beat (2)

Pop Pop Pop Beat (2)

Pop Pride Beat (1)

Pop Pushy Beat (1)

Pop Relaxed Beat (1)

Pop Ripple Ticker Beat (5)

Pop Routine Beat (1)

Pop Sassy Way Beat (1)

Pop Shake It Beat (1)

Pop Slide Strut Beat (1)

Pop Slip and Fall Beat (1)

Pop Slow Rocking Beat (1)

Pop Super Low Beat (1)

Pop Sure Step Beat (1)

Pop Talking Drum Beat (2)

Pop Three vs. Four Beat (1)

Pop Ultra Remix Beat (2)

Pop Watch Me Beat (1)

Remix Smooth Bass (1)

Remix Action Synth (5)

Remix African Shaker (1)

Remix Air Slicer FX (4)

Remix Ancient Pipe (1)

Remix Beat Box Vocal FX (1)

Remix Bell Tree (1)

Remix Bongo Action (1)

Remix Breath Box Vocal FX (1)

Remix Broken Beat (3)

Remix Cabassa (2)

Remix Cherry Bass (2)

Remix Cherry Organ (1)

Remix Cherry Piano (1)

Remix Chord Slicer FX (21)

Remix Clap FX (3)

Remix Classic Agogo (2)

Remix Conga & Woodblock (1)

Remix Conga Drama (1)

Remix Conga Fever (12)

Remix Cowbell (2)

Remix Crazy Scratch FX (2)

Remix Dirty Drum FX (1)

Remix Distant Memory Pad (1)

Remix Doppler In Space FX (1)

Remix Dragon Harp Synth (1)

Remix Eastern Drone (2)

Remix Egyptian FX (2)

Remix Fast Funk Bass (1)

Remix Finger Rhythms (2)

Remix Glacier Pad (1)

Remix Gravel Synth (2)

Remix Guitar FX (7)

Remix Guitar Hit FX (1)

Remix Hypnotic Bass (10)

Remix Hypnotist Pad (5)

Remix Indian Tabla (2)

Remix Jazz Bass (2)

Remix Jazz Flute (1)

Remix Jazz Organ (3)

Remix Jazz Piano (3)

Remix Jazz Strings (1)

Remix Jazz Synth (2)

Remix Layer Synth (2)

Remix Liquid Waves Synth (1)

Remix Mercury Drops Pad (1)

Remix Noisy Percussion (4)

Remix Noisy Scratch FX (1)

Remix Party Crowd FX (1)

Remix Phasing Away Bass (1)

Remix Punctuation FX (12)

Remix Radio Vocoder FX (1)

Remix Resonant Blast FX (1)

Remix Resonate Hats (1)

Remix Reverse Vocal FX (1)

Remix Rock Funk Bass (3)

Remix Rocking Congas Beat (1)

Remix Saucer FX (1)

Remix Sci Fi Synth FX (1)

Remix Shaker (6)

Remix Shields Up FX (1)

Remix Shimmery Synth (9)

Remix Simple Clav (1)

Remix Simple Hats (1)

Remix Siren FX (1)

Remix Slicer FX (2)

Remix Slicer Synth (3)

Remix Snowing Pad (1)

Remix Spacey Piano (4)

Remix Spanish Bass (3)

Remix Stakeout Bass (1)

Remix Suspense Begins Pad (1)

Remix Sweeping Synth (5)

Remix Synth Slicer (6)

Remix Synthetic Noise (1)

Remix Synthetic Wind FX (1)

Remix Tambora (3)

Remix Tambourine (3)

Remix Tambourine FX (1)

Remix Timpani FX (1)

Remix Toca (2)

Remix Turntable FX (2)

Remix Udu (2)

Remix Underground Beat (4)

Remix Vacuum FX (1)

Remix Vacuum Synth (2)

Remix Vocal Warp FX (4)

Remix Vox Electronic (2)

Remix Vox FX (1)

Remix Vox Slicer (1)

Remix Vox Slicer FX (1)

Remix Warm Glow Slicer (4)

Remix Warm Vocoder (1)

Remix Warm Vox Chords (1)

Remix Wood Block (2)

RnB Arabian Night Beat (2)

RnB Candles and Wine Beat (1)

RnB Finding Someone Piano (1)

RnB Flow Bass (2)

RnB Hot Enough Beat (1)

RnB Jam To It Beat (1)

RnB Lay It Down Beat (1)

RnB Listen Carefully Beat (1)

RnB Lock and Rock Beat (1)

RnB Red Cherries Beat (1)

RnB Rock the Bells (1)

RnB Seduction Beat (1)

RnB Shift Around Beat (1)

RnB Simple Love Beat (2)

RnB Slow and Low Beat (1)

RnB Smokey Acoustic Bass (1)

RnB Sweet Talk Piano (2)

RnB Walking Beat (1)

RnB What She Said Beat (1)

Satellite Calling (4)

She Spy Electric Bass (9)

She Spy Electric Piano (2)

Squeezing Resonance FX (1)

TR-606 RnB Beat (1)

TR-808 Classic Beat (3)

TR-808 Hip Hop Beat (17)

TR-808 RnB Beat (3)

TR-909 Classic Beat (4)

Techno 8 Bit Beat (4)

Techno Alert Bass (1)

Techno Alert Synth (3)

Techno Anticipate Beat (2)

Techno Aquatic Beat (1)

Techno Automata Beat (1)

Techno Bang Bang Beat (4)

Techno Battle Bot Beat (6)

Techno Big Shot Beat (2)

Techno Binary Beat (5)

Techno Bleep Beat (6)

Techno Breeze Beat (1)

Techno Bubble Beat (4)

Techno Conga Beat (4)

Techno Crying For Synth (1)

Techno Dark Sky Bass (1)

Techno Dark Sky FX (2)

Techno Dark Sky Synth (3)

Techno Festival Bass (1)

Techno Festival Beat (1)

Techno Festival FX (1)

Techno Festival Piano (1)

Techno Festival Synth (6)

Techno Folds Upon Beat (1)

Techno Hopscotch Beat (2)

Techno Inner Bass (2)

Techno Inner Synth (6)

Techno Jackhammer Beat (4)

Techno Latin Bot Beat (4)

Techno Liquid Beat (2)

Techno Locomotive Beat (4)

Techno Morse Future Synth (1)

Techno Mutant Beat (4)

Techno No Escape Beat (1)

Techno Phase Bass (2)

Techno Razor Beat (2)

Techno Reactor Beat (4)

Techno Reverse Beat (4)

Techno Robot Vox Beat (2)

Techno Rolling Beat (4)

Techno Runner Beat (8)

Techno Soft Step Beat (2)

Techno Spin Cycle Beat (2)

Techno Spokes Beat (4)

Techno Storm Beat (2)

Techno Stretcher Beat (2)

Techno Substance Beat (2)

Techno Sweeper Beat (4)

Techno Tribal Beat (2)

Trance Balancing Beat (4)

Trance Cluster Synth (1)

Trance Daze Bass (3)

Trance Daze Piano (1)

Trance Daze Synth (2)

Trance Deep India Beat (4)

Trance Deep Space Beat (4)

Trance Dripper Beat (8)

Trance Europa Beat (4)

Trance Get On The Beat (4)

Trance Hypnotic Beat (4)

Trance In and Out Beat (4)

Trance Jazzman Beat (4)

Trance On It Beat (1)

Trance Plastic Beat (8)

Trance Reflection Beat (1)

Trance Space Bass (3)

Trance Stride Beat (7)

Trance Sudden Bass (3)

Trance Sudden FX (1)

Trance Sudden Pad (2)

Trance Sudden Piano (1)

Trance Sudden Synth (3)

Trance Travel Synth (2)

Trance Tunnel Bass (2)

Trance Tunnel FX (5)

Trance Tunnel Organ (1)

Trance Tunnel Pad (1)

Trance Tunnel Synth (2)

Trance Vaporized Beat (8)

Trance Vinyl Beat (8)

Trip Hop (1)

Trip Hop Airhead Beat (1)

Trip Hop Ally Beat (1)

Trip Hop Antarctica Beat (1)

Trip Hop Arrival Pad (2)

Trip Hop Back Beat (1)

Trip Hop Bell Drama FX (1)

Trip Hop Bell Tap Beat (1)

Trip Hop Big Banger Beat (1)

Trip Hop Broken Guitar (1)

Trip Hop Buckle Beat (1)

Trip Hop Candy Eater Beat (1)

Trip Hop Chill Out Beat (1)

Trip Hop Circle Back Vibe (1)

Trip Hop Clutter Beat (1)

Trip Hop Creatures Beat (1)

Trip Hop Darkness Beat (2)

Trip Hop Delay Trick Beat (1)

Trip Hop Devotion Beat (2)

Trip Hop Diver Beat (6)

Trip Hop Dub Beat (1)

Trip Hop Dub City Beat (1)

Trip Hop Dub Drummer Beat (1)

Trip Hop Dub Zone Beat (1)

Trip Hop Dusty Town Hook (1)

Trip Hop Eastern Beat (1)

Trip Hop Expand Bass (3)

Trip Hop Expand Beat (1)

Trip Hop Expand Clav (1)

Trip Hop Freestyle Beat (1)

Trip Hop Full Rim Beat (1)

Trip Hop Glide Beat (1)

Trip Hop Idle Beat (1)

Trip Hop Jungle Beat (2)

Trip Hop Jungle Boat Beat (1)

Trip Hop Kicking Beat (1)

Trip Hop Laidback Beat (2)

Trip Hop Lander FX (1)

Trip Hop Lazy Beat (2)

Trip Hop Live Beat (1)

Trip Hop Lonely Beat (1)

Trip Hop Lonely Guitar (1)

Trip Hop Lonestar Guitar (1)

Trip Hop Lost Beat (1)

Trip Hop Low Blow Beat (1)

Trip Hop Low Rocker Beat (1)

Trip Hop Morse Beat (2)

Trip Hop Mover Beat (3)

Trip Hop Old Record Beat (1)

Trip Hop Pipes FX (1)

Trip Hop Player Beat (1)

Trip Hop Pop Beat (2)

Trip Hop Potent Beat (1)

Trip Hop Potion Beat (2)

Trip Hop Pumper Beat (1)

Trip Hop Quiet Calm Beat (1)

Trip Hop Ragga Beat (1)

Trip Hop Relaxing Beat (1)

Trip Hop Ride Down Beat (1)

Trip Hop Roll Away Beat (1)

Trip Hop Sandpaper Beat (1)

Trip Hop Seeker Synth (1)

Trip Hop Shaman Beat (11)

Trip Hop Smart Beat (2)

Trip Hop Sneak Out Beat (1)

Trip Hop Soak Up Beat (2)

Trip Hop Spy Bass (1)

Trip Hop Steady Beat (2)

Trip Hop Stick Trick Beat (1)

Trip Hop Suspense FX (1)

Trip Hop Sympathy FX (1)

Trip Hop Tap Beat (1)

Trip Hop Telephone Beat (1)

Trip Hop Thick Space Beat (1)

Trip Hop Tiny Jam Beat (1)

Trip Hop Tip Top Beat (2)

Trip Hop Too Fat Beat (2)

Trip Hop Tribal Beat (1)

Trip Hop Tube Beat (1)

Trip Hop Underwater Beat (1)

Trip Hop Velvet Beat (3)

Trip Hop Vinyl Beat (1)

Trip Hop Vocal Chatter FX (1)

Trip Hop Want to Be Beat (1)

Trip Hop Woodpecker Beat (1)

Warm Nighttime Pads (2)

World Traveler Pad (4)

World Music

Sounds from all over the world are brought together in this Jam Pack. All corners of the globe and all traditions are represented, from Klezmer to Indian and from Chinese to Irish. This Jam Pack is for everyone who wants to add some musical ethnicity to their productions. The authenticity with which these Software Instruments and loops are rendered is breathtaking. Check out how much you can do with the modulation wheel on your keyboard to achieve some of the cool "alt" sounds that each of these fine instruments was created to be able to make. See Chapter 6 and the section called "Using the Editor for Editing MIDI Information" for more information about the special "flourishes" available within of many of these sounds.

Afganistan Sand Rabab (31)

African Chant Mbira (14)

African Crash Box (5)

African Dance Marimba (18)

African Ghana Kalimba (11)

African Ghana Kit (10)

African Ghost Bells (6)

African Ghost Drum (10)

African Ghost Kit (18)

African King Atenteben (10)

African King Axatse (1)

African King Ensemble (25)

African King Gyl (12)

African King Tsonshi (5)

African Lion Atsimevu (11)

African Lion Axatse (2)

African Lion Gankogui (2)

African Lion Kaganu (2)

African Lion Kidi (5)

African Lion Sogo (6)

African Marimba (3)

African Mist Gankogui (1)

African Mist Kpanlogo (13)

African Mist Voice (14)

African Monkey Drum (4)

African Rain Caxixi (5)

African Rain Crashbox (7)

African River Kalimba (18)

African Seed Caxixi (8)

African Skies Kit (13)

African Skies Marimba (4)

African Skies Voices (2)

African Talking Drum (26)

African Udu Drum (14)

African Zebra Log Drum (18)

African Zebra Mbira (4)

African Zulu Harp (6)

African Zulu Kalimba (4)

African Zulu Kit (8)

Andean Stroll Drum (2)

Andean Stroll Dulcimer (1)

Andean Stroll Guitar (6)

Andean Stroll Guitarron (1)

Andean Stroll Lute (2)

Andean Stroll Panpipe (9)

Andean Stroll Ukulele (1)

Arabian Nights Gombri (9)

Argentine Accordion (8)

Argentine Tango Bass (2)

Argentine Tango Piano (7)

Asian Parade Bass (7)

Asian Parade Di Zi (6)

Asian Parade Erhu (8)

Asian Parade Kit (5)

Asian Pond Di Zi (8)

Asian Pond Kit (3)

Asian Pond Zither (5)

Australian Didgeridoo (16)

Balkan Sea Riq (4)

Bavarian Accordion (10)

Bavarian Bass (4)

Bavarian Drums (6)

Beltane Bass (2)

Beltane Celtic Harp (4)

Beltane Chimes (2)

Beltane Dulcimer (3)

Beltane Lute (2)

Beltane Percussion (2)

Beltane Recorder (2)

Beltane Tamburin (7)

Beltane Whistle (5)

Bosnian Sunset Bass (13)

Bosnian Sunset Drumset (12)

Bosnian Sunset Guitar (16)

Bosnian Sunset Violin (24)

Brazilian Ago-go (1)

Brazilian Apito (2)

Brazilian Bass (9)

Brazilian Berimbau (11)

Brazilian Bossa Bass (11)

Brazilian Bossa Drums (3)

Brazilian Bossa Guitar (6)

Brazilian Bossa Piano (22)

Brazilian Caixa (2)

Brazilian Cavaquinho (7)

Brazilian Cuica (4)

Brazilian Drumset (7)

Brazilian Ganza (2)

Brazilian Guitar (10)

Brazilian Panderio (2)

Brazilian Repique (19)

Brazilian Sun Bass (3)

Brazilian Sun Drums (7)

Brazilian Sun Guitar (5)

Brazilian Sun Panderio (6)

Brazilian Sun Shaker (4)

Brazilian Sun Voice (2)

Brazilian Sun Zambuma (9)

Brazilian Surdo Drum (5)

Brazilian Tamborim (3)

Chinese Dawn Yueqin (12)

Chinese Moon Drum (4)

Chinese Moon Flute (3)

Chinese Moon Guitar (1)

Chinese Moon Zither (9)

Chinese Reeds Di Zi (11)

Chinese Reeds Erhu (11)

Chinese Winds Di Xiao (7)

Chinese Winds Di Zi (12)

Cuban Bass Upright Fun (20)

Cuban Cha Cha Clave (4)

Cuban Cha Cha Guitar (7)

Cuban Cha Cha Piano (9)

Cuban Fun Bongo (19)

Cuban Fun Clave (2)

Cuban Fun Conga (13)

Cuban Fun Cowbell (10)

Cuban Fun Flute (1)

Cuban Fun Guiro (2)

Cuban Fun Horn (9)

Cuban Fun Maracas (5)

Cuban Fun Timbale (6)

Cuban Fun Trombone (3)

Cuban Fun Trumpet (1)

Cuban Fun Voices (5)

Cuban Guaba Piano (8)

Cuban Guabachoso Piano (6)

Cuban Salsa Piano (12)

Cuban Son Bass (10)

Cuban Son Horns (3)

Cuban Son Percussion (18)

Cuban Son Sax (3)

Cuban Timba Bass (14)

Cuban Timba Conga (12)

Cuban Timba Drumset (16)

Cuban Timba Guitar (3)

Cuban Timba Maraca (1)

Cuban Timba Trumpet (3)

Cuban Timba Voice (4)

Eastern Gold Oud (27)

Eastern Gold Voice (6)

Eastern Storm Oud (11)

Eastern Storm Violin (10)

Eastern Storm Voice (3)

Egyptian Darbouka (1)

Egyptian Fingers Drum (13)

Egyptian Fingers Zil (13)

Egyptian Nile Darbouka (27)

Egyptian Nile Lute (5)

English Court Drum (3)

English Court Flute (9)

English Court Harp (3)

English Court Lute (7)

Europa Waltz Accordion (4)

Europa Waltz Bass (1)

European Jam Accordion (2)

European Jam Dulcimer (8)

European Jam Harp (2)

European Jam Whistle (2)

Greek Dance Bouzouki (31)

Greek Sirtos Bass (8)

Greek Sirtos Doumbek (22)

Greek Sirtos Guitar (4)

Greek Sirtos Riqq (13)

Greek Sirtos Violin (10)

Havana Bass (10)

Havana Cabasa (1)

Havana Claves (2)

Havana Congas (2)

Havana Cowbell (4)

Havana Flamenco (6)

Havana Guiro (1)

Havana High Hats (4)

Havana Horns (4)

Havana Maracas (2)

Havana Piano (9)

Havana Snare (1)

Havana Timbales (2)

Havana Toms (1)

Havana Triangle (1)

Havana Trumpet (8)

Hawaiian Luau Bass (1)

Hawaiian Luau Drums (3)

Hawaiian Luau Guitar (5)

Hawaiian Luau Ukulele (1)

Hawaiian Wave Ukulele (6)

Highland Keep Dulcimer (7)

Highland Keep Harp (9)

Highland Keep Whistle (10)

Indian Bhangra Choir (1)

Indian Bhangra Drum (8)

Indian Bhangra Flute (8)

Indian Bhangra Santoor (7)

Indian Bhangra Sitar (11)

Indian Chant Subahar (18)

Indian Curry Ganjira (6)

Indian Dandiya Drum (10)

Indian Dholak Drum (40)

Indian Khol Drum (10)

Indian Mridangam Drum (19)

Indian Pakawaj Drum (18)

Indian Raga Drums (6)

Indian Raga Oboe (1)

Indian Raga Sitar (9)

Indian Raga Tabla (10)

Indian Rajah Bansuri (4)

Indian Rajah Sarod (30)

Indian Rajah Sitar (41)

Indian Rajah Tabla (37)

Indonesian Chi Erhu (5)

Indonesian Chi Flute (3)

Indonesian Chi Gamelan (25)

Indonesian Chi Kit (8)

Indonesian Gamelan (7)

Indonesian Rey Gamelan (3)

Indonesian Te Balinese (3)

Indonesian Te Di Zi (7)

Indonesian Te Gamelan (7)

Irish A Rún Violin (11)

Irish Athair Harp (8)

Irish Bay Bouzouki (4)

Irish Bluegrass Bouzouki (1)

Irish Breton Harp (9)

Irish Brionglóid Harp (15)

Irish Chante Bodhran (4)

Irish Chante Guitar (4)

Irish Chante Malodeon (6)

Irish Chante Violin (6)

Irish Chiann Flute (1)

Irish Chiann Harp (20)

Irish Chiann Violin (8)

Irish Chiann Whistle (3)

Irish Comp Bouzouki (3)

Irish Cooley Bouzouki (1)

Irish Delight Harp (2)

Irish Dew Melodeon (8)

Irish Frost Bodhran (6)

Irish Frost Flute (7)

Irish Frost Harp (4)

Irish Frost Violin (8)

Irish Frost Voice (2)

Irish Ginger Bouzouki (2)

Irish Jig Violin (11)

Irish Land Bodhran (3)

Irish Land Harp (2)

Irish Land Mandola (4)

Irish Lore Bodhran (7)

Irish Lore Voice (4)

Irish Nag Harp (3)

Irish Nag Mandolin (3)

Irish Póg Bodhran (2)

Irish Póg Harp (4)

Irish Póg Mandola (4)

Irish Reel Bouzouki (3)

Irish Strum Acoustic (5)

Irish Strum Guitar (5)

Jacaranda Bansuri (1)

Jacaranda Conga (1)

Jacaranda Finger Zimble (1)

Jacaranda Marimba (3)

Jacaranda Percussion (2)

Jacaranda Shaker (4)

Jacaranda Shakuhachi (1)

Jacaranda Singers (6)

Jacaranda Udu (1)

Jamaican Anis Bass (2)

Jamaican Anis Fill (2)

Jamaican Anis Guitar (3)

Jamaican Anis Kabasa (1)

Jamaican Anis Organ (4)

Jamaican Clav Anis (1)

Jamaican Crash Anis (1)

Jamaican Drums Anis (1)

Jamaican Duck Bass (4)

Jamaican Duck Cowbell (2)

Jamaican Duck Crash (1)

Jamaican Duck Drumset (2)

Jamaican Duck Fill (3)

Jamaican Duck Guitar (5)

Jamaican Duck Rhodes (3)

Jamaican Egret Bass (3)

Jamaican Egret Cowbell (2)

Jamaican Egret Drumset (5)

Jamaican Egret Fill (3)

Jamaican Egret Guitar (5)

Jamaican Egret Organ (1)

Jamaican Egret Shaker (1)

Jamaican Frog Anis (1)

Jamaican Ibis Bass (3)

Jamaican Ibis Cowbell (1)

Jamaican Ibis Crash (1)

Jamaican Ibis Drumset (3)

Jamaican Ibis Fill (3)

Jamaican Ibis Guitar (7)

Jamaican Ibis Organ (2)

Jamaican Ibis Rhodes (4)

Jamaican Ibis Shaker (1)

Jamaican Jaeger Bass (2)

Jamaican Jaeger Clav (2)

Jamaican Jaeger Drum (4)

Jamaican Jaeger Fill (1)

Jamaican Jaeger Flextone (1)

Jamaican Jaeger Guitar (4)

Jamaican Jaeger Organ (2)

Jamaican Jaeger Shaker (1)

Jamaican Jaeger Vibbra (1)

Jamaican Rail Guiro (1)

Jamaican Rail Organ (4)

Jamaican Ruff Bass (2)

Jamaican Ruff Drumset (5)

Jamaican Ruff Fill (1)

Jamaican Ruff Frog (1)

Jamaican Ruff Guitar (4)

Jamaican Ruff Kabasa (1)

Jamaican Ruff Organ (2)

Jamaican Ruff Rhodes (2)

Jamaican Ruff Shaker (1)

Jamaican Sora Bass (3)

Jamaican Sora Drumset (6)

Jamaican Sora Fill (1)

Jamaican Sora Shaker (1)

Japanese Garden Koto (8)

Japanese Katana Drums (11)

Japanese Katana Flute (2)

Japanese Katana Guitar (2)

Japanese Katana Koto (10)

Japanese Katana Zither (6)

Japanese Spring Drum (9)

Kiev Eve Accordion (6)

Kiev Eve Balalaika (4)

Kiev Eve Bass (2)

Klezmer Bend Bass (15)

Klezmer Bend Clarinet (32)

Klezmer Bend Drums (26)

Klezmer Bend Guitar (11)

Klezmer Bend Horn (24)

Klezmer Bend Saxophone (27)

Klezmer Bend Violin (11)

La Marca Accordion (13)

La Marca Bass (11)

La Marca Cabasa (7)

La Marca Flamenco (10)

La Marca Guiro (2)

La Marca Piano (6)

La Marca Tamburin (1)

La Marca Triangle (2)

Latin Baby Bass (5)

Latin Bembe Conga (16)

Latin Bembe Cowbell (1)

Latin Bolero Bass (3)

Latin Danza Bass (7)

Latin Danza Drumset (10)

Latin Danza Guitar (2)

Latin Danza Horn (2)

Latin Danza Shaker (5)

Latin Day Bass (8)

Latin Day Block (2)

Latin Day Bongo (7)

Latin Day Conga (7)

Latin Day Cowbell (6)

Latin Day Cymbal (1)

Latin Day Guiro (4)

Latin Day Horns (7)

Latin Day Maracas (2)

Latin Day Timbale (6)

Latin Day Voice (3)

Latin Dulce Bass (9)

Latin Dulce Brass (2)

Latin Dulce Percussion (11)

Latin El Clan Bass (1)

Latin El Clan Drum (3)

Latin El Clan Guitar (20)

Latin El Clan Piano (12)

Latin Fire Bass (8)

Latin Fire Percussion (18)

Latin Funk Bass (2)

Latin Heart Guitar (6)

Latin Jam Bass (9)

Latin Jam Guitar (6)

Latin Merengue Bass (12)

Latin Roja Bass (1)

Latin Roja Percussion (5)

Latin Roja Piano (12)

Latin Spice Percussion (17)

Lebanese Jbail Oboe (4)

Lebanese Jbail Santoor (17)

Lebanese Jbail Zither (6)

Lotus Cymbals (1)

Lotus Di Zi (4)

Lotus Drums (4)

Lotus Erhu (4)

Lotus Gongs (2)

Lotus Guzheng (6)

Lotus Percussion (2)

Lotus Ruan (3)

Lotus Stings Ensemble (2)

Macedonian Clarinet (3)

Macedonian Rise Violin (10)

Macedonian Violin (2)

Mexican Mariachi Bass (1)

Mexican Mariachi Drums (6)

Mexican Mariachi Horns (12)

Mexican Ole Guitarron (6)

Mitzvah River Bass (14)

Mitzvah River Clarinet (8)

Mitzvah River Drum (1)

Mitzvah River Guitar (15)

Mitzvah River Sax (11)

Mitzvah River Violin (15)

Moscow Snow Balalaika (2)

Moscow Snow Bass (5)

Native American Drum (2)

Native American Flute (5)

Nian Hua Bass (4)

Nian Hua Cymbals (4)

Nian Hua Di Zi (3)

Nian Hua Erhu (2)

Nian Hua Gong (1)

Nian Hua Guzheng (8)

Nian Hua Ruan (5)

Nian Hua Ruan Chords (5)

Nian Hua WoodBlocks (4)

Persian Charm Clarinet (11)

Persian Dayereh (13)

Persian Market Tar (19)

Sanskrit Bansuri (4)

Sanskrit Bass (1)

Sanskrit Darabuka (1)

Sanskrit Manjira (5)

Sanskrit Santoor (5)

Sanskrit Shehnai (2)

Sanskrit Sitar (3)

Sanskrit Tablas (4)

Sanskrit Tamburin (1)

Sanskrit Tanpura (2)

Sanskrit Udu (3)

Scottish Bass Drum (4)

Scottish Bog Accordion (4)

Scottish Bog Fiddle (2)

Scottish Bog Harp (11)

Scottish Bog Whistle (3)

Scottish Flute (2)

Scottish Ides Bagpipes (5)

Scottish Ides Drum (3)

Scottish March Snare (5)

Shetland Bagpipe (6)

Shetland Bass Drum (7)

Shetland Fiddle (3)

Shetland Field Drums (3)

Shetland Shaker (1)

Shetland Snare (1)

Shetland String (2)

Shetland Tamurin (4)

Shetland Toms (1)

Shetland Whistle (2)

Shogun Bass (1)

Shogun Di Zi (3)

Shogun Fill (3)

Shogun Groove (3)

Shogun Guzheng (8)

Shogun Koto (4)

Shogun Shakuhachi (5)

Shogun Toms (1)

Shogun Woodblock (1)

Swedish Ni Nyckelharpa (8)

Swedish Nyckelharpa (7)

Tango Rose Accordion (21)

Tibetan Peace Bowl (13)

Tibetan Peace Drum (10)

Tibetan Temple Gongs (4)

Tibetian Temple Gong (1)

Tigris Arco Strings (2)

Tigris Bass (4)

Tigris Boghran (4)

Tigris Darabuka (6)

Tigris Izmir (1)

Tigris Oud (5)

Tigris Santoor (5)

Tigris Saz (5)

Tigris Shehnai (1)

Tigris String Ensemble (2)

Tigris Tamburin (2)

Tigris Udu (2)

Tigris Zimble (8)

Turkish Calm Riq (10)

Turkish Morning Drum (4)

Turkish Morning Flute (12)

Turkish Morning Oboe (8)

Turkish Morning Oud (11)

Turkish Spice Saz (25)

Turkish Winter Riqq (2)

Turkish Winter Violin (20)

Ukranian Solo Violin (10)

Software Instruments

African Kalimba

African Kit

African Marimba

Afro-Cuban Upright Piano

Asian Kit

Indonesian Gamelan

Celtic Hammered Dulcimer

Celtic Harp

Celtic Tin Whistle

Chinese Di Zi Flute

Chinese Erhu Violin

Chinese Guzheng Zither

Chinese Ruan Moon Guitar

Chinese Xiao Flute

European Folk Kit

Hawaiian Ukulele

Highland Bagpipes

Indian & Middle Eastern Kit

Indian Bansuri Flute

Indian Shehnai Oboe

Indian Sitar

Irish Bouzouki

Irish Fiddle

Japanese Koto

Japanese Shakuhachi Flute

Latin Baby Bass

Latin Kit

Medieval Lute

Medieval Recorder

Mexican Guitarron

Native American Flute

Persian Santoor

Peruvian Panpipes

Polka Accordion

Russian Balalaika

South African Singers

South African Voice Effects

Spanish Flamenco Guitar

Tango Accordion

Tibetan Singing Bowls

Turkish Oud Lute

Turkish Saz Lute

Voices

Jams, shouts, raps, backup oohs—this Jam Pack has everything you need to layer in the backup singers you always wished you had!

Andre Background (24)

Andre Improv (28)

Andre Lyric (31)

Bailey Background (14)

Bailey Improv (8)

Bailey Lyric (3)

Bailey Melody (9)

Beatbox (23)

Beatbox Old School (14)

Bollywood Lyric (23)

Boys Choir Background (30)

Brahms Lyric (1)

Byron Background (15)

Byron Improv (10)

Byron Lyric (3)

Byron Melody (16)

Candy Improv (8)

Candy Lyric (1)

Carla Background (9)

Carla Improv (20)

Carla Lyric (3)

Carla Melody (31)

Christy Background (16)

Christy Improv (7)

Christy Lyric (19)

Christy Melody (1)

Classic Choir Lyric (19)

Classical Background (30)

Clyde Improv (1)

Clyde Lyric (12)

Clyde Melody (8)

Cody Background (6)

Cody Improv (6)

Cody Lyric (37)

Cody Melody (3)

Conor Background (13)

Darcy Background (5)

Darcy Improv (15)

Darcy Lyric (1)

Darcy Melody (33)

Devon Background (14)

Devon Improv (34)

Devon Lyric (18)

Devon Melody (4)

Donna Background (18)

Donna Improv (7)

Donna Lyric (1)

Donna Melody (4)

Dustin Background (18)

Dustin Improv (15)

Earl Lyric (58)

Emery Background (10)

Emery Improv (9)

Emery Melody (16)

Feuertrunken Lyric (2)

Fledermaus Lyric (2)

Fynn Background (10)

Fynn Improv (13)

Fynn Lyric (32)

Gospel Background (6)

Gospel Improv (9)

Gospel Lyric (26)

Gregorian Latin Lyric (19)

Gregorian Melody (16)

Hallelujah Lyric (8)

Hanna Background (5)

Hanna Melody (4)

Inara Improv (1)

Inara Lyric (4)

Inara Melody (3)

Jack Improv (3)

Janice Improv (2)

Janice Lyric (5)

Jax Improv (1)

Jax Lyric (11)

Jeron Background (6)

Jeron Melody (1)

Jessi Background (12)

Jessi Improv (5)

Jessi Lyric (6)

Jessi Melody (18)

Jordon Lyric (10)

Jordon Melody (3)

Kara Background (21)

Katie Background (5)

Kayla Background (21)

Kayla Improv (1)

Kayla Lyric (1)

Kayla Melody (9)

Keith Background (3)

Leena Improv (13)

Leena Lyric (1)

Leena Melody (42)

Levi Background (10)

Levi Improv (7)

Levi Lyric (5)

Levi Melody (3)

Mikal Improv (10)

Mikal Lyric (58)

Mozart Lyric (8)

Nathan Improv (14)

Nathan Lyric (46)

Owen Background (3)

Pearl Melody (14)

Rachel Improv (12)

Rachel Lyric (1)

Rachel Melody (4)

Ricky Improv (2)

Ricky Lyric (18)

Roger Improv (3)

Roger Lyric (2)

Ruth Background (8)

Sean Lyric (2)

Sean Melody (7)

Seth Background (37)

Seth Improv (2)

Seth Lyric (30)

Shana Improv (2)

Shana Lyric (2)

Shana Melody (1)

Sophie Background (1)

Sophie Improv (21)

Sophie Lyric (9)

Sophie Melody (5)

Stone Improv (2)

Theo Improv (2)

Tia Improv (1)

Tia Lyric (16)

Tom Improv (6)

Tom Lyric (20)

Tonya Background (9)

Tonya Improv (1)

Tonya Melody (1)

Tristan Background (4)

Tristan Lyric (1)

Tristan Melody (3)

Tyson Background (9)

Tyson Improv (23)

Tyson Lyric (18)

Vera Background (2)

Vera Improv (16)

Vera Melody (17)

Verdi Lyric (3)

Vinnie Lyric (4)

Vocoder Lyric (6)

Whistle Improv (20)

Wilson Background (2)

Wilson Melody (1)

Wynn Improv (10)

Wynn Lyric (1)

Yasmin Background (6)

Yasmin Melody (8)

Software Instruments

Boys Chamber Swells

Gospel Ensemble

Boys Chamber Ensemble

Chamber Female Ensemble

Chamber Female Swells

Chamber Male Ensemble

Chamber Male Swells

Chamber Ensemble

Chamber Ensemble Swells

Classical Ensemble Swells

Classical Ensemble

Classical Female Ensemble

Classical Female Swells

Classical Male Ensemble

Classical Male Swells

Eastern Solo

Gospel Ensemble Swells

Gospel Voice Effects

Gregorian Ensemble Swells

Gregorian Ensemble

Human Beat Box

Human Body Sound Effects

Human Body Rhythm Effects

Human Bass

Synth Soprano Solo

Vocal Shout Effects

Vocal Shouts

Whistler

GarageBand '09 Keyboard Shortcuts

Keyboard shortcuts are an easy way to execute many of the functions and alter the views within GarageBand, and many proficient users will argue that there is no reason whatsoever to use the menus along the top of your screen to access these features once you learn the keystrokes that represent the functions you use most. Just like you press the Shift key and then the letter T to type a capital T instead of a lowercase t, most keyboard shortcuts are combinations of keys. This is why people often refer to these keyboard-driven commands as *key combos* or *hot keys*. Many keyboard shortcuts incorporate a modifier key, such as Shift, Command, or Option, and one or more other keys to execute the command, such as Command+Shift+N to create a new track in GarageBand. Others are only the single press of a single key, such as M to mute or unmute a selected track. Use the reference list below to learn the keyboard shortcuts for your favorite GarageBand functions, and see your productivity and fluidity increase while you incorporate these new habits into your workflow.

Keyboard Shortcut Comprehensive Reference Guide
Playback and Navigation

ACTION	SHORTCUT
Start or stop playback	Spacebar
Go to beginning	Return or Z or Home
Go to end	Option+Z or End
Move back in smaller increments	Left arrow
Move forward in smaller increments	Right arrow
Move back in larger increments	Option+left arrow
Move forward in larger increments	Option+right arrow
Move back the visible width of the timeline	Page up
Move forward the visible width of the timeline	Page down
Zoom in	Control+left arrow
Zoom out	Control+right arrow

Tracks

ACTION	SHORTCUT
Create a new track	Command+Option+N
Create a new Basic track	Command+Shift+N
Duplicate the selected track	Command+D
Delete the selected track	Command+Delete
Select the next higher track	Up arrow
Select the next lower track	Down arrow
Mute/unmute the selected track	M
Solo/unsolo the selected track	S
Lock/unlock the selected track	L
Show/hide the track's automation curves	A
Unmute all tracks	Option-click Mute button
Unsolo all tracks	Option-click Solo button
Show/Hide the Arrange Track	Command+Shift+A
Show/Hide the Master Track	Command+B
Show/Hide the Podcast Track	Command+Shift+B
Show/Hide the Movie Track	Command+Option+B

Track Info Panel

ACTION	SHORTCUT
Show/Hide the Track Info panel	Command+I
Select the next higher category or instrument (when the Track Info panel is open and a category or instrument is selected)	Up arrow
Select the next lower category or instrument (when the Track Info panel is open and a category or instrument is selected)	Down arrow
Move from instrument list to category list (when the Track Info panel is open and an instrument is selected)	Left arrow
Move from category list to instrument list (when the Track Info panel is open and a category is selected)	Right arrow

Learning to Play

ACTION	SHORTCUT
Automatic notation view	1 (in a Learn to Play lesson)
Show chord names	2 (in a Learn to Play lesson)
Show chord grids (guitar) / Show left hand only (piano)	3 (in a Learn to Play lesson)
Show tablature (guitar) / Show right hand only (piano)	4 (in a Learn to Play lesson)
Show tablature and standard notation (guitar) / Show both hands (piano)	5 (in a Learn to Play lesson)
Show notation and instrument	8 (in a Learn to Play lesson)
Show instrument only	9 (in a Learn to Play lesson)
Show notation only	0 (in a Learn to Play lesson)
Easy view (piano)	E (in a Learn to Play lesson)

Arranging and Editing

ACTION	SHORTCUT
Undo	Command+Z
Redo	Command+Shift+Z
Cut	Command+X
Copy	Command+C
Paste	Command+V
Delete	Delete
Select all	Command+A
Split selected region at the playhead	Command+T
Join selected regions	Command+J
Turn snap to grid on/off	Command+G
Show/hide alignment guides	Command+Shift+G
Lock automation curves to regions	Command+Option+A
Delete selected arrange region and its timeline content	Command+Option+Delete
Delete selected region and fill in time	Control+Delete
Add marker to Podcast/Movie Track	P
Turn ducking on/off	Command+Shift+R

Recording

ACTION	SHORTCUT
Start or stop recording	R
Turn the cycle region on/off	C
Turn the metronome on/off	Command+U
Turn count in on/off	Command+Shift+U

Score View

ACTION	SHORTCUT
Move selected notes to previous grid position	Left arrow
Move selected notes to next grid position	Right arrow
Move selected notes back one measure	Shift+left arrow
Move selected notes forward one measure	Shift+right arrow
Send selected object up one semitone	Up arrow
Transpose selected notes down one semitone	Down arrow
Transpose selected notes up one octave	Shift+up arrow
Transpose selected notes down one octave	Shift+down arrow
Print notation (must be visible in editor)	Command+P

Adjusting Master Volume

ACTION	SHORTCUT
Raise master volume	Command+up arrow
Lower master volume	Command+down arrow

Showing Windows and Editors

ACTION	SHORTCUT
Show Track Mixer	Command+Y
Show Track Info panel	Command+I
Show editor	Command+E
Show Loop Browser	Command+L
Show Media Browser	Command+R
Show onscreen keyboard	Command+K
Show Musical Typing window	Command+Shift+K
Minimize GarageBand window	Command+M

LCD Mode Commands

ACTION	SHORTCUT
Show Chord mode in LCD (with Software Instrument track selected)	Command+F
Show Tuner mode in LCD (with Real Instrument track selected)	Command+F
Show Time mode in LCD	Command+Shift+F
Show Measures mode in LCD	Command+Option+F
Show Tempo mode in LCD	Command+Control+F

File Menu Commands

ACTION	SHORTCUT
Create new project	Command+N
Open an existing project	Command+O
Close the current project	Command+W
Save the current project	Command+S
Save As	Command+Shift+S
Print notation (must be visible in editor)	Command+P

Application Menu Commands

ACTION	SHORTCUT
Show GarageBand preferences	Command+comma (,)
Hide GarageBand	Command+H
Hide other applications	Command+Option+H
Quit GarageBand	Command+Q

Help Menu Commands

ACTION	SHORTCUT
Open GarageBand Help	Command+?

Index

A

About GarageBand, 62
acoustic guitars, 23. *See also* guitars; instruments
adagio, 39. *See also* tempo
Add Automation menu, 299–302
adding
    loops to timelines, 183–184
    movie scores, 27
    notes, 164
    parts to songs, 45
Add Marker button, 262
Advanced Preferences, 59–60
Advisory field, 266
album art, 260
American Federation of Musicians, 244
amps, Electric Guitar tracks, 120–123
Amp Simulation plug-in, 283
analog to digital converters, 9
Apple Discussions, 10
Apple Loops, 167–168
    editing, 188
    favorites, 189–190
    formatting, 185–186
    installing, 182
    Loop Browser, 173–183
    overview of, 169–173
    preferences, 183
    regions, 168–169
    swapping, 186–188
    timeline, adding loops to, 183–184
Apple Support, 11
Apple website, 1
Application menu commands, 402
applying
    Jam Packs, 345–346
    Track Editor, 134
archiving projects, 320–321
arrangements
    creating, 241, 248–253
    keyboard shortcuts, 399
    opening, 253–254
    songs, 243–248
arrange regions
    copying, 252–253
    creating, 249
    deleting, 250
    moving, 250–252
    naming, 249–250
    resizing, 250
Arrange Track, 248–253
Arrange window, 71–73
Artist Lessons, 31–32, 337–341
artwork, episodes, 261

Artwork Editor, 265
AU (Audio Unit) effects, 293–294
audio
    ducking, 263–264
    forums, 11
    loops, 97–102
    Media Browser, 74
    mixing, 270–273
    recording, 83–84
    regions, 90
    trimming, 97–102
Audio Input, 55
Audio Line In, 8–9
Audio/MIDI Preferences window, 150
Audio Output, 55
Audio Preview, 52–54
Audio Unit (AU) effects, 293–294
auditioning bands, 229–235
Auto-Funk stompbox effect, 126–127
Automatic Filter effect, 284
automating, 269
    Add Automation menu, 299–302
    formatting, 294–299
    Master Track, 107, 305–306
    pitch, 306–307
    Show/Hide Automation
        buttons, 105
    tempo, 306–307
    tracks, 105–108
Auto Normalize, 59
Auto Wah effect, 283–284

B

backgrounds, 91
baked projects, 310
bands, 229–235. *See also* GarageBand
Basic Lessons, 329–337
Bass Amp effect, 285
Basslines, 172
Bass Reduction effect, 285–286
beats, 94
    drums, building, 156–159
    metronomes, 47–50
    musical time, 82
Bitcrusher effect, 286
Blue Echo stompbox effect, 127
Blues, 32, 195, 198–201, 230
bouncing, 310
breakdowns, definition of, 246
breaks, definition of, 246
bridge, definition of, 246
Browse mode, 154
buffer sizes, 56

builds, definition of, 247
burning songs to CDs, 319
buttons
　Add Marker, 262
　Cancel, 89
　Change Genre, 229
　Choose, 19
　Close, 36
　Create New Arrange Region, 248
　Create New Track, 88
　Cycle Region, 140, 277–278
　Learn, 332
　Lock, 105
　Mute, 105
　My Apple Loops, 58
　Pause, 51
　Play, 332–337
　Preview, 32, 196
　Quit, 36
　Reset, 178
　Show/Hide Automation, 105
　Solo, 105
　Stop, 51
　Track Icon Selection, 153
buzzes, 104

C

Cancel button, 89
CDs
　burning songs to, 319
　quality, 60
Change Genre button, 229
chirps, 104
Choose button, 19
Chord view, 83
chorus, definition of, 245
Chorus effect, 286–287
chrome, 91
click tracks, 48
clipping, 104
Close button, 36
Column view, 175
combining
　recording passes, 154
　takes, 143–144
Command key, 164
commands
　Application menu, 402
　File menu, 401
　Help menu, 402
　LCD mode, 401
Command+Z key command, 275
compacting projects, 322–323
compatibility, 1
comping, 138
compression, 107
configuring
　Advanced Preferences, 59–60
　Apple Loops, 183, 185–186
　arrangements, 248–253
　Audio/MIDI Preferences, 54–59
　Audio Preview, 52–54

　automation, 106
　Cycle Recording option, 50–52
　effects, 115–120
　episodes, 256–257
　General Preferences, 47–54
　guitar lessons, 335–336
　Input Source, 113
　keyboards, 57
　keys, 40–41
　Magic GarageBand, 197–229
　metronomes, 47–50
　Monitor, 114
　My Apple Loops, 58
　My Info Preferences, 60–61
　nodes, 294–299
　optimization, 56
　piano lessons, 333–334
　podcasting, 256–260
　projects, 19–26
　Recording Level control, 114–115
　signatures, 39
　Software Instrument tracks, 149–151, 151
　System Preferences, 12–16,
　　111–112
　templates, 26–27
　tempo, 39
　tracks, 83–84, 88–89
connecting devices, 9–11. *See also* connection
　protocols
connection protocols, 5–11
　Audio Line In, 8–9
　FireWire (IEEE 1394), 6–7
　MIDI (Musical Instrument Digital Interface), 7–8
　USB (Universal Serial Bus), 6
Control menu, 67–69
controls
　playback, 93
　Recording Level, 114–115
　Track Mixer, 102–105
　Transport, 73, 92
copying
　Apple Loops, 185–186
　arrange regions, 252–253
　tracks, 90
costs
　Lesson Store, 29–30
　of software, 1
country, 32, 195, 208–211
　song structures, 232
Create New Arrange Region button, 248
Create New Track button, 88
Create New Track dialog box, 151
customizing
　parameters, 109
　projects, 19–26
　ringtones, 33–35
　System Preferences, 2, 12–16
　templates, 26–27
　views, 74
cuts, 87
cutting regions, 135
Cycle function, 51
Cycle Record function, 33

Cycle Recording option, 50–52
Cycle Region button, 140, 277–278
cycle regions, 51

D

data, MIDI, 8
delay, 56, 291
Delete Unused Takes, 143
deleting
    arrange regions, 250
    nodes, 298–299
    tracks, 91–92
Description field, 266
devices, connecting, 9–11. *See also* connection protocols
dialog boxes
    Create New Track, 151
    Export Song to Disk, 267
    New MIDI Input Detected, 151
    New Project, 5, 194, 256
    Open, 36
    Save As, 38, 322
DI boxes, 9
disabling
    effects, 118
    recording, 104–105
disks, exporting songs, 319
Distortion effect, 287
distortion pedals, 10
dividing regions, 135
documents, 54. *See also* files
double-tracking, 131
downloading
    Artist Lessons, 31–32
    lessons, 29–30
    loops, 172
drums
    beats, building, 156–159
    tracks, viewing, 165
ducking
    audio, 263–264
    tracks, 265
Ducking function, 107–108
duplicating tracks, 90–91

E

Echo effect, 116
editing
    Apple Loops, 188
    effects, 117
    keyboard shortcuts, 399, 401
    markers, 265
    MIDI, 159–160
    songs, 45
    Track Editor, 134
    tracks, 89–90
Edit menu, 65–66
editors
    nondestructive, 101
    Track Editor, 74
effects, 115–120
    Audio Unit (AU), 293–294
    Automatic Filter, 284

Auto Wah, 283–284
Bass Amp, 285
Bass Reduction, 285–286
Bitcrusher, 286
Chorus, 286–287
disabling, 118
Distortion, 287
Flanger, 287–288
Master Track, 305
mixing, 281–293
Overdrive, 288
Phaser, 288–289
post-processing, 130–131
presets *versus*, 281–282
Sound Effects tab, 12–14
Speech Enhancer, 289–290
stompbox, 123–128
stompbox, modifying, 293
Track Echo, 291
Track Reverb, 291
Treble Reduction, 291–292
Tremolo, 292
Visual EQ, 302–305
Vocal Transformer, 292–293
electric guitars, 20. *See also* guitars
Electric Guitar tracks, 89
    amps, 120–123
    stompbox effects, 123–128
enabling recording, 104–105
enhancers
    podcasts, 257
    timing, 144–146
    tuning, 145–146
entering metadata, 266
episodes
    artwork, 261
    creating, 256–257
    exporting, 266–267
    podcasting, 264–266
EQs, Visual EQ effect, 302–305
Example Ringtone project template, 34
examples of ringtones, 33
existing files, opening, 35–36
exporting
    podcasting, 266–267
    songs to disks, 319
Export Song to Disk dialog box, 267

F

favorites, Apple Loops, 189–190
File menu, 63–64
    commands, 401
files. *See also* songs
    moving, 25
    opening, 35–36
    previewing, 53
filters, Automatic Filter effect, 284
FireWire (IEEE 1394), 6–7
Flanger effect, 287–288
flattening out levels, 275–276
focusing microphones, 10
folders, 53

format shifters, 292
formatting
    Advanced Preferences, 59–60
    Apple Loops, 183, 185–186
    arrangements, 241, 248–253
    arrange regions, 249
    Audio/MIDI Preferences, 54–59
    Audio Preview, 52–54
    automation, 106
    Cycle Recording option, 50–52
    effects, 115–120
    episodes, 256–257
    General Preferences, 47–54
    guitar lessons, 335–336
    keyboards, 57
    keys, 40–41
    Magic GarageBand, 197–229
    metronomes, 47–50
    Monitor, 114
    My Apple Loops, 58
    My Info Preferences, 60–61
    nodes, 294–299
    optimization, 56
    piano lessons, 333–334
    podcasting, 256–260
    projects, 19–26
    Recording Level control, 114–115
    ringtones, 33–35
    signatures, 39
    Software Instrument tracks, 149–151
    System Preferences, 12–16
    templates, 26–27
    tempo, 39
    tracks, 83–84, 88–89
forms
    modifying, 45
    songs, 243–248
forums, 11
functions
    Cycle, 51
    Cycle Record, 33
    Ducking, 107–108
    monitoring, 103
Funk, 32, 196, 215–218, 232–234
fuzziness, 104
Fuzz Machine stompbox effect, 125

G

GarageBand
    effects. See effects
    installing, 4–5
    interfaces, navigating, 71–83
    menus, 62–63
    mixing, 273–274
GarageDoor, The, 172
Gate effect, 116
General Preferences, 47–54
genres, selecting, 194–197
Google.com, 11
gradual automation changes over time, 297–298
grids, timelines, 93–96
Grinder stompbox effect, 124–125
guitars
    amps, modifying, 293
    Electric Guitar track, 89
    Intro to Guitar lesson, 329
    lessons, 29, 30–31, 331
    selecting, 20
    tuners, 337
Guitar Track presets, 122

H

hardware
    selecting, 9
    system requirements, 3–4
head, 244
    of regions, 100
Help menu, 71
    commands, 402
hiding, Show/Hide Automation buttons, 105
hot keys, 397–402

I

iCompositions, 172
icons, 155
iDVD, sending movies to, 318–319
IEEE 1394 (FireWire), 6–7
iLife '09, 2
    installing, 3
    troubleshooting, 10–11
images, Media Browser, 74–76
importing loops, 181–183
information, episode, 264–266
Input
    tabs, 15–16
input
    Audio Input, 55
Input Source, configuring, 113
installing, 1–5
    Apple Loops, 182
    GarageBand, 4–5
    iLife '09, 3
    Jam Packs, 344–345
Instrument Generators, 280
instruments
    effects. See effects
    Magic GarageBand, 32, 197–229
    Real Instrument loops, 58
    Real Instrument tracks, 86, 87–88
    selecting, 44
    Software Instrument tracks, 86, 87–88
interfaces
    backgrounds, 91
    GarageBand, navigating, 71–83
    Lexicon Omega USB audio, 13
    Loop Browser, 57–58, 73–74, 173–183
    Media Browser, 53, 74–77
    MIDI. See MIDI
    New Project, 17–36
    Software Instrument tracks, 149–151
Internal Speakers, 13
intro, definition of, 245
Intro to Guitar lesson, 329
Intro to Piano lesson, 328–329
iPhone ringtones, 33–35
iPods, 42. See also podcasts
iTunes
    movies, sending, 315

podcasts, sending, 318
podcasts, submitting, 267
ringtones, sending, 315–318
songs, sending, 311–315

J

jacks
    Audio Line In, 8–9
    USB (Universal Serial Bus), 6
Jam Packs, 172, 343
    applying, 345–346
    installing, 344–345
    overview of, 348–395
    troubleshooting, 346–348
jams, definition of, 247
Jazz, 32, 195, 205–208, 231–232, 244

K

Keyboard Collection, selecting, 21–23
keyboards
    layouts, 58
    MIDI (Musical Instrument Digital Interface), 10
    QWERTY, 7
    sensitivity, 57
    shortcuts, 51, 397–402
    tracking, 152–153
keys, 40–41
    combos, 397–402
    modifying, 239–241

L

language change, 243
larghetto, 39. *See also* tempo
largo, 39. *See also* tempo
latency, 56
Latin, 32, 196, 219–222
    song structures, 234–235
layouts, keyboards, 58
LCD (liquid crystal display)
    displays, 77–79
    mode commands, 401
leading tones, 181
Learn button, 332
Learn to Play, 327–329
    keyboard shortcuts, 399
    options, 27–29
LED level meters, 104–105
Lee, Geddy, 139
lessons
    downloading, 29–30
    guitars, 29, 30–31, 331
    Intro to Guitar, 329
    Intro to Piano, 328–329
    Learn to Play, 27–29, 327–329
    Lesson Store, 29–30
    pianos, 29, 30–31, 331
    songs, 338–340
Lesson Store
    Artist Lessons, 31–32, 337–341
    Basic Lessons, 329–337
levels, flattening out, 275–276
Lexicon Omega USB audio interface, 13
LFO (low-frequency oscillator), 288

libraries, Track Icons, 155
licenses, 1
Lifeson, Alex, 139
liquid crystal display. *See* LCD
Lock button, 105
Logic Pro
    projects, opening, 253–254
    projects, sharing with, 323–324
Loop Browser, 57–58, 73–74, 173–183
Loop Ringtone project template, 34
loops
    Apple Loops. *See* Apple Loops
    audio, 97–102
    cursors, 101
    downloading, 172
    importing, 181–183
    preferences, 57–58
    previewing, 74
    Real Instrument, 58
    recording, 51
    REX Loops, 170
    ringtones, 33
    searching, 175
    selecting, 21
    sorting, 174
    viewing, 175
low-frequency oscillator (LFO), 288

M

Mac Box Set, 2
Macidol, 172
MacJams, 172
Macloops, 172
Magic GarageBand, 32–33, 43–45
    arrangements, creating, 241
    options, 197–229
    overdubbing, 235–238
    overview of, 193–194
    projects, creating, 229–235
    song genres, selecting, 194–197
major scales, 180
managing tracks, 92
Manual preset, 119
markers, 243
    Add Marker button, 262
    editing, 265
    podcasting, 262–263
mash-ups, mixing, 307–308
Master Track, 107
    automating, 305–306
    effects, 305
    metronomes, 47
measures, 94
Measures view, 78, 82
Media Browser, 53, 74–77
    podcasting, 259–260
memory, 11
menus, 61–71
    Add Automation, 299–302
    Control, 67–69
    Edit, 65–66
    File, 63–64
    GarageBand, 62–63
    Help, 71

menus (*Continued*)
    Multiple Takes, 142
    Share, 69–70, 310–319
    Sound Generator, 280
    Timeline Grid Value, 95
    track, 66–67
    Voices, 280
    Window, 70–71
    Windows, 7
metadata, entering, 266
metronomes, 47–50
    starting, 140
microphones, focusing, 10
middle eight, definition of, 246
middle section, definition of, 246
MIDI (Musical Instrument Digital Interface), 7–8
    Audio/MIDI Preferences, 54–59
    controllers, tracking, 152–153
    editing, 159–160
    forums, 11
    keyboards, 10
    recording, 153–155
    regions, 90
    Software Instrument tracks, 149–151
    Status, 56
minor scales, 181
mixdowns, 310
mixing, 269
    audio, 270–273
    effects, 281–293
    GarageBand, 273–274
    guitar lessons, 336
    mash-ups, 307–308
    piano lessons, 334–335
    processes, 274–278
    skills, 269–270
    Software Instrument tracks, 278–281
    Track Mixer, 276
modifying
    forms, 45
    keys, 239–241
    pitch, 107
    resolution, 133
    stompbox effects, 293
    tempo, 239–241
Monitor, configuring, 114
monitoring functions, 103
mono audio regions, 99
movies
    iDVD, sending, 318–319
    iTunes, sending, 315
    Media browser, 76–77
    scores, adding, 27
    selecting, 25–26
moving
    Apple Loops, 185–186
    arrange regions, 250–252
    files, 25
    loops, 181–183
multiple takes
    Cycle Recording Using Multiple Takes, 156–159
    recording, 138–144
Multiple Takes menu, 142

music
    forums, 11
    lessons. *See* lessons
    projects, 37–41. *See also* projects
Musical Button view, 177
Musical Instrument Digital Interface. *See* MIDI
musical time, 82
musical typing, 7
Mute button, 105
muting
    metronome tracks, 48
    mixing, 278
My Apple Loops button, 58
My Info Preferences, 60–61

N

naming
    arrange regions, 249–250
    regions, 159
    tracks, 89–90
navigating
    GarageBand interfaces, 71–83
    keyboard shortcuts, 397
    Loop Browser, 73–74, 173–183
    Media Browser, 74–77
    menus, 61–71
    New Project interface, 17–36
    Preferences window, 47–61
    Share menu, 310–319
    timelines, 92–102
    tracks, 85–87
New MIDI Input Detected dialog box, 151
New Project dialog box, 5, 194, 256
New Project interface, 17–36
New Project window, 19
nodes
    automating, 106
    creating, 294–299
    deleting, 298–299
nondestructive editors, 101
normal selection cursor, 99
notes
    adding, 164
    MIDI (Musical Instrument Digital Interface), 7

O

one-click syndication, 257
Open dialog box, 36
opening
    arrangements, 253–254
    files, 35–36
Open in GarageBand, 238–239
operating system versions, 1
optimization, 56
options
    Advanced Preferences, 59–60
    Apple Loops, 183
    Audio/MIDI Preferences, 54–59
    Audio Preview, 52–54
    Cycle Recording, 50–52
    effects, 115–120
    episodes, 256–257

General Preferences, 47–54
guitar lessons, 335–336
Input Source, 113
keys, 40–41
Learn to Play, 27–29
Magic GarageBand, 197–229
metronomes, 47–50
Monitor, 114
My Apple Loops, 58
My Info Preferences, 60–61
nodes, 294–299
optimization, 56
piano lessons, 333–334
Play Feedback When Volume Is Changed, 14
Play User Interface Sound Effects, 13
podcasting, 256–260
projects, 19–26
Recording Level control, 114–115
ringtones, 33–35
signatures, 39
Software Instrument tracks, 149–151
System Preferences, 2, 12–16
templates, 26–27
tempo, 39
orchestration, 244
ordering tracks, 92
ostinato, 170
output, Audio Output, 55
Output tab, 14
outro, definition of, 247
Overdrive effect, 288
overdubbing, 44, 49, 86
Magic GarageBand, 235–238

P

panels
System Preferences Sound control, 112
Track Info, 74, 108–110
panning, 104, 299
parameters, customizing, 109
passes, mixing, 276–277
Pause button, 51
peaking, 104
Peart, Neil, 139
Phaser effect, 288–289
Phase Tripper stompbox effect, 123–124
photos, Media Browser, 74–76
Piano Roll view, 160–164
pianos
Intro to Piano lesson, 328–329
lessons, 29, 30–31, 331
selecting, 20
pitch
automating, 306–307
modifying, 107
playback
controls, 93
keyboard shortcuts, 397
Play button, 332–337
Play Feedback When Volume Is Changed option, 14
playheads, 51, 93–96

playing
Learn to Play options, 27–29
songs, 340–341
Play User Interface Sound Effects option, 13
plug-ins. See also effects
Amp Simulation, 283
Speech Enhancer, 119
podcasts, 41–43, 255–256
audio, ducking, 263–264
creating, 256–260
episodes, 264–266
exporting, 266–267
iTunes, sending, 318
markers, 262–263
Media Browser, 259–260
selecting, 25
tracks, 260–263
video, 257–259
Podcast Sounds view, 178
polyphony, 59
ports
Audio Line In, 8–9
USB (Universal Serial Bus), 6
positioning
microphones, 10
tracks, 92
post-processing, 130–131, 281–293
pre-amplification, 8
pre-chorus, definition of, 245
preferences
Advanced Preferences, 59–60
Apple Loops, 183
Audio/MIDI Preferences, 54–59
Audio Preview, 52–54
Cycle Recording option, 50–52
effects, 115–120
episodes, 256–257
General Preferences, 47–54
guitar lessons, 335–336
Input Source, 113
keys, 40–41
loops, 57–58
Magic GarageBand, 197–229
metronomes, 47–50
Monitor, 114
My Apple Loops, 58
My Info Preferences, 60–61
nodes, 294–299
optimization, 56
piano lessons, 333–334
podcasting, 256–260
projects, 19–26
Recording Level control, 114–115
ringtones, 33–35
signatures, 39
Software Instrument tracks, 149–151
System Preferences, 2, 12–16, 111–112
templates, 26–27
tempo, 39
Preferences window, navigating, 47–61
presets
effects, 115
versus effects, 281–282

presets (*Continued*)
Guitar Track, 122
Manual, 119
Speech Enhancer, 119
prestissimo, 39. *See also* tempo
Preview button, 32, 196
previewing
Audio Preview, 52–54
loops, 74
processes, mixing, 274–278. *See also* mixing
projects
compacting, 322–323
exporting, 266–267
files, opening existing, 35–36
formatting, 19–26
iPhone ringtones, 33–35
lessons. *See* lessons
Logic Pro, sharing with, 323–324
Magic GarageBand, 32–33, 43–45, 229–235
music, 37–41
opening, 253–254
podcasts, 41–43
saving, 320–321
selecting, 17
sharing, 310–319
templates, creating, 26–27
types, 36–45
Project view, 83
protocol connections, 5–11
punching in, 131–134
purchasing lessons, 29–30. *See also* lessons

Q

quality of CDs, 60
quantizing, 74, 145
quarter notes, 94
Quit button, 36
QWERTY keyboards, 7

R

RAM (random access memory), 11
random access memory. *See* RAM
Real Instrument
loops, 58
tracks, 86, 87–88
really simple syndication (RSS), 257
real-world instruments, 10
recording
audio, 83–84
Cycle Recording Using Multiple Takes, 156–159
disabling, 104–105
enabling, 104–105
keyboard shortcuts, 400
loops, 51
multiple takes, 138–144
post-processing, 130–131
punching in, 131–134
regions, splitting, 135–138
ringtones, 33–35
sampling, 169
Software Instrument tracks, 153–155
tracks, 110, 128–129
Recording Level control, 114–115

refrain, definition of, 247
reggae, 32, 196, 212–215, 232
regions, 85
Apple Loops, 168–169
arrange. *See* arrange regions
audio, 90, 97–102
cycle, 51
Cycle Region button, 277–278
MIDI, 90
renaming, 159
splitting, 135–138
renaming
regions, 159
tracks, 90
reordering tracks, 92
requirements, system, 1–4
Re-Record command, 129–130
Reset button, 178
resizing arrange regions, 250
resolution, 60, 133
resources, 10–11, 325–326
Retro Chorus stompbox effect, 125
returns, 117
Reverb effect, 116
REX Loops, 170
rhythm, 49
ringtones
examples, 33
iPhone, 33–35
iTunes, sending, 315–318
loops, 33
voices, 33–35
rippling, 250
Robo Flanger stompbox effect, 125–126
rock, 32, 195, 201–204, 231
roots rock, 32, 196, 222–225, 235
RSS (really simple syndication), 257

S

Samples4.com, 172
sampling, 169
Save As dialog box, 38, 322
saving projects, 320–321
scales, 179–181
scores, adding movie, 27
Score view, 164–165, 400
scratches, 104
scrolling, 96–97. *See also* navigating
searching loops, 175
selecting
acoustic instruments, 23
electric guitars, 20
hardware, 9
instruments, 44
Keyboard Collection, 21–23
loops, 21
movies, 25–26
pianos, 20
podcasts, 25
projects, 17
song genres, 194–197
Songwriting, 23–24
System Preferences, 2
takes, 142–143

tempo, 39
voices, 20–21
semitones, 57
sending
movies to iDVD, 318–319
movies to iTunes, 315
podcasts to iTunes, 318
ringtones to iTunes, 315–318
songs to iTunes, 311–315
sensitivity, keyboards, 57
setup
guitar lessons, 335–336
piano lessons, 333–334
Share menu, 69–70, 310–319
sharing
projects, 310–319
projects with Logic Pro, 323–324
shortcuts, keyboards, 51, 397–402
Show/Hide Automation button, 105
Show/Hide Loop Browser icon, 174
signatures, 39
Silicon Beats, 172
sizing buffers, 56
skills, mixing, 269–270
sliders, zoom, 97
slow blues, 32, 196, 226–229, 235
Smart Loops, 172
software
system requirements, 1–3
updating, 2
Software Instrument tracks, 87–88, 149
Apple Loops, 171. *See also* Apple Loops
creating, 151
Cycle Recording Using Multiple Takes, 156–159
MIDI, editing, 159–160
MIDI preferences, 149–151
mixing, 278–281
Piano Roll view, 160–164
recording, 153–155
regions, renaming, 159
Score view, 164–165
workflow, 152–153
Solo button, 105
solos
definition of, 246
mixing, 278
recording, 138–139
songs, 37–41. *See also* music
arrangements, 243–248
CDs, burning to, 319
disks, exporting, 319
editing, 45
forms, 243–248
genres, selecting, 194–197
iTunes, sending, 311–315
lessons, 338–340
playing, 340–341
previewing, 53
Songwriting, selecting, 23–24
sorting loops, 174
Sound Effects tab, 12–14
sound forums, 11
Sound Generator menu, 280
Sound pane, 150
speakers, Internal Speakers, 13

Speech Enhancer effect, 119, 289–290
spiking, 104
splitting
Apple Loops, 185–186
regions, 135–138
Squash Compressor stompbox effect, 128
starting metronomes, 140
Status (MIDI), 56
stereo audio regions, 99
stereotypes, 195
stompbox effects, 123–128, 293
Stop button, 51
story, 341
structure, song, 243–248
styles, Magic GarageBand, 197–229
submenus, 62. *See also* menus
subscribing to podcasts, 266
swapping Apple Loops, 186–188
synchronization, 26
syndication, 42, 257
System Preferences, 12–16
configuring, 111–112
selecting, 2
system requirements, 1–4

T

tail of regions, 100
takes
combining, 143–144
Cycle Recording Using Multiple Takes, 156–159
recording multiple, 138–144
selecting, 142–143
templates
Example Ringtone project, 34
formatting, 26–27
Loop Ringtone project, 34
Voice Ringtone project, 35
tempo
Apple Loops, 170
automating, 306–307
modifying, 239–241
selecting, 39
thumbnails, Audio Preview, 52–54
Time Left cursor, 100
Timeline Grid Value menu, 95
timelines, 71
grids, 93–96
loops, adding, 183–184
podcasting, 263
tracks, 92–102
Timeline window, 51
Time view, 78, 79–82
timing
enhancers, 144–146
metronomes, 47–50
musical time, 82
tones, leading, 181
tools
Apple Loops Utility, 170
Magic GarageBand, 43–45
Track Echo effect, 291
Track Editor, 32, 73, 133, 134
Track Icon Selection button, 153

Track Info panel, 74, 108–110,
        398
tracking it live, 49
Track menu, 66–67
Track Mixer, 102–105, 276
Track Reverb effect, 291
tracks, 85
        Arrange Track, 248–253
        automating, 105–108
        Create New Track button, 88
        creating, 83–84, 88–89
        deleting, 91–92
        double-tracking, 131
        duplicating, 90–91
        Electric Guitar, 89
        Electric Guitar, amps,
                120–123
        keyboard shortcuts, 398
        Master Track, 107
        mixing, 270. *See also* mixing
        naming, 89–90
        navigating, 85–87
        panning, 299
        podcasting, 260–263
        post-processing, 130–131
        presets, 122
        Real Instrument, 86, 87–88
        recording, 110, 128–129
        renaming, 90
        reordering, 92
        Software Instrument, 87–88, 149. *See also*
                Software Instrument tracks
        stompbox effects, 123–128
        timelines, 92–102
        Track Mixer controls, 102–105
        volume, 103–104,
                295–297
Transport controls, 73, 92
Treble Reduction effect, 291–292
Tremolo effect, 292
trimming audio, 97–102
troubleshooting
        iLife '09, 10–11
        Jam Packs, 346–348
Tuned Percussion, 280
tuners, guitars, 337
Tuner view, 82–83
tuning enhancers, 145–146
types
        of Jam Packs, 348–395
        of projects, 36–45

U

Undo command, 129–130, 250
        mixing, 275
unity gain, 104
Universal Serial Bus. *See* USB
updating software, 2
USB (Universal Serial Bus), 6

V

vamp, definition of, 245
verse, definition of, 245
versions, operating systems, 1
Vibe stompbox effect, 126
video, podcasting, 257–259
Video Game, 43
viewing
        Apple Loops, 189–190
        loops, 175
views
        Chord, 83
        Column, 175
        customizing, 74
        Measures, 78, 82
        Musical Button, 177
        Piano Roll, 160–164
        Podcast Sounds, 178
        Project, 83
        Score, 164–165
        Time, 79–82
        Tuner, 82–83
Vintage Drive stompbox
        effect, 124
Visual EQ effect, 302–305
Vocal Transformer effect,
        292–293
Voice Per Instrument setting, 59
Voice Ringtone project template, 35
voices
        ringtones, 33–35
        selecting, 20–21
Voices menu, 280
volume
        automating, 107
        keyboard shortcuts, 400
        tracks, 103–104, 295–297

W

Welcome to GarageBand window, 17
whole steps, 57
Window menu, 70–71
windows
        Arrange, 71–73
        Audio/MIDI Preferences, 150
        keyboard shortcuts, 401
        Loop Browser, 174
        New Project, 19
        Preferences, navigating, 47–61
        Timeline, 51
        Welcome to GarageBand, 17
Windows menu, 7
workflow, Software Instrument tracks, 152–153

Z

zeroing out levels, 275–276
zooming, 96–97. *See also* navigating